SPARTAN EDUCATION

SPARTAN EDUCATION

Youth and Society in the Classical Period

Jean Ducat

Translated by
Emma Stafford, P.-J. Shaw and Anton Powell

The Classical Press of Wales

First published in 2006 by
The Classical Press of Wales
15 Rosehill Terrace, Swansea SA1 6JN
Tel: +44 (0)1792 458397
Fax: +44 (0)1792 464067
www.classicalpressofwales.co.uk

Distributor in the United States of America:
The David Brown Book Co.
PO Box 511, Oakville, CT 06779
Tel: +1 (860) 945–9329
Fax: +1 (860) 945–9468

ISBN 1–905125-07-0

A catalogue record for this book is available from the British Library

Typeset by Ernest Buckley, Clunton, Shropshire
Printed and bound in the UK by Gomer Press, Llandysul, Ceredigion, Wales

---

The Classical Press of Wales, an independent venture, was founded in 1993, initially to support the work of classicists and ancient historians in Wales and their collaborators from further afield. More recently it has published work initiated by scholars internationally. While retaining a special loyalty to Wales and the Celtic countries, the Press welcomes scholarly contributions from all parts of the world.

The symbol of the Press is the Red Kite. This bird, once widespread in Britain, was reduced by 1905 to some five individuals confined to a small area known as 'The Desert of Wales' – the upper Tywi valley. Geneticists report that the stock was saved from terminal inbreeding by the arrival of one stray female bird from Germany. After much careful protection, the Red Kite now thrives – in Wales and beyond.

CONTENTS

ACKNOWLEDGEMENTS

This book would not exist without the initiative and the constant encouragement of Anton Powell, who acted as inspirer as well as publisher. The work of translation was done by Emma Stafford (Introduction, and Chs. 1, 2, 4 and 6), Pamela-Jane Shaw (Chs. 5, 7 and 9) and Anton Powell (Chs. 3, 8 and Conclusion). The process of translation has proved to be a true collaboration between colleagues. I similarly thank Mme Jacqueline Manessy for her help on the subject of certain Spartan names for age-categories.

INTRODUCTION

SPARTAN EDUCATION HAS A HISTORY

In the Roman period, the only reality of the ancient Spartan order (*kosmos*) which survived as a whole was the education system. The Spartans believed that this had remained unchanged since Lycurgus, and visitors were convinced that the festivals and ceremonies which they attended dated back to the earliest times.[1] This was, in antiquity, one of the fundamentals of the Spartan myth. Modern historians do not make the same mistake. They have said for a long time that Spartan education has a history, that it was restored by Cleomenes III around 226, after having more or less fallen into disuse, that it was abolished by Philopoimen in 188, and re-established some years later, and that the form in which it was resurrected in the imperial period was certainly very different from what it was in the classical period. But one of the main objectives of Kennell's study (1995) has been to denounce scholars' lack of logic in this respect, because, according to him, they have not drawn the methodological conclusions which follow from these observations. In their study of Spartan education, Kennell accuses them of using what he calls 'a synchronistic approach' (p. 7), to the extent of exhibiting what Cartledge has rightly called 'methodological holism'.[2] This cruel remark is largely justified by the way in which, before Kennell, accounts of Spartan education have made use of the sources. Whether these date from the fourth century BC, like Xenophon and Plato, or from the second century AD, like Plutarch and Pausanias, or whether their content is practically undatable, like most of the glosses, scholia and lexicographical notices, scholars combine and use them as a whole, as though the reality to which they refer had remained identical through the centuries. This is because people readily believe that, over and above any changes the educational system might have undergone as an institution, there shines an eternal education, like a Platonic idea, an original model (unconscious avatar of the myth of Lycurgus) to which all the texts would refer. This is to forget that the model itself could have changed: an 'eternal' education is as every century envisages it. Plutarch is the most deeply implicated: it is on the account which he gave of Spartan education in the *Life of Lycurgus* that historians' reconstructions are for the most part based, to the extent that often Xenophon, less articulate and less picturesque, is practically forgotten. Den Boer's study (1954) provides a typical example: chapter 2, 'The Spartan *agōgē*' (233–98), consists solely of a discussion, interesting in itself, of various passages of Plutarch; but it has to be conceded to Kennell that everyone has fallen into this error to a greater or lesser degree.[3]

Kennell presents himself, in opposition to this traditional approach, as the intransigent defender of a diachronic orthodoxy, something of which one can but approve. But what is striking in his vision of the history of Spartan education is that it rests on the idea of discontinuity. Twice, according to him (Kennell 1995, 9–14), there must have been a complete break in the functioning of the education system, and for quite a long period: once in the third century BC, once in the second; moreover, its reinstatement must have been accompanied by profound modifications. Thus the later history of the system would have been radically divorced from its roots in the classical period. To pick up the archaeological metaphor by which Kennell characterizes his method, for him, everything happens as though sterile strata of abandonment lie in between the classical education system and that of the end of the third century BC, then again between this and the system of the Roman period, completely isolating the periods. It is this hypothesis of discontinuity that I wish to examine to begin with.[4]

The problem of interruptions

According to Kennell, when, around 226, Cleomenes dealt with the education system, it had ceased to function since a date which, without being able to be more precise, he places between 270 and 250, so during the twenty-five to forty-five years which correspond to one or two generations.[5] This is not a new idea. Porter (1935, 13) too talks about one or two generations; Shimron (1972, 8 n.9) found this excessive, while estimating that, without having been abolished as such (p. 20), the system 'had fallen into disuse by neglect' (p. 26). In the same way, Piper (1986, 54) declares: 'it had been in disuse for so many years'. This then is the common opinion of specialists in the period. But all this is simply deduced from the fact that, according to what Plutarch tells us, Cleomenes had to restore the educational system. This does not necessarily imply that it had ceased to function, but only that, like the *syssitia*,[6] it was not functioning well, perhaps, for example, for lack of citizens with the means to have their sons brought up in this way; in which case the remedy would have been to rebuild a true civic community – which is what Cleomenes tried to do. A passage in a dialogue by Teles of Megara,[7] datable between 240 and 229, which uses the present tense in connection with the *agōgē*, seems indeed to confirm that it was still functioning at this date. Without proof, the interruption is unlikely: every society considers its educational system as something fundamental, as the very vehicle of its identity; there would have to be some compulsion for it to have been given up.

This is what happened in 189/8, for here the reality of an interruption seems to be indisputable. Livy (38.34.1–3) reports only that Philopoimen made the Spartans give up the laws of Lycurgus and adopt Achaean institutions (which is partially confirmed by two inscriptions, *IG* 5.1.4 and 5); Pausanias (8.51.3) and Plutarch (*Philopoimen* 16.8) state clearly that the training of the young was included in this measure (Pausanias is in fact talking solely about training). What is more doubtful is the duration which Kennell attributes to this interruption. For him, the traditional education system could not have been re-established until Sparta had become a *civitas libera*, in 146; this duration, of more than 40 years, allows him to hypothesize some profound modifications for the restoration. Before Kennell, people generally accepted that this restoration had taken place much earlier, in 184/3 or in 179/8.[8] I believe that this traditional view is preferable, not so much because of a passage of Livy (45.28.4) often adduced in this connection, but which in fact is rather vague and rhetorical, as in accordance with an argument put forward by Lévy (1997, 153): Plutarch (*Philopoimen* 16.9) specifies that it was following a request made to the Romans, and accepted by them, that the Spartans were able to recover their own institutions; whereas in 146 they would not have needed Roman support for this. So the interruption may only have lasted a dozen or so years at the most, which would not in itself have meant upheavals.

The problem of reform

It seems natural to assume that resumption after an interruption is a favourable moment to effect change, but, on reflection, this is not at all self-evident. Change requires society to feel the necessity for this reform, and that there should be someone to see it through. We do not hear anything of the sort in connection with the restoration which followed the interruption caused by Philopoimen, and Kennell himself (1995, 101), although he deliberately prolongs the duration, does not seem to think that there was an important modification of the educational system at this point, since he presents the *ephēbeia* of the Roman period as the direct descendant of the hellenistic *agōgē*. It is to Cleomenes, therefore, that he attributes the decisive reform, the reform which cuts the history of Spartan education into two separate parts.

Here too it is not a case of a new idea, and Kennell refers at length to Ollier's study (1936) of Sphairos' role in Cleomenes' reform.[9] Shimron (1972, 44) too, for the same reason, the presence of Sphairos, suggests that the education system was fundamentally changed at this period. For Kennell, we have better documentation than one might think for Cleomenes' education system: not only does he relate the scholia to Herodotos and Strabo on the age classes to Cleomenes, as well as Hesychius' gloss on *boua*, but he believes that in entries 1 to 17 of the *Instituta Laconica* we possess nothing less than extracts, cited verbatim, from Sphairos' treatise on the institutions of Sparta. These texts will be examined later; for the moment let us be content with a preliminary question: was there a 'Cleomenean education system' entirely different from the classical system? The question is important for us, because a positive reply entails refraining from using any later source (including, of course, the texts which Kennell attributes to Sphairos) in a reconstruction of the classical education system.

A few texts seem to state clearly that the reforming kings of the third century accorded a very special place to education in their concerns and in their deeds. It is generally accepted that Agis, in 242, did not have time to carry out his intentions; but, according to Plutarch (*Agis* 4.2), 'he used to say that he had no time for royalty if he could not use it to restore the laws and the ancestral *agōgē* (εἰ μὴ δι' αὐτὴν ἀναλήψοιτο τοὺς νόμους καὶ τὴν πάτριον ἀγωγήν).' Cleomenes, on the other hand, was able to progress to action (around 226). Plutarch first describes his procedure (*Cleomenes* 11.3–4): 'He turned to the education of the young and what is called the *agōgē*, on most aspects of which Sphairos, who was there, worked with him' (ἐπὶ τὴν παιδείαν τῶν νέων ἐτράπη καὶ τὴν λεγομένην ἀγωγὴν, ἧς τὰ πλεῖστα παρὼν ὁ Σφαῖρος αὐτῷ συγκαθίστη). The last phrase is especially important, as it is this which alludes to Sphairos' role. At *Cleomenes* 18.4, Plutarch describes how the Spartans greeted the reform: 'A little while later, when they had just taken up their ancestral customs again and were following the tracks of this *agōgē*, they showed as much courage and obedience as if Lycurgus was there directing the city with them' (ὀλίγου δὲ χρόνου διελθόντος, ἁψάμενοι μόνον τῶν πατρίων ἐθῶν καὶ καταστάντες εἰς ἴχνος ἐκείνης τῆς αγωγῆς, ὥσπερ παρόντι καὶ συμπολιτευομένῳ τῷ Λυκούργῳ πολλὴν ἐπίδειξιν ἀνδρείας ἐποιοῦντο καὶ πειθαρχίας). In these three passages education is certainly present (11.3: 'he turned to the education of the young'), and this is natural: any restoration of the Lycurgan order which neglected education would be bound to fail, and Sphairos, who had read Plato and Aristotle (as Cleomenes certainly had too), understood that here was the beginning of everything. But education is only mentioned in passing, as an element included in the whole. In fact it would be wrong to accept without discussion that in these texts the term ἀγωγή always means education. This depends on our accepting that the Spartan education system was in fact called this. However, as we shall see later (p. 69), *agōgē* is not a local term, but a common Greek word which is widely polysemic. It can designate education, but also, more vaguely, the collection of 'Lycurgan' customs and institutions which we can only really render as Spartan 'discipline'. The only determinative which allows us to be sure that it really means education is 'of children', ἡ τῶν παίδων ἀγωγή; none of the others (πάτριος, λεγομένη, Λακωνική, Λυκουργεία) is decisive and, as in the case of the substantive used alone, it is the context which indicates the meaning. In the case of Agis' projects, ἀγωγή is coupled with οἱ νόμοι: it would be very surprising if in such a general context the word referred to the precise reality of the education system. At *Cleomenes* 11.3–4, *agōgē* is the second term in a list where the first is education (*paideia*). Certainly καί, which links the two, can in some cases mark equivalence (with a sense close to 'i.e., that is'), but this usage is relatively rare, and it is much more natural for the copulative to link two different things, 'education' (a detail) and 'discipline' (the whole of which this detail is part). This passage is important, because it is here that Sphairos appears; moreover the phrase clearly indicates that it is in the re-establishment of 'discipline' that Sphairos collaborated, and not specifically in that of the education system.[10] The remainder of the phrase, which is the first evocation (before 18.4) of the Spartans' reaction to the proposed reform, confirms that *agōgē* does indeed have its wider sense: 'they re-established for them, as was vital, the organization of the gymnasia and of the common meals, and applied themselves, some under compulsion and force, but the majority voluntarily, to the simplicity of the Laconian way of life'; εἰς τὴν εὐτελῆ καὶ Λακωνικὴν ἐκείνην δίαιταν is a developed reprise of τὴν λεγομένην ἀγωγήν.

Τὴν...ἐκείνην δίαιταν is echoed, at 18.4, by the formula καταστάντες εἰς ἴχνος ἐκείνης τῆς ἀγωγῆς, to which Kennell accorded such importance that he made it the title of his first chapter. It does not mean 'in the track of the famous *agōgē*' (in the sense of 'education'). As at 11.4, ἐκείνη simply refers to what precedes, and ἀγωγή here refers to πάτρια ἔθη; it is, once again, 'discipline'. The expression ἐπὶ τὴν παιδείαν ἐτράπη at 11.3 is, then, the only one which definitely designates education. It is clear that Cleomenes took an interest in education, but only as one of the instruments allowing him to restore the traditional way of life (as well as a powerful symbol of that way of life). As for Sphairos, I am entirely in agreement with Powell's comment[11] that Kennell, following Ollier, surely overestimated his role. He could have been an inspiration and an adviser for Cleomenes, but the king's aim (at least his advertised aim) was not to put a new system into place; he wanted to restore the 'Lycurgan customs'. For Kennell (1995, 102), proof that the philosopher took a particular interest in the training of the young is that, already during Cleomenes' own youth, 'Sphaerus had lectured extensively at Sparta on education'. But the text (Plutarch, *Cleomenes* 2.2) on which this statement rests does not say this; it says that Sphairos 'conversed passionately with the youths and the ephebes'. Sphairos' role, then, was at the same time wider and more limited than people say: wider, because he was interested in the whole collection of 'Lycurgan customs', and more limited because he was only an adviser and because it was only a matter of a restoration. So his work consisted above all of collecting information, as much oral as written, on what society could have been like according to Lycurgus, and in order to do this he certainly used works which we do not possess, starting with those of Critias and of king Pausanias. That said, under the camouflage of restoration real novelties can be introduced, and there are multiple ways of reconstructing the past; so it is possible that Sphairos used the occasion to put some of his own ideas into practice. I am not then denying that the Cleomenean restoration could have brought about some modifications in the education system relative to the classical period; but I do not believe in a systematic rupture in its essentials.

Change and continuity

The period when the Spartan education system could have been most profoundly modified is rather the second century BC. Between about 188 and 178 there was an interruption, the existence of which is assured, as we have seen; but I am not persuaded that the re-establishment which followed is the best context for change; in such an emergency, a return to what existed before is more likely. If we take the *corpus* of dedications made by the victors in the ephebic games, we can note that the earliest references to what are called *moa* and *keloia* date to the second half of the second century. As for the word *kynagetas*, designating another contest (which would, from the Flavian period, be called *kattheratorion*), Kennell has demonstrated that it is a creation based on the model of the common Greek *kunēgetēs* ('the hunter') and probably dating to the late hellenistic period. The most convincing document seems to me to be the stele of Xenokles (*Artemis Orthia* no. 2). This dedication, which is dated to the second half (probably the end) of the second century BC, shows the existence at this period, in addition to the contest called the *moa*, of two characteristic traits of the *ephēbeia* of the Roman period, the system of *kasen* and, in the annual classes, the year of *prat*[*opam*]*pais*. This is why I think that it is in the second half of the second century BC that, having become a *civitas libera* in 146, and living in a now more peaceful world, Sparta reorganized her education system, instituting an *ephēbeia* as in other cities; this is not far from the date, 146, adopted by Kennell.

It remains to assess the extent of this transformation, and this is not easy. At first we might be tempted to judge it a complete metamorphosis. What the inscriptions show us in the Roman period (republican and especially imperial) is no longer a *paideia* but an *ephēbeia*.[12] Compared to what they were before, the names of the annual age classes are (slightly) modified, and the *cursus* is shortened by the first two years. A new type of group, the *boua*, appears; its leader, the *bouagos*, is a member of the group. The agonistic aspect is very pronounced, with numerous contests, organized either by age categories or for all. The games and exercises have a brutal, even savage, character: at the altar of Orthia, the theft of cheeses has become a regulated flagellation, capable, Cicero and Plutarch tell us, of bringing about death; the game of Platanistas, as Pausanias describes it, includes several important elements which can hardly be earlier than the late hellenistic period, and must therefore have been radically transformed, at the least; the game of ball has become an official test, a test which Kennell thinks qualified ephebes to enter adult status.

We should not, however, minimize the continuity which links this *ephēbeia* to the *paideia* of preceding centuries. It lasts five years, which makes it much closer to the system described by the glosses on the annual classes than to what happened in other cities at this period. Moreover, there is nothing to preclude its having been preceded by a period of public training for children. This is in any case what a passage of Dion of Prusa suggests (*Discourse* 25.3): 'As he (Lycurgus) prescribed, even now the Lacedaemonians are whipped, live out of doors, go naked, and endure much other treatment which would seem harsh to anyone else.' Of course, fidelity to the laws of Lycurgus is just a commonplace, but the text evokes precise customs as still real. That the ephebes of the imperial period underwent 'training periods' outside the city is very possible; that they went naked is clearly less so, and it is rather during childhood, as is described by Xenophon, that such conduct is envisageable. In the classical period, too, children were organized into 'teams': since no text gives us their local name, it is not impossible that these were already the *boua*. The dedication of Arexippos[13] shows that already in the fourth century contests were organized amongst the *paides*; but we do not know their names. Likewise, Xenophon[14] shows that the game of ball was already very popular in his time, and in the *Laws* (1.633b) Plato makes a fairly obscure allusion to what could be the classical period's counterpart of the Platanistas combat. Altogether, one gets the impression that, more than the education system itself, it is its environment, in other words society as a whole, which was transformed between the classical and the imperial periods. In this transformation the Spartans used all means, including an artificial and archaizing re-creation (being very sensitive in vocabulary, for example, according to Kennell's analyses), to ensure that the education system would give the impression of remaining unchanged. This was not in the least, as has been too often claimed, to attract foreign visitors (even if, effectively, it did attract them), but, as Kennell has very rightly said, because the Spartans thought of their education as an inheritance, fundamental to their identity.[15] My opinion is, then, that up to and including the imperial period it is continuity which prevails in the history of Spartan education; this seems to me to be normal for an area which is in every society essentially dedicated to permanence.

The reader will doubtless be convinced that the considerations which have just been expounded are intended as advance justification for a study of Spartan education in the classical period based on the use of all existing sources, without consideration of date, and conducted as if their object were an immutable ideal and not a historical reality, and so subject to change. This is not the case. To me, Kennell's work marks a turning and provides a lesson which is essential even to those who accept neither his cutting into slices of the history of Spartan education, nor his often rash theses on such and such a point of this history or on such and such a source. Neither is it certain that the Spartan education system was completely transformed over the centuries, nor that an author of the Roman imperial period like Plutarch describes, as Kennell maintains on several occasions,[16] what existed in his own time; thus presented, these hypotheses seem improbable. They nonetheless show the necessity of the greatest prudence in the handling of the sources. This is why I have decided to confine my discussion to the education of a particular period, the classical one (basically the fourth century), using, for important points, only contemporary sources (especially Xenophon). However this does not mean, in my opinion, that I have to dismiss out of hand all other sources on principle; it is possible, for example, that there may be information in Plutarch which goes back to fourth-century authors in the final analysis, and which it would be a pity to deny oneself. A careful examination, case by case, will be necessary in order to sift out what can be used, by means of constant confrontation with sources from the classical period.

I have chosen the classical period, first because it is what interests me, and also because, despite everything which today's historian may be able to reproach him with, Xenophon's account provides a basis for which one would be hard put to find an equivalent in the third century, for example. Spartan education has indeed recently given rise to two valuable books. That of Birgalias[17] employs the global approach rightly criticized by Kennell and, what is more important to my eyes, is principally interested in the history of the image of Sparta through the ages. As for that of Kennell, since he considers Xenophon to be worthy of little credence, and takes History back-to-front, he is led to consign most of his development to later periods, and has nothing much to say when, at the end of his perilous enterprise, he finally reaches the classical period (1995, 115–42). This is why I think there is room for a third work.

Notes

[1] Cf. Cicero, *Pro Flacco* 63, for whom the Spartans are 'the only people in the world who have lived now for more than seven hundred years with one and the same set of customs and unchanging laws' (tr. Kennell 1995, 6). Some inscriptions call the education system τὰ Λυκούργεια ἔθη.

[2] Review of Kennell's book, Cartledge 1997, 100.

[3] There are of course exceptions; most notable is the lucid warning in Powell 2001, 223.

[4] For a detailed critique of Kennell's theories, cf. Lévy 1997, whose opinion I entirely share.

[5] This idea of an interruption to education in the 3rd century is accepted by Hodkinson 2000, especially 434.

[6] Phylarchos, in Athenaeus 4.141f–142b.

[7] Teles, ed. Hense (1909), 28. Kennell's argument (1995, 12) is not concerned with the use of the present tense in this text.

[8] References in Kennell 1995, 173, n. 24.

[9] On Sphairos, see Kennell's exposition (1995, 98–102).

[10] The antecedent of ἧς is ἀγωγή.

[11] Powell 1998, 173–4, reviewing Kennell's work. Similarly Lupi 2000, 45 n. 56.

[12] Description in Kennell 1995, chapters 1 and 2.

[13] *Artemis Orthia* 206 no. 1; see below, pp. 210–12.

[14] *Lak. Pol.* 9.5.

[15] Kennell 1995, 48: 'Through all the cataclysmic changes the city had suffered, the *agōgē* had been preserved as a link with Sparta's heritage.'

[16] For example 1995, 31, 33, 38, 42. He does not always say this, either. Thus he affirms (205 n. 81) that when Plutarch makes education begin at 7 years old, he is talking about the classical period, hellenistic education beginning (according to him) at 14, and the *ephēbeia* at 16. Fair enough, but it seems to me that from this remark Kennell should have drawn the conclusion that *everything* Plutarch reports about education before the age of 14 relates to the classical period.

[17] Birgalias 1999 – but for the most part the text is that of a thesis submitted in 1993, and the bibliography does not really go beyond around 1988.

1

DOCUMENTARY SOURCES

By 'documentary sources' I mean those which are capable (although this hope may be disappointed) of giving us information on the functioning and the content of Spartan education in the classical period.

Xenophon

The chapters of the *Lakedaimonion Politeia* devoted to education are an exceptionally important source for us, because they constitute the only systematic account of this period. It has been equally possible to describe them either as a remarkably substantial account, or as an essentially idealistic discourse, lacking in real information, especially on the subject of organization. Each to his own; both these visions are true. The first is relatively true: in relation to the state of documentation on Sparta, an account of education in the classical period running to several pages, by a contemporary author, is a rarity of inestimable value. The second is absolutely true, that is in relation to what, in our opinion, a historical document ought to be. Now, the historian is a professional doubter of absolute truths, because he knows that truth is only a word, and that absolute truths, without confessing it, are in reality relative.

It would not be useful to provide yet another note here on the *Lak. Pol.* Suffice it to note that the attribution to Xenophon is now no longer doubted; on its date, discussion continues, with answers ranging between *c.* 390, date of Xenophon's installation at Skillous, and 378; for present purposes, this uncertainty is not too much of a problem.[1] The account of the education system occupies chapters 2 to 4, with an appendix in chapter 6.1–2. Below will be found, chapter by chapter, the text (following Dindorf's edition, Leipzig 1883, which I find preferable to that of Rühl, which replaced it in 1912 in the Teubner), a new translation, and what I shall call an analysis. This is not a commentary: that can be found in the body of this work; for the time being, my aim is simply to render intelligible the flow of the text, its intentions, the articulation of ideas and arguments.

The beginning of chapter 1 (§§1 and 2) provides a kind of Introduction, where the general idea of the treatise is explained. The author's point of departure is the paradox of Sparta, which, despite being a city with 'the lowest population', is nevertheless the most powerful and glorious of Greece, something which demonstrates that there are efficiencies other than that of number. The reason for this superiority: τὰ ἐπιτηδεύματα τῶν Σπαρτιατῶν ('the Spartans' customs', 'their rules of conduct'). It is very probable that Xenophon indicates here, in accordance with the custom of the period, what constitutes the 'title' of his treatise; it is also the Greek title given to Plutarch's *Instituta Laconica*. All the merit is attributed to Lycurgus, 'who established for them the laws, respect for which has ensured their prosperity' (θέντα αὐτοῖς τοὺς νόμους οἷς πειθόμενοι ηὐδαιμόνησαν).[2] Lycurgus was supremely σόφος, says Xenophon, who thus approaches the institutions of Sparta from a philosophical point of view, and with an eye to permanence. He demonstrated his σοφία by making laws not only different, but even opposite to those of other cities. This opposition is the major theme of the work. Sparta's individuality was an argument in propaganda against the city from the fifth century on; Xenophon turns this on its head and makes it into a eulogistic motif: Lycurgus did the opposite, *and he was right*. The rest of chapter 1 (§§3–10) treats the *teknopoiia* (production of children), first illustration of Sparta's originality, as §10 notes.

Chapter 2

1. ἐγὼ μέντοι, ἐπεὶ καὶ περὶ γενέσεως ἐξήγημαι, βούλομαι καὶ τὴν παιδείαν ἑκατέρων σαφηνίσαι. τῶν μὲν τοίνυν ἄλλων Ἑλλήνων οἱ φάσκοντες κάλλιστα τοὺς υἱεῖς παιδεύειν, ἐπειδὰν τάχιστα αὐτοῖς οἱ παῖδες τὰ λεγόμενα ξυνιῶσιν, εὐθὺς μὲν ἐπ' αὐτοῖς παιδαγωγοὺς θεράποντας ἐφιστᾶσιν, εὐθὺς δὲ πέμπουσιν εἰς διδασκάλων μαθησομένους καὶ γράμματα καὶ μουσικὴν καὶ τὰ ἐν παλαίστρᾳ. πρὸς δὲ τούτοις τῶν παίδων πόδας μὲν ὑποδήμασιν ἁπαλύνουσι, σώματα δὲ ἱματίων μεταβολαῖς διαθρύπτουσι· σίτου γε μὴν αὐτοῖς γαστέρα μέτρον νομίζουσιν. 2. ὁ δὲ Λυκοῦργος ἀντὶ μὲν τοῦ ἰδίᾳ ἕκαστον παιδαγωγοὺς δούλους ἐφιστάναι ἄνδρα ἐπέστησε κρατεῖν αὐτῶν ἐξ ὧνπερ αἱ μέγισται ἀρχαὶ καθίστανται, ὃς δὴ καὶ παιδονόμος καλεῖται. τοῦτον δὲ κύριον ἐποίησε καὶ ἁθροίζειν τοὺς παῖδας, καὶ ἐπισκοποῦντα, εἴ τις ῥᾳδιουργοίη, ἰσχυρῶς κολάζειν. ἔδωκε δ' αὐτῷ καὶ τῶν ἡβώντων μαστιγοφόρους, ὅπως τιμωροῖεν ὅτε δέοι. ὥστε πολλὴν μὲν αἰδῶ, πολλὴν δὲ πειθὼ ἐκεῖ συμπαρεῖναι. 3. ἀντί γε μὴν τοῦ ἁπαλύνειν τοὺς πόδας ὑποδήμασιν ἔταξεν ἀνυποδησίᾳ κρατύνειν, νομίζων, εἰ τοῦτ' ἀσκήσειαν, πολὺ μὲν ῥᾷον ἂν ὀρθιάδε βαίνειν, ἀσφαλέστερον δὲ πρανῆ καταβαίνειν, καὶ πηδῆσαι δὲ καὶ ἀναθορεῖν καὶ δραμεῖν θᾶττον ἀνυπόδητον, εἰ ἠσκηκὼς εἴη τοὺς πόδας, ἢ ὑποδεδεμένον. 4. καὶ ἀντί γε τοῦ ἱματίοις διαθρύπτεσθαι ἐνόμισεν ἑνὶ ἱματίῳ δι' ἔτους προσεθίζεσθαι, νομίζων οὕτως καὶ πρὸς ψύχη καὶ πρὸς θάλπη ἄμεινον ἂν παρεσκευάσθαι. 5. σῖτόν γε μὴν ἔταξε τοσοῦτον ἔχοντα συμβολεύειν τὸν εἴρενα ὡς ὑπὸ πλησμονῆς μὲν μήποτε βαρύνεσθαι, τοῦ δὲ ἐνδεεστέρως διάγειν μὴ ἀπείρως ἔχειν, νομίζων τοὺς οὕτω παιδευομένους μᾶλλον μὲν ἂν δύνασθαι, εἰ δεήσειεν, ἀσιτήσαντας

ἐπιπονῆσαι, μᾶλλον δ' ἄν, εἰ παραγγελθείη, ἀπὸ τοῦ αὐτοῦ σίτου πλείω χρόνον ἐπιταθῆναι, ἧττον δ' ἂν ὄψου δεῖσθαι, εὐχερέστερον δὲ πρὸς πᾶν ἔχειν βρῶμα, καὶ ὑγιεινοτέρως δ' ἂν διάγειν, καὶ εἰς μῆκος ἂν αὐξάνεσθαι τὴν ῥαδινὰ τὰ σώματα ποιοῦσαν τροφὴν μᾶλλον συλλαμβάνειν ἡγήσατο ἢ τὴν διαπλατύνουσαν τῷ σίτῳ. 6. ὡς δὲ μὴ ὑπὸ λιμοῦ ἄγαν αὖ πιέζοιντο, ἀπραγμόνως μὲν αὐτοῖς οὐκ ἔδωκε λαμβάνειν ὧν ἂν προσδέωνται, κλέπτειν δ' ἐφῆκεν ἔστιν ἃ τῷ λιμῷ ἐπικουροῦντας. 7. καὶ ὡς μὲν οὐκ ἀπορῶν ὅ,τι δοίη ἐφῆκεν αὐτοῖς γε μηχανᾶσθαι τὴν τροφήν οὐδένα οἶμαι τοῦτο ἀγνοεῖν· δῆλον δ' ὅτι τὸν μέλλοντα κλωπεύειν καὶ νυκτὸς ἀγρυπνεῖν δεῖ καὶ μεθ' ἡμέραν ἀπατᾶν καὶ ἐνεδρεύειν, καὶ κατασκόπους δὲ ἑτοιμάζειν τὸν μέλλοντά τι λήψεσθαι. ταῦτα οὖν δὴ πάντα δῆλον ὅτι μηχανικωτέρους τῶν ἐπιτηδείων βουλόμενος τοὺς παῖδας ποιεῖν καὶ πολεμικωτέρους οὕτως ἐπαίδευσεν. 8. εἴποι δ' ἂν οὖν τις, τί δῆτα, εἴπερ τὸ κλέπτειν ἀγαθὸν ἐνόμιζε, πολλὰς πληγὰς ἐπέβαλε τῷ ἁλισκομένῳ; ὅτι, φημὶ ἐγώ, καὶ τἆλλα ὅσα ἄνθρωποι διδάσκουσι κολάζουσι τὸν μὴ καλῶς ὑπηρετοῦντα. κἀκεῖνοι οὖν τοὺς ἁλισκομένους ὡς κακῶς κλέπτοντας τιμωροῦνται. 9. καὶ ὡς πλείστους δὴ ἁρπάσαι τυροὺς παρ' Ὀρθίας καλὸν θείς, μαστιγοῦν τούτους ἄλλοις ἐπέταξε, τοῦτο δὴ δηλῶσαι καὶ ἐν τούτῳ βουλόμενος ὅτι ἔστιν ὀλίγον χρόνον ἀλγήσαντα πολὺν χρόνον εὐδοκιμοῦντα εὐφραίνεσθαι. δηλοῦται δὲ ἐν τούτῳ ὅτι καὶ ὅπου τάχους δεῖ ὁ βλακεύων ἐλάχιστα μὲν ὠφελεῖται, πλεῖστα δὲ πράγματα λαμβάνει. 10. ὅπως δὲ μηδ' εἰ ὁ παιδονόμος ἀπέλθοι, ἔρημοί ποτε οἱ παῖδες εἶεν ἄρχοντος, ἐποίησε τὸν ἀεὶ παρόντα τῶν πολιτῶν κύριον εἶναι καὶ ἐπιτάττειν τοῖς παισὶν ὅ,τι [ἂν] ἀγαθὸν δοκοίη εἶναι, καὶ κολάζειν, εἴ τι ἁμαρτάνοιεν. τοῦτο δὲ ποιήσας διέπραξε καὶ αἰδημονεστέρους εἶναι τοὺς παῖδας· οὐδὲν γὰρ οὕτως αἰδοῦνται οὔτε παῖδες οὔτε ἄνδρες ὡς τοὺς ἄρχοντας. 11. ὡς δὲ καὶ εἴ ποτε μηδεὶς τύχοι ἀνὴρ παρών, μηδ' ὣς ἔρημοι οἱ παῖδες ἄρχοντος εἶεν, ἔθηκε τῆς ἴλης ἑκάστης τὸν τορώτατον τῶν εἰρένων ἄρχειν· ὥστε οὐδέποτε ἐκεῖ οἱ παῖδες ἔρημοι ἄρχοντός εἰσι. 12. Λεκτέον δέ μοι δοκεῖ εἶναι καὶ περὶ τῶν παιδικῶν ἐρώτων· ἔστι γάρ τι καὶ τοῦτο πρὸς παιδείαν. οἱ μὲν τοίνυν ἄλλοι Ἕλληνες ἢ ὥσπερ Βοιωτοὶ ἀνὴρ καὶ παῖς συζυγέντες ὁμιλοῦσιν, ἢ ὥσπερ Ἠλεῖοι διὰ χαρίτων τῇ ὥρᾳ χρῶνται· εἰσὶ δὲ καὶ οἳ παντάπασι τοῦ διαλέγεσθαι τοὺς ἐραστὰς εἴργουσιν ἀπὸ τῶν παίδων. 13. ὁ δὲ Λυκοῦργος ἐναντία καὶ τούτοις πᾶσι γνούς, εἰ μέν τις αὐτὸς ὢν οἷον δεῖ ἀγασθεὶς ψυχὴν παιδὸς πειρῷτο ἄμεμπτον φίλον ἀποτελέσασθαι καὶ συνεῖναι, ἐπῄνει καὶ καλλίστην παιδείαν ταύτην ἐνόμιζεν· εἰ δέ τις παιδὸς σώματος ὀρεγόμενος φανείη, αἴσχιστον τοῦτο θεὶς ἐποίησεν ἐν Λακεδαίμονι μηδὲν ἧττον ἐραστὰς παιδικῶν ἀπέχεσθαι ἢ γονεῖς παίδων ἢ καὶ ἀδελφοὶ ἀδελφῶν εἰς ἀφροδίσια ἀπέχονται. 14. τὸ μέντοι ταῦτα ἀπιστεῖσθαι ὑπό τινων οὐ θαυμάζω· ἐν πολλαῖς γὰρ τῶν πόλεων οἱ νόμοι οὐκ ἐναντιοῦνται ταῖς πρὸς τοὺς παῖδας ἐπιθυμίαις. ἡ μὲν δὴ παιδεία εἴρηται ἥ τε Λακωνικὴ καὶ ἡ τῶν ἄλλων Ἑλλήνων· ἐξ ὁποτέρας δ' αὐτῶν καὶ εὐπειθέστεροι καὶ αἰδημονέστεροι καὶ ὧν δεῖ ἐγκρατέστεροι ἄνδρες ἀποτελοῦνται, ὁ βουλόμενος καὶ ταῦτα ἐπισκοπείσθω.

1. Having finished my account of procreation, I want to explain too how children on both sides are educated. Those other Greeks who claim to give their sons the best education, as soon as they are of an age to understand what people say to them, immediately submit them to pedagogues of servile status, and immediately send them to teachers to learn their letters, *mousikē* and

gymnastic exercises. Moreover, they soften the boys' feet by putting shoes on them, and make their bodies effeminate by having them change their cloaks; as for food, their measure is the capacity of their stomachs. 2. Lycurgus, on the contrary, instead of letting each one assign slaves on a private basis as pedagogues, put in command of the boys a citizen from amongst those who occupied the highest magistracies; he is called the *paidonomos*. He gave this man the power to assemble the boys, to supervise them, and to punish severely those who misbehaved. He also appointed as his assistants whip-bearers taken from among the *hēbōntes*, to administer the necessary punishments; as a result, there is as much respect as obedience at Sparta. 3. Instead of softening their feet by putting shoes on them, he prescribed that the boys should harden them by making them go bare-foot, thinking that if they endured this training, they would climb steep slopes more quickly and would be safer in their descents, and that, with training, they would jump, dash and run more quickly bare-foot than with shoes. 4. Instead of making them effeminate by giving them several cloaks, he made it a rule that they should be accustomed to have only one throughout the whole year, thinking that in this way they would be better prepared to endure the cold as well as the heat. 5. As for food, Lycurgus prescribed that the *eirēn* should gather the quantity necessary so that they would never be weighed down by satiety, and so that they might be accustomed to a certain lack; he thought that those who were brought up like this would be more capable, at need, of making an effort without eating, could, if they were ordered to, last longer on the same rations, would have less need of eating well, would be more easily satisfied with any kind of food, and would only be the better for it. He also considered that a diet which makes the body slim would further a growth in height more than one which fattened them with food. 6. However, so that they might not be too gnawed by hunger, without authorizing them to take what they lacked without worrying, Lycurgus permitted them to steal the wherewithal to ward hunger off. 7. I think everyone realizes that it was not because he did not know what to give them to eat that he allowed them to manage in this way. It is clear that someone who wants to steal must stay awake at night, and must scheme and remain on the look-out during the day; and that anyone who wants to help himself to something must also post spies. In any case, clearly, his intention was to make the boys more astute in procuring necessities, and thus he trained them to be better warriors. 8. Why, then, someone might ask, if he considered stealing to be a good thing, did he give a sound beating to anyone who was caught? My reply is that in all kinds of education the disobedient pupil is punished. So it is at Sparta: those who are caught because they have stolen badly are punished. 9. In the same way, while deciding that it would be fine to snatch as many cheeses as possible at the sanctuary of Orthia, Lycurgus prescribed that others should whip the thieves; by this, too, he wished to demonstrate that a short period of suffering can bring about long-lasting glory. This also demonstrates that when speed is absolutely necessary, he who acts sluggishly, far from gaining advantage by it, on the contrary incurs the maximum difficulties. 10. So that, even if the *paidonomos* was absent, the boys would never be without a leader, he granted any citizen who found himself there the authority to give any order he judged appropriate, and to punish the disobedient. By doing this he made the boys even more respectful: for at Sparta there is nothing that all, boys and men alike, respect as much as the magistrates. 11. And in order that, should it happen that no man was present, even so the boys should never be without a leader, he laid down that the most intelligent of the *eirenes* should command each *ilē*: thus the boys there are never without a leader. 12. I think I must also say something about the love of boys, because this too is relevant to education. Amongst other Greeks, either, as in Boeotia, a mature man and a boy live together as a couple, or, as amongst the Eleans, possession of a young body is bought with presents; but there are also cities where it is absolutely forbidden for lovers to talk to boys. 13. Lycurgus, though, adopted a position different from that of all these people, too. When a man who was himself completely respectable was seized with admiration for a boy's soul and tried to befriend him without dishonour and to keep company with him, Lycurgus approved this and considered it to be the finest education; but if it was clearly the boy's body which interested him, Lycurgus condemned this as a terrible disgrace; so much so that at Sparta lovers abstain from physical relations with their beloveds as rigorously as do parents with their children, brothers with their brothers. 14. Some people, indeed, do not believe this, and this does not surprise me: for in many other cities the laws do not oppose lust for boys. Such is my account of education amongst the Spartans and amongst other Greeks. Which of the two creates the more obedient and respectful men, and the more capable of control whenever circumstance demands, is for each to form his opinion on, if he wants to.

Structure of the account

There are two underlying principles. The first, and most obvious, is none other than the central idea of the whole of the first part of the treatise (up to and including chapter 10), the *contrast* between Sparta and the rest of the Greeks; this principle is emphasized at the beginning and the end of the chapter, using the technique of 'ring composition'. Xenophon has therefore to contrast Spartan education to a normal education point by point. §1 is devoted to an account of this normal education, which is already in itself implicity critical. ἐπειδὰν τάχιστα, εὐθύς place repeated emphasis on the haste of the 'other Greeks' to rid themselves of the reponsibility of educating their children. It would seem that this is done a little dishonestly, because a normal education usually begins at around seven years of age, not 'as soon as children understand what is being said to them' (which would be about three years old); and education seems not to start any later at Sparta. This insistence on 'haste', then, is not immediately understandable. On the other hand, the implicit criticism of the fact that the *paidagōgoi* are slaves is much better founded, and, feeling himself to be on firm ground, Xenophon returns to it, not without complaisance, at the beginning of §2, where he will add a supplementary criticism to the passage, the fact that the pedagogues are a purely private affair (ἰδίᾳ ἕκαστον). Criticism is much less evident in the phrase 'they send them to teachers to learn their letters, *mousikē* and gymnastic exercises'. It cannot be about the list of subjects, unless Xenophon means to suggest the absence of 'civic' education; perhaps he is also aiming at the *didaskaloi*, inasmuch as they are salaried, but it does not appear that this is any different at Sparta. The author next attacks the laxity and luxury of a normal education. It is not immediately apparent in what respect giving children shoes and several cloaks is blameworthy; this will only become clear in the comparison with Sparta. On the other hand, we understand straightaway that their diet is too plentiful.

Each of these points is taken up again in what follows, with contrasts and repetition of terms. In §2, παιδαγωγοὺς δούλους ἐφιστάναι recalls παιδαγωγοὺς θεράποντας ἐφιστᾶσιν. In §3, ἀντὶ τοῦ ἁπαλύνειν τοὺς πόδας recalls πόδας ὑποδήμασιν ἁπαλύνουσι. In §4, ἀντὶ τοῦ ἱματίοις διαθρύπτεσθαι recalls (and is explained by) σώματα ἱματίων μεταβολαῖς διαθρύπτουσι. Such an echo technique is not used after this.

The second principle of the account is that of *justification*. To demonstrate point by point that the Spartans do the opposite to others would not be sufficient and could even be used against them; it is also necessary to show that they are right in doing so. The attribution, repeated every time, of each custom to Lycurgus already functions as a justification in itself, by presenting it as an element in a planned and considered work, and not as a bizarre anonymous custom. This is the purpose served by the technique of 'interior deliberation' attributed to Lycurgus on a whole series of points (νομίζων in §§3, 4, 5, ἡγήσατο and βουλόμενος in §§7 and 9).[3] But this is not enough, and, on each point, Xenophon gives an explanation and shows what the aim, the *good* aim, of the measure presented is. From the second point (the absence of shoes) onwards the explanation, which was very brief for the *paidonomos* because this institution hardly needed justifying, begins to exceed the account of the facts in length. Thus presented and repeated, the explanation appears not so much as a eulogy (which the effect of the refrain might suggest) but as an apology, that is a *defence speech*. This defensive aspect is striking throughout the chapter. Xenophon's real intention is to reply to the detractors of Spartan education by tackling them on their own ground, taking up their argumentation point by point. This can be found in the text's counterpoint: the young Spartans are badly dressed, they are bare-foot and starving; they are taught to steal; the authority of fathers is destroyed; physical pederasty is practised. To answer all these points successfully was no easy thing.

§2 *The* paidonomos

It is logical to begin by saying who is in charge of the Spartan education system; moreover, this allows Xenophon to start on solid ground. Instead of pedagogues of servile status, it is to one of the most important magistrates that the children are entrusted. His role is to 'assemble the boys' (recalling the Cretan *agretas*), which indirectly evokes the fact that they are organized in 'teams'; also to supervise them, and punish the disobedient. Like the *agōnothetēs*, he has assistants equipped with whips. The result is obedience, which is easily understood, and 'reserve', *aidōs*, which is more the product of the whole system than of the particular action of the *paidonomos*.

§3 *Absence of shoes*

Here justification suddenly becomes difficult, and it occupies the whole exposition. The idea is that it is good to harden the boys' feet so that later, during their adult life, they can, when this might be useful, go bare-foot. This end is apparently athletic, but its application must surely be understood as military: thus it would be for forest and mountain warfare that the youths were being prepared (Xenophon emphasizes the steepness of the slopes), which, at first sight, does not at all resemble traditional hoplite combat. It is generally agreed amongst the Greeks that in difficult terrain men are more sure-footed without shoes, as demonstrated by the Plataeans' escape in Thucydides (3.22.2).

§4 *Sparsity of clothes*

According to Kennell, Plutarch,[4] or his source, wrongly interpreted this piece of information as meaning only one cloak for the whole year, without any other garment, so no *chitōn*.[5] Sure enough; but does Xenophon really mean to speak of a single cloak for the year, as Kennell believes? It is not clear what sense there would be in this, and it does not accord with the justification presented by Xenophon, which is training to endure the heat and the cold. The expression 'a single cloak' is contrasted to 'changes of cloak' (ἱματίων μεταβολαί) practised in other cities (§1). This means, then: a single *type* of cloak, which would be at once too hot in summer and too cold in winter; in this way the desired training would be achieved. Of course, for the poorest a single type of cloak would in fact be equivalent to a single cloak.

I think that in these two paragraphs Xenophon has in mind his memory of the expedition of the Ten Thousand, during which the Greek warriors had to advance and fight in difficult terrain, and to endure intensely cold temperatures. He knew from experience that it was *also* necessary to prepare oneself for this. The characteristics described in §§3 and 4 are likewise found in Cretan education as expounded by Ephoros (70F149), quoted by Strabo (10.4): walking on sloping terrain in §16; the single cloak in §20.

§5 *Diet*

'He prescribed that the *eirēn* should gather...': I have adopted the most commonly agreed text (that of Dindorf 1883, Ollier 1934, and Marchant 1968), which includes two corrections; I shall return to this point later (p. 83). The justification for this paradoxical practice, an intentionally insufficient supply of food, is multiple and infiltrates the whole exposition. In the first place, it takes the form of a consecutive double proposition defining the quantity of food provided by the desired result: what is necessary for them not to be weighed down (is this in order to encourage growth, as at the end of the section, or activity, a theme which is taken up again a little later?) and to accustom them to lack of food.

This justification is given new impetus by a reflection (νομίζων) attributed to Lycurgus. An insufficient diet first develops specific abilities in the boys, that is ones linked to the training they are pursuing: the ability to make an effort even without having eaten; the ability to hold out longer (than others) on a specified ration. We find here, and up to the end of the exposition, a whole series of comparatives,[6] which express the idea of a kind of competition between Spartan boys and others, where the Spartans, thanks to their education, prevail on every point. The Spartan *boys*: because, contrary to what one might think, Xenophon seems to keep strictly to the chronological framework of the education system; the *present* participle τοὺς οὕτως παιδευόμενους shows, I think, that he is not looking forward to an age when the adult will reap the benefits of the regimen. It is indeed already at the stage of training during childhood that the results are apparent. But it is of course impossible for the mind not to jump from the present to the military end; the vocabulary suggests it, σῖτος, πόνος (contained in ἐπιπονῆσαι), παραγγέλλω (which frequently has a military sense). Furthermore, *Inst. Lac.* 13, which is inspired on the subject by this passage to the point of literally reproducing an expression from it, clearly exposes this military end.[7] But, continues Xenophon, a controlled diet also has benefits which become apparent in a more general way, throughout life: ability to eat less, ability to adapt to any kind of diet, with better health as a bonus. These general advantages strongly recall the praise of temperance by Socrates in the *Memorabilia* (1.5); but we may detect there too, as before, the memory of his experience in the Ten Thousand: to the extent that we might ask whether it was not this which 'converted' Xenophon to Spartan education.

It is noticeable that all these benefits, while including the psychological dimension of endurance, are essentially physical and even physiological. So it is not surprising to find this paragraph ending with a medical remark which is indeed introduced by ὑγιεινοτέρως. Hippocrates was a contemporary of Xenophon, and the treatise *On Regimen* (whether or not it is by him) is usually dated to the end of the fifth century or the beginning of the fourth; the regimen, which has to be adapted for each individual, is a result of the combination of diet and exercises. In recommending a restricted diet and numerous harsh exercises *at the same time*, Xenophon is applying the master's teachings in a rather strange manner. What he says here is considerably developed in *Inst. Lac.* 13 and in Plutarch, *Lyc.* 17.8; but if these texts add some jargon, they do not provide any supplementary ideas.[8]

§§6–9 *Stealing*

Xenophon seems to think that Lycurgus, with extreme skill, killed two birds with one stone: not only did he force the young Spartans to profit from the benefits of a restricted diet, but in doing this he pushed them to practise an occupation which is no less educational: stealing. This is indeed presented as the young people's defence against hunger; so as a rule it is food which they steal. We might be tempted to charge Xenophon with illogicality, insofar as these larcenies are a means of escaping from the much-vaunted diet; but there is no real contradiction, so evident is it that the author thinks that the few food supplements thus acquired do not change the essential in any way, no more than the supplements brought to the common meals by hunting, where the 'extras' (*epaikla*) do not compromise the austerity. In fact, since hunger and stealing are *a priori* equally incomprehensible forms of behaviour for us in an educational context, it seems to me impossible to shed light on the one by the other.

For Xenophon, stealing is a consequence of hunger, but it also has its own justification: this is, once again, the military end. For him, the good soldier is one who can combine individual initiative with discipline and team spirit. Likewise, the young thief must both act by himself, to conceive the theft, put the plan into action, participate in its realization, and at the same time command the team who are helping him; thus will he serve his apprenticeship in command. If the skill with which Xenophon (alone against all, it is true) defends the educational value of children's theft at Sparta is indisputable,[9] we cannot say as much of his sincerity.[10] What makes me think this is not so much the discussion in the *Anabasis* (4.6.14–15) between Xenophon and the Spartan Cheirisophos, *à propos* a military position which they have to capture, concerning the respective aptitudes of the Spartans and the Athenians for stealing: for this clearly develops in a joking tone, between two men who know each other well and respect each other; it remains on the surface of things and does not provide any real criticism. On the other hand, in a passage of the *Cyropaedia* (1.6.31 ff.), where the question of whether the teaching of deceit and cunning should be part of education is very seriously posed and discussed, the answer is clearly negative. The position which he adopts here, then, does not correspond with his personal opinion; it is dictated to him both by his apologetic aim and by the anxiety, common amongst all writers, that his argument be coherent, an argument which maintains that, wherever it departs from the common Greek way of doing things, Spartan practice is right.

In §8, the exposition takes the form (very common in the 'Old Oligarch') of a discussion with an imaginary interlocutor. The paradox of the punishment of thieves (they are compelled to steal, then they are punished for so doing) is explained with ease. It is in this connection that the allusion to the theft of cheeses 'at the sanctuary of Orthia' occurs in §9. The juxtaposition shows that Lycurgus acted in a coherent manner: there too it is compulsory to steal, and there too one is 'punished' (with the difference that *all* definitely receive blows, as is shown later by the reference to suffering). Having been explained by its classification under the rubric of prescribed and punished theft, the rite is also justified in itself: it is a test. Whoever passes it best gains a double benefit: he acquires lasting glory (which makes it possible that the title 'victor at the altar', *bōmonikas*, already existed and was highly valued in the classical period), and, in proving his agility and determination, he succeeds both in taking more cheeses and in receiving fewer lashes. We find the same idea again in connection with war, in 9.2, and earlier in Tyrtaios (fr. 11.11–13 W): those who fight the best have the best chances of survival.

§§10–11 *The delegation of authority*

This theme is introduced by what looks like a return to §2, on the *paidonomos*. Xenophon indicated there that the *paidonomos* was accompanied by assistants carrying whips; he seems here to pursue this account by adding that he also had other deputies, which all citizens are, matters being presented as if, as a rule, the *paidonomos* was supposed to be present wherever there were boys. Thus any citizen who finds himself present automatically becomes the magistrate's delegate: this is what is meant by the phrase at the end of §10 about respect for magistrates at Sparta (a theme which will be developed in chapter 8).

Here Xenophon might appear to diverge from his main theme, which is, we must remember, Sparta's originality. But there is another exposition of the delegation of authority, in 6.1–2, and this is clearly subordinated to the theme.

> 6.1. ἐναντία γε μὴν ἔγνω καὶ τάδε τοῖς πλείστοις. ἐν μὲν γὰρ ταῖς ἄλλαις πόλεσι τῶν ἑαυτοῦ ἕκαστος καὶ παίδων καὶ οἰκετῶν καὶ χρημάτων ἄρχουσιν· ὁ δὲ Λυκοῦργος, κατασκευάσαι βουλόμενος ὡς ἂν μηδὲν βλάπτοντες ἀπολαύοιέν τι οἱ πολῖται ἀλλήλων ἀγαθόν, ἐποίησε παίδων ἕκαστον ὁμοίως τῶν ἑαυτοῦ καὶ τῶν ἀλλοτρίων ἄρχειν. 2. ὅταν δέ τις εἰδῇ ὅτι οὗτοι πατέρες εἰσὶ τῶν

παίδων, ὧν αὐτὸς ἄρχει, ἀνάγκη οὕτως ἄρχειν ὥσπερ ἂν καὶ τῶν ἑαυτοῦ ἄρχεσθαι βούλοιτο. ἢν δέ τις παῖς ποτε πληγὰς λαβὼν ὑπ' ἄλλου κατείπῃ πρὸς τὸν πατέρα, αἰσχρόν ἐστι μὴ οὐκ ἄλλας πληγὰς ἐμβάλλειν τῷ υἱεῖ. οὕτω πιστεύουσιν ἀλλήλοις μηδὲν αἰσχρὸν προστάττειν τοῖς παισίν.

6.1. Here are some more points where Lycurgus decided the opposite to most people. For in other cities, each is master of his own children and slaves and possessions; but Lycurgus, wanting to arrange things so that citizens, without doing any harm, might to some extent gain mutual enjoyment from their possessions, decided that each man would have control over other men's children just as over his own. 2. Nonetheless, when someone knows that the children over whom he has control themselves have fathers who have the same right, he is obliged to control them as he would want others to control his own. If a child who has been beaten by another father reports this to his own, the latter is obliged, on pain of dishonour, to give him further blows; so great is their confidence in one another that no one will ever give any dishonourable order to the children.

What we have here is another facet of the subject treated in 2.10: it is no longer the delegation to every citizen of the *paidonomos*' authority (and so that of the city), but the communization of paternal authority. The context is, moreover, what we might call 'communal practices' in regard to certain categories of owned property (slaves, dogs, horses, provisions), possessions which children are thus considered to be part of.[11] The frame of reference, then, is not the same: in 2.10 the scene is necessarily set out of doors, while in 6.1 it is rather inside the *oikos*. In 6.2, Xenophon carefully lays out how the reversibility of the community relationship automatically works against any abuse of authority. This custom is evidently a striking novelty in relation to the norm in Greek cities. The delegation of the *paidonomos*' authority seems less peculiar, but what it suggests is less a communization of children than anxiety for constant surveillance, which is indeed a distinctive feature of Spartan education. This is so true that Xenophon seems to explain the organization of the boys into groups (the *ilai*), placed under the authority of the *eirenes*, exclusively by this same anxiety.[12] In reality, anxiety for permanent authority explains neither the existence of these groups nor the *eirēn*'s command: they are teams which have a certain autonomy, the absence of adults is not occasional but structural, and they do indeed need a leader. What might need explaining is the fact that this leader is not an adult, nor a member of the group; there is something here which stems from the very status of the *eirēn* in society.

§§12–14 *Pederasty*

It is not by chance that this point is approached last and rather reluctantly by Xenophon. This is, I would say, the author's most serious difficulty. It is not the greatest, because justifying the fact that theft was included in the 'compulsory subjects' was technically more difficult, while for pederasty there existed an obvious answer, the very one which Xenophon gives. But it is the most serious, because if theft might look like a rather outlandish side-issue, pederasty matters a great deal more. A pederastic relationship (that is, between a boy between, say, twelve and eighteen years old and an adult) could only be approved, by a philosophical disciple of Socrates, as a kind of crowning of the educational process, on the imperative condition that it remained chaste: this is precisely, he says, what happened at Sparta.[13] He qualifies it as 'the finest education' (καλλίστη παιδεία, §13): that is, for him it played an essential role in education. However, *in fine* he shows himself rather defeatist about his ability to convey his convictions concerning chastity at Sparta, doubtless because he was very aware of going against the tide.

Here, Xenophon cannot easily maintain that the Spartans' practice (as he presents it) was the opposite of other Greeks'. Indeed he says himself, with supporting examples, that cities' approaches to the subject were extremely diverse. What the Spartans do is rather exactly in the middle: neither absolute prohibition nor complete licence. On the other hand, the pederastic relationship is not presented here as compulsory, nor as institutionalized, which obviously would make it more difficult to justify. It is described as the result of free choice – and this being, apparently, the act of the single adult: this last point surely corresponds to reality.

The concluding formula 'such is my account of education amongst the Spartans and amongst other Greeks' seems to indicate the *end* of the discussion of education in the *Lak. Pol.*; the discussion is all the more firmly closed because this phrase makes a 'ring' with that of the beginning: 'I want to explain too how children on both sides are educated.' However, the most widespread view is that we only have here the account of the education of *paides*, and that chapters 3 and 4 provide the sequel concerning the other age categories. We must then ask ourselves about the status of this chapter 2 and its function in the treatise.

There is no doubt that, although there may be no (or little) further mention of them later, some of the aspects of education described and justified here are again present at later stages: the authority of the *paidonomos*, the delegation of authority, and above all the pederastic relationship.[14] On other points, at least as far as the *paidiskoi* are concerned, the case ranges from doubtful to probable, without being confirmed: belonging to a 'team', sparsity of clothing, practice of theft (at least in the form of the theft of cheeses). It is tempting to say, then, that in chapter 2, rather than simply the education of *paides* (a term which can indeed, taken in its wider sense, include *paidiskoi*), it is either the most striking features[15] or, perhaps rather, the most criticized aspects of the education system *as a whole* which are explained and justified; and that the discussion of education is pursued later in the exposition of features particular to each age in turn. But why, then, this concluding formula at the end of chapter 2? Do we have here something like hesitation on Xenophon's part in the conduct of his account? It is not necessary to posit such a thing: we can rather say that at the end of chapter 2 'properly so-called' (or rather 'commonly so-called') *paideia* finishes, that of *paides*. At the age reached at the beginning of chapter 3 *paideia* amongst other Greeks finishes, as §1 of this chapter strongly emphasizes. From here on, therefore, it becomes impossible to make a systematic comparison between Spartan education and the systems of other cities, because in them past this age there is no longer any education at all.

Chapter 3

1. ὅταν γε μὴν ἐκ παίδων εἰς τὸ μειρακιοῦσθαι ἐκβαίνωσι, τηνικαῦτα οἱ μὲν ἄλλοι παύουσι μὲν ἀπὸ παιδαγωγῶν, παύουσι δὲ ἀπὸ διδασκάλων, ἄρχουσι δὲ οὐδένες ἔτι αὐτῶν, ἀλλ' αὐτονόμους ἀφιᾶσιν· ὁ δὲ Λυκοῦργος καὶ τούτων τἀναντία ἔγνω. 2. καταμαθὼν γὰρ τοῖς τηλικούτοις μέγιστον μὲν φρόνημα ἐμφυόμενον, μάλιστα δὲ ὕβριν ἐπιπολάζουσαν, ἰσχυροτάτας δὲ ἐπιθυμίας τῶν ἡδονῶν παρισταμένας, τηνικαῦτα πλείστους μὲν πόνους αὐτοῖς ἐπέβαλε, πλείστην δὲ ἀσχολίαν ἐμηχανήσατο. 3. ἐπιθεὶς δὲ καὶ εἴ τις ταῦτα φύγοι, μηδενὸς ἔτι τῶν καλῶν τυγχάνειν, ἐποίησε μὴ μόνον τοὺς ἐκ δημοσίου ἀλλὰ καὶ τοὺς κηδομένους ἑκάστων ἐπιμελεῖσθαι ὡς μὴ ἀποδειλιάσαντες ἀδόκιμοι παντάπασιν ἐν τῇ πόλει γένοιντο. 4. πρὸς δὲ τούτοις τὸ αἰδεῖσθαι ἰσχυρῶς ἐμφυσιῶσαι βουλόμενος αὐτοῖς καὶ ἐν ταῖς ὁδοῖς ἐπέταξεν ἐντὸς μὲν τοῦ ἱματίου τὼ χεῖρε ἔχειν, σιγῇ δὲ πορεύεσθαι, περιβλέπειν δὲ μηδαμοῖ, ἀλλ' αὐτὰ τὰ πρὸ τῶν ποδῶν ὁρᾶν. ἔνθα δὴ καὶ δῆλον γεγένηται ὅτι τὸ ἄρρεν φῦλον καὶ εἰς τὸ σωφρονεῖν ἰσχυρότερόν ἐστι τῆς θηλείας φύσεως. 5. ἐκείνων γοῦν ἧττον μὲν ἂν φωνὴν ἀκούσαις ἢ τῶν λιθίνων, ἧττον δ' ἂν ὄμματα μεταστρέψαις ἢ τῶν χαλκῶν, αἰδημονεστέρους δ' ἂν αὐτοὺς ἡγήσαιο καὶ αὐτῶν τῶν ἐν τοῖς θαλάμοις παρθένων. καὶ ἐπειδὰν εἰς τὸ φιλίτιόν γε ἀφίκωνται, ἀγαπητὸν αὐτῶν καὶ τὸ ἐρωτηθὲν ἀκοῦσαι. καὶ τῶν μὲν αὖ παιδίσκων οὕτως ἐπεμελήθη.

1. When they leave the category of children and enter adolescence, this is, amongst other Greeks, the end of pedagogues, the end of teachers; no one is in charge of them any more, they are left free. On this point too Lycurgus took the opposite decision. 2. For having noticed that it is at this age that the temperament is the most arrogant, insolence the most frequent, and desires the most violent, it is on these that he most imposed harsh exercises, for these that he organized the most complete absence of respite. 3. In prescribing also that anyone who shirked these obligations would have no further share in the 'good things', he contrived that not only the city representatives but also those responsible for each boy would see to it that he avoided bringing complete dishonour on himself in the city by cowardice. 4. Furthermore, wishing firmly

> to inculcate reserve, he prescribed that even in the street they should keep their hands under their cloak, walk in silence, and, instead of looking around them, they should keep their gaze fixed in front of their feet. In this way he proved that the masculine sex prevails over the feminine sex even in modesty. 5. In any case, you would hear stone statues talking sooner than these youths, and see bronze statues turning their eyes; you would judge them even more reserved than virgins in their wedding chamber. And when they come to the common meals, they confine themselves to answering the questions put to them. This then is the way in which Lycurgus dealt with *paidiskoi.*

Like the one before, this chapter is clearly delineated by ring composition: 'when they leave the category of children and enter adolescence…this then is the way in which Lycurgus dealt with *paidiskoi*'. This chapter too is constructed on the contrast between Sparta and other cities, but this contrast changes in nature: it no longer operates separately on each point, but concerns the chapter as a whole, for, says Xenophon, outside Sparta there would be nothing to say about the education of adolescents, because there is none. Thus formulated the declaration is perhaps surprising: Xenophon knew very well that at Athens, for example, education extended through adolescence for some young men. However, what the author has in mind is not simply education but the fact that the city deals with these youths, that it is compulsory and that strict discipline is imposed on them. As in chapter 2, it is not a matter of instruction but of real education.

The structure of the exposition is simple: §1, the contrast between Sparta and other cities; §2, the severity of discipline and its motives; §3, punishments (the nature of these shows that at this age things become serious, and that this period already has implications for the whole future of the citizen-to-be); §§4–5, the *eukosmia* of *paidiskoi*, first in the street (a long exposition), then at the *syssition*.

At the beginning I have, like Ollier, kept the text of the manuscripts, ἐκ παίδων εἰς τὸ μειρακιοῦσθαι ἐκβαίνωσι, although Cobet, who has been followed by many others, athetises εἰς τὸ μειρακιοῦσθαι; I shall explain myself below (p. 89). I also keep, further on, the manuscript reading τῶν ἐν τοῖς θαλάμοις παρθένων. Ollier argued in favour of the text quoted by Stobaeus and by Pseudo-Longinus, τῶν ἐν τοῖς ὀφθαλμοῖς παρθένων,[16] but his reasoning seems to me to come up against two objections: first, the pupil of the eye is designated by κορή and not by παρθένος, and we would have to posit that Xenophon had superimposed a play on words on top of a metaphor; second, and most importantly, he is here simply picking up the idea expressed in §4, that the masculine sex prevails over the feminine sex even in modesty, which shows that young girls are indeed relevant here. As we shall see later, Ollier misunderstood the exact tone of the text.

On the level of content, this chapter is even more disappointing than the previous for those who are in search of information. In §2, the intemperance of adolescents is a commonplace. It would be interesting to know what the 'harsh exercises' (πόνοι) consisted of, the 'ceaseless occupations' (ἀσχολία) of the *paidiskoi*; should we understand them to be more or less the same as for the *paides*? Every commentator has picked up on the extremely rhetorical character of §§4 and 5. The tone is that of a eulogy: 5 simply reprises 4, despite the variety introduced by the address to the reader and the statue metaphor. The portrait of the reserved adolescent is itself also a commonplace, which reappears in every period: hands held under the cloak can be found in Dion of Prusa and Artemidoros;[17] eyes lowered, in a fragment of an anonymous comic writer quoted by Lucian;[18] silence[19] is already in Aristophanes.[20] This is nothing other than the stereotype of the perfectly educated young boy, like Plato's Charmides. What, for Xenophon, is particular to Sparta is that this model is imposed by law, and that everyone conforms to it, and not just a few members of the elite as elsewhere.[21]

What gives this very conventional portrait a certain evocative power is its discretely erotic atmosphere. Xenophon, who in the previous chapter pleads the cause of chastity, surely has not done this on purpose; but the simple act of sketching the portrait of modest and reserved young boys, as produced by a very strict education, necessarily had erotic resonances, the Greeks being what they were, as much in the author's unconscious as for his readers or listeners. It is to such boys, timid and blushing, like Charmides in Plato's dialogue, that men wanted to pay court, this virginal modesty that men wanted to force; such a conquest alone brought the prize. This latent eroticism is also contributed to by the heterosexual comparisons and allusions (it is not by chance that the virgins are evoked 'in their wedding chambers', ἐν τοῖς θαλάμοις, something Ollier did not understand), by means of which the boys are appreciated, according to their virtue, as objects of desire just as much, and even more (end of §4), than girls. If this commentary arouses some scepticism, refer to the words of the Just Argument in the *Clouds* (961–83); this portrait of well brought up boys produced by the old education is strewn with erotic allusions which are completely intentional and not in the least bit veiled. So this ending to chapter 3, like that of chapter 2, is placed under the sign of Eros.

Stricto sensu, as we have seen, this chapter is not about education, a subject which Xenophon says he has exhausted in chapter 2. Here it is 'how Lycurgus dealt with' youths, who at the beginning are implicitly called *meirakia* and at the end explicitly *paidiskoi*.[22] However, several details show that this chapter is indeed part of the account of education in a broad sense. First, there is the contrast between Sparta and other cities. Amongst other Greeks, says

Xenophon, *paideia* stops at adolescence; whereas, he continues, Lycurgus did the opposite. In other words, then, the lawgiver, according to him, *prolonged paideia* throughout this age range (at least). Next there are, as we have seen, the features described in chapter 2 which surely lasted (even if this is not said) throughout adolescence. Finally, there is this 'programme' of 'harsh exercises' imposed on adolescents by the city, which Xenophon says left them no leisure time: here is something which very much resembles education.

Chapter 4

1. περί γε μὴν τῶν ἡβώντων πολὺ μάλιστα ἐσπούδασε, νομίζων τούτους, εἰ γένοιντο οἵους δεῖ, πλεῖστον ῥέπειν ἐπὶ τὸ ἀγαθὸν τῇ πόλει. 2. ὁρῶν οὖν, οἷς ἂν μάλιστα φιλονικία ἐγγένηται, τούτων καὶ χοροὺς ἀξιακροατοτάτους γιγνομένους, καὶ γυμνικοὺς ἀγῶνας ἀξιοθεατοτάτους, ἐνόμιζεν, εἰ καὶ τοὺς ἡβῶντας συμβάλλοι εἰς ἔριν περὶ ἀρετῆς, οὕτως ἂν καὶ τούτους ἐπὶ πλεῖστον ἀφικνεῖσθαι ἀνδραγαθίας. ὡς οὖν τούτους αὖ συνέβαλεν, ἐξηγήσομαι. 3. αἱροῦνται τοίνυν αὐτῶν οἱ ἔφοροι ἐκ τῶν ἀκμαζόντων τρεῖς ἄνδρας· οὗτοι δὲ ἱππαγρέται καλοῦνται. τούτων δ' ἕκαστος ἄνδρας ἑκατὸν καταλέγει, διασαφηνίζων ὅτου ἕνεκα τοὺς μὲν προτιμᾷ, τοὺς δὲ ἀποδοκιμάζει. 4. οἱ οὖν μὴ τυγχάνοντες τῶν καλῶν πολεμοῦσι τοῖς τε ἀποστείλασιν αὐτοὺς καὶ τοῖς αἱρεθεῖσιν ἀνθ' αὐτῶν καὶ παραφυλάττουσιν ἀλλήλους, ἐάν τι παρὰ τὰ καλὰ νομιζόμενα ῥᾳδιουργῶσι. 5. καὶ αὕτη δὴ γίγνεται ἡ θεοφιλεστάτη τε καὶ πολιτικωτάτη ἔρις, ἐν ᾗ ἀποδέδεικται μὲν ἃ δεῖ ποιεῖν τὸν ἀγαθόν, χωρὶς δ' ἑκάτεροι ἀσκοῦσιν ὅπως ἀεὶ κράτιστοι ἔσονται, ἐὰν δέ τι δέῃ, καθ' ἕνα ἀρήξουσι τῇ πόλει παντὶ σθένει. 6. ἀνάγκη δ' αὐτοῖς καὶ εὐεξίας ἐπιμελεῖσθαι. καὶ γὰρ πυκτεύουσι διὰ τὴν ἔριν ὅπου ἂν συμβάλωσι· διαλύειν μέντοι τοὺς μαχομένους πᾶς ὁ παραγενόμενος κύριος. ἢν δέ τις ἀπειθῇ τῷ διαλύοντι, ἄγει αὐτὸν ὁ παιδονόμος ἐπὶ τοὺς ἐφόρους· οἱ δὲ ζημιοῦσι μεγαλείως, καθιστάναι βουλόμενοι εἰς τὸ μήποτε ὀργὴν τοῦ μὴ πείθεσθαι τοῖς νόμοις κρατῆσαι. 7. τοῖς γε μὴν τὴν ἡβητικὴν ἡλικίαν πεπερακόσιν, ἐξ ὧν ἤδη καὶ αἱ μέγισται ἀρχαὶ καθίστανται, οἱ μὲν ἄλλοι Ἕλληνες ἀφελόντες αὐτῶν τὸ ἰσχύος ἔτι ἐπιμελεῖσθαι στρατεύεσθαι ὅμως αὐτοῖς ἐπιτάττουσιν, ὁ δὲ Λυκοῦργος τοῖς τηλικούτοις νόμιμον ἐποίησε κάλλιστον εἶναι τὸ θηρᾶν, εἰ μή τι δημόσιον κωλύοι, ὅπως δύναιντο καὶ οὗτοι μηδὲν ἧττον τῶν ἡβώντων στρατιωτικοὺς πόνους ὑποφέρειν.

1. The *hēbōntes* were the object of his greatest concern, on the principle that if they were to become what they should, they would clearly incline the city towards good. 2. So, seeing that it is when the strongest competitive spirit exists that choirs are most worth listening to and gymnastic competitions most worth watching, he thought that if he made the *hēbōntes* also compete in virtue, they would achieve the height of valour. I shall explain how he achieved this. 3. Amongst those of them who are at the height of their development, the ephors chose three men; these are called *hippagretai*. Each of them draws up a list of a hundred men, explaining why he is choosing some and leaving others aside. 4. Those who do not win this honour think of both those who have left

> them aside and those who have been chosen in their stead as their enemies; because of this, they mutually spy on each other, in order to see if they are committing some act contrary to what is considered good. 5. This is how the rivalry dearest to the gods and most worthy of citizens is instilled; it makes clear what a good man must do; each of the two groups trains independently to be as good as possible and to defend the city, if the need arises, with all their might. 6. They also have to watch their physical fitness. Indeed, their rivalry pushes them to fist-fights wherever they encounter one another. However, anyone who comes upon them has the right to separate the combatants. If one of them refuses to obey this arbiter, the *paidonomos* brings him before the ephors; they punish him with a heavy fine, with the intention of inducing him never to let anger prevent him from obeying the laws.

In §1, Xenophon announces an account of the way in which Lycurgus organized the category of *hēbōntes*. The content of the chapter does not match this programme. The account really just develops one theme, that of rivalry between the young people.[23] Everything we know about Spartan society shows that competition was a permanent feature from childhood to election to the *Gerousia*; but Xenophon thinks that it is at the age of the *hēbōntes* that it is the most pitiless, because it is then that the 'career' of those who are only future citizens becomes apparent (something which is entirely possible). It is probable that what struck him most about the *hēbōntes* was the extreme tension which ruled amongst them, and he wants to show that this tension is not a result of the young men's temperament, but that it is intended and organized by the laws themselves. This is a paradox, for the laws generally organize order and concord rather, and Sparta built her reputation on precisely this (*eunomia*). That is why Xenophon insists so much on the fact that it is a 'good rivalry', the best for the gods and for the city (ἡ θεοφιλεστάτη τε καὶ πολιτικωτάτη ἔρις) because its object is the city's good, and because of this it points the city towards good. It is not enough to say, as Ollier does,[24] that Xenophon here 'recalls' a passage of Hesiod (*Works and Days* 17–26): it is a *reference*; he borrows the idea from it by transposing to the political sphere what the poet applied to the sphere of work and the craftsman.[25] It remains for Xenophon to demonstrate that this rivalry results from love for the city and not from individual ambition, and that it is a good thing to direct all the energy of both those who are recruited as *hippeis* and those who are rejected (because he strongly emphasizes this reciprocity) towards the preparation and execution of apparently pointless confrontations.

This theme is implemented in a particularly rigorous fashion in a structure which alternates theoretical considerations on the good civic *eris* and concrete facts – for there is in this chapter some real information, as much about the selection of the *hippeis* as about the brawls amongst the youths.

§2, theoretical: the usefulness of emulation, familiar in the case of choirs and sporting contests, less so in the case of the good of the city. In each case, it results in a raising of the level of performance.
§§3–4, application to Sparta: the recruitment of *hippeis* and the rivalries which ensue.
§5, theoretical: these rivalries benefit the city, because they make everyone aspire to excellence, especially in combat.
§6, application to Sparta: the physical aspect and its limitations.

This to-ing and fro-ing between theory and practice is effective, and, if you accept the author's presuppositions, convincing.

The choice of the theme, and the fact that Xenophon sticks to it rigorously, have curious consequences. The *hēbōntes* surely did have numerous and important activities; but Xenophon chooses only to mention these rivalries and brawls, as if these were their only occupation. Because of this, the *hippeis*' tasks and the importance of their role in the functioning of the state are completely obscured. Not only does the author suppress everything but the fact, the process, and above all the consequences of selection, but the institution is presented in such a way that we might think the setting of the youths in competition was its only aim. To the unsuspecting reader, the *hippeis* are thus in danger of appearing to be a pseudo-institution, a 'joke' institution – which is evidently not what Xenophon thinks, who knew it and understood its importance, as is shown by his account of the way in which the conspiracy of Cinadon was put down (*Hell.* 3.3.9). Such is the distortion produced by the fact that here, as throughout the treatise but perhaps even more clearly here, his discussion is entirely governed by ideology. The *hippeis* are not even named (as in *Hell.* 3.3.9, their name has to be deduced from that of the *hippagretai*), a typical example of the author's intellectual attitude, which is not at all concerned with transmitting information: this is assumed to be familiar.

Why has he chosen this theme of rivalry? Doubtless, as I have said, he was really struck by the tension prevalent amongst the *hēbōntes* – we can credit him with this. But he had other reasons, connected to the logic of his account. First, this theme fits perfectly with his general idea, which is that Lycurgus did completely the opposite to other Greeks. In other cities, the ideal is harmony amongst citizens and submission to the authorities: here we see the young vowing surely fierce and durable hatreds against one another, and rebelling against the choice made by the authorities. The other reason for this choice, less evident but undoubtedly decisive, is Xenophon's desire to reply, without saying so, as he does elsewhere, to the critics.[26] It is easy to imagine how Sparta's adversaries who were familiar with these customs might have exploited them, protesting against the perversion represented by the obligation placed on the youths, including those who had been chosen, to devote all their energy to these quarrels; against the spying and, absolutely without doubt, the informing which it entailed;[27] against the physical brutality which was deployed therein.[28] He is particularly careful to reply to this last point, by showing that this use of force was beneficial to the physical condition of those concerned, and that it was limited by very precise rules, so that it could not entail serious consequences.

In the end, Xenophon comes out rather well from this dangerous exercise, but he cannot remedy the weakness of his thesis itself, that the behaviour imposed on the *hēbōntes* by custom is an example par excellence of the good *eris*. As Birgalias has shown,[29] there is not a great deal in common between the agonistic spirit cited as a model in §2 and the rivalries of the Spartan youths. The *agōn* takes place between two men placed on an equal footing in which the better man wins; here there is no equality, because the choice of the better man is made *beforehand*. To be sound, rivalry has to take place before the decision, and this, taken under conditions accepted by all, puts an end to the competition; here, on the contrary, competition is *born of the decision* and takes place in a ghastly context, in a spirit of revenge and jealousy. Informing, ambushes and evil blows of all kinds take the place of rules of the game. These practices, which Xenophon wants to make us accept as bouts of virtue, in reality show Spartan education in its worst light. Transposed to the political sphere, such behaviour would make of each election to a post of responsibility the start of an endless struggle where anything, or almost anything, would go.

Conclusion

Is it legitimate to make chapters 2–4 (with 6.1–2), thought of as a whole, into an account of the Spartan education system? If this was the case, it would be the longest section of the treatise after that on military matters, and this length would have to be explained either by Xenophon's early awareness (before Plato and Aristotle) of the importance of the role of education in the city's system, or (perhaps rather) by the number of criticisms which were current on the subject. We have seen that the concluding formula of chapter 2 announces the end of the account of *paideia*; on the other hand, the introductory phrase of chapter 5, 'I have explained in outline the measures enacted by Lycurgus concerning each age-group (ἃ μὲν οὖν ἑκάστῃ ἡλικίᾳ ἐνομοτέθησεν σχεδὸν εἴρηται)', indicates that for the author, if chapters 2–4 do indeed form a whole, its subject is not exactly education, but the regulation specific to each age-group,[30] chapter 2 alone treating of *paideia* proper. In practice, it seems to me that this comes to the same thing. Certain features, as we have seen, link chapter 3 to this account of *paideia*, and do so even in the author's mind. The same goes for the *hēbōntes*: of course, they are physically adults and fight in the army, so much so that it might seem strange to talk of *paideia* in connection with them; but they still do not lead an independent life, they are closely supervised and they undergo a 'breaking in'. The most significant thing, as far as they are concerned, is the role of the *paidonomos* in §6: for Xenophon, it goes without saying that the *hēbōntes* are his responsibility, even if he does not have the power to punish them and for that he has to transfer them to the ephors. All in all, then, I believe that it is legitimate to think that, for Xenophon, final departure from the education system only took place on departure from the category of *hēbōntes*; but this departure was progressive, as their introduction into the life of the city was progressive.

The apologetic aspect

Xenophon's aim was certainly not to *describe* the Spartan education system, even summarily. There is no information in his text on the annual age classes, on the age of entry into his categories, on the way time was spent and the subjects taught.[31] He keeps to the programme announced at the beginning: to show the singularity and the excellence of Lycurgus' laws, only possible cause of Sparta's greatness. This theme structures the treatise until 10.8, where his account seems to be closed by the phrase 'however ancient they may be, [these laws] are still at present completely novel for other Greeks; the most surprising thing of all, everyone praises such customs, but no city can imitate them'.[32] In fact, this theme is absent from chapters 11–14, but it reappears briefly in 15.1. Up until the end of chapter 10, then, the account is conducted with the rigour of a demonstration, in which chapters 2–4 are just a step.

This theme is a theme of praise, and, in fact, the tone is sometimes the eloquent one of the *enkōmion*; for example, on the discipline of the *paidiskoi*. But the discussion is most often a defence plea, the organization of which seems to be dictated less by the logic of a plan than by the argumentation, in the form of a list of critical points, of Sparta's detractors; whence the often enumerative pace of the exposition. Is this defensive character specific to the account of education? It is difficult to say, because we do not have any other criteria for judging it than what we gauge to be the *tone* of each passage. It seems to me that the defensive tone can be found in other places in the whole made up by the ten first chapters: in 1.3–4 (physical exercises for girls and women; justification – *teknopoiia*); 1.7–9 (sharing of women; same justification); 5.7 (absence of torches; justification – it makes temperance indispensable); 7.5–6 (nature of coinage; justification – to prevent secret enrichment); 10.1 (gerontocracy; justification – it encourages the practice of virtue right up to old age). But it also seems to me that it is in the account of education, especially in chapters 2 and 4, that the defensive attitude is the most frequent. This might correspond to the fact that Sparta's adversaries in the fourth century particularly concentrated their fire on her education system: this is a point we shall have to verify.

On reflection, this defensive discourse of Xenophon's has some strange aspects. We might expect that, against arguments which were for the most part received wisdom, when they were not pure myths, he would re-establish 'the truth about Sparta', by explaining that in reality things were not such as were believed, or at least that they were not so clear-cut. For example, *à propos* theft, he could have said that the boys did not steal all the time, but only on particular occasions; and (for he knew this, since he says it at *Anabasis* 4.6.14) that they could only steal a certain category of objects. Not at all; he takes generally accepted ideas just as they are, and tries to turn them around by making their contents into stages of a eulogistic argument. Yes, the boys are poorly dressed, and malnourished; yes, they steal all the time, and have a pederastic relationship forced upon them; yes, the young men spend their time spying on and fighting against each other; but it is precisely this which is excellent.

Documentary value

As a consequence of this choice, the *Lak. Pol.* is often very disappointing as a documentary source. This is not *always* the case. In chapter 2 we find some precise but allusive information, given as if unintentionally, for example on the *paidonomos* and his assistants, on the ritual at Orthia's sanctuary, on the role of the *eirenes*, on the delegation of authority; the same in chapter 4, on the selection of the *hippeis* and on the limits imposed on the brawls. But, alongside this, chapter 3 is almost pure rhetoric, the only information worthy of mention being the introduction to the *syssition*. In chapter 2 we find quite an alarming catalogue of generally accepted ideas reproduced wholesale, which might make us doubt whether the author had ever actually been to Sparta and was really familiar with Spartan education.[33] It is not that I really doubt that Xenophon is the author of the *Lak. Pol.*, far from it; but he believes that it is possible to convince without informing.

Insofar as Xenophon does so, what sort of Sparta does he describe? It is generally thought that, beyond the Lycurgan fiction, it is the Sparta that he knows, the Sparta of his time. The beginning of the treatise clearly indicates this: the situation he is reflecting upon is the *current* situation, that of a city very poor in citizens. Chapters 11–13 and 14, on the kings and the army, manifestly describe contemporary reality. In the chapters on education, the tense employed is the present, but this is fairly rare when it comes down to it (2.8 and 10; 3.5), except in chapter 4, where, in §§3–6, it is systematic. Xenophon most frequently adopts 'Lycurgus' point of view', which leads him to use a past tense; this interweaving of tenses clearly demonstrates that for him there is no difference between the Sparta he knows and that of Lycurgus.[34]

Such is our principal, and almost sole, source.

Aristotle

Lakedaimonion Politeia

All that is left of the exposition which Aristotle, in his *Lakedaimonion Politeia*, devoted to education is the very brief extract-summary preserved by a second-century BC epitomizer, Herakleides Lembos (fr. 13 Dilts = fr. 611.13 Rose).

> τρέφουσι δὲ τὰ τέκνα ὥστε μηδέποτε πληροῦν, ἵνα ἐθίζωνται δύνασθαι πεινῆν. ἐθίζουσι δὲ αὐτοὺς καὶ κλέπτειν, καὶ τὸν ἁλόντα κολάζουσι πληγαῖς, ἵν' ἐκ τούτου πονεῖν καὶ ἀγρυπνεῖν δύνωνται ἐν τοῖς πολεμίοις· μελετῶσι δὲ εὐθὺς ἐκ παίδων βραχυλογεῖν, εἶτα ἐμμελῶς καὶ σκώπτειν καὶ σκώπτεσθαι.

> They feed the children in such a way that they are never full, so that they learn to endure hunger. They also teach them to steal, and punish with blows anyone who lets himself be caught, to make them better able to endure fatigue and lack of sleep in the face of the enemy. From childhood they learn to speak briefly, and then both to joke and be the subject of jokes.

This fragment is rather disappointing, both in its brevity and because it does not add any (for us) new information. It is divided into two parts. The first, on diet and theft, is directly inspired by Xenophon, both in its meaning and, partly, its formulation.

> μηδέποτε πληροῦν, cf. ὡς ὑπὸ πλησμονῆς μήποτε βαρύνεσθαι (2.5);
> ἀγρυπνεῖν, cf. καὶ νυκτὸς ἀγρυπνεῖν (2.7);
> ἐν τοῖς πολεμίοις, cf. πολεμικωτέρους (2.7);
> τὸν ἁλοντα κολάζουσι πληγαῖς, cf. πολλὰς πληγὰς ἐπέβαλε τῷ ἁλισκομένῳ (2.8).

The second part treats a subject which is not tackled by Xenophon, and which we might be tempted to say only appears for us in Plutarch; but this would be to forget Plato's eulogy of the teaching of 'laconism', which he considers to be Sparta's great success (*Protagoras* 342d–343c). Plato also speaks of joking words, but not jokes made *ad hominem*. Plutarch will recapitulate the two themes of brief speech and joking.

The main interest of this extract is to attest that Aristotle devoted an exposition to education in his *Lak. Pol.*; the opposite would indeed be surprising, Spartan education being the subject of eulogies in the fourth century, but also of criticisms, and Aristotle, following Plato, being persuaded of the importance of education for anyone who wants to build a stable society.

These few phrases do not allow us to construct a precise idea of what this exposition looked like. We can see that it was not solely devoted to customs linked to education, but also evoked, at least in part, related teachings. Did it also tackle its structures and organization? Herakleides' inadequate extracts do not tell us. It is probable, in any case, that Aristotle's account was used by hellenistic authors, and perhaps also by Plutarch.

Plutarch

Life of Lycurgus

The problem which concerns us here is establishing whether Plutarch's text transmits, at least on certain points, information dating back to the fourth century, and can because of this be used as a complement to Xenophon to reconstruct a picture of the classical education system. It is in any case evident that in *Lycurgus* he is following Xenophon very closely on the subject, especially borrowing his plan, to the extent that we get the impression that while writing he had Xenophon's treatise if not before his eyes, at least in his memory. But he adds a great deal, especially on the subject of organization, and nowhere is he content simply to copy. A significant example is given by what he says about the rite at Orthia's altar (18.2). He talks about it because Xenophon talks about it, but there the resemblance ceases. He cannot say the same thing, he cannot use it in the same way, because, in the meantime, the ritual has been profoundly modified (so much so that what Xenophon says about it must have seemed enigmatic to him). He does not talk about it in connection with theft, but in connection with hardening to suffering – a theme which Xenophon also develops, but in the commentary which follows the reference to the ceremony. Nothing could better show how far Plutarch is from being a servile imitator.

The gap between Plutarch and Xenophon

This gap is immediately obvious: a difference, first, between the literary genres used, each with very strong constraints; a difference of period too, which means different points of view – on the one hand, that of the involved theorist, on the other, that of the antiquarian. The two authors have in common, however, an important characteristic: admiration for Lycurgus' Sparta. But what Plutarch says about education is much closer to a description. Information is not assumed to be known, it is supplied, if necessary by means of autopsy.[35] A few fragments of justification are present, and come from Xenophon: on theft (17.6); on the dietary regime, but with a developed and updated medical commentary (17.7–8). Naturally, Plutarch's text does not have the defensive tone of Xenophon's, since the Spartan education system was no longer under attack in his time.

At the level of information, one of the most important differences between the two authors concerns organization. In Plutarch, we find no trace of Xenophon's *paidiskoi* and *hēbōntes*. Now it is just a matter of *paides*, from their start at seven years of age to their final year, the nineteenth, when they are *melleirenes* (17.3–4); and at twenty, education seems to be finished. There is a break in this very long *paides* stage at the age of twelve, while a comparable break in Xenophon only comes between the *paides* and the *paidiskoi*, the verb μειρακιοῦσθαι suggesting, as we shall see, that it happened at about fourteen years of age. Kennell (1995, 33–5) has tried to demonstrate that there was no break in Plutarch, and that at 16.12 he only meant to speak, on a precise issue (clothing), of a hardening of discipline around the age of twelve. His argument does not seem convincing to me unless one takes this passage alone. But what follows shows that, for Plutarch, at this age there are other new things: dirtiness (16.12), and camping out (16.13). The impression that there really is a break is confirmed by the expression τοῖς τηλικούτοις, 'the youths of this age', which at 17.1 introduces another and much more important novelty, the pederastic relationship. This novelty has nothing to do with hardship, and represents on the contrary an essential promotion for the youth.

Another detail, at 17.2, seems to me to be decisive. Here Plutarch says that the *agelē* is commanded by an *eirēn*, while before the age of twelve its leader is one of its members. Den Boer (1954, 249) has argued that for Plutarch the leader of the 'little boys' was also an *eirēn*, but the interpretation is not acceptable. In this case the phrase at 16.8 would be incomprehensible: the *eirēn* does not appear until 17.2, and he is immediately defined. Above all, the argument misconstrues the grammatical structure: τῆς ἀγέλης is the complement of τὸν διαφέροντα καὶ θυμοειδέστατον, which shows that the leader is indeed one of the members of the *agelē*. Moreover, it is not possible to supply 'the Spartans' as an implied subject for παρίσταντο: in the preceding phrase, the subject is singular (Lycurgus), and, in what follows, the plural verbs (ἀφεώρων and ἠκροῶντο) clearly have the young boys as their subject. It is they who choose their leader, and we should write αὐτοῖς. So there is indeed an organizational difference in Plutarch concerning the command of the *agelē*, between the *paides* of less and more than twelve years old.

The fact that Xenophon does not give a precise age for moving from the *paides* category to that of *paidiskoi* of course makes a reconciliation between his system and Plutarch's theoretically possible. This route has been explored by Lupi (2000, 40–1). Noting rightly that what Plutarch says about the boys of more than twelve is on the whole a reprise of what Xenophon says about the *paides*, he deduces that Xenophon did not take the period from seven to twelve years old into account in his treatise, doubtless because it did not seem to him (but why so?) to form part of the collective education of the state. On this hypothesis, the two systems would still not be identical, since they would place the beginning of education at ages very far removed from one another; but they would have in common the existence of an important break at age twelve. I shall discuss the difficulties that Lupi's thesis raises below (p. 86); they are so great that it is better, I think, to retain the traditional opinion, that Xenophon's and Plutarch's systems differ profoundly on this point.[36]

The ways of life depicted or suggested likewise include important differences, which have of course been forgotten by those who seek to combine the texts of these two authors. Plutarch presents the life of the children as wholly collective. For him they are entirely removed from their families. Between the ages of seven and twelve, he says, Lycurgus already makes them live, eat, play and study in common (καὶ συννόμους ποιῶν καὶ συντρόφους μετ᾽ ἀλλήλων εἴθιζε συμπαίζειν καὶ συσχολάζειν, 16.7). After twelve years old, in addition, they sleep together (ἐκάθευδον δ᾽ ὁμοῦ κατ᾽ ἴλην καὶ κατ᾽ ἀγέλην, 16.13). The constant supervision described in the last phrase of 17.1 is only possible in the context of a collective life; how else could so many scattered individuals be supervised? At 17.4 and 18.3–8, it is the whole team who, under the direction of the *eirēn*, prepare and doubtless also take their meal in common. This idea of the communal life is not entirely absent from Xenophon, but it only appears in the form of the communal meal organized by the *eirēn* (2.5) and the existence of troups (ἴλη) also directed by an *eirēn*. We could say, then, that in a sense Xenophon is the origin of this aspect of the presentation of the education system in Plutarch; but we emphatically do not find the idea of a wholly collective life in his account.

Another aspect of the way of life where a similarly marked difference appears is what I call *the savage life*. This has several components. The first is the fighting. In Plutarch, the boys pass their time in fighting one another. Before the age of twelve: at 16.8, the boys choose as leader 'the most resolute at fighting', θυμοειδέστατον ἐν τῷ μάχεσθαι; in 16.9, the 'older boys' encourage 'constant fighting and rivalry', μάχας τινὰς ἀεὶ καὶ φιλονεικίας; at 16.10, they are taught to 'win in combat', νικᾶν μαχόμενον. This does not stop after twelve years old; at 17.1, we see the 'eldest' present at their fights (μαχομένοις); at 17.2, the members of the *agelē* choose as leader the *eirēn* who fights the best, μαχιμώτατον (so this must continue amongst the *eirenes*!); in 17.4, the *eirēn* leads them 'in their battles', ἐν ταῖς μάχαις, that is the battles between 'bands' of boys; in 18.8, a boy has said a bad word 'while fighting', ἐν τῷ μάχεσθαι. Omnipresent in Plutarch, this theme is remarkably absent from Xenophon, which shows at least that these brutalities were not a major theme of criticism against Sparta at the very beginning of the fourth century;

we only see these brawls taking place amongst the *hēbōntes*, in whose life, if we are to believe Xenophon, they played a great role. Such conduct might even appear entirely unthinkable on the part of the *paidiskoi* as he presents them. We could say, then, that in Xenophon education during childhood and adolescence is an apprenticeship in self-control, while in Plutarch it is an apprenticeship in aggression.

Another component of the savage life is the 'camping', or life in the natural wild. Plutarch paints its picture at the beginning of his exposition on the way of life of those above the age of twelve (16.13–14 = *Inst. Lac.* 6). The most striking feature is the sleeping on a kind of straw mattresses (*stibades*) made of reeds gathered by hand (return to primitive humanity) from the bed of the Eurotas. Of course, these 'mattresses' could have been installed indoors, but the key-word, *stibas*, has very precise connotations which are all linked to the idea of primitive or improvised sleeping arrangements, in the open air or in a tent, especially in the context of vagrancy or of the military life. Plutarch really gives the impression of believing that the boys lived like this all the time; however, other passages of the description go against this vision. It is hard to imagine that the 'elders', whoever they are, who are constantly supervising the boys (16.9; 17.1; 18.6), accompany them in their 'camping'. Is it in the wilds that they learn their letters (16.10), Laconian eloquence (19–20), *mousikē* (21)? Their communal meals take place in a building (κατ' οἶκον, 17.4), where the *eirēn* is reclining (κατακείμενος, 18.3). They do not live constantly in the forest, since they are told to be well informed about what is happening in the city (18.4). We can, then, use Plutarch as his own corrective.[37] This theme of the savage life is absent from Xenophon's text, even if it is true that the training of young boys can happen in the mountains (2.3), and that theft (2.7) seems to take place mostly in the country or in gardens.

A final aspect of the savage life is underlined by Plutarch: dirtiness. While Xenophon talked only of 'a single cloak' (2.4), in the sense, as we have seen, of a single type of cloak for the whole year, Plutarch adds (16.12) not only the absence of a tunic, but also bodily dirtiness (αὐχμηροὶ τὰ σώματα), due to the absence of baths and rub-downs (λουτρῶν καὶ ἀλειμμάτων ἄπειροι). This feature belongs with the savage life because it aims to present the existence of the young Spartans as deprived of everything which contributes to the pleasure of civilized life (τῆς τοιαύτης φιλανθρωπίας).

This way of seeing Spartan education seems to be characteristic of Plutarch's period. It can be found, indeed, in an even more extreme form in the epitome made by Justin of the work of Pompeius Trogus, both in its evocation of this education (3.3.6)[38] and in its more detailed description of that of the Lucanians (23.1), which he says is similar to that of the Spartans. 'Justin' goes so far that we might wonder whether he has not conflated *paideia* with the

Crypteia.[39] It is possible that this vision of 'Lycurgan' education is influenced by what Spartan education had become in the imperial period. It seems indeed, to judge by the transformation undergone by the rite carried out at Orthia's altar, or, to take other examples, by the form taken by the Platanistas combat and by the institutional importance given to the game of ball, that the *paideia* of the imperial period had, by a kind of archaizing regression, taken on a more physical, and even more brutal, character than that of the classical period. However, education in the imperial period was surely not as 'savage' as 'Justin' and even Plutarch say. It is also possible (and the two explanations are of course not mutually exclusive) that it is a question of image. The education system which Plutarch sees is richer in local colour and in picturesque, archaizing details because this suits the taste of the period. We must, then, ask ourselves how Plutarch's text is situated in relation to the two realities, that of the classical period and that of the imperial period.

What is Plutarch describing?

If we compare the education described in the *Life of Lycurgus* with the picture drawn by Kennell (1995, 28–97), on the basis of inscriptions, of the *ephēbeia* of the Roman period, we are particularly struck by the differences, especially in the area of organization of the whole and of the age categories (the *ephēbeia* begins at sixteen years old, not at twelve). Plutarch says nothing about contests, omnipresent in inscriptions from the sanctuary of Orthia, nor about the game of ball, which, according to Kennell, ended the *ephēbeia*, nor about the Platanistas combat, which Pausanias and Lucian describe (Kennell 1995, 55–9). So, if certain elements of Plutarch's description seem to correspond to what existed in his time, as is the case for flagellation, which he says he has seen (18.2), this is obviously not true for everything. Moreover, it is entirely clear that it is not this contemporary education which Plutarch intends to describe: it is that of Lycurgus, and he is sufficiently well informed to know that the two are not the same. This Lycurgan education can only be a scholarly reconstruction using elements which are very diverse as much in their date as in their degree of reality. We might be tempted to decide that only the elements directly borrowed from Xenophon date back to the classical period, but this would be to misunderstand the recognized fact that Plutarch also used other fourth-century works which are lost to us, such as Aristotle's treatise.

To distinguish in the *Life of Lycurgus* what, concerning education, is contemporary with the author and what is earlier, Kennell (1995, 24–5) proposed a simple and seductive criterion, that of the tense of the verbs. He noted that the tense used by Plutarch on this subject is normally the past, the present only appearing from 17.3 to 18.2. This exposition in the present begins with the definition of the *melleirēn* and the *eirēn*, presents the command of the *agelē* by an *eirēn*, (17.2), includes everything concerning theft and the dietary regime, and ends with the allusion to flagellation. Kennell deduces from this, then, that theft was still practised in Plutarch's time. In reality, this is not certain, for, returning to the *eirēn*'s command (18.3), Plutarch uses first the aorist, then, in everything that follows, the imperfect.[40] It seems rather that the present tense – used for the definition of the *eirēn* because this was still valid – so to speak spreads through the rest of the exposition by pure stylistic contagion, until Plutarch corrects himself by returning to the past. Conversely, we can note that he uses the imperfect, at 16.12–13, for features (clothing, bare feet, life in the open air) which Dion of Prusa (*Speeches* 25.3)[41] explicitly attests (by ἔτι νῦν) as existing still in his time. So it seems that it would be very dangerous to think of the tenses used by Plutarch as a historical criterion in something which is presented as a biography of Lycurgus.

Wondering what period Plutarch's text reflects is perhaps posing the problem the wrong way, and succumbing to the positivist illusion which lies in wait for us all. It does not reflect a period, nor even periods, but the sources which the author used. He was not the first to wish to describe Lycurgus' education system; it is surely what all those who treated Spartan education before him wanted – to begin with the only one whose text has come down to us, Xenophon. In addition to the real elements borrowed from periods which we may suppose to be diverse, these reconstructions were also according a (varying) place, we must not forget, to utopia. In Plutarch's text, it has been possible to verify this on one point, the selection of infants (*Lyc.* 16.1–2). In a very convincing study, Marc Huys (1996) compared with this passage a small group of texts describing the selective sorting of the newborn and the putting to death, by active or passive euthanasia, of those excluded. All these texts belong to the utopian sphere. Two are the works of philosophers describing their ideal city (Plato, *Rep.* 5.460c and Aristotle, *Pol.* 7.1335b18–20). The two others belong in genre to the ethnographic utopia, that of Onesikritos, concerning the Indian kingdom of Sopeithes, and that of Iamboulos, which locates a strange variant of this practice in his Island of the People of the Sun. I cannot agree with all of Huys' hypotheses. It seems unlikely to me that the Spartan model, which is only known from Plutarch, would be the oldest in this tradition of good infanticide; it is at least equally probable that this element was introduced into the Spartan legend under the influence of the Cynics and the Stoics, who were very interested in this city. But what is crucial here is that this prescription, preliminary to the upbringing and education of children, is shown to fall within the sphere of myth.[42]

For the historian, then, Plutarch's text is very difficult to use because it is composite. Let us take as an example the savage life. What the author says about it could have three origins and probably combines all three. It could be in part an older reality, which might even date back to the classical period, the criterion being comparison with Xenophon's text. A part might correspond to a reality contemporary with the author, whether some practices had remained since the fifth century, or had been revived in a more or less artificial, more or less archaizing manner. And finally, we must take into account the systematization, the going to extremes, which are characteristics of the imaginary. In fact, some aspects of the 'savage life' can already be found in Xenophon. That this aspect existed also in the imperial period is attested by Dion of Prusa; as for systematization, it is clear in the fact that, to read Plutarch, we might believe that the boys *always* lived in this way, while Hesychius' gloss on the word φουάξιρ shows that it is actually just a 'stage' (preparatory, according to this gloss, to flagellation), and that Plutarch's text itself represents the boys leading an urban life elsewhere. Prudence, then, dictates that we consider the *Life of Lycurgus* as fundamentally a fiction, that is as an intellectual construction made up of disparate elements, the logical coherence of which, a result of the author's savoir-faire, makes sense and produces an effect of reality. What Plutarch says about Spartan education should not be accepted or rejected as a whole. Only comparison with other sources, when possible, will let us know how to use it.

Instituta Laconica

I would certainly not have devoted a note to this short treatise if Kennell had not accorded it exceptional importance. One of the points to which he is visibly most attached, for he often returns to it, is that he thinks he has demonstrated that numbers 1 to 17 of these *Instituta* (of which nos. 4–13 concern education, and 14–17 music) are nothing less than fragments, quoted *verbatim*, of Sphairos' treatise on the institutions of Sparta. If these texts had really been written around 225, they would be of great interest for us. Of course, they might be programmatic texts, in which Sphairos explains his vision of what the future education system, restored by Cleomenes, should be; but it would be more likely that he presented the Lycurgan system, as far as his researches allowed him to reconstruct it, which would mean we could look here for information on what it was like in the classical period. But we do not have to examine these two possibilities, because the link between these *Instituta* and Sphairos seems to be pure hypothesis.

The *Instituta* form a separate collection in the *Spartan Sayings*, even if it is only in modern editions that they are presented in autonomous form. No. 2 alone is in something vaguely resembling apophthegmatic form; the only thing these notes have in common with apophthegms is their fragmented character and the absence of a logical order (with some exceptions, and Kennell is right to say that 4–13 are an exception). Neither do they constitute a treatise; they are morsels chosen and copied, *excerpta*.

I shall not rehearse Kennell's argument; it is better, I think, to return to the texts without preconceived ideas, in order to see what they look like and how they were constructed. Besides, as they are not apophthegms, what is generally agreed about the origins and nature of the Plutarchan *Sayings* does not necessarily apply to the *Instituta*.

The origins of most of notes nos. 4–17 can be determined with certainty.

Xenophon (adapted)

No. 7 (love). Contents identical to 2.13, but completely different in expression, with only the pair ψυχή/σῶμα in common.

No. 10 (delegation of authority). Contents as 6.1, with some similarities of wording; dependence is obvious.

No. 11 (same subject). Closely related to 6.2, with both similarities of wording and an attempt at variation.

No. 13, from οὕτω γὰρ ᾤοντο[43] το τὰ σώματα: corresponds with 2.5, with some similarities of wording (ἀσιτήσαντες ἐπιπονῆσαι in common; πλείω χρόνον in common; ἀνοψίαν, cf. ἧττον ὄψου; βρῶμα τὸ τυχὸν, cf. πᾶν βρῶμα; ὑγιαινότερα, cf. ὑγιαινοτέρως; εὐαυξῆ, cf. αὐξάνεσθαι; πλάτος, cf. διαπλατύνουσαν).

The passages of Xenophon on which these texts are based are always very short; generally they are no more than expressions. There is a real but superficial attempt to differentiate from the original.

Aristotle (according to Herakleides)

No. 13, second phrase. Compare καὶ ἵν' ἐθίζωνται μηδέποτε γίνεσθαι πλήρεις, δύνασθαι δὲ πεινῆν with ὥστε μηδέποτε πληροῦν, ἵνα ἐθίζωνται δύνασθαι πεινῆν.

Of course, since Aristotle's text is not preserved, there could be (I would willingly say: there certainly were) other similarities.

Plutarch, verbatim

No. 4 (teaching), first phrase = *Lyc.* 16.10

No. 5 (clothing, dirtiness) = *Lyc.* 16.12

No. 6 (sleeping arrangements) = *Lyc.* 16.13–14

No. 12 (theft and diet) = *Lyc.* 17.6

No. 13 (diet), first phrase = first phrase of *Lyc.* 17.7; εἰς βάθος τε καὶ πλάτος μὴ πιεζόμενα = *Lyc.* 17.7; καὶ καλὰ δὲ κτλ. = *Lyc.* 17.8

No. 14 (poetry and song) = *Lyc.* 21.1–2, with some variants

No. 15 (*trichoria*) = *Lyc.* 21.3, except the first phrase, which is missing
Plutarch, adapted
No. 9 (punishment): cf. *Lyc.* 15.2, which describes the punishment of men who remain single
No. 16 (music): cf. *Lyc.* 21.4 and 7, with some similarities of wording
No. 13 (diet): in addition to the identical phrases cited above, the whole is very similar

The most complex case is that of no. 13, which incorporates literal borrowings from Xenophon, Aristotle and Plutarch into an argument essentially based on Plutarch.

Original remainders, in our current state of knowledge
No. 4, except the first phrase: *xenēlasia* of matters other than *grammata* (a happy phrase), education's military end.
No. 8: an interesting note on supervision by their 'elders' of the youths' movements, and punishments relating to this. Probably to be juxtaposed with the mysterious no. 38, although this juxtaposition does not shed much light on it. This supervision recalls that to which the *paidiskoi* are subject in Xenophon.
No. 16, the phrase ὁ γὰρ Λυκοῦργος...ἁρμονίαν ἔχῃ. Another interesting note: music as calming the excesses of the warrior temper.
No. 17, anecdotes about Terpander and Timotheos.

I am not claiming to establish who edited these notes, and how, but only, in the light of the obvious comparisons made above, to look at the case for Sphairos. We might accept that Sphairos adapted Xenophon and more or less copied Aristotle. But numerous passages are identical, word-for-word, to passages of Plutarch. That Plutarch could, in his preparatory work, have taken notes copied *verbatim* from some authors is possible; but that he introduced into one of his *Lives* whole copied phrases from Sphairos' *Lak. Pol.*, without citing him, this seems to me impossible to concede.

Moreover, as has been noted for a long time, some of the passages identical to the Plutarch passages include errors which, of course, are not there in the original: καί in no. 12, and notably the nominatives in no. 14. These errors are a consequence of breaks or of slight modifications made in the course of copying. The nature of these errors makes it clear that it is not Plutarch who has copied the author of the *Inst. Lac.*, but *vice versa*. The hypothetical collection made up of nos. 4 to 17 cannot, then, represent a series of notes taken by Plutarch from such or such a work, with a view to the *Life of Lycurgus* or a treatise. It is rather the work of a successor, who had undertaken to compose a treatise based on excerpts taken from Plutarch, supplementing them with Xenophon, Aristotle and other authors, one of whom could have been Sphairos.[44]

In any case, Kennell's Sphairos is ghostly. All the passages which he considers to be characteristic, those where he thinks he recognizes his vocabulary and his Stoic ideas, belong to the category of extracts taken from Plutarch *verbatim*; their Stoic flavour is thus quite naturally explained, and the medical vocabulary of no. 13, for example, corresponds with the language of the imperial period.

Notes

[1] The most recent article on the question, to my knowledge, is that of Bianco (1996); she favours the date upheld by Ollier, a little after 394. Luppino-Manes (1988, 19–31) inclines to favour a process of writing beginning around 390 and taken up again around 378; see also Rebenich (1998) for 378.

[2] Note the aorist, which seems to point to chapter 14.

[3] The technique continues in the following chapters: καταμαθών in ch. 3.2, βουλόμενος in 3.4, νομίζων in 4.1, ὁρῶν and ἐνόμιζεν in 4.2.

[4] *Lyc.* 16.12; *Inst. Lac.* 5, *Mor.* 237b.

[5] Cf. Kennell (1995, 34), who demonstrates that this interpretation is wrong. It could also be that the custom had changed over time, because the *himation* worn alone is characteristic of philosophers, especially Cynics, who hold such trivial things in contempt; the Spartans could have reinforced the austerity of their education on this model (probably in the 3rd century).

[6] μᾶλλον μέν…μᾶλλον δέ…ἧττον δέ…εὐχερέστερον δέ…ὑγιεινοτέρως δέ…μᾶλλον.

[7] οὕτω γὰρ ᾤοντο καὶ εἰς τὸν πόλεμον χρησιμωτέρους ἔσεσθαι, εἰ δύναιντο καὶ ἀσιτήσαντες ἐπιπονῆσαι.

[8] For an analysis of the vocabulary of these texts, cf. Kennell 1995, 104; but it does not seem at all evident to me that that of the *Inst. Lac.* 13 points to a much earlier date than that of *Lyc.* 17.6.

[9] On this skill, see below, pp. 142–3.

[10] Cf. the remarks of Ollier (1934, xxxiii and 28), who nonetheless, in the inverse of what I am doing, seems to call into question Xenophon's veracity rather than his sincerity.

[11] Plutarch understood this very well (*Lyc.* 15.14): 'Lycurgus considered that children did not belong exclusively to their fathers (οὐκ ἰδίους τῶν πατέρων), but that they were the common property of the city (ἀλλὰ κοινοὺς τῆς πόλεως).' An analogous formula can be found in Plato, *Laws* 7.804d (below, p. 54).

[12] Here, as at §5, I have adopted the correction εἰρένων, which goes back to Cragius. For an explanation, cf. below, p. 96.

[13] On this chastity, cf. *Inst. Lac.* 7, which recapitulates Xenophon's (admittedly very commonplace) idea. Curiously enough, Plutarch (*Lyc.* 17.1 and 18.7–8) refrains from posing the chastity problem: does this reserve betray scepticism about its reality in Lycurgus' Sparta?

[14] A remark already made, on this last point, by Tazelaar 1967, 148 n. 1.

[15] Cf. Kennell (1995, 126), who thinks that here Xenophon is giving 'a general description of the highlights of Spartan education'.

[16] Ollier 1934, 6 and 18 n. 1. Pierleoni had also adopted this reading (Berlin 1905; Rome 1937).

[17] Dion, *Speech* 36 (the 'Borysthenic'), 7–8; Artemidoros 1.54 p. 61 Pack. Ollier rightly points out that the reverse of Attic vases of the fifth and fourth centuries often represents young men in this attitude.

[18] Lucian, *Loves* 44 (portrait of a young man of good family).

[19] On silence cf. David 1999.

[20] *Clouds* 963–4 (the Old Education).

[21] With this portrait of *paidiskoi* we might compare the description, in the *Cyropaedia* (1.4.6), of the extreme timidity which seizes Cyrus when, from being a *pais,* he becomes an ephebe.

[22] The manuscripts have παιδικῶν; but Haase's correction παιδίσκων is necessary, not so much as the *lectio difficilior* as because of *Hell.* 5.4.32 (on the subject of Sphodrias): παῖς τε ὢν καὶ παιδίσκος καὶ ἡβῶν.

[23] An excellent commentary can be found on the way in which Xenophon has utilized and twisted this idea here in the article by Birgalias 1997, 35–44 (the rest of the article is a discussion of the *hippeis,* with which I am much less in agreement).

[24] Ollier 1934, 34.

[25] Birgalias 1997, 38.

[26] This point was perceived by Ollier (1934, 34–5).

[27] For an indirect criticism of the 'spying' on private life at Sparta, cf. Thucydides 2.37.2.

[28] Cf. Plato and especially Aristotle (below, p. 63).

[29] Birgalias 1997, 39–41.

[30] Ch. 2, *paides*; ch. 3, *paidiskoi*; ch. 4.1–6, *hēbōntes*; ch. 4.7–ch. 10, citizens.

[31] Throughout the treatise it is often the case that Spartan realities are mentioned without being explained in the slightest, something which occasionally makes these allusions extremely obscure. Examples: in 2.5 and 11, the *eirenes*; in 2.9, the ritual at Orthia's sanctuary; in 4.3, the *hippeis* are not even named; in the portrait of the 'Tremblers' in ch. 9, the game of ball, the places said to be ignominious for dancing, the fine; in 12.3, the Skirites; in 13.11, the *hellanodikai*. All this is assumed to be familiar.

[32] On this 'break' at the end of chapter 10, cf. Ollier 1934, xii. Note ἐπιτηδεύματα.

[33] Although there is a tradition according to which Xenophon had his own sons educated there. It is true that we do not have to believe this to be genuine (below, p. 153).

[34] Of course, chapter 14 disrupts this fine harmony.

[35] 'I have seen', at 18.2, in connection with flagellation. It is possible that the detail of the shaved head, at 16.11, which is not in Xenophon, is also the result of personal observation.

[36] For a hypothesis about the origin of this difference, cf. below, p. 91.

[37] In the same sense, Birgalias 1999, 75.

[38] Cf. below, p. 184.

[39] Birgalias 1999, 75.

[40] Same remark in Lupi 2000, 38.

[41] Text cited above, p. xv.

[42] We may particularly note that neither Plato nor Aristotle makes reference to Sparta in this connection, which they would surely have done if this regulation had really been

in use there.

[43] The text of the *Inst. Lac.* is always cited first.

[44] This conclusion follows the same lines as the observations recently presented by Pelling (2002, 65–90) *à propos* the *Apophthegms of Kings and Generals*: contrary to received opinion, he thinks that this collection was edited after and adapted from the Lives, using other material too gathered by Plutarch in his preparatory files. The difference is that Pelling believes this work was done by Plutarch himself, which to me hardly seems possible for the *Instituta*.

2

THE IMAGE OF SPARTAN EDUCATION IN THE FIFTH AND FOURTH CENTURIES

Simonides, writing at the end of the sixth century and beginning of the fifth, is generally taken to be the first author to mention Spartan education. In fact, this reference amounts for us to a single word, the epithet δαμασίμβροτος, 'tamer of mortals', which he applies to Sparta. If this were the case, it would be very interesting, because it would show that from the end of the archaic period Greek writers were clearly aware of the originality of the Spartan educational system and of its role in the city's success; Sparta was qualified as 'tamer of mortals' *because of* its educational system. Furthermore, it would show that at this period there was already an understanding that the essential feature of this system was its aim, and that this aim was the training of the citizen, thought of as a 'taming'. In this idea Simonides would have preceded Plato by a century and a half – Plato who, moreover, denies this quality to Sparta, and castigates her precisely for not having sufficiently 'broken in' her young (*Laws* 2.666e; below, p. 59). It seems it is not until the third century, in Stoic thinking, that this image of Sparta became current, before becoming an established idea.

In order to attribute such lucidity to Simonides, we would have to be sure of our premises. I do not think that we can. The single-adjective fragment is preserved for us by Plutarch. At the beginning of his *Life of Agesilaos* (1.3), commenting on the fact that, because he was not destined to reign, his hero had followed the common education system for Spartan citizens, the biographer reports Simonides' word. Insufficient attention has perhaps been paid to the manner in which he does this. His presentation (διὸ καί φασιν ὑπὸ Σιμονίδου τὴν Σπαρτὴν προσηγορεῦσθαι δαμασίμβροτον, 'this is why people also say that Simonides called Sparta tamer of mortals') shows not only that he had no context at his disposal, and only cites the poet on the basis of what he found in his sources, but further that for these sources themselves the explanation of the formula 'Sparta, tamer of mortals' as referring to the city's education system was only a hypothesis. The latter is of course entirely acceptable, and if we take Spartan education as our starting point the idea of applying the epithet 'tamer of mortals' to it seems natural – but if we have as our only starting point the expression 'Sparta tamer of mortals', we must admit that usually this would lead us in a completely different direction than the treatment the city imposed on its own citizens. δαμασίμβροτος naturally evokes death, or at least a crushing military victory, which annihilates the enemy. Pindar uses it of Achilles' 'murderous lance', δαμασιμβρότου αἰχμᾶς (*Ol.* 9.79), and Simonides himself characterizes sleep as δαμασίφως, a term which has the same sense and was perhaps, like δαμασίμβροτος, coined by him (it is cited by a scholion on *Iliad* 24.5). In the form δαμασίμβροτος, the element δαμα- has a very strong force, as δαμάζω often does; not just 'tame, subject', but reduce someone's body to an inert state. It seems to me that this expression 'Sparta, tamer of mortals' more probably alluded to her military effectiveness (in particular the conquest of Messenia) rather than her educational system; the explanation passed on by Plutarch and accepted without discussion by modern scholars would seem to be just an erudite interpretation dating from the hellenistic period.

Fifth-century authors

Aristophanes

(Clouds *961–1023)*

This is not a text about Spartan education, but there are reasons for thinking that Spartan education provides most of the background. We are talking about the famous *agōn* which takes places between two personifications, which the list of *dramatis personae* names as Δίκαιος Λόγος ('Just Argument') and Ἄδικος Λόγος ('Unjust Argument'), but which in the text call themselves Κρείττων Λόγος ('Strong Argument', l. 990) and Ἥττων Λόγος ('Weak Argument'; so called by himself, l. 1038, and by his adversary, l. 893). The debate concerns education, unsurprisingly, the winner having to gain Pheidippides' business – the chorus plays the role of competition judge. Weak Argument (let us call him that) sings the praises of the 'new education' (τὴν καινὴν παίδευσιν, ll. 936–7), the education of the sophists, which could make the weakest idea triumph (whence the name of the character). Strong Argument praises the 'old education' (τὴν ἀρχαίαν παιδείαν, l. 961) also called that of 'people of the past' (οἱ πρότεροι, ll. 935 and 1029), or that of 'the men of Marathon' (l. 986). It is not what we would call children who are evoked in the speech of Strong Argument, but adolescents: they have reached their ἥβη (l. 976), as confirmed by many physiological details (ll. 975–8) with overtly erotic connotations.

Some characteristics of the Old Education can hardly fail to call Spartan education to mind.[1] The young men whom Strong Argument describes have been perfectly educated. This is indicated by their absolute silence (l. 963), their manner of walking in order in the street (l. 964), their reserved and modest demeanour (ll. 965, 973–5: not hiding their sex would be interpreted as an invitation); the same goes for their behaviour at table (ll. 981–3). The similarity to the portrait of the *paidiskoi* (likewise older adolescents) in chapter two of Xenophon's *Lacedaimonion Politeia* is striking. We must, however, be wary of drawing too hasty a conclusion from this similarity, because, as we have seen in relation to this text (above, p. 15), we are in both cases in the presence of the same stereotype, to which the erotic allusions also belong. One detail perhaps has more evidential value. Strong Argument says that the pupils of the old days got up from their seats when older people came in (καὶ τῶν θάκων τοῖς πρεσβυτέροις ὑπανίστασθαι προσιοῦσιν, l. 993); now this was a custom very much honoured at Sparta, to the extent that Herodotos even says that amongst the Greeks it was respected there alone.[2]

On the 'subjects taught', Strong Argument is not very forthcoming. He does not even mention the study of literacy. This shows that at the very least he does not want to emphasize this point, something which could be compared with the reputation the Spartans had for not being interested in this matter. On the other hand, we see children going to the kitharist (l. 964), and, especially, practising physical exercises: with the *paidotribēs* (ll. 973–6) and at the gymnasium (ll. 1002–8); as at Sparta, their favourite exercise is running. In order to be effective, this education is tough – blows rain on the recalcitrant (l. 972), the children have no right to hot baths (ll. 1044–6), 'because', explains Strong Argument, 'this is a very bad practice which makes men cowardly' (l. 1046). The absence of baths (at all, although this is surely either an exaggeration or, rather, a way of saying the same thing) for Spartan children does not appear in Xenophon, but only in Plutarch. Should we deduce from this that here we have a detail on which sources specific to Plutarch go back to the classical period? I would not insist on this, as it is a commonplace applied to any harsh education system.

In sum, it is impossible to arrive at certainty because of the weight of stereotypes.[3] However, apart from the relevance of a particular custom like that of rising from one's seat before one's elders, we should ask ourselves what reality Aristophanes could have referred to in order to paint a picture of a traditional education. To information collected in Athens? This would be to consider the picture historical, when it is certainly completely fictional. The influence of the Spartan model seems, then, more than probable. Moreover, we encounter this model again at line 1373 of *Knights*, which says that 'no young man will go to do his shopping in the Agora', a prescription comparable with that reported by Plutarch (*Lyc.* 25.1) concerning Spartiates aged less than 30 (below, p. 107). Sparta was regarded as an ideal by some Athenians, nostalgic for a largely imaginary past;[4] this is the past which Weak Argument associates in spiritual terms with such cultural antiquities as the Dipoleia, the Bouphonia and the 'cicadas' (ll. 984–5). As in Pericles' Funeral Speech, Sparta is the opposite of Athens (see e.g. ll. 1003–4), but here it is Sparta which is preferred. But it would have been difficult to present their enemies to the Athenians as models (we are in 423 BC): so Aristophanes had to make sure that no characteristic would allow a formal identification of Sparta in these lines. In this context the word λιπαρός (applied to a young boy in the gymnasium, l. 1002) is perhaps particularly meaningful; as we shall see (below, p. 336) this is a qualifier typical of Sparta's young and of her citizens.

Thucydides

Although they are not explicitly linked, and were spoken by different people in different circumstances, two speeches in Thucydides evoke Spartan education in a symmetrical manner.

Archidamos' speech (1.84.3)

A debate took place at Sparta in 431 BC in which the Corinthians and the Athenians spoke in turn; after this the foreign delegates withdrew and Archidamos explained his thoughts to the Spartan citizens (80–5). He judges Sparta's situation to be inferior to that of Athens for the moment, and advises the Spartans to wait two or three years before engaging either in a war or in more serious negotiations. In chapter 84, the speech tackles the criticism of slowness and timidity levelled against the Spartans by the Corinthians, and turns this criticism into praise – but praise which is not without ambiguity. For Archidamos, reflection and wisdom are Spartan assets, and it is to their education that they owe these qualities.

> Our discipline (τὸ εὔκοσμον) makes us at the same time good warriors and wise men. We get the first quality from the fact that reserve (αἰδώς) is very close to self-control (σωφροσύνη), and courage to shame at acting badly. And if we are wise, it is because our education leaves us too ignorant to think of snapping our fingers at the laws, and, thanks to its toughness, too self-controlled (σωφρονέστερον) to disobey them.

In the first phrase, γιγνόμεθα shows that from the very start it is the training of the citizen which is at stake, which will be explicitly mentioned only later – Archidamos thinks (as will Plato) that moderation and wisdom cannot be innate, but they must be acquired. The same phrase characterizes the result of this training as τὸ εὔκοσμον, which is the equivalent for each citizen of what εὐνομία is for the city, the good order born of respect for the law. The σωφροσύνη in which the young Spartiate is trained puts him on the path of αἰδώς, the respect due to others and to oneself; and αἰσχύνη, a concept associated with αἰδώς,[5] is close to military valour, because of the fear that by being cowardly one will be dishonoured in the eyes of others. Archidamos thus analyses the military effectiveness of the education system in uniquely psychological and ethical terms, by enumerating the qualities which it develops.

The third phrase presents two other aspects of this education system. Let us start with the most simple, which comes last. Education at Sparta is effective because it is harsh; this is why it inculcates self-control, and so control of all passions which might push the citizen to infringe the law. Here we are very close to Xenophon (*LP* 4.6): the ephors punish a recalcitrant 'with the intention of teaching him never to allow anger to prevent him from obeying the laws'. The beginning of the phrase is not without irony and can only be understood by an implicit comparison with Athenian education. The Athenians boast of the high intellectual level of their education, but what use is this to them, except to make them believe themselves too intellectual to obey the laws, like those, for example, who demonstrate that the laws are relative and have no inherent value? Amongst us, says Archidamos, this is not the case: perhaps we are not brilliant intellectually, but because of this we do not place ourselves above the laws and we submit ourselves to collective discipline. Here we are close to the debate of the *Clouds* between the old and the new education: does not the Weak Argument pride himself on teaching people how to overturn the law without risk? But it is very probable that an enlightenment spirit like Thucydides would not entirely espouse Archidamos' argument, and we may think we see in his point something like second-degree irony: because what he makes him say, in sum, is that the Spartans are stupid but disciplined, and that they are disciplined because they are stupid – something which is certainly not an ideal for Thucydides. All in all, the image of Spartan education to which this text bears witness is that of a harsh education, which disciplines more than it teaches, which prefers integration of the individual into the collective to his own development, and which disciplines above all because it scarcely teaches. We find something analogous in the second speech.

Pericles' Funeral Speech (2.39.1–2)

The subject treated in this chapter of the speech is preparation for war: Pericles wants to show the Athenians that, contrary to popular opinion, they have nothing to envy the Spartans for in this regard.

> As for our educational systems (ἐν ταῖς παιδείαις), while the Spartans can only attain courage at the price of a laborious training (ἐπιπόνῳ ἀσκήσει), which begins in their youth, for us, it is by living without constraint that we learn how to face similar dangers, and no worse than they... Surely, if it is by living without care rather than by training to excess, if it is with a courage which we derive less

> from our laws than from our character that we choose to meet danger, so much the better for us: we are at an advantage in not having to suffer in advance for future trials, without showing less audacity when they are upon us than those who are permanently in training.

Spartan education is not tackled here on its supposed weak point, its intellectual level, but on what everyone agrees in viewing as its strong point, preparation for war. Pericles does not dispute the efficacity of Spartan education in this respect. He contrasts two kinds of Greek citizens: those (the Spartans) whose education and training are organized with this end in view, programming them to be war-machines and nothing more, and those (the Athenians) who lead a free life and only fight well for their city because they are good citizens. It is evidently the second who lead a life most in keeping with the ideal of the city. Pericles also contrasts two kinds of men: those who only attain courage at the cost of forced training, and those who reach the same result simply by their natural dispositions and by living normally. It is the second who have the most beautiful life, aesthetically and humanly speaking. In sum, it is finer to make war as amateurs than as professionals. Pericles further suggests, by twice using the figure of litotes, that even in terms of military effectiveness the second sort are winners, doubtless because they keep the spirit of initiative and inventiveness which in the others is smothered by over-heavy discipline.[6]

Aristophanes and Thucydides apply contrasting assessments to Spartan education. Where the former praises an education 'of the good old days', uncontaminated by the current intellectual 'modernism', the latter sees a harsh, constraining system, which is in the end less efficient than is claimed even in its preferred area, preparation for war. But the images which they give agree in one essential respect: Spartan education, in their view, forms a coherent whole, a 'system', which not only by its content but already in itself contrasts with the 'liberal' method of education which functions at Athens as in most cities. It is particularly clear in Thucydides that each method of education reflects and at the same time conditions the political and social system of the city in which it functions; something which Plato and Aristotle will later restate. These assessments rest on fairly schematic global visions, fed on established ideas. What remains to be instituted is a real *discussion*, based on detailed information and focusing on concrete realities.

The missing link

There is a phrase in Xenophon's *Lak. Pol.*, in connection with the boys' diet (2.7), which has not received the attention it deserves, doubtless because it has been seen, rather hastily, as a purely rhetorical turn of phrase: 'I think everyone realizes that it was not because he [Lycurgus] did not know what to give them to eat that he allowed them to manage in this way.' We can interpret this in different ways, but it is not its exact sense which concerns us for the moment; it is its very existence. It implies that in the period when Xenophon was composing his treatise, not only did numerous Greeks know that a distinctive *paideia* existed at Sparta, but this knowledge and the discussions to which it led extended to a good deal of detail. For this to have formed a part of the shared knowledge of cultivated Greeks around 390–80, works treating Spartan education – amongst other systems – must have circulated amongst the public, spreading information, supporting adopted positions and contributing in a decisive manner to shaping the image which people had of this *paideia*.[7] As we possess nothing of the kind, these treatises must have disappeared, as at least in the two following cases.

Critias

Lakedaimonion Politeia

A Critias composed one or two treatises to which this title has been given, perhaps one in verse, the other in prose; four fragments of the first and six or seven of the second have come down to us.[8] That this Critias is the same as (a) the political man, leader of the Thirty and (b) the disciple of Socrates, son of Kallaischros and a character in several of Plato's dialogues, without being formally established, is very generally accepted; his style, in any case, is right for this period, and his ideas agree with those of (a) as much as (b). His *Constitutions* are in fact eulogies, apparently without reservations, less of the Spartans' institutions, moreover, than of their way of life. One of the fragments of the *Constitution* in prose seems to be its opening:

> I begin with the conception of a man. How can he be most physically healthy and strong? If his father practises gymnastics, eats solidly and trains his body, and if the mother of the future child strengthens her body and practises gymnastics. (fr. 32, *apud* Clement of Alexandria, *Stromates* 6.9)

This text closely resembles the passage in Xenophon's *Lak. Pol.* which constitutes the real start of the development (1.3–4): 'For example, *à propos teknopoiia*, to begin at the beginning…'; in the rest of the phrase, too, Xenophon has clearly followed Critias very closely. After treating reproduction and marriage, Xenophon quite naturally passes on to the education of the children thus conceived; it can be inferred from this that Critias did the same. Indeed, he could hardly have done otherwise: to what can an exposition on procreation lead if not to an account of education? There is a logical progression here, and one which seems inevitable. So it is practically certain that Critias, like Xenophon, devoted his second chapter to education. We are completely ignorant of its content, because no fragment of it has been transmitted; I believe that it must have differed from that of Xenophon at least in tone, which, given what we think we know of Critias' character, must have been very assertive, and offensive rather than defensive.

The treatise of king Pausanias

It is not without hesitation that I approach this subject, which, having for a long time been the preserve of a few specialists, has become almost a commonplace of Spartan history of the period. My problem will be to be as brief as possible; I shall content myself with giving my point of view, without being able really to argue it. Those who know the literature will easily supplement this insufficiency.[9]

The documentary base is a passage of Ephoros (*FGH* 70 F 118) 'quoted' (in fact, summarized in an indirect style) by Strabo (8.5.5); the text, in the manuscripts, is lacunose, but it has been possible to complete it thanks to a Vatican palimpsest (Vat. Gr. 2306 and 2061A), the reading of which, due to G. Cozza-Luzi, deputy librarian at the Vatican at the end of the nineteenth century, was first reproduced by Ehrenberg in 1924, then by Aly in 1950, the document having become indecipherable in the meantime. I would translate thus:

> Pausanias, banished by the other royal house, composed during his exile a treatise against the laws of Lycurgus, the latter having belonged to the house which had driven him out, a treatise where he cites even the oracles given to Lycurgus, of which the majority contain eulogies of him.[10]

The issue which has until now been the subject of dispute is the 'title' of the treatise. 'Against the laws of Lycurgus' (κατὰ τῶν Λυκούργου νόμων, Cozza-Luzi's reading) is in fact very strange, and it has been rightly asserted that to entitle a pamphlet thus was not only provocative – which would not be very surprising on the part of a character such as king Pausanias seems to have been – but politically suicidal.

I do not intend to discuss here David's very convincing argument of historical probability. Because for me the problem should not be primarily a historical problem (that kind of discussion only comes *afterwards*), but a problem with the Greek text. From this point of view, my opinion is that the reading κατὰ, 'against', is the one which gives the Greek text the best sense – more, the only one which really gives it a sense in all its parts: which means there is no reason to have recourse to the *correction* περί. This is why.

The first, obvious, reason is the genitive absolute ὄντος τῆς ἐκβαλούσης οἰκίας. Adopting περί obliges us to give it a concessive value: Pausanias would have written a treatise 'on' the laws of Lycurgus, although the latter had belonged to the house which had driven him out. But if it is true that a genitive absolute can have a concessive value in itself, the sense has to depend on the evidence of the context.[11] This would be the case if the latter had said that the treatise was *in favour* of the laws of Lycurgus; but περί being neutral, there is no opposition between the title thus formulated and the hostility of Pausanias towards Lycurgus. There would hardly be any sense in saying that Pausanias had written a treatise *on* the laws of Lycurgus (neither for, nor against: on), *although* in other respects he had every reason to detest him.

The second reason is the final relative clause, ἐν ᾧ καὶ τοὺς χρησμοὺς λέγειν τοὺς δοθέντας αὐτῷ ἐπ' ἐγκωμίῳ πλείστους. It is καί which underlines the logical articulation of the text. If the text had previously said that Pausanias was the author of a treatise *on* the laws of Lycurgus (neither for, nor against: on), what sense would there be in saying that in this treatise he cited *even* oracles which eulogized the great man?[12] If, on the contrary, the treatise was presented as hostile to the lawgiver, the adversative value of καὶ becomes not only intelligible, but necessary. The final words, ἐπ' ἐγκωμίῳ πλείστους, are the other significant element of this relative clause. The point thus made, that most of the oracles cited by Pausanias included eulogies of Lycurgus, would be without interest if the treatise was presented as neutral (and even more so if it was favourable); if on the contrary it was presented as hostile, this detail becomes remarkable and sums up the meaning of the whole passage. Ephoros' assertion is moreover far from being exact,[13] to judge by those oracles which have come down to us:[14] of these six oracles only the first, already cited in part by Herodotos (1.65), consists of a eulogy of Lycurgus. All this is demonstrative of the way in which Ephoros manipulates information.

These, then, are the reasons relating to the text itself, in its formulation and its logic, which seem to me to necessitate the reading κατά. We must remember the context of this long quotation of Ephoros: he is arguing against Hellanikos, who was removing paternity of the fundamental laws of Sparta from Lycurgus in order to attribute it to Eurysthenes and Prokles, the founders of the city. His first argument is that the Spartans of his time continued to pay great honours to Lycurgus, while to the descendants of Eurysthenes and Prokles they had not even given collective appellations formed from their names. Next comes the argument drawn from Pausanias' treatise. What Ephoros means is that even the king Pausanias, although he hated the Eurypontids, whom he considered responsible for his exile, and for this reason composed a treatise against Lycurgus, considered to be a Eurypontid, was nevertheless induced to cite oracles given to Lycurgus in his treatise, oracles which not only confirmed his status as lawgiver, but even included eulogies in his honour, something which is not common in oracles. For all that, I am not claiming that the reading περί is impossible; if it was, it would not have been supported by such good scholars; but I find that it weakens the text excessively and does not explain the reasoning followed therein. It seems to me that it accords less importance to an attentive consideration of the text than to arguments of historical verisimilitude, which are sound but not compelling: it is possible, for example, that his death-sentence turned Pausanias' attitude towards his city's institutions upside-down. I think that if Ehrenberg, Baladié and, after the publication of David's article, Nafissi, amongst others, have followed Cozza-Luzi's reading, it is because they have been sensitive above all to the logical progression of the text itself.

There is another point which has perhaps not been accorded sufficient attention:[15] the question of the title. If Pausanias had really *entitled* his treatise 'Against the laws of Lycurgus', we might indeed have been surprised; but this is very improbable. The custom for a writer to inscribe a title at the head of the work which he would communicate, in one form or another, to the public, was not yet established at the beginning of the fourth century; a formula appearing in the *incipit* took its place, and the titles which we find as headings in the manuscripts were added later. I think that Pausanias himself did not entitle his treatise either 'on' or 'against': he did not give it a title *at all*. As it included amongst other things criticisms concerning Spartan laws and customs, it was easy for those who did not share his point of view to claim in a fairly malicious way (a malice which Ephoros likewise demonstrates when he presents the king as motivated solely by his hatred of the Eurypontids, which leads him also to say that he had been exiled *by* them) that the treatise had been composed 'against the laws of Lycurgus'.

After these over-long explanations, I return to what interests us here: that Pausanias' treatise consisted of criticisms of 'the laws' of Sparta. These criticisms certainly extended beyond the domain of political institutions; what were called 'the laws of Lycurgus' were essentially the customs which regulated the life of the city. It is possible, then, that Pausanias criticized the education system, because of the key role that education played in the Spartan system, and also because, as Xenophon's treatise clearly, if indirectly, shows, it could be criticized and certainly was (as Thucydides confirms), in a period when Sparta was hardly popular. This criticism would have had a considerable impact, not only because of the identity of its author (not an ordinary Spartiate – the first Spartiate to take issue with Lycurgus – but a king of Sparta), but also because instead of reproaching the Spartans for their error in no longer respecting the laws of Lycurgus, it was the legislation itself which he was attacking, head-on. In this way Pausanias had inaugurated a train of thought which would later be followed by Plato, and more explicitly still Aristotle, whose extreme critical vigour, as far as education is concerned, would thus be explained.

Where should we place Xenophon's treatise in relation to that of Pausanias? It is tempting to think that when Xenophon is defending the Spartan education system against accusations which he considers to be malicious and unfounded, he is not reacting against opinions disseminated through the world anonymously, but against the arguments of Pausanias; that, for example, and to return to our point of departure, it was Pausanias who had asserted ironically that Lycurgus appeared to have had no food to give the children of Sparta (which Xenophon could have taken literally). It could have been the same with the scepticism professed 'by some' (ὑπό τινων) about the chastity of the pederastic relationship (2.14). But this remains only a suggestion, because there is no proof that Xenophon's treatise was a response to Pausanias', and, for all that we know, it could just as well have been the other way round.[16]

Orators

Two rhetorical texts composed in the third quarter of the fourth century allude to the Spartan education system. The first, that of Isocrates, is a virulent criticism of it.

Isocrates

Panathenaicus §§209–13 and 216 (c. 342–339 BC)

In the first part of the work (§§40–199), which is presented as a formal speech of the usual type, combining the traditional praise of Athens with a counterpoint of often violent attacks on Sparta, education does not arise. This theme is only introduced in the second part (§§200–32), where it is presented in a very logical fashion. Isocrates recounts that after he had composed the preceding speech, he had summoned one of his former pupils, whom he knew to have pro-Spartan leanings, so that, he says, he could read through his text and tell him if, in his opinion, Isocrates had made any errors concerning Sparta. In a rather surprising way, the pupil finds the speech excellent (§201), but declares that he admires the Spartans, because in his opinion they invented τὰ κάλλιστα τῶν ἐπιτηδευμάτων, 'the finest rules of life' (§202). It is this expression which gives the speech new impetus; from here on the subject will be these *epitēdeumata*, to the extent that κάλλιστα ἐπιτηδεύματα becomes its leitmotif. Whenever a new subject is introduced (§§204, 205, 207, 210), Isocrates addresses his pupil, saying more or less: these are the people who behave in a such a way, whom you praise for having invented the *kallista epitēdeumata*? Since this term is the very one which, according to my argument, represents the true 'title' of Xenophon's treatise (cf. above, p. 2), we might ask ourselves whether it is in fact this author who is aimed at via the pupil. Indeed, the pupil's intervention is obviously a fiction, and it must be the case that this word *epitēdeumata*, which relaunches the speech, had meaning for Isocrates' readers as a reference.

The education system is the principal target of this new wave of attacks. First criticism: the dramatic insufficiency of its intellectual side. §208: the Spartans 'are so behind in the ways of common education and knowledge (τῆς κοινῆς παιδείας καὶ φιλοσοφίας) that they do not even learn their letters'. This is clearly excessive.[17] Xenophon does not address this aspect, but we shall see later that the Spartans were certainly as literate as most Greeks. That said, we should recognize that the criticism was traditional at this period.

Second criticism: the Spartan education system develops only a spirit of domination and conquest. §210: 'They accustom their children to pursue occupations which they do not expect to make them benefactors to other men, but to make them as harmful as possible towards the Greeks.' The formulation is extremely cantankerous, but at bottom it is a serious criticism: the usually laudatory theme of military efficiency is turned on its head into an accusation of imperialism; we shall find this again a few years later in Aristotle.

Third criticism: theft. This is the longest exposition:

> 211. Those people, every day, as soon as they get up, they send their children, with companions of their own choice, in theory to hunt, in reality to steal from those who live in the countryside. 212. The result is that those who are caught pay a fine (ἀργύριον ἀποτίνειν) and receive blows, while those who knew how to commit the greatest infamies without being caught win a reputation superior to others amongst the children, and when they become men, if they remain faithful to the habits acquired during childhood, are well on the way to attaining the highest offices.

It is then easy for Isocrates to get indignant. For example:

> 214. Others consider wrongdoers and thieves as the worst kind of slaves; these men judge the best of their children to be those who have won first place in such exercises, and they honour them more than all the rest.

The orator attacks very strongly at the weakest point, the point which Xenophon had the greatest difficulty justifying; without the least charity, he happily gives his all to it. The excessiveness of the argument is at first striking, as is a certain dishonesty which was not really necessary;[18] even while noting this, however, we must remain fair and try to understand. Isocrates is presenting theft as one of the children's everyday activities; this is certainly false, but Xenophon himself introduces no qualification on this point, and the only real difference is that for him the exercise seems to take place rather at night (ἀγρύπνειν). He goes further in insisting on the haste with which the Spartans send their children off. He presents it as the principle and even the only occupation of the young. He completely distorts reality (if we take it that what Xenophon says is reality) by passing in silence over the lack of food: this is another reproach which he could have levelled against Spartan education, but he refrains from doing so because that could to a certain extent have excused the theft. The result is that, to read Isocrates, we might believe that Spartan children would steal anything, whereas Xenophon clearly explains that only food is involved.[19] Isocrates probably knows this, since he speaks of 'those who live in the countryside'; it is indeed there that fruit, vegetables, cereals and farmyard animals are most easily found. He is even more malicious when he claims that the children are classified, and the best held in great esteem, according (solely) to the results obtained in this exercise. It is true that, in the passage of the *Anabasis* where Xenophon is conversing with Cheirisophos,[20] the Athenian emphasizes that at Sparta the children's stealing is considered to be a 'good thing' (οὐκ αἰσχρὸν ἀλλὰ καλόν), but this is a deliberate exaggeration: the whole tirade is spoken in a jocular tone (Cheirisophos will respond in the same way, and with a very 'Laconian' aptness), and, in the *Lak. Pol.*, stealing is not depicted as a good thing, but as a *test* to which the youth is *compelled* to submit. For all that, I do not believe that this assertion concerning the honours given to the best thieves, and, especially, at §214, concerning the fact that these honours have an influence on the youth's entire future 'career', is just a delirious exaggeration. I would think rather that Isocrates has conflated with 'ordinary' theft a very particular theft, that of the cheeses from the altar of Orthia, a competition whose victors probably indeed won a lasting renown (this is what Xenophon 2.9 indicates).

This example demonstrates that Isocrates is without doubt exaggerating, distorting and amalgamating, but not inventing. This is why I think we should stress what makes this text interesting, rather than its rhetorical amplifications.[21] We must first ask ourselves who, according to Isocrates, sends the children to steal, and, in consequence, where they are supposed to be sleeping (ἐξ εὐνῆς). In the text, the subject is ἐκεῖνοι, 'those people', that is the Spartans in general, as in the whole exposition. But there are two possibilities: it is either a question of the parents, which means that the children are thought of as sleeping at home, or of the Spartiates as a collective, i.e. the state, and the children could be sleeping either at home or, rather, communally (and perhaps already in the countryside). The expression ἐκεῖνοι... ἐκπέμπουσι τοὺς παῖδας rather gives the impression that we should understand '*their* children' (a standard Greek turn of phrase), but this is not at all certain.

Another preliminary question is that of the bands of children. By 'with companions of their own choice', Isocrates sketches a picture of bands which form themselves around a leader, with the single aim of engaging in theft. It is naturally tempting to think that here we have a serious distortion of the reality, which is made up of stable and institutional groups, like Xenophon's *ilē*, into which the children are organized. But we must remember what Xenophon says (2.7), that whoever wants to steal has to get help from some of his little companions: so it seems indeed true that, for each operation, whoever was its leader had to form a team under his command, perhaps within his group, but made up of companions whom he chose; Isocrates, basically, is saying exactly this.

The reference to hunting is interesting and should not be overlooked; Xenophon does not talk about this, but he says nothing of the children's everyday activities. For Isocrates, hunting is just a pretext and the word serves only to disguise the reality of stealing, the two activities having in common the fact that they happen outside the city. But this presentation of the matter is contradictory: if stealing was, as he says, held in high esteem at Sparta, neither parents nor the state would have reason to try to hide the fact that it was to this exercise that they were sending the children. If hunting appears here, it is because it really was an important occupation for Spartan boys, and familiar to all the Greeks whom Isocrates is addressing. This is not pure speculation. Amongst the competitions between children whose existence is attested by inscriptions of the Roman period, one is called *katthēratorion*, a term which Kennell translates 'the little hunter's contest';[22] this was certainly not a real hunt, but a dance or mime of hunting. Kennell proposes putting alongside this activity another of these competitions, called the *keloia*, and he notes 'this prominence of hunting' in the *agōgē* of the imperial period. The Isocrates passage seems to me to show that the same was already the case (though perhaps in different forms) in the classical period: change *and* continuity, as ever.

The monetary fine immediately appears highly improbable, as such a punishment obviously could not be applied to children. But Isocrates knew this as well as we do, and doubtless he means that this fine was paid by the parents.[23] Thus the latter would be associated with the shame of their son, shame not for having stolen, but for having been caught.

Isocrates has in any case noted something which is entirely true: that education at Sparta is a permanent competition (though not, it would seem from reading Xenophon, in the case of stealing), and that performances achieved during this stage of life partly condition the future of each individual. It is possible, moreover, that the distortion introduced by Isocrates is linked to the fact that he takes (or pretends to take) seriously Xenophon's joke at the end of his conversation with Cheirisophos: 'This is the moment to demonstrate your education (καιρός ἐστιν ἐπιδείξασθαι τὴν παιδείαν).'[24]

The pupil does not avow himself entirely convinced and takes up the argument to explain exactly why he praises the Spartans for having invented τὰ κάλλιστα ἐπιτηδεύματα (§217):

> When I said that I was not thinking of the piety, the justice and the wisdom of which you spoke, but of the gymnastic exercises that are practised there, of the training in courage, of the solidarity, in short, of the preparation for war, occupations which one can but praise, and of which one can say that they are supremely honoured amongst them.

Not only does this point of view completely lack originality, but its choice as a line of defence by the pupil quickly turns out to be disastrous: Isocrates takes pleasure in pushing against this open door (§§219–29).

Lycurgus

Against Leocrates 106 (331/330 BC)

Leocrates had fled Athens the day after Chaeroneia, and thus avoided the call-up. The whole of the second half of the speech (§§74–130) is a kind of anthology of patriotism and cowardice; Lycurgus goes so far as to appeal to Sparta to lend him Tyrtaios, of whom he quotes, at §107, the long fragment 10 West (6–7 Prato). But this is, for him, just tit for tat, for in reality Tyrtaios was originally from Athens:

> Who among the Greeks does not know that the Spartans received Tyrtaios from Athens to be their general, thanks to whom they overcame the enemy and organized the education of the young (τὴν περὶ τοὺς νέους ἐπιμελείαν)? It was a good decision, not only for the danger that they were in then, but for all time; for he left them elegies of his own composition, which they are made to recite to educate them in courage (παιδεύονται πρὸς ἀνδρείαν).

Thus it is Tyrtaios, and not Lycurgus (whom the Athenians would not easily have been able to claim), who is presented here as the creator of Spartan *paideia*, on the sole basis of the content of his verses, which is, as Jäger used to say, 'a grandiose educational ethos'. It is true that they are addressed primarily to young men of an age to fight: line 15 of the fragment which Lycurgus goes on to quote begins with the apostrophe ὦ νέοι. This theory is nonetheless surprising, and it did not have much success. On the other hand, the theory which makes Tyrtaios an Athenian by origin is quite widespread (at Athens, naturally) in the fourth century: we find it first in Plato (*Laws* 1.629a), and Philochoros (328F215) specifies that he was a native of Aphidna.[25] On the education system in itself, the only point to note is the interpretation by its military aim – a banal idea: Lycurgus is not Isocrates.

Philosophers

Spartan education attracted the attention of the two great philosophers of the century, Plato and Aristotle.

Plato

Socratic dialogues

The first dialogue, in the generally accepted chronological order, where this question is broached is the *Hippias Major*,[26] almost at the beginning of the discussion (282b–6a). Hippias has no difficulty in recognizing that the value of a sophist is assessed in terms of the money he makes; this means that he himself makes a really great deal of it, and even in the most out-of-the-way places.

> – So, says Socrates, at Sparta, where you go often, you must surely break the records.
> – Not at all, replies Hippias, I have never made anything there.
> – Astonishing, says Socrates; but the Spartans want to learn, and they do not lack money. Would this be because, having an education system better than yours, they have no need of your services?

This is how the discussion takes the turn which for a moment directs it towards education systems, envisaged as preparations for virtue: the system which the Spartans have always had, and the one which Hippias would like to sell them. Of course, the sophist could not accept the explanation which Socrates has just proposed, and he finds other reasons for the Spartans' obstinate refusal.

First reason: 'It is because the Lacedaemonians are not accustomed to meddle with the laws, and to give their sons an education which deviates from the custom (οὐδὲ παρὰ τὰ εἰωθότα παιδεύειν τοὺς ὑεῖς)' (284b). Hippias thus adduces the Spartans' conservatism, in all things and in particular in the area of education. To his great frustration, they absolutely do not want to be 'modern'.

Second reason: 'For them, it is contrary to custom to give an education of foreign type (ξενικὴν παίδευσιν οὐ νόμιμον αὐτοῖς παιδεύειν)' (284c). Now it is a matter of the Spartans' particularity, we might say their 'nationalism'; this remark calls to mind a phrase in *Inst. Lac.* 4 (above, p. 31) which uses the metaphor of *xenēlasia* in this connection.

Next they discuss the lecture subjects appreciated by the Spartans (who are not totally insensitive to intellectual problems): not astronomy, nor geometry, nor arithmetic,[27] nor the art of speaking, Hippias' strong points, but, let us say, ancient history in general (πάσης τῆς ἀρχαιολογίας); this has compelled him to work on this subject. But there is also education: 'Even more recently, I had great success there when I expounded the rules of conduct to which the young man must apply himself (ἃ χρὴ τὸν νέον ἐπιτηδεύειν)' (286a); the *epitēdeumata* again!

In this dialogue, then, Plato already shows a marked interest in Spartan education. But his aim is less to talk about it (it remains at the level of generalities) than to use this theme to ridicule Hippias, which Socrates does at length. Spartan education here serves him as a foil. It is clear that in Plato's eyes the Spartans are right to prefer their good old system, which works well for them, to the so-called modernity (see previously the ironic discussion of the notion of progress) of that sold by Hippias. The philosopher's attitude is thus comparable to that of Aristophanes in the *Clouds*; it does not go very far, Spartan education appearing only as the classic example of a traditional education.

In the *Protagoras*, which, while being an eminently 'Socratic' dialogue, is probably a little later (around 390 BC?), there is a long passage (342a–c) about Spartan education, viewed not as itself but in its results.[28] We are, in a debate rich in about-turns, at the moment where, after an interruption provoked by Socrates, the discussion starts up again, Protagoras agreeing from now on to abandon sustained argument in order to pose questions. So he uses one of his favourite procedures, the exposition of a text. It is a poem of Simonides, in which he sees a contradiction in connection with virtue. Socrates, who, likewise, is rather good at expounding texts, does not agree; he explains his interpretation. He begins with praise of brevity, and this leads him to talk about Sparta. 'Of all Greece,' he asserts, 'it is Crete and Sparta which are the places where philosophy[29] has been practised the longest and the most assiduously...' A surprising assertion, which we at once suspect of irony; however, the association of Crete with Sparta makes us think that the 'philosophy' concerned could well be related to the adoption of wise laws and a good constitution. This is not at all impossible: the ultimate aim of philosophy, for Plato, could well be this, and it is philosophers who direct his ideal city. But Socrates immediately adds '...and it is the place in the world where there are most sophists'. There is, then, no more doubt: he is joking. What follows develops this ironic paradox by presenting various well-known aspects of Spartan civilization as proofs of what he has suggested. In order to philosophize quietly and without anyone knowing, the Spartans pretend to be ignorant, and not to aspire to anything other than military superiority. In order to have leisurely discussions with the sophists amongst them, they expel strangers: whence their famous *xenēlasia*. Finally, they forbid their young men to go abroad 'so that they do not un-learn what they themselves have taught them'. This phrase focuses the argument, which no longer bears on Spartan culture in general, but on education, which is at once its expression and its source. These, then, are some of the aspects of the Spartans' conduct, at the same time the strangest and the best known, which are agreeably explained by the fact that they are philosophers, not without knowing it (for they know it perfectly well), but wishing, secretive as they are, it not to be known.

After this brilliantly conducted paradox, the tone changes and the discussion passes on to serious matters. 'In these cities,' says Socrates, 'there are not only men but even women who are proud of their education (ἐπὶ παιδεύσει μέγα φρονοῦντες)' (342d). There is no discernible trace of irony or joking here. The argument does not seem really paradoxical, if one thinks of the role played by certain women of Spartan high society in the fourth century and later. It appears, then, that when Socrates said earlier (342b) that the Spartans pass themselves off as ignorant (ἀμαθεῖς), this was not a way of saying that they were so really, and that when he said that they cultivated the image of war specialists, this does not come down to saying, in a critical fashion (as Plato does in the *Laws*), that they occupied themselves with this alone.

> Here is the proof that what I say is true, and that the Lacedaemonians are excellently trained in philosophy and in speaking. If you want to have a good discussion with the most ordinary Lacedaemonian, you will find him at first, in general, rather weak in his arguments; but then, wherever you may have got to in the discussion, suddenly, like a javelin expert, he throws in a word full of sense, brief and concise, so well that his interlocutor seems to be little better than a child. Both now and in the past many people have understood that laconism was much more philosophy than sport, given that the ability to deliver such words is the deed of none but the perfectly educated man (τελέως πεπαιδευμένου ἀνθρώπου).

Spartan education is viewed here as intellectual training; it proves its efficacy by its results. Socrates strongly emphasizes that it is not only a question of brevity, but also of pertinence, and that the brevity reinforces the pertinence, making the word as effective as an act. ὥσπερ δεινὸς ἀκοντίστης: thus the Spartan fights with words. There is no doubt in my mind that this praise is entirely serious. It leads towards what Socrates says further on, to conclude the exposition before returning to Simonides: 'Why do I say this? Because such was the character of the philosophy of the ancients: a laconic brevity.' This does not mean that the opening formula, that the Cretans and the Spartans are the best philosophers, should itself be taken seriously: for if, in order to be a true philosopher according to Socrates, it is necessary to hate verbosity and cultivate brevity and absolute pertinence, this does not mean that this is sufficient. But, with their ability in speaking, which rests on an ability in thinking, the Spartans are well on the way, thanks to their education.

Something else which confirms that the praise is serious is that it is closely related to what Socrates said earlier against verbosity (334c–d), when he refused to listen any longer to what Protagoras was saying: 'Protagoras, I am a man without memory; when people talk to me at length, I forget the subject of the conversation.' Moreover, this is a Laconian saying. In 3.46, Herodotos gives an account of the embassy to Sparta of some Samians exiled by Polycrates. They address to the *archontes* (doubtless the ephors) a long and impassioned speech, to which the latter respond that 'they had forgotten the beginning of the speech and had not understood the rest'. Socrates' allusion was certainly transparent for Plato's public: it was a way of implicitly invoking Spartan patronage. This question of brevity is not a coquetry on Socrates' part. What he means to make clear is the implacable opposition between two philosophical practices. That of the sophists uses sustained argument, which aims to seduce or to convince a passive audience. That of Socrates is dialectic; it can either guide the interlocutor of good faith towards the truth, or compel anyone who resists to surrender, at the end of a real struggle. It is this opposition which is the true subject of the *Protagoras*. The praise of Laconian brevity is directly related to this subject.

This text is chronologically the first to talk about Spartan education *as an intellectual training*, and this is in order to praise one particular aspect of it. It is the source of Plutarch's exposition of the same subject (*Lyc.* 19–20), an exposition which concludes with the formula of 342e: τὸ λακωνίζειν πολὺ μᾶλλον ἐστιν φιλοσοφεῖν ἢ φιλογυμναστεῖν, quoted almost verbatim. Plutarch, too, took Plato's argument here seriously.

We might be tempted to conclude from these two 'Socratic' dialogues, the *Hippias Major* and the *Protagoras*, that at this period (*c.* 390 BC?) Plato had an entirely favourable opinion of Spartan education. This is perhaps true, and we might accept that it was the reflections which accompanied the writing of the *Republic* which led him seriously to qualify this opinion. But it is also possible that what we have here is an essentially tactical attitude, and that he chose, amongst all the features of this education, those which, because he approved of them, could serve his argument against the sophists.

The Laws

If we judged the case only on the aspects of Spartan education of which Plato explicitly declares his approval, we would think that in the *Laws* criticism largely outweighs praise. In fact, we only find a single positive reference, and this concerns a relatively marginal trait, the absolute prohibition of young men from questioning the value of the laws.

> 'In your city,' says Socrates to Megillos and Kleinias, 'however wise your laws may be in general, one of the best is that which absolutely forbids the young (νέοι) from asking questions about what good or bad your legislation contains, which commands them to proclaim with one voice, with one mouth, that everything about it is excellent, since its authors are the gods; and, if one of them says otherwise, to refuse obstinately to listen to him.' (1.634d–e)

The celebrated *unanimity* (*homonoia*) of the Spartans is, then, for Plato the result of a systematic training; he is not talking about a duty to denounce, but this is almost a matter of course. However, dispute is not forbidden to adults, on condition that they respect certain conventions: 'If someone older finds something to criticize in your institutions, he will only address such arguments to a magistrate or to a man of his own age, when no young man is present.' This is what Plato approves of strongly.

In addition to this, there are numerous points in the education system which Plato is imagining for his ideal city which seem to be inspired by the Spartan model, which obviously means that he approves of them. Elsewhere (8.836b) he acknowledges, in a general way, his debt to Sparta and Crete. This can be seen, first of all, in the aim which he assigns to education: not essentially to inculcate in the youth a certain amount of basic knowledge, but to prepare him to be a good citizen, entirely devoted to his city:

> [Our discussion] calls by this name the kind of education which leads towards virtue from childhood, by inspiring the desire and the passion to become an accomplished citizen, who knows how to give and to take orders in accordance with justice (τὴν δὲ πρὸς ἀρετὴν ἐκ παίδων παιδείαν, ποιοῦσαν ἐπιθυμητήν τε καὶ ἐραστὴν τοῦ πολίτην γενέσθαι τέλεον, ἄρχειν τε καὶ ἄρχεσθαι ἐπιστάμενον μετὰ δίκης). (1.643e)

Of course, this is the ideal of every city, and Thucydides' Pericles also talks of the citizen 'in love' with his city; but Spartan education is, much more than the 'liberal' education of the Athenians, entirely directed towards this end.

To arrive at this, it is advisable for this education to be compulsory, identical for all and organized by the city. This is, in a sense, what happens at Sparta, and the importance of this principle has been strongly felt by Plato, who takes it up for his city. He has just been talking about 'school buildings', class-rooms and gymnasia, that the state will construct in the city, and where resident foreigners will be paid to teach.

> It should not be the case that the boy whom his father wishes to send to school attends, while the boy whose father does not want to should be excused from education. No, it is, as they say, every man and boy who, as far as possible, seeing that they belong to the city rather than to their parents (ὡς τῆς πόλεως μᾶλλον ἢ τῶν γεννητόρων ὄντας), should receive a compulsory education. (7.804d)

The idea of a state education is so strongly linked to Sparta in Greek thought that Plutarch recapitulated Plato's formula, attributing it to Lycurgus, concerning children as property of the city: 'Lycurgus considered that children did not belong to their fathers, but in common to the city (οὐκ ἰδίους ἡγεῖτο τῶν πατέρων τοὺς παῖδας, ἀλλὰ κοινοὺς τῆς πόλεως ὁ Λυκοῦργος)' (*Lyc.* 15.14).

How far does this public character extend? The question must be asked first in relation to Sparta. Comparing its education system to that of Plato,

Piérart considers it self-evident that if, in this city, education was public, teaching, i.e. basic apprenticeships, was private: and this, for him, renders the Platonic city totally original.[30] In this he is just following common opinion, and he is probably right; but in fact the matter is more problematic than he allows. This point will be examined later;[31] perhaps then we shall find the Spartan practice of teaching, as far as school-houses as well as the teachers are concerned, less far removed than he thinks from that of the city of the *Laws*.

In a general way, the organization of the course of schooling in Plato's city resembles what we know about Sparta: its commencement at six years old, the age at which the sexes are separated; the importance of physical exercises and the handling of arms; the exceptional place accorded to *mousikē* (poetry, singing, dance); the active participation in the city's festivals. But we might think of such a programme as the norm amongst Greeks; what perhaps more precisely indicates a Spartan influence is the strictly traditional and conservative character which Plato assigns to each of the exercises which constitute *mousikē*.

One of the most distinguishing traits of Spartan education is that it aims constantly to select the best. This is also a major concern of the Platonic city. It is expounded as one of the fundamental principles of social organization, in both the *Republic* (3.413c–e: the selection of leaders amongst the Guardians) and the *Statesman* (308c–d). In the *Laws* (12.969b–c), this selection is explicitly related to education.

In order to pick out the best, the Spartans were not content with a few tests scattered throughout the course; to this end – and also, more prosaically, to impose discipline – the children are continuously observed. Since those responsible for this task cannot assure absolute continuity, the principle of supervision is complemented, as we have seen in reading Xenophon, by that of the delegation of authority. Something similar happens in the Platonic city. When it is slaves to whom the children are entrusted, be they pedagogues or teachers:

> any free man who appears shall punish both the child and the pedagogue or master, if one of them commits a fault. If anyone, finding himself present, does not impose the appropriate punishment, first let him incur the greatest dishonour, and then let the guardian of the laws who has been chosen as responsible for children examine the case of the man who came across the wrongdoers without punishing them, when he should have done, or punishing them in an inappropriate way. (7.808e–809a)

In a completely different 'teaching' structure from that at Sparta (at least according to Xenophon), we find again, applied with the same rigour, the principle which makes each citizen responsible for all children, at the same time as the technique of supervised supervisors.

This text has the magistrate whom Plato puts in charge of the education system intervening.[32] Here (809a) he is called, in a rather complicated way and one which sounds like an official title, ὁ τῶν νομοφυλάκων ἐπὶ τὴν τῶν παίδων ἀρχὴν ᾑρημένος; earlier we find a simpler but apparently unofficial designation, 'the *epimelētēs* of all education (ὁ τῆς παιδείας ἐπιμελητὴς πάσης)' (6.765d). In this passage, in order to explain this magistrate Plato emphasizes the great importance he attributes to him: it will be a case of a single magistrate, not a committee; he must be at least fifty years old, and be the father of legitimate children, if possible both boys and girls; 'let the man chosen and the man choosing be aware that this magistracy is by far the most important amongst the city's highest magistracies' (765e). He comes back to the point a little further on: the man who should be chosen is τῶν ἐν τῇ πόλει ὃς ἂν ἄριστος εἰς πάντα ᾖ, 'he who is the best in the city in every way' (766a). This insistence is the exact counterpart of Xenophon's insistence on the *paidonomos*: 'Lycurgus…put in command of the boys a citizen from amongst those who occupied the highest magistracies; he is called the *paidonomos*' (2.2). To avoid appearing to be dependent on an existing model, which would damage his enterprise, Plato has clearly deliberately not made use of the Spartan magistrate's title; but he has obviously been inspired by it. Like the *paidonomos*, his *epimelētes* has responsiblity not only for directing the children but also for punishing them (7.809a). For Piérart, his functions are even more extensive, since they also embrace all teaching; but it seems to me improbable that the Spartan *paidonomos* had no role in this area.

There are other details in the Platonic education which call Sparta to mind. To excite his citizens' patriotism, the philosopher establishes three choirs, one of children ('choir of the Muses'), one of young men ('choir of Apollo') and the third of citizens between thirty and sixty years old ('choir of Dionysos'); they have to take part in festivals in this order (2.664c–e). We can hardly avoid comparing this *trichoria* with that described by Plutarch (*Lyc.* 21.3 = *Inst. Lac.* 15), which likewise took part 'in the festivals' (ἐν ταῖς ἑορταῖς), with slightly different age categories.[33] More unexpected on the part of a man who, as we shall see, considered Spartan education too violent, is his decision to organize real exercises in fighting, which, doubtless, especially involved the young:

> As for the 'major' exercises, those in arms, let them take place at least once a month; let them fight against one another over the whole territory, with assaults on positions and ambushes, imitating military behaviour; let them fight seriously, with gauntlets and projectiles which resemble real ones as closely as possible while being less dangerous… (8.830d–e)

Plato then insists on the fact that these mock battles should involve risk, including that of death. The true model for these exercises is certainly Crete, to judge by the description given by Ephoros (in Strabo 10.4.20); but Plato's reader could not help but think also of Sparta, where such regulated battles existed: that of the Platanistas, if it existed in the classical period, and those to which Megillos alludes in 1.633b; and also the Crypteia, which is not a battle between youths, but where young men are armed, go all over the terrritory, and, probably, kill.

I have left till last another passage of the *Laws* (8.845b) which is even more surprising.[34] Here the 'theft' of fruit from countryside properties is under discussion.

> As for pears, apples, pomegranates and all produce of this type, let there be no shame in picking these on the quiet, but if he is caught doing it, let any man aged less than thirty be beaten and driven away, as long as this is without wounding; there will be no recourse for the free man against blows received under these conditions.

The arrangements are less bizarre which concern passing foreigners, who can pick fruit freely, by way of gifts of hospitality, and for men aged more than thirty, who must eat on the spot and not take anything away. For the young men the strangeness is double: first, while it is *permitted* to them by law, they *must* 'steal' (λάθρᾳ λαμβάνειν), that is try not to let themselves be seen; secondly, if he surprises the thieves, the owner of the place *must* put up opposition to what they are doing, even by using violence, *but* a limited, regulated violence, which does not entail injury. It is thus a kind of game, a theft with opposition. I do not see how we can explain that Plato took the trouble to reflect in detail on this question, and at the same time that he opted for such a strange regulation, but one which he presents as entirely natural, other than by a kind of imitation of the children's stealing at Sparta. For the context of this prescription is not theft at all; it is, on the contrary, the placing of certain products of the land, under certain conditions, at certain times, at the disposal of all. So it is a community practice which, though different, recalls the making available of provisions in countryside houses described by Xenophon (*LP* 6.4). In these conditions the 'theft' prescribed by Plato appears as an almost ritual form imposed, in a way which seems entirely arbitrary to us, on a practice which belongs in reality to a making available of supplies. It all looks as though Plato was absolutely determined to introduce the youths' stealing into his legislation, but ridding it of the shocking aspects it had at Sparta.

There are, then, a certain number of principles and details of Spartan education which Plato takes up, and so approves. There are also others, less numerous but very important, which he condemns. His first criticism is well known. He does not deny that this education prepares for virtue; but virtue, while being a unity, has many forms. He distinguishes four of them: intelligence, which enables one to perceive the Good, moderation, justice and courage. Now, Spartan education only takes one of these forms as its objective, courage, which moreover is the most inferior form. Plato thinks, too, that this criticism is valid for Sparta's (and Crete's) institutions as a whole: 'What you both,' says the Athenian to Kleinias and Megillos, 'ordered the good law-giver was to set war as the objective of all your institutions' (3.688a). Such being his interpretation of the principal institutions of Sparta, it is logical that the philosopher considers Spartan education as preparing essentially for war. This conception was already that of Thucydides (above, p. 40), but his Pericles did not make the same use of it: he did not criticize the thing in itself, but showed that as far as preparation for war goes, Athenian practice was better. Plato is not criticizing the Spartans for preparing for war, for he knows that this is necessary for the survival of the city, but for preparing for nothing else. What is needed, by contrast, is:

> an education (παιδοτροφία) which makes him (the child) not only a good soldier, but someone who will be able to direct a city and towns; and such a man, of whom we said at the start that he was a better soldier than Tyrtaios' soldiers, will hence always honour courage as the fourth element of virtue, not the first. (2.666e–7a)

By only preparing for military valour, besides, Spartan education misses its mark, for those who have been educated in virtue as a whole will be superior in this area too (this is more or less what Thucydides makes Pericles say).

Plato's second fundamental criticism is expressed in several passages of the *Laws*; I shall present it here in the manner of a sustained argument, whose theme might be: savagery and civilization. Gentleness in man is not natural:

> Man is, as they say, a civilized being. Certainly, if he receives a correct education and has a good nature, he usually becomes an altogether god-like and civilized being; but if his education is insufficient or bad, he becomes the most savage creature the earth has produced. (6.765e–6a)

The same idea is taken up further on:

> The child is the most difficult of all wild beasts to tame. The origin of thought, not yet brought under control, is so powerful in him that it makes him a cunning animal, cruel and extremely violent, so he must be chained, as it were, with multiple bonds: first, when he leaves wet-nurses and mothers, with pedagogues to direct his boyhood and his early years; then with masters to instruct him in all kinds of subjects. (7.808d–e)

Man's humanity is not innate; it is a conquest brought about by education.[35] It all looks as though each child re-lived for himself the whole of man's evolution since his first appearance on earth, from the savagery of the earliest ages to the civilization of the city. Such a conception was natural for the Greeks, for whom the same word, *paideia*, designated education and civilization. So it is, it would appear, in two ways that, for Plato, education is the foundation of the city: because it teaches how to live in a city, and because it teaches how to be a man; in reality, the two come down to the same thing, since only he who lives in a city is truly a man. Now, in this regard Sparta commits a major error:

> 'Your institutions,' says the Athenian to Kleinias and Megillos, 'are those of a military camp and not that of men living in towns. Your young are like foals grazing in the meadow in compact herds (οἷον ἀθρόους πώλους ἐν ἀγέλῃ νεμομένους φορβάδας τοὺς νέους κέκτησθε). In your cities no one can be seen taking his own, snatching him away, all savage and furious, from his companions, in order to place him with a personal groom, calming him and taming him, in short giving all his care to an education which would make of him not only a good soldier...' (2.666e; the rest has been cited above, p. 58)

The insistence of the vocabulary (ἀθρόους, ἐν ἀγέλῃ) shows it clearly: what Plato criticizes here above all about Spartan education is that it is *collective*. For him, children can live and play in groups up to a certain age (six years old: 7.794a); but at this age it is necessary, despite their resistance, to snatch them away (σπάσας) from the group, in order to entrust each one individually to a 'trainer'. Far from finding Spartan education too harsh, like many people, Plato finds it too permissive; he thinks that children brought up in troops do what they want, and do not learn to obey.

The horse-taming metaphor is all the more natural here because πῶλος is a term which, in poetry and notably in tragedy, can be used to designate young people. But it is wrong that it should take the place of demonstration, for what Plato says is far from being self-evident. If it is true that one cannot tame a whole herd of horses *en masse*, nothing proves that it is impossible to educate a group of children. The philosopher's attitude is all the more surprising because, as we have seen, he recommends that education be organized by the state: it seems natural that it should be collective in this case. Having reached this point, Plato abandons his state model in favour of adopting a practice which appears to us rather characteristic of the 'liberal' model (of the Athenian type, for example), that of the pedagogue. Several times over Plato asserts that at this stage of education (around six years old) he considers the role of the pedagogue absolutely fundamental,[36] that is the role of an adult who takes personal charge of the child, though without giving him any teaching.[37] If he recommends this solution, it is from necessity rather than choice; it is the child's native savagery which makes this solution the only one possible, because it is so strong that each young person needs a 'trainer' who is concerned with him alone. Plato is not unaware of Xenophon's objection (*LP* 2.1–2) to pedagogues, that they are slaves. His answer is that in his city these slaves will be continually supervised, thanks to the system of collective competence (7.808e; cf. above, p. 55). This answer does not indeed completely cancel out the objection; but this imperfection has little weight, for the philosopher, in comparison to the major risk of collective education, which is savagery. In proscribing pedagogues (for the horse-taming metaphor, in the passage cited above, shows that Plato accepts what Xenophon asserts on this point), Spartan education once again misses its mark. In teaching only the fourth element of virtue, military valour, it fails to make perfect citizens; here the failure is even more serious, for it fails to make men.

The third criticism concerns pederasty. In two passages, 1.636b and 8.836b, Sparta and Crete are condemned for favouring physical love between males. In the first, the Athenian analyses the inconveniences of the communal life of men in the *syssitia* and the gymnasia; pederasty is one of them, and 'it is upon your cities,' he says to Kleinias and Megillos, 'that the essential responsibility is incumbent.' In the second, to numerous points in relation to which he has been inspired by Sparta and Crete he opposes this practice, with which he asserts his complete disagreement. There are two reasons for this condemnation. First, this type of love is against nature. In 1.636c, the Athenian explains that sexual pleasure has been accorded to man solely with a view to reproduction, 'while the copulation of males with males or females with females is against nature'. This argument is taken up again in 8.836, 838e, 841d. The second motif is that this practice is far from conducive to virtue. Whoever plays the role of the male certainly does not learn moderation, nor does whoever plays the female learn courage; the latter, on the contrary, has a tendency to become soft and effeminate (8.836d). This deviation results from an insufficient education, which teaches resistance to suffering but not to pleasure: 'it is the excessive appetite for pleasure which inspired such an act in those who first dared it' (1.636c).

It is clear that Plato does not take at all seriously the justification given by Xenophon for the pederastic relationship at Sparta, maintaining that it was free of any physical aspect. He neither explains nor refutes it; for him it seems to be self-evident that such a thesis is simply improbable. Perhaps he had not always thought thus: it is probable that when, in the *Symposium*, he makes Pausanias say (182b, in the manuscript texts) that at Sparta as at Athens the *nomos* concerning love (pederastic, understood) is 'complex' (*poikilos*), this means that for him it is practised and even encouraged there, but that the sexual aspect is forbidden.[38]

If Plato approves of Spartan education explicitly only on one point, he takes up numerous important aspects of it in his own system, even at the level of organizational principles. So we cannot really say that his opinion is globally unfavourable. But the criticisms which he makes of it, explicitly this time, are of considerable weight. It is not a case of attacking details by singling out a few incomprehensible and easily-condemned practices like theft or the deprivation of food. No, the philosopher takes on essential subjects, and because of this the *Laws* represents a turning-point in the history of the image of Spartan education. It opens the way for Aristotle, who will be even more radical.

Aristotle

Politics

I shall start with two passages which concern Spartan education, though it is impossible to say at once whether they are praising or criticizing.

The first relates to its egalitarian aspect (4.1294a19–24). Some, says Aristotle, want to define the Spartan government as a democracy, and the first feature that they adduce is the way in which children are brought up (τὴν τροφὴν τῶν παίδων): 'in fact, the children of the rich are brought up in the same way as those of the poor; moreover, they receive an education which the children of the poor could receive too'. Plato had already said that education should be organized by the city (above, p. 54), but without mentioning Sparta explicitly. Aristotle's presentation also differs in the emphasis he places on the polarity rich/poor. He does not give his judgement openly, but the second half of the phrase, by presenting this noted uniformity as a kind of levelling to the lowest (and almost as the revenge of the poor on the rich, a revenge which would indeed be in the spirit of democracy as he conceives it), at the very least demonstrates reserve.

The other passage treats of a less hot topic: music. Should there be a place for music in education? That depends, says Aristotle, on the judgement you apply to it: if music is a simple game or relaxation, the answer is no; if you think that music can lead to virtue, or that it is the accompaniment of a noble life, we can give it a place. But what place? 8.1339b1–4: is it necessary for children to learn to play an instrument,

> whereas if they only listen to others they will gain authentic pleasure from it and will be able to give a precise judgement, like the Laconians? These, in fact, without learning to play, are no less able, it is said [or 'they claim'] to judge good and bad tunes.

We might think that Aristotle here is approving the conduct that he attributes to the Spartans, in that they turn their backs on an apprenticeship which is purely technical and almost manual; this opinion seems verified when we see him a little further on reporting the opinion that professional musicians are simple drudges. But the rest of the exposition shows that such is not his real opinion, and that, under certain conditions, he makes the practice of an instrument (of certain instruments) an educational subject. So, he does not approve Spartan custom on this point, though we cannot speak of a condemnation either. The question arises, moreover, whether such was really the rule at Sparta. The description (in the second century, it is true) of the Hyakinthia by Polykrates, cited by Athenaeus (4.139e; below, p. 263), shows the young Spartans as virtuoso instrumentalists.

The other passages where Aristotle evokes Spartan education concern much more important points, on which his opinion on the whole follows that of Plato, but with personal arguments or inflexions. Like Plato, he approves the fact that at Sparta education is organized by the city (8.1337a).[39] At lines 4–5, he asks the question: does education belong to the community, or to private initiative? The answer comes twice. He first asserts that the law-giver should concern himself with education, both because it must be adapted to the spirit (ἦθος) of the constitution, in order to assure its preservation, and because another aim of education is to train in virtue, something which is a primary concern for the law-giver. This first stage already announces the final response, for it would be astonishing if the law-giver's only concern with education was to say that each citizen is free to organize it as he pleases. Effectively, Aristotle's opinion is that it is the community's business, and that it must be the same for everyone. On this point too he gives two reasons: first that the city has a single and common aim, and assures its continuance by education (what is common calls for a common training, ll. 26–7); second that the citizen belongs to the city (an idea taken up from Plato, *Laws* 11.923), which is also true for children. The text ends with praise of the conduct of the Spartans: 'On this point too we might praise the Lacedaemonians, for they take the greatest care of their children and make this a communal concern' (ll. 31–2), a phrase which recapitulates the two stages of the reply.

This praise is entirely provisional: it is not enough that the education system should be organized and directed by the state for it to be good; it must also have good as its aim (πρὸς τὸ βέλτιστον τέλος, 7.1333b7; τὸ καλὸν δεῖ πρωταγωνιστεῖν, 8.1338b29–30), and, if this is not the case, its public and communal character becomes, on the contrary, an aggravating factor. Now, Aristotle says clearly, and even with a certain vehemence, Spartan education has the good neither as its objective nor as its result. This negative judgement rests on two observations.

The first is repeated from Plato (the reference is given by Aristotle himself, 2.1271b1): Spartan education prepares only for war. Four passages treat this subject, with different developments: 2.1271b1–6, 7.1324b3–9, 7.1333b5–23, 8.1338b9–38. Aristotle is ironic about those who praise this orientation towards war (6.1333b11–21). Like Plato, he asserts that at Sparta they are only interested in one part of virtue, military courage (2.1271b, where the assertion concerns the legislation as a whole; 7.1333b8–9, where legislation and education are associated; 8.1339b14–16). But he goes further. In training its youth for war, the city prepares its domination over other Greeks (we have already seen this idea in Isocrates): 7.1324b associates legislation and education, as above; 7.1333b11–26 emphasizes that history has clearly shown, now that the Spartans have lost their hegemony, the harmfulness of such a project. This cruel opposition between the Spartans' hegemonic ambitions and the result to which they led recurs at 8.1338b26–9, expanded into the sporting domain too. The result is that the Spartans have not prospered (οὐκ εὐδαίμονες), because they had a bad law-giver (οὐδ' ὁ νομοθέτης ἀγαθός, 7.1333b22–3), and the end of the phrase, which emphasizes that in doing this the Spartans had only been conforming to the laws of Lycurgus, seems aimed at Xenophon's *Lak. Pol.*, both in its *incipit* and in its celebrated chapter 14. The Spartans' appetite for domination had radically tainted their practice of education, since the latter does not have the good as its aim, but the enrichment which domination permits (7.1333b9–10 and 16–21). The Spartans sacrifice their children to their cupidity: what they have is exactly the opposite of *paideia*.

Aristotle's exposition arrives at the same conclusion with regard to what he calls 'savagery', τὸ θηριῶδες. This theme is, moreover, linked to the one before, since 'savagery' is itself a consequence of the priority accorded to preparation for war; this is why, in this exposition (8.1338b9–38), the two themes are interlaced. But Aristotle gives it a certain autonomy. The origin of this criticism is also probably to be found in Plato, in the passage of the *Laws* (2.666e) analysed above (p. 59), where the young Spartans are compared to foals. But Aristotle's idea is different, and his criticism radical. While Plato criticizes Spartan education for not sufficiently holding in check, because it is collective, the savage instincts of children, Aristotle thinks that it creates and develops savagery voluntarily, because the city sees military efficiency in this. In this, however, it is deceived: 'Even this aim it misses' (ll. 16–17). Indeed, taking up the idea formulated by Thucydides' Pericles (above, p. 40; it is perhaps this reference which is indicated by the formula ὥς φησιν ὁ λόγος, l.36; but the idea can also be found in Plato, *Laws* 2.667a), Aristotle asserts that Sparta's soldiers are not the best. Here the criticism inherited from Plato, and recapitulated in the same passage, of being concerned with only a part of virtue, is largely overtaken: in the θηριῶδες, he would not recognize the least virtue. From this point of view, too, Spartan education is revealed as the opposite of a *paideia*; it makes the child savage rather than civilizing him.

What does Aristotle mean by this term *thēriōdes*? He seems to me to be referring to three pairs of antinomic ideas. First, savagery/civilization; this is probably the most important element, since the word which indicates education corresponds also more or less to what we call civilization. Next, bestiality/humanity: θῆρ is the brute beast, and the education which the young Spartan experiences restores him to this level. Finally, ferocity/gentleness; Aristotle recalls in this passage that true courage (he gives as example that of the lion) is not ferocity, but is accompanied, on the contrary, by a certain gentleness.

What does this attack rest on, whose vigour has no equivalent in the *Politics*, even in the long passage (2.1269a29–1271b19) where Aristotle systematically criticizes Spartan society and institutions? He gives two clues to what, according to him, is responsible for this en-savaging. First he calls into question the tests (πόνοι) which are imposed on children: 'By the tests which they impose upon them, they make their children like savage beasts', θηριώδεις ἀπεργάζονται τοῖς πόνοις (ll. 12–13); it is a kind of back-to-front training, which could be compared to that which gladiators would have. Then he takes up the accusation which we have seen in Thucydides (Archidamos' speech) and in Isocrates, and which was clearly very much current in the fourth century, that they neglect all intellectual and moral training worthy of the name: 'In refusing training in what is indispensable, they make them truly labourers (βαναύσους κατεργάζονται), by making them capable, in the life of the city, of just a single activity' (ll. 33–5). However, beyond these justifications, there is in this attack a passion which denotes the philosopher's personal engagement. His conviction is partly explained by the importance which, like Plato, he accords to education in the city; these faults rouse him to indignation like crimes against humanity. It is equally probable that his characterization of Spartan education as a school in savagery comes from the impression which he might have gained on the subject when he was collecting information in order to write the *Lak. Pol.* In any case, his attacks could not have reached this intensity if his analysis had not taken as a point of departure the assumption, unanimously accepted in the fourth century, of the essentially military aim of Spartan education.

If we expected to discover any precise information about the Spartan education system from this survey of texts of the classical period, we would have reason to be disappointed. In fact, even from this point of view the result is not entirely negative. One of the themes which makes the education described by Plutarch appear different from that which Xenophon defends is what I have called 'the savage life'. This theme is present, in various forms, in some of the texts we have studied. To be sure, there are no clear references to 'camping', but when Plato compares the young Spartans to foals grazing in the meadow (φορβάδας), when Isocrates sites the practice of stealing in the countryside, it is indeed this kind of life that they evoke. Dirtiness, in the supposedly positive form of the deprivation of hot baths, can be found in Aristophanes. The young men's fights are welcomed in his city by the author of the *Laws*, which calls to mind that, in relation to the *hēbōntes*, Xenophon talks of almost nothing else. But it is the philosophers above all who denounce the savagery of Spartan education, and Aristotle names it: it is *to thēriōdes*.

The real object of this chapter, though, was something else: to trace the evolution of the image of Spartan education from the end of the fifth and through the fourth century. In fact none of the texts we possess is documentary in character; such things existed (if only in Aristotle's *Constitution*), but they have not come down to us. Our authors' intention was not to transmit information, but to *use* Spartan education, either to attack Sparta (Isocrates) or to praise her (Xenophon), or in the framework of reflection on the ideal city. In this last case the difference between Plato and Aristotle is noticeable. In Plato, on the surface (that is at the explicit level), the criticisms (it prepares only for war, does not sufficiently control the child's native savagery, encourages sexual relations contrary to nature), though not numerous, have more weight than the praise (its traditional character, it teaches the practice of brief speech full of sense, inculcates unanimous obedience to the laws, is public and identical for all); but the fact that, without acknowledging it, Plato borrows several characteristics of Spartan education for his city restores a certain equilibrium. This is evidently not the case for Aristotle. It seems, then, that progress in precise knowledge about the Spartan education system was not beneficial to its image – to say the least. In the course of the fourth century, this image is dramatically degraded, to an extent which is in proportion to the disasters suffered by the city; for here, without doubt, lies the deepest cause of this evolution. We might ask ourselves whether, without the Cynics and above all the Stoics, this image would have recovered from the blows struck by Aristotle.

Notes

1 In this sense, David 1999, 136 n.7.

2 Herodotos 2.80: οἱ νεώτεροι αὐτῶν τοῖσι πρεσβυτέροισι…ἐπιοῦσι ἐξ ἕδρης ὑπανιστέανται. Even the words are similar (although this is not proof).

3 An aspect emphasized by Jeanmaire 1939, 508.

[4] In reality, as Ollier (1934, 33) points out, the education evoked here had not completely disappeared at Athens even in the age of Plato, or, at least, the age in which he sets his dialogues (*Protagoras* 325e; *Charmides* 159b).

[5] In these four ideas, εὔκοσμον, σωφροσύνη, αἰδώς, αἰσχύνη, all practically untranslatable, we have a summary of Spartan morality. Cf. Richer 1998b and 1999.

[6] Aristotle, as we shall see, returns to this argument (below, p. 63).

[7] In the same sense, cf. Christien 1997, 46.

[8] Text and translation: Diels-Krantz, *Die Fragmente der Vorsokratiker* II (Berlin 1960), no. 88, frs. 6–9 (in verse), 32–7 and possibly 60 (in prose). Cf. Stephens, *Critias: Life and literary remains* (1939).

[9] It is easy enough to become conversant, thanks to the excellent account of David 1979, who upholds a very definite thesis, but clearly explains the elements of the problem; see also the notes of Baladié in his edition of book 8 of Strabo (1978), 45–6. See these studies for bibliography.

[10] I translate on the whole as Baladié does, but athetising τῶν Εὐρυποντίδων, as a marginal gloss introduced into the text, not at the place it relates to (τῆς ἑτέρας οἰκίας), but at the beginning of the line opposite which it was written.

[11] Busolt indeed felt this, and *added* καίπερ: cf. David 1979, n. 15.

[12] Baladié emphasizes this opposition: 'he goes so far as to cite'.

[13] The same goes for his presentation of Pausanias as exiled *by* the other royal house, which is not entirely false, but distorts reality – unless this is meant to reflect the thought of the deposed king.

[14] Either via Diodorus (Book 7, fr. 12 Vogel), or, in one case, via Eusebius (*Prep. Evang.* 5.28.3).

[15] Though cf. – but very allusively, and with some misunderstanding of David's intentions – Nafissi 1991, 61.

[16] The same uncertainty surrounds Thibron's treatise, but in this case it is even more radical: all we know of it is from a passing allusion in Aristotle (*Pol.* 7.1333b18–21 = Jacoby 581 T 1), and it is not even certain that this Thibron should be identified with the Spartan military leader of the years 400–391.

[17] In a turn-about which completes the originality of the speech and gives it a particular depth, Isocrates, in §232, acknowledges and deplores this excessiveness.

[18] Birgalias (1999, 83–4) perceives only this aspect of the text, which leads him to a rather strange speech in defence of Spartan education.

[19] Elsewhere (*Anabasis* 4.6.14) he specifies that the law determines what the children can (must?) steal (ὅσα μὴ κωλύει νόμος). Plutarch (logically) adds wood to the food (*Lyc.* 17.4).

[20] Cf. the previous note. It seems to me that it is this passage of the *Anabasis*, much more than *LP* 2.7–9, which Isocrates has used.

[21] Hodkinson (2000, 204) is to my knowledge the only historian to have perceived the interest of this text. He notes the localization in the countryside and the use of ability in theft for classifying the children.

[22] Kennell 1995, 52–3.

[23] Birgalias (1999, 93 n. 3) deems this improbable because the stealing was imposed on the children. This is not a reason: Xenophon explains with great care that this exercise was imposed and punished *at the same time*.

[24] We know that a word of the same family, ἀπόδειξις, is the technical term used of the

exhibition of young men on their graduation from the *ephēbeia*.

[25] This is doubtless the origin of the theory, because there is an Aphidna in Laconia. As for Tyrtaios the military leader, he appears again elsewhere (Strabo 8.4.10).

[26] I leave aside the problem of the dialogue's authenticity.

[27] Hippias goes so far as to assert (285c) that many Spartans do not even know how to count. We shall accord this declaration the same welcome as that of Isocrates, that 'they do not even learn their letters' (above, p. 46).

[28] This text was the object of a study by Richer (2001).

[29] It is clear that this word does not have exactly the same sense for Plato as for us, but I shall not attempt to translate it.

[30] Piérart 1974, 364 and 369–71.

[31] Cf. below, pp. 129–34.

[32] On the magistrate, cf. Piérart 1974, 365–72; comparison with the Spartan *paidonomos*, 370–1; the same comparison is made in Christien 1997, 56.

[33] I shall return to the Spartan *trichoria* later (pp. 268–9).

[34] Plato was very much aware of the strangeness of his laws: νόμους ἀλλοίους τῶν πολλῶν τρόπων, he says a little earlier (8.836b).

[35] This idea of the domestication of man in education recurs in some modern philosophers: 'man the rearer of man' (Nietzsche, who no doubt was thinking of this passage of Plato); the self-domestication of man (Foucault).

[36] Cf. 7.808d: 'Just as neither sheep nor any other herds can live without a shepherd, in the same way children cannot do without a pedagogue, nor slaves without a master.'

[37] This is the role of the school-master, διδάσκαλος; this teaching is, of course, collective, and takes place in locations built by the city. In this way Plato reconciles the two models, public and private.

[38] This is the interpretation maintained by Cartledge 2001, 95. Cf. below, p. 198.

[39] We might compare *Eth. Nic.* 10.1180a25–9, where the life of citizens in general is under discussion, but where certain details (τροφή, παίδων in the quotation of Homer) suggest that he was thinking in particular of education. On this point, cf. Curren 2000.

3

STRUCTURE AND ORGANIZATION

Our knowledge of Spartan education in the classical period is so limited that this chapter necessarily amounts to a catalogue of problems, and to a statement of the current position of scholarship thereon.

The term ἀγωγή (*agōgē*)

Kennell is right to say (1995, 113–14) that the term ἀγωγή *is never found in the classical period* with the meaning of the Spartan education system. Its occurrence in the apophthegm attributed to the ephor Eteokles cannot be taken as historical.[1] In general, the text of these apophthegms has a long – and largely obscure – history. Not only was this particular apophthegm probably fabricated in the third century; in its Plutarchan form it is certainly later still, as is shown by the use of the verb ἀτευκτεῖν which belongs to the vocabulary of the Roman imperial period. The first established occurrence of the term in our sense comes in a speech of Teles of Megara, dating probably to the period 240–230.[2] The term is there used without any qualification, which shows that its sense was familiar at the time. The metaphor of animal-training developed by Plato in connection with young Spartans need not be understood as an implicit reference to the term *agōgē*.[3] Rather, what underlies his metaphor is the word πῶλος, commonly used in poetry as meaning 'boy' or 'girl'. However, we part company with Kennell on the question why the word ἀγωγή is not found in the classical period.

First, the absence of the word ἀγωγή from surviving texts need not mean that it did not yet bear the sense in question. Relevant texts are few in number, and none of them – not even (as we have seen) Xenophon's – amounts to a technical account of Spartan education. Such an account probably did form part of Aristotle's *Constitution*, but which term he used there is unknown. Further, even if the term ἀγωγή was not used in the classical period, that would not mean that Spartan education was not seen at the time as something special. Kennell (1995,116) considers that, so long as the term is not found, Spartan education is not individualized, and is perceived only as a closely-integrated element in the general Spartan way of life (δίαιτα). Such reasoning seems dubious. Admittedly education is conceived as part of a way of life. Indeed, it could hardly be otherwise, given that it was the embodiment *par excellence* of the particular quality of that way of life and also the guarantee that this quality would be transmitted down the generations. But an education system was an eminently distinct part of a way of life. It was the stage of life at which the citizen was shaped, and thus it has a name attested from Thucydides onwards: *paideia*. But that is the general Greek word for education: should we therefore conclude that Greek vocabulary withheld any recognition for the existence of a special Laconian form of education? Certainly not. Spartan education, from the classical period onwards, is not only seen as distinct from, but actually as opposed to, other forms of education: it is opposed to Athenian education in the Periclean funeral speech in Thucydides, and in Xenophon to every other system of education. Vocabulary, therefore, is not the whole story; a term may be commonplace while referring to something which is clearly conceived as unique.

But we should go further, and challenge the currently-accepted idea that the term *agōgē*, when indeed it is used, is virtually the technical term for the Spartan education system. In its origin, of course, the word is commonplace Greek for 'leading', 'directing'. As Kennell notes (1995, 116), 'it can be used just as easily in connection with horses, ships, or water, as with children' – or with armies, one might add. 'Leading', not 'taming',[4] though in the case of animals there is inevitably a connection. For that reason, in a Spartan context the word does not mean necessarily 'education', but just as often – probably more often – it means something we might rather inadequately render as Spartan 'discipline'.[5] Since the word is used without qualification, its meaning can only be determined by context. And context not only does not always allow one particular sense, but quite often gives the impression that the author's meaning lies somewhere between the two senses, or indeed may very well include both.[6] Often the word ἀγωγή is qualified by an adjective. Thus we find ἡ πάτριος ἀγωγή, ἡ Λακωνικὴ ἀγωγή, ἡ Λυκουργεῖος ἀγωγή, ἡ λεγομένη ἀγωγή. But in all these cases the addition of the adjective is not sufficient to make the sense clear. [7] Finally, the only case to be perfectly clear is ἡ τῶν παίδων ἀγωγή (Plut. *Inst. Lac.* 21, *Mor.* 238e; Aelian *VH* 12.43).

Plutarch's account of Spartan education in the *Lycurgus* does not in fact contain the word ἀγωγή. At 16.8 and 16.10 he uses παιδεία, at 16.11 ἄσκησις, and at 24.1 παιδεία again. We do indeed find ἀγωγή at 22.1, but the sense approaches 'discipline', corresponding to δίαιτα at 22.3. It appears, then, that the true meaning of ἀγωγή is 'discipline'. In something like half of its occurrences the word refers to education; but that is because education is discipline applied to children, as well as being discipline par excellence. Take, for example, the apophthegm of Eteokles (Plut., *Apophth. Lac.*, Anon. 54, *Mor.* 235b). The ephor refuses to send children to Antipatros as hostages ἵνα μὴ ἀπαίδευτοι γένωνται, τῆς πατρίου ἀγωγῆς ἀτευκτήσαντες. If ἀγωγή here meant 'education', the expression would amount to tautology. It is much better to take the sense as 'to prevent them remaining uneducated, deprived of the ancestral discipline'. The 'discipline' imparted in this case, the discipline shared by all Spartans, is only one part of their education – as we shall see below. But it is a necessary part; there can be no education without it (education being understood as the result of the process). I believe that here we come close to the true relationship between the *agōgē* and education. In any case that the two concepts were originally distinct seems to me certain. It was possibly due to the Stoics, and their insistance on the element of taming in Spartan education, that the two ideas were so closely assimilated; in their eyes education was the main basis of the Lycurgan discipline.

The annual age-classes

Texts of the classical period relating to Spartan education make no apparent reference to any system of annual age-classes. What we do find is an organization of *age-categories*: the lives of the young as divided into fairly long periods (in Hippocrates they last for seven years), corresponding to the main stages of physical development. Thus Xenophon, as we have seen, divides his account into three periods: *paides*, *paidiskoi*, and *hēbōntes*. Plutarch, much later, is aware of only two: *paides* and *neoi*, but within the category of *paides* he has a threshold at the age of twelve. This categorization of human development is universal among Greeks, both in ordinary vocabulary and in more technical language. We have already noted the case of medicine; competitions also normally had three categories: *paides*, *ageneioi* (from the fourth century onwards) and *andres*.[8]

Age-classes are something quite different; our first problem will be to determine whether they existed in the Spartan education system of the classical period. In the imperial period they are well attested, by numerous inscriptions, within the *ephēbeia*. Otherwise, the only sources to mention them are two glosses of unknown date, which in their surviving form are Medieval; in studying them, our aim will be to see whether we can identify the era to which these glosses refer.[9] The first text is a note in a work entitled Λέξεις παρεκβληθεῖσαι ἀπὸ τῆς βίβλοῦ τοῦ Ἡροδότου κατ' ἀλφάβητον ('Words extracted from the book of Herodotos, in alphabetical order'), which takes the form of a dictionary. The note aims to explain the term εἰρήν, albeit a term which so far as we know does not occur in Herodotos.[10] The text is as follows:[11]

> Εἰρήν· παρὰ Λακεδαιμονίοις ἐν τῷ πρώτῳ ἐνιαυτῷ ὁ παῖς ῥωβίδας καλεῖται, τῷ δευτέρῳ προκομιζόμενος, τῷ τρίτῳ μικιζόμενος, τῷ τετάρτῳ πρόπαις, τῷ πέμπτῳ παῖς, τῷ ἕκτῳ μελείρην. ἐφηβεύει δὲ ὁ παῖς παρ' αὐτοῖς ἀπὸ ἐτῶν

δεκατεσσάρων μέχρι καὶ εἴκοσιν. βαρυτόνως δὲ τὸ μελείρην, ὥσπερ πυθμὴν ἀπύθμην, αὐχὴν ὑψαύχην.

Several things are odd about this note. It is supposed to explain the word *eirēn*, but does not do so; the term itself does not occur in the text as we have it. Instead of an explanation, we have first a list of names of age-classes, and only after this comes information on the total length of the *ephēbeia*, which might to some extent make the list intelligible (though the δέ is discouraging); finally, as if that were not enough, there is a remark on the accentuation not of εἰρήν but of μελλείρην – something which has no obvious point in this context. That is why, until the publication of the second gloss in 1941,[12] the text was interpreted in a variety of ways, with the adversative value of the word δέ following ἐφηβεύει leaving obscure the relation between the list of years and the total duration of the *ephēbeia*.[13]

The second text is a marginal note found in the oldest known manuscript of Strabo (Parisinus 1397, fol. 225v–226r, of the tenth century, though the note itself dates only from the fifteenth or sixteenth; cf. Den Boer 1954, 250 n. 4). It begins with a long comment on the respective accents of nouns in -ην and of their compounds, the latter being non-oxytone. It gives a list of examples, which ends as follows:

...εἰρὴν μελλείρην, παρὰ Λακεδαιμονίοις ὁ μέλλων εἰρὴν ἔσεσθαι. ἐφηβεύει μὲν γὰρ παρὰ Λακεδαιμονίοις ὁ παῖς ἀπὸ ἐτῶν ιδ΄ μέχρι κ΄. καλεῖται δὲ τῷ πρώτῳ ἐνιαυτῷ ῥωβίδας, τῷ δὲ δευτέρῳ προκομιζόμενος, τῷ τρίτῳ μικιζόμενος, τῷ δ΄ πρόπαις, τῷ ε΄ παῖς, τῷ ζ΄ μελλείρην, τῷ ξ΄ εἰρήν·

It is immediately apparent that we are dealing with the same note, composed of the same elements but in this case in a different order, making the note fully intelligible.[14] In the first place, its subject matter is an aspect of accentuation, the shift to the grave accent (barytonesis). Cited by way of an example, the pair *melleirēn-eirēn* attracts a note on the total length of the Spartan *ephēbeia*, the relevance of which to the preceding text is not clear (in spite of the γάρ) – until once again we reach the pair *melleirēn-eirēn*, at the end of the list. The note on the Spartan *ephēbeia* appears to be a quite artificial addition to a text which is solely concerned with grammar, but such is often the case with marginal glosses. Given that its structure is in every way more logical, and makes wholly comprehensible the list of ordinal numbers (the numbers of the years within the period from 14 to 20 years), this text appears at first sight simply 'superior' to the other.

Combining the ordinal numbers of the years with the cardinal numbers concerning duration, we get the following:

year 14: ῥωβίδας
year 15: προκομιζόμενος

year 16: μικιζόμενος
year 17: πρόπαις
year 18: παῖς
year 19: μελλείρην
year 20: εἰρήν.

We have used expressions such as 'year 14' so as not to prejudge the question of chronology. There are two ways of expressing a person's age in Greek: either by including the year in progress ('he is in his 15th year'), or by excluding it ('he is 14 years old'). In Greek as in modern languages, the system being used is shown by the type of number employed: ordinal for inclusive counting and cardinal for exclusive. Here, however, we are faced with a combination of both systems: cardinal numbers for the period taken as a whole and ordinals for the particular years.[15] Also, as Tazelaar pointed out, the counting has in any case gone wrong in the 'better' text, that of Strabo. Both texts state that the *ephēbeia* begins at 14 years and ends at 20, which only allows for six years (15th–20th). The gloss on Strabo is therefore wrong to give the names of seven years. We should exclude the year of the *eirēn* (it does not appear in the Herodotean gloss, which on this point therefore is better), and assume that the author added it so as to recover the pair *melleirēn-eirēn* which was his starting point. (The author of the other note had no such concern.) Thus the grade of *eirēn* did not form part of the *ephēbeia*; it was the first grade of adult life.

Leaving aside for the moment these problems of arithmetic, our immediate concern is to identify the period at which the system described by the glosses was operating. If it cannot have existed in the classical period, further discussion here would be pointless. The sources of these glosses can be identified with some probability. Stein has suggested that the source for the list of age-classes and for the length of the *ephēbeia* was the work of Aristophanes of Byzantion Περὶ ὀνομασίας ἡλικιῶν ('The names of age-groups').[16] Aristophanes was the first to show a systematic interest in the names of the various social categories, kinship bonds and age classes. That these lists are found combined, in the glosses, with a comment on grammar, means, as Diller has shown, that the information given by Aristophanes was transmitted via the work of a grammarian, almost certainly Herodian.[17] But what matters now is Aristophanes: the fact that he is the ultimate source of the glosses shows that the system which they describe dates at the latest from the third century. Kennell, who believes that the working of the Spartan education system was interrupted before the reign of Agis IV, is convinced that we are dealing here with the system created by 'Sphairos' reform'.[18] However, since we do not believe in an interruption of this kind, such an idea would be too dogmatic; in our view this system of age-classes may (only 'may') go back to the classical period.[19] Two further points need to be made. First, it is difficult to see how a state education system such as Sparta's, which was compulsory and identical in form for the sons of all citizens, and led eventually to acceptance into the army, could have functioned without some form of collective promotion for young people of the same age, corresponding with what modern societies themselves call 'classes'. For young people in considerable numbers, educated collectively, such a system seems inevitable. It is not something which any statesman can reasonably be supposed to have invented at a particular moment. So, for the classical period the question is not so much whether age-classes existed but rather how they were named. That question in itself is of some importance.

Our second point is this: subsequent reality, that is the information on Spartan age-classes given by inscriptions of the imperial period, shows a striking continuity with the system described by the glosses. The names may change, but the system itself goes on.[20] Structurally, the main difference is that in the imperial period the *ephēbeia* begins at 16 and the two first year-groups accordingly disappear. Thus the corresponding names are as follows:

mikizomenos	*mikkichizomenos*
propais	*pratopampais*
pais	*hatropampais*
melleirēn	*melleirēn*
eirēn	*eirēn*

The last two names remained unchanged. The changes to the others have been well explained by Kennell 1995, 93, as follows: *mikizomenos* (a better form would be μικκ-) has been strengthened by the diminutive suffix -ιχ. *Propais* and *pais* have undergone both strengthening and artificial laconizing.[21] This tendency to over-laconize is commonplace during the imperial period in vocabulary concerning ephebes. Thus the evolution of the names of age-classes corresponds exactly with what the general evolution of ephebic vocabulary would lead us to expect. This evolution is superficial, and should not distract us from the basic continuity involved. Thus between the third and the first centuries Sparta underwent changes so marked that some scholars have spoken of two separate cities, whereas the names of the age-classes remained remarkably consistent in their general sense. (This was of course a way for Spartans to affirm their identity, in both senses of that word.) There is every chance, therefore, that the names did not greatly change from the fourth to the third centuries, when no drastic change occurred and the reform of Cleomenes was represented as a return to tradition.

To come back to the list: it is clear that the names are presented there in a logical manner. After the year of the *rhōbidas*,[22] which can be seen as a year of transition, there were evidently three pairs of years, with the first year of each pair being conceived as preparatory to the second. However, since the year of the *eirēn* apparently was not considered as part of the *ephēbeia*, it is better to see the year of the *melleirēn*, like that of the *rhōbidas*, as a year of transition – to the status of adult. Oddly enough, this structure with its very pedagogic look (one probably quite unlike the actual contents of the system) is reminiscent of primary education in France. The latter has an introductory – preparatory – year, followed by two pairs of years: Elementary 1 and 2, and Intermediate 1 and 2. These terms, however, are very far from having the flavour of their Spartan counterparts.

The Spartan names make a point relentlessly: the boys are just juveniles. It is as if the beginning of adolescence required that the boys be reminded very firmly indeed that they were still only small. Den Boer finds persuasive parallels in the Anglo-American university system (1954, 251–2). But the Spartan system of names also needs to be seen from a different angle, as Tazelaar has observed (1967, 152). By giving them such a low status when they entered, the system presented children with a progression. The culmination of the progression was the term *melleirēn*, one which had about it nothing of the child. That term contained the promise of a very different status.

The word προκομιζόμενος presents a problem. It seems to be the first element of a pair (parallel to παῖς/πρόπαις) with μικιζόμενος as the second element. (The latter term is confirmed by inscriptions.) Logically, then, one is inclined to emend it to προμικιζόμενος, as most historians have done – in my opinion rightly. However, Den Boer (1954, 255) keeps the reading προκομιζόμενος which is found in both glosses and therefore was also the reading of their source. For Den Boer the term would mean 'one who has been presented' (to the Spartans, that is) and would refer to a presentation ceremony occurring at the end of the *rhōbidas* year – a ceremony possibly resembling the presentation to the phratry at Athens. Unfortunately for this hypothesis, the word προκομίζειν does not have the required sense. Its only attested meaning in the classical period is 'to carry away'; in the imperial period it means 'to bring forward', 'to publish', 'to carry in procession'. The verb κομίζειν on its own does have, as one of its various meanings, the sense of 'to introduce', but only with reference to things previously unknown (coinage, philosophy) which are brought in from elsewhere. Den Boer's suggestion must therefore be rejected.

Finally, can we identify the *ages* which corresponded to the years in question? The difficulty arising from the combination of exclusive and inclusive counting is compounded by the fact that we are dealing here not with individuals but with classes. For the individual the case is simple: after his 14th birthday, for example, he can be described either as 14 years old or as in his 15th year. But what of the case of a group of children, whose birthdays are spread over a whole year? The only answer is to regard all children born during the one year as being of the same age (ἡλικιῶται). That is the inevitable way to form an age-class. [23] One may, with Christien (1997, 54), go further and speculate as to whether the Spartan age-classes were brought together at the end of their first year of life, during the Tithenidia. The above reconstruction seems to be reflected in the distinction between ἔτος and ἐνιαυτός in the gloss on Strabo. The latter term, ἐνιαυτός, means the astronomical year, which was also the civil year. The former, ἔτος, can have the same meaning, but is the only term used (often with γεγονώς) to express age numerically from the date of birth.

When an age-class is formed in this way, how should it be given a number? For the '14 year-old' class, for example, one way is to have all those who will reach the age of 14 during the year. The other is to have all those who are already 14, and who will therefore have their 15th birthday during the year. In this context, it might seem that we could rule out the second method, because at the start of the system it would require there to be a 'year zero', for children under a year old. But that is in fact what happened where individuals were concerned; a child was described as 'one year old' (ἓν ἔτος γεγονώς) only when it had passed its first birthday. Before that point it was simply referred to as 'born' (γεγονώς). It would be reasonable to expect the same logic to be applied to groups: in each civil year the 'class of one-year-olds' would include all those who on the first day of that year had already had their first birthday, and so on. Thus in the class labelled '14-year-olds' there would be, as the year went on, more and more children who had passed their 15th birthday and so were into their 16th year. What counted was not the changing ages of individuals, but the situation on the first day of the year.

We are now in a position to give a table of our results, based on the glosses, as follows. It also reflects the prevailing scholarly opinion at the present time.[24]

'14-year-olds' = 15th year of life = *rhōbidas*
'15-year-olds' = 16th year of life = *promikkizomenos*
'16-year-olds' = 17th year of life = *mikkizomenos*
'17-year-olds' = 18th year of life = *propais*
'18-year-olds' = 19th year of life = *pais*
'19-year-olds' = 20th year of life = *melleirēn*

The *eirēn* no longer counted as an ephebe, or as a *pais* in the normal sense, according to the glosses. This table applies in all probability to the third century, but, as we have seen, there had very likely been no major changes since the fourth.

What was the *role* of these age-classes in the Spartan education system? On this the glosses, our only immediate source, have nothing to say. The role of the age-classes must, however, have depended largely on the numbers in each class. Luckily, since we make no claim to precision, there is no need to engage in elaborate calculations, which would inevitably have been based on the highly controversial subject of the numbers of men in the army. We must be content with an order of magnitude. In 418, on Singor's calculation,[25] there were about 120 in each educational year-group. Between then and 370 numbers must have declined by at least half. But whichever period one considers, the group was too large to be the basic unit for teaching, the 'set' as we shall now call it.

Although the age-group was not the same as this 'set', it could still have had an important and well-defined role. It was their age-class that dictated the activities and exercises of the young. It was also probably within their age-class that the children competed, as in the Roman imperial period. The fourth-century stele of Arexippos refers to 'gatherings of children', σύνοδοι παίδων, at the temple of Orthia (*AO*, no.1). There will have been many other occasions on which the whole age-class was assembled in one place; thus the vital solidarity within each 'year' could be created. It is even possible that there were annual age-classes, each with its own name, for children between 7 and 13. The glosses do not mention them. But since what gave rise to the glosses was the pair *melleirēn-eirēn*, they were only concerned with the period which ended with those two stages. It would have made sense for year-groups to have provided the framework for the whole period of Spartan education.

Children's sets

The everyday activities of children took place in their sets. But on the important subjects of how those sets were formed, and how they functioned, we are exceptionally short of information.

First, *what were the sets called*? We might well expect to find several names, since there were several possible ways of dividing the children into sets. There may have been large composite groups combining several smaller units, as in the army. There may also have been groups of *paides*, and others, with different names, of *paidiskoi* (to use Xenophon's term). In addition there may have been groups organized horizontally, made up of children from the same year-group, and others organized vertically, with children of different ages – as within a family – within a particular age-range or of all ages. Moreover, the names of sets may have changed over the centuries. Several names are in fact known. But how authentic are they?

The best candidate as name for a set of children is *agela*, which several texts use concerning Sparta. In support of this term are three considerations, of unequal force. First, the term existed in Crete, where according to our sources it was applied to sets of young people of 17 years and upward. It is attested of numerous Cretan communities, and also – at widely varying dates – in

Asia Minor.[26] Second, this is the term regularly used by Plutarch,[27] though we should note that at one point (*Lyc.* 16.13 = *Inst. Lac.* 6) it is linked with ἴλη. Finally, Plato uses this word, and it is tempting to think that he does so in a precise, technical sense.[28] For these reasons most modern historians have thought it certain that ἀγέλα was the name given to a set of children at Sparta. However, this idea is far from secure. The usages cited above have a quite straightforward explanation: ἀγέλη is a common Greek word, an everyday term for 'herd' ('something that is led'). And in the passage of Plato cited, there is no need to look for any allusion. As Kennell has rightly emphasized (1995, 108), there is no evidence that ἀγέλα was the name for a set of children at Sparta. Indeed, the oft-cited gloss in Hesychius, βοῦα· ἀγέλη παίδων, suggests quite the opposite: it implies that *boua* is the local equivalent of what elsewhere has the regular name ἀγέλη. The reason why Plutarch used this term is that it was the commonest Greek way of referring to a set of children.

Significant too is the fact that Xenophon does not use the term. His word is ἴλη. Admittedly this word occurs only once in the *Lak. Pol.* (2.11), in keeping with the author's lack of interest in matters of organization. *Ilē* is like *agelē* : neither is a local 'technical' term; rather, *ilē* is regular Greek meaning 'group', with a strong military overtone. It has the special sense of 'a troop of cavalry', a branch of the military with which Xenophon was particularly familiar. It is unlikely that the Spartans, who had no cavalry before 424, used this word for their groups of children. In fact, if we compare the two passages of Xenophon and Plutarch on the authority of the *eirēn* (*Lak. Pol.* 2.11 and *Lyc.* 17.2), we realize that Xenophon uses *ilē* in precisely the way that Plutarch uses *agelē*.

Finally there is the term βοῦα, derived from the word for cattle (βοῦς). It is attested only from the Roman imperial period, and then only indirectly; it is implied by the term for a leader, βουαγός, which occurs in 35 dedications between AD 80 and 240. The name of the group itself is found only in Hesychius, but clearly the fact of βουαγός presupposes the existence of βοῦα. Can we infer that the latter term had existed earlier? Kennell does so, on the assumption that the glosses βοῦα, βουαγόρ in Hesychius derived from Aristophanes of Byzantium. He may be right; but why limit oneself to the hellenistic period[29] and not suppose that the phenomenon already existed in classical times? Admittedly, this case is different from the names of the age-groups. Here it is far more doubtful whether the source was Aristophanes of Byzantium, and the word-form given by Hesychius, with its rhotacism, hardly favours a third-century dating.[30] That the title *bouagos* does not appear in inscriptions until the second half of the first century AD suggests rather that it is an artificial archaism.[31]

We reach a disappointing conclusion: we have not after all identified a number of Spartan technical terms. In fact, none has been identified with certainty. But further investigation is still justified: children were undoubtedly divided into sets, and we can still enquire as to the *nature of those sets and how they operated.*

Plutarch suggests that there existed two kinds of set, one for 'little boys' and one for 'big boys' (those over 12); they differed in the way they chose their leader, but in both cases it was the boys themselves who did the choosing. The little boys, we are told, 'themselves chose as their leader the boy from their *agelē* who was the most intelligent and the bravest in a fight' (*Lyc.* 16.8). The big boys 'themselves in each *agelē* chose as their leader the *eirēn* who had the most self-control and the most courage' (17.2). Thus the leader of the former was himself one of the boys, whereas the leader of the latter was an *eirēn*. The little boys were the group with the greatest autonomy. This distinction is understandably not found in Xenophon, who makes only one reference to the appointment of a leader, in connection with the *paides*: 'He [Lycurgus] ordered that each *ilē* should be commanded by the most intelligent of the *eirenes*' (*Lak. Pol.* 2.11). Xenophon does not say whether the children themselves chose this leader; and here – as so often – it may not be right to use Plutarch to supplement Xenophon. What is surprising here is that Plutarch, while clearly basing himself on Xenophon's sentence, differs substantially in one respect: for Xenophon it was the little boys (*paides*) who were commanded by an *eirēn*, while for Plutarch it was the big boys.

In Xenophon's system, how was the *eirēn* chosen as leader? We might expect that for each *ilē* either the children within it or the Spartan authorities would choose from the class of *eirenes* the one they judged best. But that is not what Xenophon says. He writes: ἔθηκε τῆς ἴλης ἑκάστης τὸν τορώτατον τῶν εἰρένων ἄρχειν , and this seems to mean that *within* each *ilē* there were several *eirenes* and that the choice was made from them. Has Xenophon simply expressed himself badly here, while meaning in fact that for each *ilē* there was selected the best of the *eirenes* who remained available, i.e. of those who had not been chosen by or for another *ilē*? Probably. But there is another possibility to be considered. Did Xenophon envisage the *ilē* as structured vertically, as made up of young males of all ages, from the age of *pais* up to that of *eirēn*?

Plutarch may seem to support this latter possibility. This at least is what Kennell (1995, 42) infers from the passage in which Plutarch describes how the children of the *agelē* prepared meals, under the direction of the *eirēn*: 'he orders the bigger boys (ἁδροῖς) to fetch wood, and the smaller ones (μικροτέροις) vegetables' (*Lyc.* 17.4). Kennell's interpretation seems hard to challenge; such a clear distinction between big and small, especially with the word μικροτέροις, could hardly be made between children of the same age. But we need to know to what period this passage applies: we can only use it to interpret Xenophon if it concerns the classical period. Kennell believes that Plutarch here is referring to his own day, and on this single passage he bases his view that in the Roman period there existed groups structured vertically, which he calls *phylai*, alongside horizontally-structured groups, the *bouai*. But for his belief that this passage refers to the Roman period Kennell's only argument is the fact that it forms part of a passage written in the present tense; such an argument, as we have already shown (pp. 27–8), is very far from reliable. It thus remains possible, though of course far from certain, that this passage of Plutarch refers to the classical period; if so, it would be relevant to the present discussion.

Vertically-structured groups can exist in every kind of education system, but they cannot operate on their own. They are not suitable for school-teaching or for physical activities; these require children to be of approximately the same age. Vertical groups can play only a complementary role, and in specific areas of activity – as, for example, in certain educational games where the older children give guidance to younger ones, or in making up groups around a meal table, as happens in a modern nursery. Now, it is meals that Plutarch is here describing, and in Xenophon the only other passage to mention an *eirēn* (2.5) concerns meals. It is thus tempting to suppose that the vertical structure was used essentially to form the children's *syssition*, just as it was for the adult *syssition*. That also would be what Xenophon had in mind when writing of the *eirēn*'s authority, and thus this practice would indeed go back to the classical period. Another 'complementary' activity to which vertical groups could have contributed was the practice of stealing, something again which was connected with food (see especially Plutarch *Lyc.* 17.5); the smallest boys could have acted, for example, as look-outs and spies (Xenophon *Lak. Pol.* 2.7). We may, then, suggest the following theory: teaching, and the main physical activities, took place in horizontal groups, under the command of one of their own members, while certain other activities, in particular those connected to any degree with food, took place in vertical groups under the command of an *eirēn*.

This theory is certainly attractive, and would tend to show Spartan teaching methods in a very good light; there is no doubt that combining vertical and horizontal groups is a very effective procedure. Sadly, it is doubtful whether the theory can be accepted. Neither Xenophon nor Plutarch gives the slightest hint that two kinds of groups co-existed. An expression used on a single occasion by Plutarch, κατ' ἴλην καὶ κατ' ἀγέλην (*Lyc.* 16.13 = *Inst. Lac.* 6, on sleeping arrangements – another 'complementary' activity, one might well think), should not be taken as evidence here.

This is the only occasion on which Plutarch uses the word *ilē*; he seems to use it here simply to signal the reference to Xenophon. And in any case for purposes of sleeping the children would necessarily have been divided into the one sort of group or the other, but not into both at once. In reading Xenophon and Plutarch it seems clear that each thought only of a single sort of group, for all activities; the former calls it *ilē*, the latter *agelē*. This is the group which in Xenophon is commanded by an *eirēn*. Apart from the two problematic passages under discussion, it also seems clear that the only kind of group compatible with the systems both of Xenophon and of Plutarch is the horizontal kind. Xenophon makes quite clear that there was a change of lifestyle between the *paidiskoi* and the *paides*. How would such have been possible if *paidiskoi* and *paides* were living together every day in the same groups? A similar change of lifestyle can be observed in Plutarch's account, but within the group of *paides*, between 'small boys' and 'big boys'. We have to conclude, then, either that our authors have misunderstood the facts, or that the groups which operated at Sparta were of the horizontal kind, subdivisions of the annual age-class.

Paides

Xenophon devotes a lengthy chapter to the category of *paides*. However, we are not in a position to see how this important stage of life was organized in general, or how a child would spend a typical day. Where did he sleep? At home? In a dormitory? In the open air? Or sometimes in one, sometimes in another? What were his activities, and how were they organized? What part was played by study? When did he go back to his family? These are elementary questions which we cannot even begin to answer. Of everyday activities there is only one aspect on which we have information, and that is *the getting of food*.

Writing of the activities of the 'bigger boys', Plutarch has a passage on food-getting (17.4–18.7) which includes two related topics: theft and the meagreness of the rations given to children. But instead of the expected description of the young people's common meal, we find something quite different: what seems to be the meal of the *eirēn*, who eats alone.[32] The children are indeed present, but are not there to eat; the *eirēn* 'uses them as servants for the meal' (ὑπηρέταις χρῆται πρὸς τὸ δεῖπνον). (This is the main meal, at the end of the afternoon.) We are told that the *eirēn* gives orders to the children to fetch wood and vegetables. At this point the account of the preparations is interrupted by the 'digressions'. We are not to be told if these improvised servants are the ones who also cook the food. The account of the meal resumes with some verbal scene-painting; this is the only point, in all of Plutarch's account of Spartan education, at which a particular scene is described in so detailed and lively a way. The meal ends – it is still, we note, referred to as 'the *eirēn*'s meal' (δειπνήσας δ' ὁ εἴρην) – and he stays stretched out on his couch. It is in this comfortable position (κατακείμενος) that he starts distributing to some children their various practical exercises. Meanwhile, we presume that the children are clearing away – apart from those of whom the *eirēn* has other things to ask.

However, Plutarch's graphic description suggests something further. Directly after the children have left, on the *eirēn*'s orders, to get the wherewithal for the meal, the 'digression' begins, mentioning first the subject of theft. This is something closely connected with the *eirēn*'s orders: καὶ φέρουσι κλέπτοντες ('what they bring is what they have stolen'). So do they steal it for the *eirēn*? Did he tell them to? Do they do the stealing and the *eirēn* the eating? All this seems illogical. But next Plutarch gives his explanation of the theft, and it is quite different: γλίσχρον γὰρ αὐτοῖς ἐστι δεῖπνον ('For their meal is a very meagre one'). From this we can infer three things. First, that the children have their own δεῖπνον, which must take place during the meal of the *eirēn*, since they are represented as going for supplies at the start of the latter and as going home when it ends. Second, that the children's own meal is (in part) provided for them. Who provided it, and how, we are not told; but the fact that 'the portions were small' shows that the meal was indeed supplied for them. And third, that it was the inadequacy of the meal provided which forced them to steal. What seemed to be a description of the *eirēn*'s meal now turns out to describe the meal of the whole group.

How are we to explain this curious duality in Plutarch's account? One possibility is, that he was combining sources and spliced a passage on stealing, derived from Xenophon, into the description of the *eirēn* eating alone and waited upon by children. Plutarch could have included the passage at this point because that is what Xenophon himself did. On this hypothesis, Plutarch would not have realized that he was interrupting the scene he was describing and creating a logical conflict. This explanation of Plutarch's procedure accords with orthodox method; we might settle for it except for the fact that there is another possibility. Plutarch may have intended to describe the meal of the whole group, and omitted to mention that the children were present – because his main interest was in the role of the *eirēn*, first as leader of the group and the person who gave orders (it is at this point that the section on stealing begins), second and more importantly as educator of the children. That the children were also eating now might go without saying. They may have taken their food while on their feet and acting as waiters, as women once did in country districts; or perhaps they took turns and sat on the ground. That this is indeed what Plutarch meant is strongly suggested by one further consideration. Ephoros has a passage describing the meal of the youngest children, at the *syssition* of adult Cretans: 'Those who are still at the youngest age are taken to the warriors' *syssitia*; they eat among the warriors, sitting on the ground...and they serve the food (διακονοῦσι) for themselves and for the adults' (70 F 149 = Strabo 10.4.20). This, in my opinion, is more or less what happened at the meal described by Plutarch. By observing this similarity we can see also that Plutarch's description probably applies to the classical period, something which I shall argue is the case for the educational session which follows in the chapter.

To return to Xenophon: his comment that the food is given to the children in meagre helpings entails, I believe, that they had their meals in common, supervised by a state official – and thus in the way envisaged by Plutarch. If they had eaten at home, control of the amount of food would not have been possible. Now, this control is referred to in a sentence of Xenophon concerning the children's meals. The sentence in question occurs in the chapter on the *paides*, but it is possible (or indeed probable; see below) that the sentence applies also to the 'bigger boys', Xenophon's *paidiskoi*. The problem is that the text has come down to us in differing versions. The best manuscripts[33] give σῖτόν γε μὴν ἔταξε (sc. ὁ Λυκοῦργος) τοσοῦτον ἔχοντα συμβουλεύειν τὸν ἄρρενα, ὡς... Some of the inferior manuscripts give σῖτόν γε μὴν ἔταξε τοσοῦτον ἔχοντα συμβολεύειν τὸν ἄρρενα, ὡς... And in Stobaeus' quotation we have σῖτόν γε μὴν τοσοῦτον ἔχειν συνεβούλευεν, ὡς...

To begin with Stobaeus: his version is coherent, but does damage to the sense. It loses the idea of a common meal, and refers to meals in general. It also loses the role of the group-leader, called the ἄρρην in the other versions.[34] Ollier's analysis (1934, 27) is full and often convincing: Stobaeus' text is in general summary and erratic; ἔχειν is impossible and should be corrected to ἐσθίειν;[35] συμβουλεύειν is no better – to give advice is not in Lycurgus' style and nowhere else in Xenophon's text is he said to do it; this last reading should not be defended by adducing the phrase of Justin *parsimoniam omnibus suasit* (3.4.10: note the verb), because Justin there refers to Spartan austerity in general.[36] The difference here between the better and the inferior manuscripts is only that the former have the verb συμβουλεύειν, the subject of which is τὸν ἄρρενα. This gives a curiously distorted sense, virtually:'Lycurgus laid down that the *arrēn* should recommend food of an amount such that...'. συμβουλεύειν is almost as unsuitable as in Stobaeus' version; the leader does not 'advise' the children, he orders them, and to 'advise' children to have insufficient food would be meaningless. Clearly emendation is needed. Now, συμβολεύειν is not conjectural. Although a *hapax*, the word is entirely regular in the way it is formed. It is found in manuscripts which overall are inferior but which preserve important readings on some points.[37] Dindorf eventually preferred the reading συμβολεύειν (proposed as long ago as 1596 by Portus) and was followed by Marchant, Ollier and Pierleoni.[38]

This verb συμβολεύειν is derived from συμβολή, one meaning of which is precisely the required contribution, in cash or kind, for a common meal, most frequently in connection with a festival. συμβολή belongs to the language of concrete experience, and as such is found in both Old Comedy (Aristophanes, *Acharnians* 1210–1) and New (Antiphanes, Alexis). Here everyday meals are clearly meant. It was not the leader of the children's *syssition*, the young adult representing the community, who provided the food.[39] His role was only to *collect* the contributions which the children brought, while seeing that its nutritional value did not exceed the legal limit. It is highly probable that, as with the adult *syssitia*, these contributions were essentially in kind. Plutarch sees them as got solely by theft; this is certainly an overdramatized view, and is not what Xenophon says. When read in context, Xenophon gives the impression that the contributions were supplied by families, that they were intended to be insufficient and that theft provided supplementary items. Theft thus played in the children's world the role which hunting did for adults. We recall what Isocrates said (above, p. 48): that at Sparta, when children were out stealing, their parents pretended that they were off hunting. Indeed, at times they might be hunting in reality; hunting might be as useful as theft in helping the children to improve on their regular rations. But above all theft was an analogue of hunting; the two activities were similar in form and had the same function. The plundering of gardens, orchards and hen-runs was a juvenile version of hunting, as if there were a tacit convention that these private spaces were in effect public.

Though brief and allusive here, Xenophon shows clearly that in the classical period the children's *syssition* was run by the *eirēn* in charge of the group. His role probably went beyond the physical organization of the meal. We are justified in applying also to Xenophon's day the educational role of the *eirēn* as described by Plutarch: his questioning of the children and his distribution of praise and punishment – especially since the content of the questions is thoroughly in keeping with the mentality of the classical *polis*. Also, Plutarch states that the meal took place indoors (κατ' οἶκον, 17.4); the questioning was done towards the end of the meal, while the *eirēn* was still reclining (δειπνήσας δ' ὁ εἴρην κατακείμενος, 18.3). The common meals were not, therefore, improvised picnics in the countryside; rather, like the adult meals, they took place in buildings furnished for the purpose which gave them a properly institutional quality.

As to the number of participants, we have no information. But presumably it was similar to that of an adult *syssition*. What that was, is itself not known for certain; here we follow the findings of the most recent study of the subject, by Singor, who reckons that the figure given by Plutarch, fifteen or so, is most likely.[40] That would in any case be entirely suitable for a group of children who, when in very large numbers, can hardly be organized or taught effectively.

There is one further point concerning Xenophon's *paides*: *at what age did children enter that category* and so at what age did education begin? Xenophon says nothing on this at 2.2. From his silence it is normally inferred that in this respect Sparta was no different from other Greek cities, and thus that Spartan education began around the age of 6 or 7. And since Plutarch (*Lyc.* 16.7) gives the figure of 7 years (after the 7th birthday, ἑπταετεῖς γενομένους, and thus in the 8th year), Xenophon's implied position is generally accepted.[41]

Xenophon is sometimes criticized for having created additional obscurity in describing, at 2.1, the time at which education began in other cities (which doubtless means in effect Athens).[42] He locates this by reference to child development: 'as soon as their children are old enough to understand what they are being told', ἐπειδὰν τάχιστα αὐτοῖς οἱ παῖδες τὰ λεγόμενα συνιῶσιν – which strictly should mean an age between 2 and 3. It is hard to think that this is what Xenophon meant. Ollier explains this apparently erroneous expression as Xenophon's response to praise of Athenian education made by Protagoras in the dialogue named after him, where a very similar expression occurs (325c): ἐπειδὰν θᾶττον συνιῇ τις τὰ λεγόμενα. But this explanation seems unsustainable. There is no obvious reason why Xenophon should have wanted to reply to the Protagoras of the dialogue, who was – we suspect – far from expressing Plato's own views. The expression συνιέναι τὰ λεγόμενα is commonplace; and if any response to that expression were involved, it could equally have been that Plato was responding to Xenophon: this is a question of chronology.

It is better to take Xenophon's phrase as an exaggeration for rhetorical effect, intended to stress how hastily the 'other Greeks' hand over responsibility for their children (ἐπειδὰν τάχιστα...εὐθὺς...εὐθὺς). In defence of Xenophon, one could also point out that 'understand what they are being told' might have meant not only understanding the limited language of daily life but also being able to take in a sustained lesson on some abstract subject, a condition which would effectively correspond with the age at which Greek education normally began.

The real difficulty here may be rather different. Xenophon's stress on the haste of the 'other Greeks' can be taken as meaning that in his view education began later at Sparta than elsewhere. We might, for example, take him as meaning that teaching (in private: learning basic literacy and so on) did indeed begin around 7, but that the education (by the state, and of a mainly non-intellectual kind) which he goes on to mention, began later, when the child's physical development made it safe. So Lupi believes:[43] noting that Plutarch's treatment of the 'big boys' is more or less a reworking of what Xenophon says on the *paides*, he infers that the education described by Xenophon began at the age at which Plutarch locates the transition from 'little boys' to 'big boys', perhaps at 12. This interpretation might appeal if taken in isolation, but it presents logical difficulties in two different directions. First, there is Xenophon's phrase 'as soon as their children are old enough to understand what they are being told' (2.1). While it is true that this applies to the 'other Greeks', we can see from what follows that – contrary to what the phrasing of 2.1 makes us expect – the contrast between the other cities and Sparta is not between haste and its opposite but between entrusting the children to slaves and hired teachers (which amounts in effect to getting rid of them) and entrusting them to one of the city's most important officials. There is, then, nothing in Xenophon's treatment to support the view that, according to him, Spartan education began at an age so unusually late as 12. The second difficulty is this: if, for Xenophon, boys entered the category of *paides* at the age of 12, at what age, in his view, would they leave it? My own response, 14, would be impossible; this vital stage could not have lasted for only two years. This is why Lupi, perhaps following Kukofka, suggests the age of 18, which would mean that the *paidiskoi* were between 18 and 20. This involves emending the text of 3.1 and omitting (as some scholars have indeed done) the words εἰς τὸ μειρακιοῦσθαι. Now strangely Lupi does not do this, but remains neutral on the point (p. 33 n. 20). Also, the system which he proposes is incompatible both with the Hippocratic age-structure and – more importantly for our purposes – with the glosses, which have the *ephēbeia* starting at 14.

In my view, then, Lupi's suggestion must be rejected; in the classical period Spartan education began when a boy reached 7.

Paidiskoi

Plutarch represents the Spartan boy as remaining in the category of *paides* up to and including his year as *melleirēn* (*Lyc.* 17.3), and thus while crossing an important threshold at the age of 12 (*Lyc.* 16.12).[44] Xenophon, on the other hand, places after the category of *paides* a different category, to which he gaves the name of *paidiskoi* (3.5), and also the implicit one of *meirakia* (3.1). The two terms are not, for all that, equivalent; *meirakion* refers to one of the main phases of a child's physical development, whereas *paidiskoi* looks more like a name for an age category. It may seem strange to find a diminutive used to refer to older children, but this accords with what the glosses show to have been Spartan practice: some of the names for boys over 14 emphasize the idea of smallness, as we have seen. Also, a gloss of Hesychius makes clear that it was commonplace in Greece to call adolescents by this name – no particular city is mentioned: παιδίσκοι· οἱ ἐκ παίδων εἰς ἄνδρας μεταβαίνοντες. Ephebes, then, are meant. And this leads to a further question concerning terms: are we dealing with a local name for young people of this age, or with a term which had the required meaning in normal Greek? *Paidiskoi* is after all a general Greek word in the classical period, and Xenophon who uses it here does avoid local terminology wherever possible. In favour of the second alternative is the fact that we know of *Laconian terms* which may have referred to the age category in question.

The first such term is *sideunas*. It is recorded once only, in a gloss of Photius concerning the word συνέφηβος. After explaining it, Photius goes on: τοὺς δὲ ἐφήβους Ἠλεῖοι μὲν Σκύθας καλοῦσι, Σπαρτιᾶται σιδεύνας ('The Eleans call ephebes "Scythians", and Spartans call them "*Sideunai*"'). He goes on to make clear that this age category, which extends to the beginning of adulthood, begins around the age of 15 or 16. This term *sideunas* is somewhat mysterious. Almost certainly it is a compound involving εὐνή, and thus means someone who 'has as a bed' the element σιδ-. Such is implied by the analogous formations χαμαιεύνης (*Iliad* 16.230, referring to the Selloi) and χαμαιευνάς, -άδος (*Odyssey* 10.243 and 14.15, referring to pigs), meaning 'who sleep on the ground'. The first element in the compound is undoubtedly the word σίδη, here taking the form σιδ- to avoid hiatus; compare the previous term, which occurs in the form χαμευνάς, -άδος as a noun meaning an animal's lair (Nicander, *Ther.* 23). 'Who sleeps on…': we think inevitably of the passage in which Plutarch reports that boys over the age of 12 used to sleep on primitive bedding (*stibades*) which they themselves created using reeds gathered from the banks of the Eurotas (*Lyc.* 16.13).

However, the word σίδη does not mean 'reed'. Its main meaning is 'pomegranate' and 'pomegranate tree' in dialects other than Ionian-Attic (where the word is ῥόα or ῥοιά). Thus the *sideunai* would be 'those who sleep on cut branches of the pomegranate tree'. This would be strange bedding indeed, hard to contrive without severely damaging all the pomegranate trees of the area, and of course entirely unattested in any written text. One might at a pinch explain the term by reference to the fact that the pomegranate is seen among other things as a fertility symbol, because of its numerous seeds, and thus often associated with Aphrodite.[45]

There is an other possible interpretation. Theophrastus (*HP* 4.10.3) describes a plant, the white water-lily, which the Boeotians – he says – used to call σίδη because of its fruit 'which, being round and with red seeds, was reminiscent of a pomegranate'.[46] The Boeotians are involved because, as Theophrastus indicates just previously (4.10.1), this plant grows on the banks of the lake of Orchomenos (Lake Copais) along with willows of different kinds and reeds. Thus the white lily was associated with reeds. But for the word σίδη to have been used at Sparta to refer to the white lily, with the same metaphor as in Boeotia, the plant in question would have needed to grow by the Eurotas, and for this there is no evidence. Further than this we cannot go. One final observation: Plutarch states that the young had to break off the reeds without the aid of iron, ἄνευ σιδήρου. Might something be made of the correspondence between σίδηρος and σίδη?

The second possibility, by way of local terminology for *paidiskoi*, involves a group of words which are clearly Laconian and formed from a single (completely obscure) root.[47] We start with the form σκυρθάλιος (Hesychius; glossed by νεανίσκος), with its variants σκυρθάλια (Hesychius; glossed by τοὺς ἐφήβους) and σκυρθάνια (Photius; glossed by τοὺς ἐφήβους οἱ Λάκωνες), as well as with σκύθραξ which Chantraine describes as the 'hypocoristic with metathesis of the liquid'.[48] With the shift, regular in Laconian dialect, from θ to σ, and dissimilation of initial σ, we get the other main – and better known – form κυρσάνιος, which occurs twice in the *Lysistrata* (ll. 983, 1248). Photius glosses the plural by τοὺς μειρακίσκους, Λάκωνες, and the neuter form κυρσάνια by Λάκωνες τὰ μειράκια; cf. κυρσίον (Hesychius; glossed by μειράκιον). That this whole group of words was used at Sparta to refer to boys of the same age as Xenophon's *paidiskoi* emerges clearly from the glosses given by the lexicographers: *meirakion*, *meirakiskos*, *ephēbos*, *neaniskos*. On the other hand, the usage of *kyrsanios* in Aristophanes seems to take us in a different direction; in line 983 the Spartan herald addresses thus a man who is an Athenian prytanis, and therefore at least 30 years old. This is presumably why Kennell (1995, 117) suggests that *kyrsanioi* was used rather of *hēbōntes*, and that only *sideunai* corresponded to Xenophon's *paidiskoi*. But even so the use of the word in the passage of Aristophanes remains strange; perhaps there was a comic intention to show how ignorant was the Spartan herald of Athenian realities and how drastically he was breaching the rules of behaviour. The word *sideunai* appears only once, fleetingly, in Photius' note; there is no proof that the word belongs to the classical period – unlike *skyrthalios*/*kyrsanios* which is there in Aristophanes. The latter term may in any event not be the exact equivalent of *paidiskos*, but can refer to only some of the *paidiskoi* – the oldest, for example.

It appears certain that the term *paidiskos* was used at Sparta *to refer to an age-category*. Xenophon uses it in a saying of Agesilaos, reported by Etymokles and concerning Sphodrias (*Hell.* 5.4.32): 'someone who, when he was *pais*, *paidiskos* and *hēbōn*' – a phrase which includes all the age-categories around which chapters 2–4 of the *Lak. Pol.* are structured. We may assume that Xenophon, without necessarily being faithful to the letter of the king's words, was careful to use words which Agesilaos could have used. But there exists evidence which is more direct and even more persuasive. An inscription from Sparta (*IG* 5.1.133) refers to a παιδισκιωρός, apparently an official concerned with the gymnasium. Le Roy published in 1961 an inscription from Teuthrone (modern Kotronas) which he dated to the second century BC; it is a dedication to Hermes made by the *paidiskoi*, with mention of the gymnasiarch and of the two hypogymnasiarchs.[49] Our study (below) of the word *hēbōn* will confirm that in all likelihood Xenophon named the categories of young people at Sparta with terms which, while being part of normal Greek and thus intelligible to all, were genuinely in use at Sparta.

At what age did a young Spartan become one of the *paidiskoi* ? On this Xenophon is fairly precise: ὅταν γε μὴν ἐκ παίδων εἰς τὸ μειρακιοῦσθαι ἐκβαίνωσι ('when they cease to count as children and reach adolescence'). Becoming *meirakion* indicates around 14 or 15 years old.[50] However, Cobet here rejected the reading εἰς τὸ μειρακιοῦσθαι, for two reasons.[51] One reason relates to vocabulary; the verb is not otherwise attested in the classical period and appears only in the Roman imperial period (Philo, Aelian). The other concerns style; the combination of εἰς with the ἐκ- of ἐκβαίνωσι is startling. Neither argument is persuasive. Even if the verb μειρακιοῦσθαι is otherwise unattested in the classical period, it is formed quite regularly and is entirely plausible. And the second argument has been refuted by Kennell (1995, 181 n. 31), who quotes a convincing parallel: οἱ παῖδες ἐκ τούτου δὲ εἰς τοὺς ἐφήβους ἐξέρχονται (*Cyrop.* 1.2.9, a passage dealing with precisely the same stage in the life of young Persians, as Xenophon conceived it). Not only is there no good literary reason to reject the expression εἰς τὸ μειρακιοῦσθαι; rather, it can be positively supported. In a passage which follows very closely the ideas expressed here by Xenophon, 'Plutarch' contrasts the *paides*, who are supervised, with the *meirakia* who are given complete freedom – which suggests that εἰς τὸ μειρακιοῦσθαι was what he read in Xenophon (*De lib. educ.* 16 = *Mor.* 12a).

The fact that in recent times numerous historians, some of them quite eminent, have accepted Cobet's emendation is not the result of close engagement with the Greek; rather, they followed Tazelaar whose study of the age groups was authoritative at the time.[52] Why did the latter himself reject εἰς τὸ μειρακιοῦσθαι? Because in his view (p. 147) the age in question corresponded to 14 or thereabouts, and he found it inconceivable that surveillance by *paidagōgoi* and masters should have ceased so early. Rather, the words ἐκ παίδων, as interpreted by Tazelaar, pointed to the age of 18. But the above-quoted passage of ps.-Plutarch shows that the age at which surveillance ceased was indeed that of the *meirakia*. It seems that what ultimately counted for Tazelaar was his desire to reconcile Xenophon, the glosses and Plutarch in a single system. To an extent he was successful in this, but gave priority to

Plutarch (especially *Lyc.* 17.3–4), with the result that in his view the *paides* extended from 7 to 18, leaving a gap of two years between the last year of that category (the year of the *melleirenes*) and the first year of adult status (that of the *eirenes*). For Tazelaar this intervening period amounted to *ephēbeia* in the strict sense, the period of Xenophon's *paidiskoi*. In support of this attempt to locate entry into the *paidiskoi* at an age definitely older than that of the *meirakia*, there are two texts which might be adduced. In the *Cyropaedia* the transition from childhood to the *ephēbeia* is put at 'around 16 or 17 years of age' (1.2.9); the text then goes on to mention the idea of permanent surveillance which is taken further at *Lak. Pol.* 3.1–2. However, while the model of Sparta is undeniably present in the *Cyropaedia*, in that text the whole system is timed quite differently: the *ephēbeia* begins around 16–17, and does not end until ten years later. The parallel, therefore, cannot be pressed; the ephebes of the *Cyropaedia* do not correspond with the *paidiskoi* of the *Lak. Pol.* Xenophon seems rather, in the *Cyropaedia*, to be influenced by thoughts of Crete, where the transition from νεώτεροι to μείζους took place at the age of 17. The second relevant text is Photius' note on the word συνέφηβος, where it is stated that the ephebes, who at Sparta are called *sideunai*, 'are separated from the younger children at the *ephēbeia*, that is at around 15 or 16'. But here too we are dealing with ephebes in the normal sense (or close to it; the usual age was around 18), which is not the case with the *paidiskoi* of Xenophon. The latter group, according to Xenophon's text and thus inescapably, began at the age of the *meirakia*, and so at around 14. That is also the starting point for the series of annual age-groups listed in the glosses, which define the period involved with the phrase ἐφηβεύει ὁ παῖς, a phrase which uses the terms 'childhood' and '*ephēbeia*' in their widest senses. This point of resemblance between two otherwise different systems – one of which, like the Hippocratic system, has regard to long expanses of existence, while the other makes fine distinctions between particular years – suggests that on the whole the information found in the glosses applies to the classical period.

If we reject Cobet's emendation, we remove also the basis for the theory put forward by Kukofka concerning the *paidiskoi*.[53] He takes as his starting point the stage in Tazelaar's system, the so-called *ephēbeia*, consisting of two years from the time a youth left the *paides* until he joined the *eirenes*. Following Tazelaar, Kukofka identifies these 'ephebes' with Xenophon's *paidiskoi*; in Kukofka's view the πλεῖστοι πόνοι imposed upon them are – the Crypteia. This theory relies upon an implausible emendation of Xenophon's text; moreover, it conflicts with the information we have concerning the Crypteia. [54] It is certain that the latter did not last for two years (the passage which gives this figure relates not to the Crypteia but to a genuinely ephebic duty), and only *some* of the *neoi* were selected for the test of the Crypteia.

We can see from the passage of the *Hellenica* (5.4.32) quoted above (p. 88) and from the glosses, that the transition around 14 from the category of *paides* to that of *paidiskoi* is not something which Xenophon invented for clarity, something which would merely correspond with the age at which 'surveillance' of the young ceased in other Greek communities. Rather, this transition was a real stage in Spartan education. We are bound to wonder why Plutarch put a transition of the same type, from 'little boys' to 'big boys', at the age of 12; how did that idea arise? Finding no precise figure in his main source (Xenophon) for the age at which this transition occurred, he must have sought elsewhere and got his information from a different author, perhaps hellenistic. It may be that at some date now unknown the age for promotion to the 'big boys' changed. Why might it have? Fundamental to Plutarch's account is the idea that at this age there were two major changes. The first, the increased severity of the discipline, is derived from Xenophon. The second is the beginning of pederastic relations (*Lyc.* 17.1, which clearly indicates the timing). Xenophon, on the other hand, gives no clear indication of when this process began; it does not correspond with any point of transition within his system. Now, pederastic relations brought with them large changes in a child's life (see below, pp. 165–6), probably including the way he spent his time. It may therefore have seemed logical, at some later date, to represent the transition to the 'big boys' as coinciding with the age when pederastic relations began.

On the subject of *how the* paidiskoi *were organized and on what they did*, Xenophon is notably reticent. His near-silence can be explained by the fact that, as we have seen,[55] at least some of the elements which he describes in chapter 2 continued into the next age-group.[56] This is certainly the case with the authority of the *paidonomos*, the pederastic relations, the existence of sets, and no doubt also of meals in common. Thus Xenophon considered that he needed merely to indicate what was specific to the *paidiskoi* and he does so, even though with regrettable brevity. First he stresses the intensified severity of the regime of exercises (§2): testing experiences are more numerous (πλείστους πόνους αὐτοῖς ἐπέβαλε, 'it is on them that he imposed the largest number of stressful exercises'), and their timetable becomes more and more onerous (πλείστην δὲ ἀσχολίαν ἐμηχανήσατο, 'they are the ones for whom he contrived the most thorough lack of respite'). This last point implies that the child does have some periods of 'respite' while he is in the *paides*; this surely must mean that the collective organization does not at that stage wholly monopolize the child, and thus that he spends a considerable part of his time with his family. It is natural that in the course of growing up he increasingly separates from the family. Thus, as represented by Xenophon, the difference between the regime of the *paidiskoi* and that of the *paides* is of the same kind as that between the regimes of the 'little boys' and 'big boys' among Plutarch's *paides*: not so much a qualitative difference as a difference of intensity. Some qualitative difference there was, however.

Xenophon indicates early on (§3) a change in the system of punishment. No doubt for normal and occasional errors they continued with the punishments which had been used among the *paides*. But the law also envisages the possibility of serious and repeated lapses, reflecting deliberate disobedience; in such cases, says Xenophon, the young person may even be deemed beyond redemption. In other words, in spite of his being young, he is losing his whole future 'career' as a citizen; he will henceforward have no share in the 'good things' (μηδενὸς ἔτι τῶν καλῶν τυγχάνειν), and in the community he will be held in complete dishonour (ὡς μὴ…ἀδόκιμοι παντάπασιν ἐν τῇ πόλει γένοιντο).[57] Matters now are serious indeed, and the young person is from this point considered as someone having full responsibility. This marks his emergence into the community as an autonomous individual.

Xenophon refers in passing to the problem of 'surveillance', and in this area too there is possibly some change. Among those with responsibility for ensuring, by their advice and their orders, that the young stay in the right path, he distinguishes two categories, each with a distinctive description. On the one hand, there are those to whom this responsibility is given by the community (οἱ ἐκ δημοσίου), a description which fits officials such as the *paidonomos* and his auxiliaries, and also 'monitors' such as the *eirenes*. Xenophon makes a distinction between these ἐκ δημοσίου and, on the other hand, οἱ κηδόμενοι, 'those who look after' the young. The latter expression is vague, and could – if taken on its own – apply just as well to the previous category. But, since the two categories are contrasted, and the former is described by a term clearly referring to the idea of 'public', we infer that the latter category is in the private sphere. The term in question may, if not connote, at least include the *erastēs* of an adolescent.[58] But my own view is that, for *paidiskoi* as for *paides*, at Sparta as elsewhere, the most natural and deeply-rooted form of authority was that of the father. Xenophon is thus recalling that, for *paidiskoi*, this authority is exercised more than ever in collaboration with representatives of the community; his expression is deliberately left vague to indicate that he is also thinking of cases where the father is no longer alive. What distinguishes this category from the *paides* is that here authority is no longer shared so markedly with every other citizen. And that, now that adolescents are involved rather than children, is entirely comprehensible.

A further significant change is not mentioned explicitly by Xenophon, but can readily be inferred from what he says: *the intensifying of pederastic relations*. Pederasty in Greece did not begin before the age of 12, as indeed

Plutarch says (*Lyc.* 17.1). Thus it was only beginning when the young were at the stage of *paides*. It was when they were *paidiskoi* that pederasty developed fully. Though encouraged by the community and virtually obligatory through custom, it was experienced as something private and between individuals. Pairing off with an older male, the *paidiskos* was to a – probably increasing – extent growing apart from the group or groups to which he had until then exclusively belonged. The effect of the pederastic bond was thus to develop his personality and to set him on the path towards personal independence. It may even be that, towards the end of their time as *paidiskoi*, boys had ceased completely to belong to a group, and were being educated exclusively by their *erastai*.

One aspect of this individual development is alluded to by Xenophon at 3.5: *introduction into the adult* syssition. However, this is not so straightforward a subject as has sometimes been thought:[59] both 'the introduction' and 'the adult *syssition*' need some discussion. The boys, according to Xenophon, already had their meals in common under the direction of the *eirēn* who was leader of the group (*ilē*), as we saw earlier. One would not expect this practice to have ceased when they became *paidiskoi*. One might therefore think that the common meal to which Xenophon alludes at 3.5 was simply that of the adolescent, that the process of questioning referred to at this point was that of the *eirēn*, and that we have the same scenario as Plutarch describes in the case of precisely his 'bigger boys' (*Lyc.* 18.3–5). All this is indeed an attractive possibility. But when Xenophon writes ἐπειδὰν εἰς τὸ φιλίτιόν γε ἀφίκωνται, it is of a common meal among adults that the reader naturally thinks. It seems doubful whether Xenophon could have used the term *philition*, without qualification, in connection with adolescents. Also, the shyness and the intense inhibition of the boys, which Xenophon so emphasizes, would be somewhat surprising unless they were 'specially invited'.[60] These various reasons make the present writer incline to the prevailing view, that Xenophon here is referring to the common meal of adults.

This leaves the question of 'admission' to the occasion. Singor gives no sign of doubting that the admission in question was permanent and virtually definitive. He even goes as far as setting at 12 the age at which this introduction took place – by combining the testimony of Xenophon with that of Plutarch.[61] But this is not how the text is normally understood.[62] Plutarch, too, writes of *paides* present at the *syssition* (*Lyc.* 12.6; in his text, as in the glosses, the category *paides* extended to the age of 20); here it is quite clear that only an occasional visit is meant. Similarly with Xenophon: the *paidiskoi* could have been invited to attend – though not necessarily to take part in – the adults' common meal.[63] A point made by Singor which is acceptable is, that every adolescent may have been introduced in this way by his *erastēs* to the latter's own *syssition*. While no text says as much, this does indeed seem probable. No doubt the adolescent had the prospect of being recruited definitively when he came of age (and when a vacancy occurred). But for the time being he was only being given an introduction; how often such invitations were given is not known.

Xenophon's way of describing the scene gives the impression that the invitation was in effect a test; doubtless the members of the *syssition* were trying to get a clearer idea of the young man, whose 'case history' they already knew. The extreme inhibition shown by the adolescent was not an attempt to evade the test; in fact he knew very well that such behaviour was exactly what was expected of him.

Xenophon's brief remarks on the *paidiskoi* leave us with the definite impression that this stage in a young person's apprenticeship marked a turning point; the youngster was becoming his own person and developing a distinctive personality, progressively leaving behind the ranks of children and taking up prolonged contact with the world of adults. At this time of transition he needed to avoid giving any impression of audacity. Instead, as he left behind the intensely collective life-style of the children and was presented at the *syssition* to the adults with whom he would one day live, this was a time to show by his behaviour how far he was from considering himself their equal. Thus the institutionalized separation of childhood life was carried on into adolescence, by something like an internalized initial probation, a process of psychological self-isolation.

Eirenes

That there existed in classical Sparta an age group named *eirenes* has been denied by Kennell. In his view the word is only found with this meaning in the glosses on Herodotos and on Strabo, and in Plutarch. He observes that in the texts of the two classical authors supposed to have mentioned the *eirenes*, Herodotos (9.85) and Xenophon (*LP* 2.5 and 11), the word is in every case an emendation, and an unconvincing one at that.[64] His inference from this is not that the term was not used in classical Sparta; in fact an inscription to be discussed below, from Geronthrai and dating from the end of the fifth century (*IG* 5.1.1120), describes a young man as *trietirēs*. But he argues that the word *eirēn*, 'a Lakonian variant of *arses*, male', had no institutional meaning, and meant simply a young male adult.[65]

Rather than the much-discussed passage of Herodotos 9.85,[66] it is the passage of Xenophon which seems most significant here. But the Herodotos passage is of some importance in that the presence or otherwise of the word εἴρην in Herodotos has a bearing on the passages of Xenophon. All the manuscripts of Herodotos have ἰρέες (and ἰρέας). ἰρένες (-ας) is an emendation first proposed by Valckenaer in 1758, accepted by Wesseling in his edition of Herodotos (1763) and generally adopted thereafter. I do not propose here to defend the manuscript reading, as Den Boer and Kennell have done, but to point out that reading ἰρένες presents formidable problems. Indeed, the problem involving Amompharetos seems unsurmountable. Even if one allows that a young man remained *eirēn* until the age of 29, which is – as we shall see – highly unlikely, we could still hardly believe that Amompharetos was both *eirēn* and *lochagos* at the same time. Xenophon states clearly (*LP* 4.7) that a Spartan could not become an elected official until he had ceased to belong to the *hēbōntes*. A *lochagos* was not only a military official, but one of the highest. This being so, one needs to question the elaborate structure of hypotheses proposed by Nafissi and Lupi (following Chrimes and Kelly). According to this, Herodotos used the term *irenes* to refer to the *hippeis*; the latter were divided into three *lochoi*, one of which was that of Pitane; the commanders of these *lochoi* were called not only *hippagretai* but also *lochagoi*; and Amompharetos was one of these. The argument is circular, because on the reading of the word *irenes* in Herodotos rests the interpretation of Amompharetos' command which makes this reading possible. In fact, Herodotos' narrative implies that Amompharetos was no beginner.[67] The meaning of the term ἰρέες in the manuscripts is unclear; but it certainly does not refer to the *eirenes*.

We come now to Xenophon *Lak. Pol.* 2.5 and 11. In both passages all the manuscripts give the word ἄρρην (τὸν ἄρρενα in §5, τῶν ἀρρένων in §11); εἴρην is an emendation. Kennell suggests returning to the manuscript reading. He argues (1995, 16) that it would be surprising if Xenophon introduced here this 'technical' term without the slightest explanation, given that he does explain, at least partially, who a παιδονόμος is (2.2) and who the ἱππαγρέται are (4.3). But Xenophon in the *Lak. Pol.* often mentions Spartan institutions or other facts about Sparta without giving the slightest explanation (above, p. 33 n. 31), as if assuming they were already known or rather perhaps as if he were responding to a work which his readers knew and where these facts were described.[68] Indeed, we might ask whether he ever gives explanations. To take the examples given by Kennell: it is not the case that Xenophon gives a definition of the παιδονόμος. That would be quite foreign to his purpose; his work is not descriptive, and his words about the magistrate in question form part of a rhetorical case in favour of the Spartan education system, contrasting the παιδονόμος with the παιδαγωγοί elsewhere. His words about the ἱππαγρέται are even more typical of his approach. Had he been concerned to be explanatory, he should have begun with the institution of the *hippeis*. But in fact he does not even name them; the ἱππαγρέται are named only because they choose the Three Hundred – this process of selection being the only thing which concerns the author.

It is quite possible, therefore, that at §5 Xenophon introduced the word *eirēn* without any special explanation. We have already seen (above, p. 83) that – quite apart from τὸν ἄρρενα – the manuscripts here do not give a satisfactory sense; whence the attempts at emendation. The only edition to retain τὸν ἄρρενα, that of Rühl, does so at the cost of drastic reshaping of the text: ἔταξε is deleted, ἔχοντα is changed to ἔχειν and τὸν ἄρρενα becomes its subject (and is given the meaning of 'the young Spartiate'), and συμβουλεύειν is changed to συνεβούλευεν. However, in spite of all these emendations the resulting text – which is largely inspired by that of Stobaeus – is still not satisfactory, because Lycurgus is hardly to be imagined as 'giving advice'. And ἄρρην is not equivalent either to ἄνηρ or to νεανίας; it means strictly 'male' as contrasted, explicitly or implicitly, with 'female'. What meaning can be given to the expression 'the male' in the manuscript text? The concept of the male has no bearing here.[69] The same point applies to §11, but in the latter case there are two further, converging, arguments. The first is raised but rejected by Kennell (1995, 17): Xenophon's words ἔθηκε τῆς ἴλης ἑκάστης τὸν τορώτατον τῶν ἀρρένων ἄρχειν correspond with those of Plutarch at *Lyc.* 17.2: κατ' ἀγέλας αὐτοὶ προΐσταντο τῶν λεγομένων εἰρένων ἀεὶ τὸν σωφρονέστατον καὶ μαχιμώτατον, 'in each *agelē* they themselves appointed as their chief that one of the so-called *eirenes* who had most self-control and most courage'. Kennell rejects this parallelism because of 'breaks between various phases of the *agōgē*', that is because of the discontinuity which he postulates in the history of Spartan education. But this amounts to a false statement of the problem. We are not dealing here with two historical realities, such that one could argue as to whether they converge or differ. We are dealing with two Greek sentences, one of which clearly transposes the other. And together they make clear that the words which Plutarch found in Xenophon's text were indeed τῶν εἰρένων.[70] The second argument is merely plain logic. What Xenophon says is this: if there is no adult present, it falls to one of the 'arrenes' who takes command of the group of children. It follows that these 'arrenes' are not themselves adults ; but neither are they children, since the law transfers to them the authority which in normal circumstances belongs to adults. Thus they must be young people...in other words, *eirenes*. That is why the emendation τῶν εἰρένων, which goes back to Cragius in 1593, has been adopted by all editors, including those who – like Rühl – retain τὸν ἄρρενα in §5. But if the emendation (or the idea that ἄρρην = εἴρην) is accepted in the one passage, why reject it in the other?

Thus *eirenes* did exist in Xenophon's day. They were an age-group and played an important role in the education system. But what age-group? *What was an eirēn*?

Plutarch defines the *eirenes* in a way which seems precise and detailed (*Lyc.*

17.3–4). His text can be divided into three separate propositions:

(a) εἴρενας δὲ καλοῦσι τοὺς ἔτος ἤδη δεύτερον ἐκ παίδων γεγονότας,
(b) μελλείρενας δὲ τῶν παίδων τοὺς πρεσβυτάτους.
(c) οὗτος οὖν ὁ εἴρην, εἴκοσιν ἔτη γεγονώς...

'The name *eirenes* is given to those who left the category of *paides* a whole year previously; the *melleirenes* are the oldest of the *paides*. Thus the above-mentioned *eirēn*, who is twenty years old...' The problems presented by these definitions emerge more clearly if we examine Plutarch's propositions in inverse order. (c) states in clear terms that the *eirēn* is 20 years old; that is, he is in his 21st year. This applies not only to the *eirēn* of the sentence which begins here, the *eirēn* who is head of a band of children, but to the *eirēn* as defined previously; that is, to the *eirenes* in general. This information agrees with what we deduce from Strabo's version of the glosses where, counting from age 14 (i.e. from the 15th year), the eirenate corresponds to age 20 (i.e. to the 21st year). (b) implies that the year of the *melleirēn* is the one preceding the eirenate. While this is not stated explicitly, it is surely implied by Plutarch's language. Since no explicit definition is given of the word *melleirēn*, its meaning should be the one which is suggested naturally by the form of the word ('he who is about to become *eirēn*'). On the other hand, (b) states clearly that the *melleirenes* form the last year in the category of *paides*. On these two points (b) is in complete agreement with the glosses.[71]

The problem arises from (a). One difficulty, more apparent than real, should be disposed of first. Some scholars have found the words ἐκ παίδων γεγονότας odd.[72] It is true that in classical Greek the perfect participle γεγονώς is only used in the sense of 'born', generally with an accusative of duration, 'born x years ago'; we find this form in (c) above. But in the imperial period γεγονώς can mean the same as γενόμενος: 'having become'.[73] That is what it means here; as the absence of the definite article shows, ἐκ παίδων... is a ready-made expression, referring to those who have left the category of *paides*.[74] The literal meaning of the phrase is thus that they are 'now in their second year since leaving the category of *paides*'. The difficulty lies in the words ἔτος ἤδη δεύτερον. It is in clear contradiction with (b), since if a person was *melleirēn* and *eirēn* in successive years, and if the year of the *melleirēn* is the last year in the category of *paides*, an *eirēn* is someone in his first – not second – year after leaving the *paides*. Moreover, Plutarch has effectively emphasized the word δεύτερον by combining it with ἤδη.

Three solutions, to our knowledge, have been proposed for this difficulty. Tazelaar disconnected the years of the *melleirēn* and *eirēn* by positing a gap between them of a whole year or, indeed, of longer. This involves giving to the explicit meaning of (a) priority over what (b) seems to imply clearly about the meaning of *melleirēn*. What makes this unacceptable as a solution is, in addition to the sense of *melleirēn*, the fact that no source mentions any such gap and that the gloss on Strabo rules out such a thing.

The second solution was proposed by Busolt and Swoboda,[75] and involves the idea that the word *paides* does not have the same meaning in (a) as it does in (b). In (a) it is to mean – as in the lists given in the glosses – an annual age-class, the one immediately preceding the year of the *melleirēn*. The meaning of (a) would fit this perfectly, since the *eirēn* has indeed spent more than a year since leaving the category in question. In (b), on the other hand, *pais* is assigned its more normal sense of a very wide category of ages, the last year of which – for Plutarch as for the glosses, on this theory – is that of the *melleirēn*. This solution involves logical acrobatics. Admittedly the glosses do use the word *pais* in both these senses, but they do so in a way which leads to no ambiguity. The present theory asks us to believe that in this passage Plutarch reproduced information from two separate sources which differed from each other in the meaning they gave to *pais*. While this is (just) possible, it is difficult to imagine Plutarch copying his sources mechanically and not realizing that they were talking of different things. However, there is a contradiction within Plutarch's text, and most probably there was some reason for it.

The third solution is the one most often accepted. It was first suggested by Chrimes (1949, 89), and adopted by Den Boer (1954, 256), MacDowell (1986, 163) and recently in substance by Kennell (1995, 36). Chrimes saw the expression ἔτος ἤδη δεύτερον as parallel to a phrase such as δευτέρῃ ἡμέρῃ 'on the second day' (Hdt. 1.82), which means 'on the day after [the event in question]'.[76] On this interpretation Plutarch would simply – and unproblematically – mean that the *eirenes* are the young people who left the *paides* the year previously. Unfortunately, the supposed parallel does not exist. Referring to the day after as 'the second day' is a perfectly normal case of inclusive counting, the kind of counting which clearly is used here since the figure is an ordinal: the day itself being the first day, the next day counts as the second. In Plutarch's expression this kind of reasoning cannot be involved, since although the form is that of inclusive counting (involving an ordinal number) the previous year cannot be included in the count; it was neither at the start of this year nor during the year that the young person 'became an ex-*pais*' but at its end. We are obliged then to see as correct the opinion of the majority of commentators, who see the words ἔτος δεύτερον as implying that between the end of the *melleirēn* year (which is thus the last year of the *paides*) and the year of the *eirēn*, there is for Plutarch another year (the 'first') – a ghost year.

We may be tempted to think of an *eirēn* having a second year in that status, i.e. to think that the status of *eirēn* lasted more than one year. But that would only be possible if in passage (a) above the *eirēn* in question was the head of the group, as is true of passage (c). But that is certainly not the case; what is meant are the *eirenes* in general, and nothing in Plutarch fits the idea that someone was *eirēn* for more than one year. Indeed, the opposite is true: passage (c) indicates a precise age (20 years, not 20 years and upwards). It is as if Plutarch had deliberately blocked every escape from the problem he poses. We are obliged to register a *non liquet*, and to move on.

Several sources indicate *the age at which one became an eirēn*; it is generally agreed to have been when the person had lived for 20 full years. Hesychius' gloss, κόρος τέλειος, hardly helps, since the problem is in knowing at what age a young Spartan was deemed to be 'a fully-fledged young man'. All other texts indicate 20 years: Plutarch *Lyc.* 17.4 (= *supra*, item (c)), εἴκοσιν ἔτη γεγονώς; the gloss to Strabo; Photius s.vv. κατὰ πρωτείρας (see below).

Plutarch and the gloss imply that a person was *eirēn* for only a single year, his 21st. But other texts seem to imply the possibility that one was *eirēn* for several years – for three years, at least. First, there are glosses in the lexicographers: Hesychius has κατὰ πρωτείρας· ἡλικίας ὄνομα οἱ πρωτείρες παρὰ Λακεδαιμονίοις (k 1358 Latte); and in Photius we find πρωτεῖραι· οἱ περὶ εἴκοσι παρὰ Λάκωσι.[77] One may well think that πρωτείρης means 'first-year *eirēn*', thus implying the existence of subsequent years. Such years have seemed to be attested by several inscriptions, none of which is from Sparta, however. These always refer to the third year, an oddity for which an explanation may nonetheless be available (see below). In *IG* 5.1.1386 (of Thouria, second century BC), one section of a list of ephebes begins with the title τριτίρενες. In the dedicatory inscription *IG* 5.1.1120 (of Geronthrai, end of fifth century BC), a list of victories won by the dedicant, occurs the phrase τριετίρης ἔον. A third inscription, published only recently,[78] is on a stele from the beginning of the first century AD found in the sanctuary of Herakles at Messene. It gives a list of τριετίρενες. Taken together, these texts, glosses and inscriptions have led some historians to believe that the status of *eirēn* at Sparta lasted for several years. The resulting systems proposed by these scholars are however widely divergent. Michell (1952, 171) believes that a person was *eirēn* from the age of 19 to that of 24, under various names – most of which are purely hypothetical: *proteires*, *dieires*, *triteires*, *tetteires* and *penteires*. Den Boer (1954, 257–8) argues for only two years, that of *eirēn* (which he takes to be the 20th year) and that of *proteirēn*. In his view the latter term would not mean 'first-year *eirēn*', as most of us assume, but something such as '*eirēn* first class'. It would indicate rank not age and would follow the *eirēn* year. Tazelaar, who puts the age of becoming an *eirēn* at 20, believes that a young man remained an *eirēn* for ten years, and thus that the *eirenes* should be identified with the *hēbōntes* of Xenophon.[79] Several other scholars have accepted his view; cf. MacDowell (1986, 164–5), Link (1994, 30) and Lupi (2000, 30).

Writing of the inscriptions, but not knowing the one from Messene (first published only in 1994), Kennell argued that they could not properly be taken in combination (1995, 119). In one way he is quite right: between Geronthrai on the one hand, and Thouria and Messene on the other, there are vital differences both of geographical relation to Sparta and of date – and thus of political and social context. But he seems mistaken to base his explanation on the linguistic difference he perceives between the term τριτίρενες used at Thouria in the second century and τριετίρης used at Geronthrai in the fifth. The first is based on the ordinal τρίτος, and the second on the compound τριέτης, which in turn is formed from the cardinal and means 'of three years'. The two terms, according to Kennell, belong to different systems of thought. The τριτίρενες of Thouria clearly refers to a normal form of hellenistic *ephēbeia*, lasting for three years; these τριτίρενες are ephebes in their third and last year,[80] and are thus very probably in their 20th year of life. On the other hand, the term τριετίρης belongs – in Kennell's view – to a system of dividing age into long periods and not to an annual categorization; he sees it as meaning that the dedicant had, two full years previously, entered an age-category which at Geronthrai was named '*eirēn*', meaning 'young man' in the same way as Xenophon's term ἡβῶν.

With the publication of the ephebic list from Messene, this opposition disappears. At Messene the word τριετίρενες is shown to have been used with exactly the same sense as the word τριτίρενες at Thouria: ephebes in their third year. What of the case of Geronthrai? Unless the inscription there is later than is claimed, it is hard to see how there could have been an *ephēbeia* of the normal hellenistic type, that is of three years. Perhaps the account which Kennell gives of the word τριετίρης in general applies to the case of Geronthrai. It may even be that at Sparta the term ἴρης, in one of its meanings, was one of the regular terms for 'young man'. But its use in Xenophon (*LP* 2.5 and 11) shows that in the classical period it could also denote a precisely-defined age-class. It would thus have the same ambiguity as the word παῖς, for example. So, Kennell's account of the word πρωτεῖραι in the glosses may be right. However this may be, my own belief is that at Sparta a youth was only *eirēn* in the strict sense for a single year, as Plutarch says, and that the text of Xenophon does not justify the identification of *eirenes* with ἡβῶντες.

In the course of this year, the young Spartiate, still subject to an educational regime, nevertheless could be chosen to play an important pedagogical role of his own as head of a group of children,[81] especially in connection with the common meals.

Hēbōntes

The word ἡβῶντες (*hebōntes*), which Xenophon uses to denote young men who while already being adult are still involved in the process of education, is a regular Greek word, the present participle of the verb ἡβᾶν. It is translated by Tazelaar (1967, 145) as 'those who have reached physical adulthood', i.e. ἥβη. Its usage in the classical period, as adjective and as noun, shows that while it can mean a young man as distinct from an old one (Aesch. *Suppl.* 775) it more often means an adult as opposed to a child or an adolescent (Ar. *Frogs* 1055, Thuc. 3.36.2). The idea of youth, however, is always present.[82] *To what age* does the word correspond?

As to when the term began to apply there is general agreement: at 20 years of age.[83] Although no text is explicit on the point, the glosses make clear that the *ephēbeia* ended at the 20th birthday. Also, our information on the period of eligibility for military service at Sparta shows that it began at 20 and lasted for 40 years (Xen. *Hell.* 5.4.13), ending at the age of 60 (at which point one became eligible for the Gerousia; Plut. *Lyc.* 26.1). Since these ages are the same as we find in Greek cities generally, they may be accepted without any problem. If the period of the *eirēn* was a single year, as I trust to have shown, it will have formed the first year of the category of *hēbōntes*.

There is also agreement on the age at which one ceased to be *hēbōn*, at 30, though that has never strictly been proved. Two facts are cited. First, the phrase τὰ δέκα ἀφ' ἥβης, used by Xenophon three times in the *Hellenika* (2.4.32; 3.4.23; 4.5.14) and once in the *Agesilaos* (1.31), meaning the body formed by the men of the first ten age classes ('the ten years following *hēbē*') present at a given place. This phrase seems to be used in a precise and regular way: the context is never the description of a military action as it unfolds, but rather of an order given before or during a battle by the commander-in-chief. The mission assigned to this body of men is always to engage either upon battle or upon pursuit. The other fact adduced is taken from Plutarch: the prohibition on those under 30 (οἱ νεώτεροι τριάκοντ' ἔτων) from entering the *agora*. The above passages of Xenophon show that the age-classes from 20 to 30 could form an independent unit on the battlefield, fulfilling specific tasks. And Plutarch shows that, at some period, citizens under the age of 30 were subject to a limitation on their rights. The age-group 20–30 did indeed, then, have a recognized existence of its own, but this does not prove beyond doubt that it should be identified with the *hēbōntes* of Xenophon. It may be that one was only *hēbōn* for part of that period, for example from 20 to 25 – especially since (as we shall see) the various restrictions and subordinations applied to the *hēbōntes* contained some which may seem very surprising in the case of men approaching the age of 30. On the other hand, we shall also meet presently evidence of the opposite tendency, and it was quite normal in the Greek world for institutions applying to 'the young' to apply to men up to the age of 30.[84] Let us leave the question open, while assuming for the time being that a man was indeed *hēbōn* until the age of 30. The *hēbōntes* were the community's young adults.

The category of *hēbōntes* presents the same question as that of *paidiskoi*: *was this the local Spartan term*, or a 'translation' by Xenophon? Three things indicate that here too we have a local term.[85] First, there is the passage of Thucydides showing that the Spartans sent out with Brasidas three citizens with orders to supervise him, who 'brought to him, against normal practice, men drawn from the *hēbōntes*' (καὶ τῶν ἡβώντων αὐτῷ παρανόμως ἄνδρας ἐξῆγον ἐκ Σπάρτης, 4.132.3). The term in question may be normal Greek, but the significance of this episode – to be analysed below – suggests rather that it is being used in a local sense. Second, there is the possibility that ἡβῶν was used in the section of the dedication by Damonon dealing with the victories of his son Enymakratidas (*IG* 5.1.213, l. 39). This restoration, by Schwartz,[86] is altogether more satisfactory than the one accepted previously, [ἐφη]β[ῶ]ν, even though it is slightly suspicious that the word ἡβῶν should appear only here in the inscription. Thirdly, this age category is found (in the form ἡβιῶν) in the Gortyn Code, although the exact age to which it applies is not clear. There is also the point that, if the Spartan term was not ἡβῶν, it is not easy to see what it could have been. Kennell has suggested κυρσάνιος (1995, 117), but the glosses in Photius, μειρακίσκος, μειράκιον, and (for σκυρθάνια) ἔφηβοι, seem to me to require that that term was applied rather to *paidiskoi*.

Once again, what Xenophon actually says about *the role of this group* appears disappointing; 4.1 leads us to expect more than in the event we are told. The chapter in question, like its predecessors, is mainly concerned to reply to criticisms of the Spartan system. On the subject of the *hēbōntes*, the latter were probably aimed at the atmosphere of rivalry and incessant struggle, and even of brawling, which characterized that stage of life – all of which might well seem a strange way to bring up young people. This, then, was the sphere in which Xenophon wished to re-assert Sparta's reputation. That is why his whole account centres on the ἔρις περὶ ἀρετῆς,[87] where the prize is selection for the 300 *hippeis*. The institution of the *hippeis* might in consequence be taken – quite wrongly – as no more than a pretext for this rivalry.

However, Xenophon's treatment of the subject is not so distorted as to be useless. As the only source for the way in which the *hippeis* were recruited, and although it was not the author's intention to be a source of that kind, his information is of great value. The atmosphere of tension created by this recruitment before the event – and also, remarkably and clearly intentionally, afterwards – certainly had a profound effect on the life of the *hēbōntes*.

Xenophon's claim, that this rivalry was a good thing for the community and also for the individuals concerned, is unconvincing. It is unlikely that the latter were motivated solely by a wish to serve the state to the exclusion of all personal ambition. The personal aspect is what made this rivalry prejudicial and even dangerous. The process of selection carried out by the *hippagretai* was a public matter, but also inevitably had a personal impact. Xenophon makes clear that the unsuccessful candidate became resentful of others: of the *hippagretas* for not selecting him, and of those who had been chosen in preference to him. Presumably the disappointed candidate would himself select a favourite target, a rival he loved to hate, on whom his loathing could be concentrated. He would then make it his job to spy on all that rival did, with the aim of discrediting him – seeking out his slightest weakness so as to report it to the authorities. In this he was motivated not just by a yearning for revenge but by a more straightforward ambition: he hoped to take the rival's place. For this system to have worked to maximum effect, I believe that the *hippeis* must have been reselected in their entirety, at least formally, at regular intervals – probably every year.[88] These rivalries operated in more than one direction. Xenophon shows that they were reciprocal (ἀλλήλους, §4; ἑκάτεροι, §5), since inevitably the *hippeis* and the *hippagretai* who were the targets of resentment would take defensive measures of their own. All, therefore, were affected by the atmosphere of tension. It seems strange that the state not only tolerated but actually made an institution of this malfunctioning: we shall try presently (pp. 172–4) to explain why.

Moreover, the selection of the *hippeis* was not the only occasion for producing rivalry. The life of the *hēbōntes* was punctuated by other forms of selection. Among the *hippeis* there was selection for this or that mission, such as the one involving Cinadon, where there was a chance to make a name for oneself. There was the choice for the Crypteia, if (as I believe) that belonged to the stage of life now in question. On leaving the *hippeis* (and the *hēbōntes* at the same time) there was selection to be *agathoergos*. And, of course, there was selection to join the body of *hippagretai* themselves. The time spent as *hēbōn* was thus less a period of education, more a period of probation. This time was therefore profoundly ambivalent. Rivalries were played out like a game with fixed rules, refereed by the citizen body in general. But what was at stake was extremely serious – the choice of the city's future elites.

There were, of course, other activities besides these rivalries for the *hēbōntes* to attend to. Indeed, some modern historians have claimed that the activities in question went on all the time, with the *hēbōntes* permanently on duty for the community and sleeping in 'barracks'.[89] This picture is wholly dependent upon the testimony of Plutarch. At *Lyc.* 25.1 we are told that 'those under 30 did not go at all to the *agora*, but arranged for their necessary purchases to be made for them by their relatives and *erastai*'. This does indeed involve a restriction upon the *hēbōntes*, but in my view the restriction involves no element of military mobilization. Indeed, the reverse is true; this individual purchase of supplies is hardly compatible with a life in 'barracks'. On the other hand, the passage *Lyc.* 15.7–8 concerning marriage is quite unambiguous: it states clearly that the young Spartiate when newly married slept in a collective setting (καθευδήσων μετὰ τῶν ἄλλων νέων) and lived day and night with the young men of his own age (τοῖς ἡλικιώταις συνδιημερεύων καὶ συναναπαυόμενος). This, then, is how Plutarch envisaged the way of life of the *hēbōn*. But there is nothing of the kind in Xenophon. He too deals with marriage (*LP* 1.5) and praises self-control; but if that had been imposed on the newly-married man by his military or civic duties, Xenophon would certainly have said so explicitly. Instead, all we find is the following: 'Seeing that when a woman marries a man, in the early stages of marriage the other Greeks were cohabiting with their wives unrestrainedly, he decided on the opposite; he decreed that it would be considered shameful to be seen either entering or leaving the women's quarters.' Moderation is produced not by some external constraint belonging to the mode of life, but by a rule which the young man has completely internalized. Any deviation entailed not punishment but shame. I believe that this is a case where using Xenophon to check Plutarch leads one to mistrust the latter, or his source. Plutarch seems to have wrongly generalized to all young Spartiates the way of life peculiar to the *hippeis*; the latter no doubt really were permanently on duty in the service of the state.[90]

It is generally agreed that the *hēbōn* was in an ambiguous position as regards citizen status. He was clearly much closer to being a citizen than was a *pais*, but still he was a long way short of full citizenship; he was thus what Aristotle terms an imperfect or incomplete citizen (*Pol.* 3.1275a17). Let us first consider the positive side, *the things which the* hēbōntes *had in common with full citizens*. Most importantly, *they fought in the army*. Even this, however, had a certain ambiguity. For one thing, the *hēbōntes* had the front ranks in the phalanx and thus were unusually exposed. Xenophon actually seems to regard them as the best trained and most vigorous soldiers (*LP* 4.7). From their number the *hippeis* were chosen, elite troops who in battle were placed around the king and who formed the only permanent military unit in the state. Also, the *hēbōntes* on occasion formed a separate unit, which Xenophon calls τὰ δεκὰ ἀφ' ἥβης, as we have seen. As such they were given precise tasks, in attack or rapid pursuit, for which their physique suited them. These tasks put them on the margin of the phalanx, as Lupi has observed;[91] the phalanx being where the outcome of battle was decided. Though armed as hoplites, they had a tactical role which resembled that of light-armed troops.[92]

A further way in which the *hēbōn* resembled a full citizen was that he was henceforward *a member of a* syssition.[93] No text says as much explicitly, but since the *syssition* was the basic structure of the army, two or three *syssitia* forming an *enōmotia*, belonging to a *syssition* would be the logical consequence of the fact that a *hēbōn* was a soldier. We shall assume here that a *hēbōn* did so belong. But there is an element of paradox, nevertheless, one which is the salient point here: strictly one would expect admission to a *syssition* to mark the successful and definitive completion of the educational curriculum.

A final respect in which *hēbōntes* resembled citizens is that both were *subject to the authority of the ephors*. But in the case of the *hēbōntes* this subordination had an ambiguity of its own; the ephors did not have exclusive authority and they were involved only as the last stage in a chain of command. Xenophon makes clear that when two *hēbōntes* were involved in a fight, any citizen had the right to intervene and stop the confrontation, and the *hēbōntes* were obliged to obey. Only if they refused did the *paidonomos* become involved (*LP* 4.6). The latter did not have the power himself to punish them (the word ζημίουσι suggests that punishment took the form of a fine, which may partly explain why the *paidonomos* lacked the power in question); rather, he brought them before the ephors. In the final analysis, the young men were punished in the same way as citizens, but the preliminary stages are revealing. Other texts suggest a further way in which the ephors had authority over the *hēbōntes*. Agatharchides of Knidos reports that 'every ten days the young men (νέοι) had to stand naked in front of the ephors', the purpose of this inspection being to check that they were not indulging in too much food. 'The ephors also checked every day their clothing and their sleeping arrangements', no doubt to see that the latter were not too luxurious and enervating.[94] These inspections were confined to the *hēbōntes*; there is no question of such for full citizens.

The relation between the *hēbōntes* and the ephors thus shows how far the former were from being treated as full adults. That the *paidonomos* still had authority, albeit limited, over them shows that, while they no longer counted as *paides*, they were still considered as subject to the *paideia*.

The ambiguous status of the *hēbōntes* also involved *certain formal incapacities*.[95] The best-known is their exclusion from magistracies; Xenophon states that the latter were open only to 'those who have passed the age of ἥβη' (*LP* 4.7), i.e. to those who have left the category of *hēbōntes*. A rather puzzling passage of Thucydides suggests the possibility of a further incapacity:[96] 'Ischagoras, Ameinias and Aristeus came personally to Brasidas, sent by the Spartans to keep an eye on the situation. Additionally, and against normal practice, they brought to him from Sparta men from among the *hēbōntes* (καὶ τῶν ἡβώντων αὐτῷ παρανόμως ἄνδρας ἐξῆγον ἐκ Σπάρτης), to instal them as governors (ἀρχόντας) of the cities, rather than leave it to chance as to who would control the latter.' It is a little surprising that *hēbōntes* could become 'superintendants' of cities, but there is no formal contradiction with their incapacity to become magistrates, since here we are dealing with administration outside Sparta.[97] The important word here is παρανόμως. It cannot here mean 'illegally', since Ischagoras and his colleagues are carrying out a mission (πεμψάντων Λακεδαιμονίων) which undoubtedly included the arrival of the young men (who may have been *hippeis*). The word therefore must mean 'against normal practice'. But just what was abnormal about this?

The structure of the sentence excludes the possibility that Thucydides meant to describe as abnormal the role which was to be assigned to these young men: rather, παρανόμως relates to τῶν ἡβώντων αὐτῷ ἄνδρας ἐξῆγον ἐκ Σπάρτης, i.e. both to ἡβώντων and ἐξῆγον. It seems, then, that what was abnormal was *to 'bring out' young men from Sparta* (note the emphasis Thucydides puts on 'leaving Sparta'). Why was this abnormal? There are six texts, four of them from the classical period, which refer to a ban on leaving Sparta, whether applied to Spartans in general or to particular categories thereof. This ban is described in various ways.[98] Four of them give a simplified, stylized, version which suggests that going abroad was always forbidden for every Spartan (Xen. *LP* 14.4; Aristotle fr. 543 Rose; Nicolaus of Damascus 90 F 103, 5; Plut. *Lyc.* 27.6 = *Inst. Lac.* 19).[99] The two other texts put the matter in a more nuanced and therefore presumably more accurate way. Isocrates (*Busiris* 18) reports 'the fact that no man subject to military mobilization (μηδένα τῶν μαχίμων) can go abroad without the permission of the authorities'.[100] Plato states that 'they do not allow any of their young people (οὐδένα τῶν νέων) to leave Sparta (ἐξιέναι; cf. Thucydides' ἐξῆγον) to go to another city' (*Protag.* 342c). These two latter texts are compatible and persuasive: men of fighting age (30 to 60) needed a 'visa' from the authorities in order to go abroad, while for the young that was completely forbidden. Not only could the latter not go abroad in a private capacity; it was not normal for them to be entrusted with a mission outside Sparta. This is the norm to which the Spartans made an exception in the case reported by Thucydides. That the Spartans had a rule of this kind is unsurprising; indeed, it would be surprising if they had not. The *hēbōntes* were in one respect always mobilized in time of war; on the other hand when abroad they would no longer have been subject to the education system and to the 'discipline' (*agōgē*), and so would have been corrupted. So once more the point is the surveillance of the young. The *hēbōntes* were not truly independent adults. Interestingly, we find in the *Inst. Lac.* (no. 8) that in Sparta itself all the movements of young people (νεώτεροι) were under the control of their elders.

A further ineligibility affecting the *hēbōntes* is mentioned by Plutarch (*Lyc.* 25.1): 'Men under 30 absolutely *never went into the* agora (τὸ παράπαν οὐ κατέβαινον εἰς ἀγόραν); it was their relatives or their *erastai* who made the necessary domestic purchases for them.' The end of the sentence makes clear that by *agora* Plutarch means the market.[101] Whence the use of κατέβαινον, which here has more an ethical than a physical sense. Formerly I inclined to the view that Plutarch here had misrepresented his source, and that the latter was using *agora* in the sense – attested from Sparta – of 'popular assembly'.[102] The comments of Lupi (2000, 52–3) on this passage of Plutarch have, however, persuaded me otherwise. Lupi cites two parallels from the classical period which show that it is indeed the *agora* as market which is meant and that the ban reported by Plutarch may go back to that period. The first is a passage of Isocrates' *Areopagiticus* (§48): while praising the *patrios politeia* of Athens, he states that formerly the young (νεώτεροι) 'so shunned the *agora* that if by chance they were obliged to cross it, they did so only in the most inhibited and disciplined manner'. This attitude is so similar to that of Xenophon's *paidiskoi* as to suggest that Isokrates had the Spartan model in mind. The second case is a law of Thebes, quoted by Aristotle,[103] which allows to become magistrates only those citizens who have 'kept away from the *agora*' for at least ten years. Further analysis is required, however. The idea of the *agora* as a place which corrupts the young is, from the classical period onwards, a commonplace of morality. Aristophanes has several references to it, most notably – on the *agora* as market – at *Knights* 1373.[104] A virtuous city is one where the young avoid the *agora*. In connection with Sparta, since Plutarch is the only source to mention such a ban, one inevitably wonders as to its historicity. One could simplify things by assuming that Plutarch's idea refers to a ban on the practice of any craft or trade, purchase or sale, by the *hēbōntes*; Thucydides reports a ban of this kind as imposed on the 'tremblers' of Sphakteria.[105] But this may be an attempted rationalization of something which is no more than a moralizing commonplace.

This passage of Plutarch raises a further question on the status of *hēbōntes*. It implies that a young man of that age *could still be* erōmenos. This has normally been taken as correct; Singor went as far as thinking that a *hēbōn* might quite possibly have – at the same time – both an *erastēs* aged over 30 and an *erōmenos* from among the *paides*.[106] But Plutarch's idea is seriously problematic, since it was normal Greek practice for a male to cease to be *erōmenos* when his beard began to grow.[107] If Plutarch were the only source on this point, one might seriously doubt him.[108] But he seems to be strongly supported by our main source on education in the classical period, Xenophon. In the *Symposion* (8.35) the latter contrasts the procedure of the

Thebans and Eleans, who station lovers together in battle, with that of the Spartans, who often separate *erastēs* from *erōmenos*. He thus implies that a person might still be *erōmenos* at the age when he began to fight in the army. The account in Xenophon's *Hellenica* of the 'Sphodrias affair' may help us understand in what circumstances the status of *erōmenos* could continue after the age of 20. At the time of Sphodrias' trial, in 378, his son Kleonymos had just left the category of *paides* (5.4.25). The latter term having probably the same sense as it does slightly later (§32), he would then have been in his fifteenth year; his having an *erastēs* – in his case, Archidamos son of Agesilaos – was thus quite normal. Now, the subsequent narrative suggests that the relationship was still ongoing when Kleonymos was killed at Leuktra in his twenty-second year, for Archidamos was both mourning for his friend and proud of his conduct (§33). I suggest accordingly that if, normally, a pederastic relationship ceased when the *erōmenos* reached the age of 20, it may have been possible in some cases, and particularly when it involved members of the upper classes (and *a fortiori* the heir apparent to a king), for it to continue beyond that age, perhaps shedding its sexual element. However, Plutarch and Xenophon (in the *Symposion*) write as if continuation beyond 20 was quite normal, and needed no comment. If that was indeed the case, we should have an additional – and particularly significant – sphere in which *hēbōntes* were treated as adolescents and not as adults.[109]

If we accepted Kennell's view, we should see the *hēbōntes* as sharing with the 'tremblers' a further incapacity, that of *contracting a marriage*.[110] On the age considered normal at Sparta for marriage, Xenophon says only, concerning both sexes, that Lycurgus 'laid down that marriages would take place between people who had reached their full physical development' (*LP* 1.6: ἔταξεν ἐν ἀκμαῖς τῶν σωμάτων τοὺς γάμους ποιεῖσθαι). What age did he mean by that? In general, it is true, the Greeks located the *akmē* around or after the age of 30.[111] But in the case of Sparta Xenophon seems not to follow this pattern: the only passage where he uses the participle-as-noun οἱ ἀκμάζοντες is concerned with the choice of *hippagretai*: 'Among those of them [i.e. the *hēbōntes*] who are at the peak of their development, the ephors choose three men (*LP* 4.3: αἱροῦνται τοίνυν αὐτῶν οἱ ἔφοροι ἐκ τῶν ἀκμαζόντων τρεῖς ἄνδρας).' The function of αὐτῶν here is to make entirely clear that the *hippagretai* are chosen from among the *hēbōntes*. It is within the latter group that Xenophon distinguishes those whom he calls οἱ ἀκμάζοντες; they are the oldest, those approaching their thirtieth year.[112] Xenophon's words at *Lak. Pol.* 1.6 do not therefore mean that in his view men at Sparta were obliged to marry after the age of 30. One may perhaps keep the view that marriage usually happened after that age, but there was no rule to that effect.

In this as in every other case, our method should be, not to follow Plutarch uncritically but instead to begin by comparing his evidence with that of Xenophon. It is only Plutarch's description of marriage (*Lyc.* 15.4–10) which allows us to form an impression of the stage of married life in which the husband has not yet reached 30 (he still sleeps with his comrades, who are called νέοι, §7). The present passage is the sole support for the hypothesis worked out by Lupi (2000, 75–90), involving a protomatrimonial – or indeed crypto-matrimonial – period.[113] This period of marriage could last for several years; according to Plutarch, it sometimes involved the birth of more than one child.[114] All this would be difficult to understand if it involved people who were fully citizens, adults more than 30 years old. Rather, it would suit the apprentice-citizen, the individual not fully emancipated: in short, the *hēbōn*.

Such is Plutarch's picture, and internally it is consistent. But when it is compared with Xenophon's information (*LP* 1.5–6), something surprising appears. On the one hand, it becomes clear that both writers are dealing with the same thing, namely the beginnings of married life according to the 'Lycurgan' norm, and that many elements of Plutarch's picture are derived from Xenophon: marriage between fully-developed adults, the furtive nature of sexual relations and the justification for this strange custom by reference to the virtue of self-control. On the other hand, however, in Xenophon there is no question of any union between young people or of any phase preliminary to the true cohabitation by which Greek marriage was defined. Xenophon is dealing with the beginnings of *every* marriage, even where such was contracted after the groom was 30; also it seems that in Xenophon's view the groom was over 30 in the great majority of cases, if not in all. Since Plutarch gives details of the wedding night which are not found in Xenophon, he clearly used additional sources, blending them with his Xenophontic material. Xenophon writes only of the virtual 'taboo' on sexual relations, and this concerns all young married couples. My own suggested conclusion is entirely in keeping with what we know from elsewhere of the working of Spartan society; to marry before 30 was not forbidden by any law, but it was not the usual practice.

Finally: *hair-style*. According to Xenophon (*LP* 11.3, the context being military organization) Lycurgus 'also allowed men beyond the age of *hēbē* to let their hair grow long (ἐφῆκε δὲ καὶ κομᾶν τοῖς ὑπὲρ τὴν ἡβητικὴν ἡλικίαν), thinking that this would make them seem taller, more free and more fearsome'. The expression ἡβητικὴ ἡλικία may at first glance seem equivalent to ἥβη, which at Sparta began at 20, as we have seen. This indeed is the view of David,[115] who inferred from this passage that the *hēbōntes* of the classical period had the right to wear their hair long; this seems logical enough, given what Xenophon reports as the purpose of the long hair and the fact that the *hēbōntes* fought in the army. Apparent support is given by another passage of the *Lak. Pol.* (13.9), but there the text seems corrupt and the meaning is unclear. The manuscripts read: ἔξεστι δὲ τῷ νέῳ καὶ κεκριμμένῳ εἰς μαχὴν συνιέναι, 'a young man is allowed to go into battle with his comrades, even if he has been judged (??)'. Some emendations import the idea of hairstyle. Thus Weiske suggested κομὴν διακεκριμένῳ, 'with the hair divided by a parting', and Sauppe proposed κεκτενισμένῳ, 'combed'. Other emendations have been drastically different: Marchant gives κεχριμένῳ [sc. ἐλαίῳ], 'anointed', a suggestion which would appeal if men went into battle naked, and if the verb χρίνειν were not first attested in the Septuagint. Den Boer, on the other hand, preserves the manuscript reading, and translates 'who has succeeded in the tests', i.e. has successfully completed his *paideia* (1954, 285). However, apart from the fact that this amounts to a gloss rather than a translation, on this version the word καὶ becomes incomprehensible (one would have to take it to mean something like 'on condition that'). Indeed, this καὶ, because apparently concessive, presents a problem for all the emendations given above. In summary, the text is certainly unsound, its meaning is not clear, and the passage cannot be used as a source for young men's hairstyle.

We return to the ἡβητικὴ ἡλικία, the age which, according to Xenophon, a man needed to have passed before he was allowed to wear his hair long. Another passage of the *Lak. Pol.* shows – beyond any doubt, in my view – that the age in question was not 20. At 4.7, after finishing his treatment of the *hēbōntes*, Xenophon states that eligibility for magistracies is given 'to those who have passed' the age in question: τοῖς τὴν ἡβητικὴν ἡλικίαν πεπερακόσι. This shows that, for Xenophon, ἡβητικὴ ἡλικία, as distinct – it now appears – from ἥβη, is the period during which one is *hēbōn*. So, for Xenophon, so far as we can tell, the *hēbōn* did not have the right to wear his hair long.

This idea, to repeat, is most surprising given the military function of hairstyle, since not only did the *hēbōntes* fight in battle but they fought in the front ranks. We should, however, need to accept the point and move on, were it not that Plutarch has the exactly opposite idea. In *Lyc.* 22.2, after stating that the Spartan discipline became rather less onerous during a campaign (as one might expect), he gives hairstyle as an example: διὸ κομῶντες εὐθὺς ἐκ τῆς τῶν ἐφήβων ἡλικίας μάλιστα παρὰ τοὺς κινδύνους ἐθεράπευον τὴν κόμην, 'for this reason, having worn their hair long since the age of *ephēbeia*, they took particular care of their hairstyle at times of danger'. Here the relaxation of the Spartan discipline consists not in being allowed to let the hair grow long – that had been the case 'since the *ephēbeia*' – but in being allowed to take great care of it. In Greece the age of *ephēbeia*, both in Plutarch's time and in the classical period and more generally, was 18–20.

Attempts have of course been made to reconcile the accounts of Xenophon and Plutarch. These have involved dissociating the two passages of Xenophon from each other: that is, claiming that the phrase τὴν ἡβητικὴν ἡλικίαν does not mean the same thing at 11.3 ὑπὲρ τὴν ἡβητικὴν ἡλικίαν (on long hair) as it does in 4.7 τοῖς τὴν ἡβητικὴν ἡλικίαν πεπερακόσι (on eligibility for magistracies). Following a suggestion of MacDowell's (1986, 167), Lupi claims that 'the age of *hēbē*' could be conceived from two different view-points (2000, 34–5). It could either be seen as a point in time (the age at which a person became *hēbōn*, i.e. the age of 20), or as a length of time (the age during which a person was *hēbōn*): context would show which. One may well concede this, but the problem remains: how are we to assign different meanings in their present respective contexts to ὑπὲρ and πεπερακότες? The former word always means that some limit, whether a precise date or a period, has been reached, passed and left behind – and that is exactly the meaning of the latter term, the perfect participle πεπερακότες.

It remains for us to explain the contradiction between the two authors. The most obvious, and most widely accepted,[116] explanation is as follows: Plutarch's expression is sufficiently similar to Xenophon's for it to have been conceivably derived from the latter, and in 'translating' τὴν ἡβητικὴν ἡλικίαν for the benefit of his contemporaries Plutarch mistook its meaning, overlooking the passage at 4.7 which would have clarified the matter. Now, this is indeed quite possible, but there does remain a difficulty. The widely-used expression εὐθὺς ἐκ παίδων does not mean 'from the time when childhood is left behind', as one might be forgiven for supposing, but 'from the time of childhood onwards'; εὐθὺς ἐκ involves inclusive counting. Thus εὐθὺς ἐκ τῆς τῶν ἐφήβων ἡλικίας means from (and including) the time of *ephēbeia*,[117] whereas if he had done no more than try to follow Xenophon, while misunderstanding him, Plutarch should have inferred from the phrase ὑπὲρ τὴν ἡβητικὴν ἡλικίαν that the age of *hēbē* was excluded. This being so, it is conceivable that Plutarch combined Xenophon with another source, which leaves open the possibility that Spartan practice had changed in the meanwhile.

That Sparta's young adults were subject to so many disqualifications, so many marks of inferiority, may cause surprise. Two considerations may help to clarify the matter. Firstly, Sparta seems to differ from other *poleis* not so much by the fact of having such features as by having so many of them. This has been observed by Kennell, and one of the texts he cites, (1995, 207 n. 14) that of Teles of Megara, gives a very good example, concerning Athens. For a man aged between 20 and 30 not to have full citizen-rights is thus, to a degree, a fact of Greek life. Secondly, our understanding of Sparta's treatment of the young has been advanced by Lupi's application of the ethnological concept of a 'generational society'. Greece in general, and

Sparta to a unique degree, was structured around three generations: sons (up to the age of 30); fathers (30–60) and the elderly (over 60). Although they were physiologically adults, the *hēbōntes* nevertheless belonged socially to the class of sons; this explains why they were not considered to have full membership of the civic community.[118]

Notes

[1] Plut. *Apophth. Lac.* Anon. 54, *Mor.* 235b. After the defeat at Megalopolis (331), Eteokles refuses to give Antipatros fifty children as hostages, because they would remain uneducated, τῆς πατρίου ἀγωγῆς ἀτευκτήσαντες.

[2] Stob. *Flor.* 40.8, p. 28 Hense². On this passage, see below (pp. 149–50) (τὸν μὲν μετασχόντα τῆς ἀγωγῆς καὶ ἐμμείναντα...)

[3] *Laws* 2.666e, on which see above (p. 59). At 659d ἀγωγή is linked with ὁλκή and means (the act of) leading.

[4] We recall that the Spartan education system is criticized by Plato precisely for not being a form of taming.

[5] *Disciplina* is, in any case, the Latin word used by Livy (45.28.4) to translate ἀγωγή.

[6] Simply 'education': Teles ap. Stob. 40.8; Plut. *Ages.* 1.2; 3.5. Rather 'education': Plut. *Cleom.* 37.14. Rather 'discipline': Plut. *Lyc.* 22.1 (referred to later, §3, as δίαιτα). Most probably 'discipline': Plut. *Cleom.* 18.4. Certainly 'discipline': Plut. *Kleom.* 3.1.

[7] ἡ πάτριος ἀγωγή: certainly 'education' at Plut. *Apophth. Lac.*, Anon. 54, *Mor.* 235b (though see below). Probably 'education': Plut. *Inst. Lac.* 11, *Mor.* 237d. Meaning 'discipline': Plut. *Inst. Lac.* 42, *Mor.* 240b, *Philop.* 16.9 (parallelling πολιτεία). ἡ Λακωνικὴ ἀγωγή occurs only at Polyb. 1.32.1 ('education'). ἡ Λυκουργεῖος ἀγωγή: certainly 'education' at Hesych. s.v. ἄφορτος. Probably 'discipline': Plut. *Philop.* 16.8 (in connection with τοῖς Λυκούργου νόμοις). ἡ λεγομένη ἀγωγή: 'education' at Plut. *Phoc.* 20.4. 'Discipline' at Plut. *Cleom.* 11.3 (cf. supra, Introd. [4–5]).

[8] Compare, in the Cretan town of Gortyn, the pairs *anēbos/hēbiōn* and *apodromos/dromeus*.

[9] The most thorough existing treatment of age-classes is that of Tazelaar 1967; MacDowell gives a simplified account (1986, 159–67), qqv. for earlier bibliography and discussion of detail.

[10] On this problem, below, pp. 94–5.

[11] According to the *editio princeps*, H. Stein, *Herodotus* (1871), II 465.

[12] Diller 1941.

[13] These interpretations are now of merely historiographic interest. They are given in Den Boer 1954, 251–2 and Birgalias 1999, 60–4.

[14] For detailed analysis of differences between the two texts, Tazelaar 1967, 132–3.

[15] In Strabonian version, ιδ' and α' could equally well correspond with ordinals (as indeed they do in what follows) as with cardinals. That we are in fact dealing with cardinals is shown by the Herodotean gloss (where the numbers are given as full words) and by the plural ἔτων.

[16] For bibliography on what follows, Kennell 1995, 20 nn. 105–6.

[17] On how the two elements were combined, Tazelaar 1967, 134–5.

[18] Above, pp. xi–xiv.

[19] Similarly Lupi 2000, 30–1 and 45; he believes that Aristophanes possessed reliable documentation on the education system of the classical period. Likewise Christien 1997, who however considers that the classes named are not year-groups.

[20] Cf. Kennell 1995, 31 with the table on his p. 39.

[21] The first stage of strengthening is the form *pampais*, found also at Lebadeia and Khalkis in the 2nd century; this is compatible with the argument above (p. xiv) on the date at which the *agōgē* was transformed into an *ephēbeia*.

[22] On the unavailing attempts of scholars to explain this word see Den Boer 1954, 254 n. 3.

[23] Tazelaar 1967, 140.

[24] Tazelaar, as we have seen, uses Plutarch to 'correct' the glosses, for which he is rightly criticized by Kennell (1995, 32).

[25] Singor 1999, 71.

[26] These communities are listed at Calame 1977, 376, and Kennell 1995, 108 (with 204 n. 62).

[27] *Lyc.* 16.7, 8, 13; 17.2.

[28] *Laws* 2.666e: οἷον ἀθρόους πώλους ἐν ἀγελῇ νεμομένους φορβάδας τοὺς νέους κέκτησθε (discussed above, p. 59).

[29] As Kennell does, for whom the *boua* 'was probably instituted as part of the hellenistic *agōgē*' (1995, 183 n. 62).

[30] On the Spartans' invention in the imperial period of a special 'agogic language', see the convincing arguments of Kennell (1995, 89–93).

[31] Thus Cartledge-Spawforth 1989, 203–4.

[32] The expression κατ' οἶκον is noteworthy. Its normal meaning is 'in the house'. Here it can only mean the children's *syssition*, in which case the latter would be housed in a permanent structure in town, like the adult *syssitia*.

[33] Mainly, *Vaticanus graecus* 1335 (12th century) and *Venetus marcianus* 511 (13th century).

[34] On this see below, in the section on the *eirenes*.

[35] As suggested by Marchant (Loeb edn 7.142 n. 1). I do not follow Ollier on this point; I find ἔχειν perfectly correct. The expression σῖτος τοσοῦτον (adv.) ἔχων seems to have been misunderstood by many editors and commentators.

[36] Rather, the section of Xenophon which corresponds to Justin's expression would be καὶ σῖτον δὲ ἔταξεν αὐτοῖς ὡς μήτε ὑπερπληροῦσθαι μήτε ἐνδεεῖς γίγνεσθαι (5.3).

[37] Ollier 1934, vii. συμβολεύειν explains why the text has ἔχοντα, and not (as in Stobaeus) ἔχειν, which is more natural with συμβουλεύειν. συμβολατεύειν must be rejected; while undoubtedly attested (Epicharmus, fr. 100 Kaibel, at Athen. 9.374e), and initially suggested here by Dindorf, it does not give suitable sense: its context seems to require something like 'to traffick'. Cf. the gloss of Hesychius: συμβολατεύειν· συναλλακτεύειν.

[38] Lipka 2002, 123 adopts the reading συμβάλλειν (a *lectio facilior*!) and deletes ἔχοντα – unnecessarily, in my view.

[39] On this idea, which some historians have adopted, see Hodkinson 2000, 198; without explicitly accepting συμβολεύειν, Hodkinson believes, like the present writer, that the members of the children's *syssition* had to finance their own meal.

[40] Singor 1999, 71–2. *Contra*, Lévy 2003, 69–72.

[41] Though note the (implicit) reasoning of Kennell (1995, 110 and n. 81): that since

the *agōgē* of the Roman period began at 16 and (Kennell's) hellenistic *agōgē* began at 14, Plutarch's reference to the age of 7 can only apply to the classical period. This is to confuse education and *ephēbeia*; I do not believe that, for example, the education of young Spartiates in the Roman period began only at 16.

42 Ollier 1934, 25–6; Kennell 1995, 117.

43 Lupi 2000, 40–2.

44 On this transition, see above, p. 24. Such is the picture given by the *Lycurgus*. However, in the *Phocion* (20.4) we see Phocion having his son educated at Sparta and 'putting the μειράκιον in with the νεανίσκοι in order to follow τὴν λεγομένην ἀγωγήν', terms more compatible with Xenophon's scheme than with Plutarch's.

45 Murr 1969, 50.

46 Amigues 1989, 275.

47 See Chantraine, *Dict. Etym.* s.v. σκυρθάλιος.

48 This form σκύθραξ seems to the present writer to shed light on the problematic Σκύθαι found in Photius' gloss on the word συνέφηβος, the subject of various modern attempts at exegesis.

49 Le Roy 1961, 223–7. Robert, *REG* 75 (1962), *Bull. Epig.* 159, dates the inscription earlier.

50 Hippocrates, *De Hebdomadibus* 5 (Littré VIII p. 636); cf. Kennell 1995, 32 and 179 n. 13.

51 Cobet 1858, 728.

52 Kennell 1995, 179 n. 7.

53 Kukofka 1993, 197–205.

54 That information is collected below, chapter 9.

55 Above, p. 12.

56 This is the explanation to which Kennell adheres (1995, 121, 125).

57 This punishment recalls that of the 'tremblers'.

58 As Richer has suggested (1999, 110, n. 106).

59 As, for example, by Singor 1999.

60 It is possible that adults other than the *eirēn* could in certain cases (involving 'inspections') have attended the young people's meal; Plut. (*Lyc.* 18.6) implies as much.

61 Singor 1999, 78: 'placing the moment of the admission formally at age 20, but *de facto* at age 12...'

62 For example, Ollier 1934, 34; Flacelière on Plut. *Lyc.* (PUF) 136 n. 2. It seems to me that Xenophon's expression, ἐπειδὰν εἰς τὸ φιλιτιόν γε ἀφίκωνται, 'each time that they go to the common meal', precisely because it implies a certain frequency, suggests also that these were only occasional visits.

63 On Crete the custom had points both of similarity and of difference. Until the age of 17 (a figure given only by a single gloss), young people attended the men's common meals. Thereafter they had their own *syssition* (Ephoros, fr. 149 ap. Strab. 10.4.20).

64 Kennell 1995, 14–17.

65 1995, 119–20. We shall see later (n. 77) that the suggested etymological connection is deemed impossible by specialists.

66 See above all Den Boer 1954, 288–98. Nafissi 1991, 302 nn. 108–9 and Lupi 2000, 47–9, attempt to justify the traditional emendation to ἰρένες. Lupi's main argument is that the division of the Spartan dead into three different graves can only have followed the criterion of age. However, since one of the graves was for helots, the criterion was

one of social class. Christien 1997, 68 n. 111 retains the reading ἱρέες.

[67] Further, it would surely be surprising if all those to whom the prize for bravery was awarded were under the age of 30.

[68] This would explain why Xenophon writes <u>τὸν</u> εἴρενα. This also applies to the text of the manuscripts.

[69] Lipka (2002, 130) argues similarly.

[70] It is theoretically possible that Xenophon used ἄρρην to 'translate' into normal Greek a Lakonian term which was (as we shall see) ἴρης. Unfortunately, this idea must be discounted, since the meaning of ἄρρην is well defined, and it is not 'young man'.

[71] See above, p. 73, on the fact that the *eirēn* does not form part of the category of *paides* – in spite of what the Strabonian version (alone) seems to say.

[72] MacDowell 1986, 162.

[73] For a similar usage, *Lyc.* 14.6.

[74] On this usage, see Kennell 1995, 36.

[75] Busolt-Swoboda 1926, 696 n. 2.

[76] In reality this system of counting applies equally to subsequent time and to previous time: it makes no difference as to which direction one moves in.

[77] Hesychius' way of declining the word – οἱ πρωτεῖρες, τοὺς πρωτείρας, as if the nominative singular were *πρωτειρ – is puzzling. However, his accusative form πρωτείρας is perfectly compatible with the nominative form πρωτεῖραι given by Photius, and the latter is thus acceptable. On the recorded forms of the word *eirēn*, cf. Den Boer 1954, 248 n. 3 and add what seems to be the authentic Laconian form, ἴρης (Kennell 1995, 120). The existence of this form ἴρης invalidates the link with ἔρσην, the Ionic form of ἄρσην/ἄρρην, on which Kennell's argument depends (Chantraine, *Dict. Etym.* s.v. εἴρην).

[78] Themelis 1999, 146–7.

[79] Tazelaar 1967, 141–3 with references there to earlier scholars of the same opinion.

[80] This may be the explanation of why they are the only ones to appear in inscriptions: about to become citizens, they are beginning to take part in public life.

[81] This is probably the role to which Hesychius refers: ἴρανες· οἱ εἴρενες, οἱ ἄρχοντες ἡλικιῶται, Λάκωνες (ἡλικιῶται is rather obscure), and perhaps also the same ἅμπαιδες ('those with the children')· οἱ τῶν παίδων ἐπιμελούμενοι παρὰ Λάκωσι – but this latter gloss may rather mean all kinds of person concerned with looking after children.

[82] We cannot therefore agree with Tazelaar (1967, 150) that one could be called ἡβῶν up till the age of 60.

[83] Tazelaar 1967, 146.

[84] Xenophon himself treats the *neoi* as a a category extending as far as the age of 30 (*Mem.* 1.2.35). This age-limit is also found at Messene in the1st century AD (inscription published by Themelis; *Prakt. Arch. Het.* 1996, 153). Likewise education in Arkadia, as described by Polybius (4.20), lasted until the age of 30.

[85] So also Hodkinson 1983, 250.

[86] Schwartz 1976, 177–8. Cf. Kennell 1995, 117.

[87] On the structure of Xenophon's argument, see above, pp. 17–18.

[88] This is confirmed by the words attributed to Pedaritos in an apophthegm which exists in three different versions (*Lyc.* 25.6; *Mor.* 191f and 231b), about the non-selection of the latter as one of the *hippeis*; 'I am delighted', he said, 'that the city has 300 citizens better than I'. Cf. Ducat 2002.

[89] Thus Ollier 1934, 34, followed by Tazelaar 1967, 142. Cf. Kennell 1995, 132.

[90] Contrast Lupi 2000, 52 who believes that the picture of a wholly collective lifestyle corresponds with the reality of the classical period.

[91] Lupi 2000, 50.

[92] According to the (particularly precise) analysis of Xenophon (*Hell.* 4.5.13–18) this unorthodox procedure gave rise to the disaster at Lechaion.

[93] Kennell 1995, 129; Singor 1999, 75.

[94] Agatharchides (2nd century BC) 86 F 10, in Athenaeus 12.550c–d. This passage is taken up by Aelian (*VH* 14.7) who adds that the ephors punished offenders. This is an extract from Agatharchides' Book 27 which, according to Jacoby, dealt with the reforms of Agis IV. In any event, the practice in question is not represented as an innovation, but as a traditional Spartan custom; given their military role, it is entirely plausible that the *hēbōntes* underwent physical inspection. (Whether the inspection needed to extend to clothing and sleeping arrangements is not so clear.)

[95] On these, Roussel 1939, 64.

[96] 4.132.3; for the various problems arising from this passage, see the commentaries of Gomme and Hornblower.

[97] The fact that posts of such importance could be entrusted to *hēbōntes* seems to me to prove that this age-category did indeed extend to the age of 30; a very young man would hardly be suitable.

[98] Cf. Rebenich 1998b, 350 and n. 92.

[99] It is surprising to see Xenophon, who knew Sparta very well, employing this extreme and obviously overstated idea; he does so to point the contrast between this ancestral custom, which he says is no longer respected, and the behaviour of Spartans in his own day.

[100] Harpokration, who preserves the fragment of Aristotle, observed the difference between the latter and Isocrates.

[101] Cf. Nilsson 1912, 311.

[102] Ducat 1999b, 64 n. 25. For *agora* as assembly, Hdt. 6.58 and also the Great Rhetra, if one accepts the emendation δᾶμω δ' ἀγορᾷ. On this interpretation cf. Tazelaar 1967, 141.

[103] *Pol.* 3.1278a25–6; 6.1321a26–31. See the commentary thereon of Lupi (2000, 53–9).

[104] 'No young man will go to do his shopping in the *agora*' (οὐδ' ἀγοράσει γ' ἀγένειος οὐδεὶς ἐν ἀγορᾷ). This is exactly the same idea as in Plutarch.

[105] This is the view of Hodkinson (2000, 85), who also makes the connection with the 'tremblers' of Sphakteria. Lupi (2000, 55–7) sees this matter as evidence of the contempt in classical Greece for vulgar and money-making activities; but this does not explain why at Sparta the ban should have been lifted at the age of 30.

[106] Singor 1999, 77; he is wrong in seeing Hodkinson as the originator of this curious concept.

[107] The problem is well discussed by Cartledge (2001, 97–8); on the beard as criterion, see the references he collects at p. 209 n. 31.

[108] So Lupi (2000, 72 n. 26).

[109] At the time of the Sphodrias affair, Archidamos, still a *hēbōn* (if indeed such categories applied to the heir apparent of a king), was the *erastēs* of Kleonymos. Should we perhaps suppose that a *hēbōn* might be either *erōmenos* or *erastēs* (though not, of course,

both at once)? Was it a question of age?

[110] Kennell 1995, 132.

[111] Kennell 1995, 207 nn. 12 and 14, quotes texts to this effect; the most conclusive is that of Teles.

[112] So Tazelaar 1967, 146. The fact that it is possible to have this distinction, among the *hēbōntes*, between the youngest and the oldest is one more point in favour of the longer, rather than the shorter, duration of that stage of youth.

[113] Lupi writes of 'hidden marriage'. I would prefer Hodkinson's expression 'furtive' (1989, 109), for what is hidden is not the fact of the marriage (the young Spartan has previously 'carried off' his wife, an official act, following an agreement reached between the two *oikoi*), but their sexual relations. In various ways Lupi appears to have extrapolated far beyond Plutarch's actual words.

[114] This shows, *pace* Lupi, that the sexual relations between the young husband and wife involved intercourse of a wholly 'normal' kind.

[115] David 1992, 13 n. 9.

[116] Cf. Kennell 1995, 207 n. 12.

[117] So Link 1994, 111 n. 23, though he appears to value Plutarch's testimony above that of Xenophon, which is not in accordance with orthodox method.

[118] Cf. the ineligibility of young adults for magistracies and, at Athens, for membership of the Boule.

4

THE HIDDEN FACE OF SPARTAN EDUCATION

The sources do not tell us everything about the Spartan education system. This is especially true of the sources from the classical period, and notably of Xenophon, the most important of them, who leaves out anything which does not fit his purpose. There are thus aspects of this education system which, though not deliberately obscured, do not appear, despite their importance. Clearly, before we look at possible interpretations, it is important to take full account of these gaps, so that we are dealing with as complete a picture as possible.

Spartan *paideia* as elementary education

Education at Sparta naturally included the acquisition of the basic competences necessary to a man and a citizen; in this respect it was a *paideia* of the usual Greek kind.

First, *reading, writing and arithmetic*. There are texts which assert that the Spartans of the classical period hardly bothered to teach these techniques to their children. The most extreme in expression is a paragraph of the *Dissoi Logoi* (2.10): 'For some it is a good thing for children not to learn *mousikē* and their letters; for the Ionians it is shameful not to know all of this.' The Spartans are not named, to be sure, but it is clear that they are intended; it has to be the Dorians who are opposed to the Ionians, and mention of Dorians immediately brings Sparta to mind. Further, this is a strange opposition; it is unusual to present the Dorians in general as uncultivated (think for example of the Cretans' reputation), even if poetry was thought of as originating in East Greece. Moreover, it is difficult to believe someone who says that the Spartans were not interested in *mousikē* (an entity made up of music, poetry, song and dance); it was generally accepted in Greece, on the contrary, that the Spartans were specialists in such activities. This text, then, discredits itself by its exaggerations. In the *Panathenaicus* (209), Isocrates, as we have seen (above, p. 46), asserts that the Spartans 'do not even learn their letters' (οὐδὲ γράμματα μανθάνουσιν). But this is in the anti-Spartan section of the speech, a section which at §232 the author recognizes to be full of exaggeration; and, at §251, the Laconophile pupil, who is not of course expressing

Isocrates' point of view, but is not for all that talking at random, implicitly contradicts his master's allegation by adducing the Spartans who read his works (something which goes a very long way beyond the simple mastery of *grammata*). Our final text concerns not letters but numbers: in the *Hippias Major* (285c), Plato (if the text is his) makes the Elean sophist say that 'many of them do not even know, so to speak, how to count' (above, p. 67 n. 27). Here too, there is much exaggeration, and the whole discussion shows that the author does not endorse this idea at all; Hippias is always talking naively, and he is constantly ridiculed. These three texts, then, all raise serious reservations, some of which are indeed suggested by the authors themselves; they nevertheless express what was clearly a commonplace in Greece: that Spartan education was dramatically insufficient from an intellectual point of view. Plutarch, who, unlike Xenophon, integrates elementary education into his account of Spartan education, states things in a much more nuanced and therefore interesting way: γράμματα μὲν οὖν ἕνεκα τῆς χρείας ἐμάνθανον (*Lyc.* 16.10). If we translate, as does Talbert, 'the boys learned to read and write no more than was necessary', this phrase is just as brutal a condemnation as the three other texts; but it seems to me that this forces the sense, which is more neutral: 'they learned their letters because of their usefulness'. There is indeed some reservation here, but it is concerned less with the quality of the apprenticeship than with its aim: the latter was, according to Plutarch, utilitarian and not cultural. This theme of 'learning what is useful' can be found in one of the Spartan sayings.[1] Others take up, in order to overturn it, the theme of Spartan 'ignorance'; they make a virtue of it. One such saying is attributed to the king Pleistoanax:[2] 'An Athenian orator was calling the Spartans ignorant (ἀμαθεῖς) in front of Pleistoanax, son of Pausanias: that is fair, said Pleistoanax, because we are the only Greeks who have learnt nothing bad from you.' Another is pronounced by Zeuxidamos, father of Archidamos:[3] 'it is better to accustom yourself to virtue than to apply yourself to the study of written texts.' This does not mean that the Spartans considered themselves to be uncultivated; these sayings are a kind of 'return of service', which uses their own arguments against malicious interlocutors.

All of this is image; what was the reality? We have no direct documentation for elementary education at Sparta, its level, the way in which it was dispensed and to whom it was addressed (all or just some?). The only way to get an idea of it is to try to assess its results, that is the average level of the Spartans' elementary education. Two enquiries were conducted simultaneously and independently into this issue, by Cartledge and Boring.[4] It is significant that they arrived at the same conclusions; it is no less so that the recent re-examination of the material by Millender[5] led her to conclude that her predecessors had tended rather to underestimate the role of writing in the Spartans' public and private life. Neither the small number of inscriptions nor the rarity of writers was related to literacy levels. These traits, at this period, were not peculiar to Sparta, and all kinds of indications show that the level of basic education there was comparable to that of other Greek cities. All we know of Spartan history in the fifth and fourth centuries suggests that the majority of citizens knew how to read and write quite sufficiently; the internal administration and external politics of a city of the first rank, which was at various moments the leader of the major part of the Greek world, would be done largely by writing and would presuppose basic knowledge. One might object that this knowledge could have been the preserve of a restricted elite. However, most of the everyday management, internal and external, was in the hands of the ephors, who were elected from amongst all the citizens; Aristotle, who is very criticical of this institution, even says: from amongst anyone who happened by, οἱ τυχόντες.[6] The rotation, resulting from the generally-agreed fact that you could only be elected ephor once in your life, effectively gave every Spartiate a real chance to become an ephor one day. This system could not have functioned if the majority of citizens had been completely ignorant. How this apprenticeship worked, we do not know; but everything suggests that it existed, and that it was effective.

But, at Sparta as in all classical cities, written expression remained secondary to *oral expression*. Moreover, according to contemporary and later Greeks, apprenticeship in oral expression – in a certain kind of oral expression – was a Spartan speciality. This form of expression was called 'laconism' (τὸ λακωνίζειν).[7] Plutarch stresses the fact that it was the object of a systematic apprenticeship during education: 'They taught the boys to express themselves in a style sharp but mixed with grace and profound in its brevity' (*Lyc.* 19.1). Aristotle had already said something similar, judging by Herakleides' paraphrase: 'From childhood they learn to speak briefly (μελετῶσι δὲ εὐθὺς ἐκ παίδων βραχυλογεῖν), and also to mock and to be mocked in a suitable fashion';[8] and Plato concludes his eulogy of Spartan brevity thus (*Protagoras* 342e): 'the ability to deliver such words is the deed of none but the perfectly educated man (τελέως πεπαιδευμένου ἀνθρώπου)'. One might have thought that apprenticeship of this sort in self-expression would have happened by absorption, as a result of living in a society which made an ideal of it; but all these texts show that it was conscious and deliberate, and that it constituted part of the *paideia*.

As the texts already cited show, laconism is not a late element of the Spartan image. It appeared perhaps already in epic: the way in which the *Iliad* (3.214) characterizes Menelaos' speech ('few words, but very clear-cut') strongly suggests an allusion to this trait. In Herodotos' time,[9] laconism is obviously something known by all, and the same goes for Ion of Chios. Then

Thucydides, Plato and Aristotle take up the theme.[10] It is Plato who puts it best. Let us re-read the *Protagoras* passage:[11] 'If you want to have a good discussion with the most ordinary Lacedaemonian, you will find him at first, in general, rather weak in his arguments; but then, wherever you may have got to in the discussion, suddenly, like a javelin expert, he throws in a word full of sense, brief and concise, so well that his interlocutor seems to be little better than a child. Both now and in the past many people have understood that laconism (τὸ λακωνίζειν) was much more philosophy than sport.' Far from being poor or hesitant speech, Laconian speech presupposes a whole philosophy of speaking. This has as its foundation a double dialectic. First, the dialectic of speech and action (evident in Thucydides 2.40.2). These two ideas are always in opposition for the Greeks, and it is true that for the Spartans indefinitely prolonged speech impeded action; but they went beyond this opposition in privileging a type of speech which, as Plato underlines by his metaphor of the javelin-thrower, is just as effective as action and is, indeed, in itself an act. A discussion is a combat, and the winner is not the one who says the most, but the one whose words reduce the other to silence. Subterfuge is also permitted: here this consists of feigning awkwardness, at the start, in order to make the interlocutor believe that he will win easily, until the moment when, just as he least expects it, a fatal 'word' nails him to the spot.

The other dialectic is that of speech and silence. David,[12] with his usual subtlety, has demonstrated the place occupied by silence in Sparta's value-system – it is tempting to speak of a fascination with silence. Laconic speech stands out against a background of silence. It is *prepared* by a phase of silence, which makes reflection possible and the preparation of effective speech. As Plutarch says (*Lyc.* 19.2): 'In the case of the currency of speech, (Lycurgus) did the opposite: by means of a few simple words he was able to express rich and subtle ideas; by the prevalence of silence he made the boys aphoristic and trained them in the art of repartee.' It also *ends* in silence, one of the interlocutors having said what he had to say in a few words, and the other being reduced to silence. One might say that laconic speech goes beyond the speech-silence opposition: its extreme concision gives the impression that silence is at the very heart of this speech, just as, in Sartre's philosophy, nothingness is at the heart of conscience. This is expressed by a saying which Stobaios attributes to Lycurgus (35.11): ' "Why do the Spartans train themselves in brevity?" "Because", he said, "it is close to silence." ' As if laconic speech combined the advantages of communication and silence.

This theory of 'laconism', formulated by Plato, is probably not Spartan in origin. For the Spartans, the brevity they practised was above all a *technique* allowing them to embue speech with a maximum of sense and thus make it a weapon – laconism, indeed, is conducive to sense. By what we might call 'the fragment effect', the fewer the words the more weight they have. But, of course, this is not enough; such speech must also be formulated with the formal perfection of a maxim. The apophthegm, which eventually became a literary form, was a Spartan speciality. The effect is further enhanced if the maxim is not heavily didactic, but ironic, light or witty: this is why Aristotle (fr. 611.13 Rose) associated apprenticeship in mockery with that in brevity. On the one hand, laconism is indeed, as David says, the linguistic form of austerity;[13] but it is also a refinement of spirit and a highly cultural product. It is, then, this complex technique which was taught to the boys; Plutarch is quite right to include his discussion of laconism in his account of education, stressing (*Lyc.* 19.1–3) the fact that laconism was not an innate gift for the Spartans but the aim and result of a long apprenticeship.[14]

Plutarch concludes his account of education with a chapter on *mousikē* (ch. 21). He begins thus: 'No less care was given to teaching them singing and poetry than to making them learn to speak with accuracy and purity.' Within *mousikē* we can distinguish several forms of expression, poetry, music proper, singing and dance; but for the Greeks these techniques were interwoven and inseparable: poetry was sung, dances could be accompanied by songs, and music was present everywhere. Here, too, we can only gain an idea of the apprenticeship by its results. While the Greeks readily called the Spartans 'uneducated', ἀμαθεῖς, it was also a universally accepted opinion that they were amongst the best connoisseurs and the best practitioners of poetry, music and dance.[15] It would be pointless to give an account here of these arts at Sparta, which would only repeat what has been said countless times before.[16] I shall confine myself to one remark: in all these fields, the great era of creation at Sparta was the archaic period; in the classical period it was already a case of an inheritance, which the Spartans could enrich, but which their primary concern was to pass on. The texts say that the Spartans applied themselves very seriously to this task; thus Athenaeus (14.632f), on music: 'among the Greeks it is the Spartans who best preserved the art of music, because they practised it a great deal, and because they had many composers. Even now they have preserved their ancient songs, and sing them with care and with art.' This transmission could only have been safeguarded by the education of the young.

All this makes it clear that Spartan education included an important element of elementary schooling, and that in this respect it was a *paideia* of the same kind and quality as that of other Greek cities. This observation, it seems to me, sheds new light on what has long conventionally been called the *agōgē* – the features described by Xenophon, on which Isocrates, Plato and Aristotle focused their attention, and which Plutarch recapitulated with new information, only paint the picture (and a partial one at that) of *one aspect* of Spartan education. Insofar as we can call them activities, they are for the most part physical activities, to which it would be natural to add traditional gymnastic activities. The other side remains in the shade (Plutarch is the only source to say a little about them); nonetheless, these intellectual and artistic activities were no less important, to the extent that they certainly occupied a greater place in the timetable of the *paides* and *paidiskoi*. However, it would not do to represent Spartan education as divided between two completely separate types of activity. A significant part of the elementary education probably took place within the framework of some of the practices described by Xenophon: at the children's communal meal, where, if we accept that what Plutarch says on the subject holds good for the classical period, the *eirēn* in charge of the group played an educator's role; in the pederastic relationship, where, with Kennell,[17] we might fairly safely assume that the *erastēs* contributed in transmitting to the *erōmenos* the knowledge and techniques which made up the cultural inheritance of the city.[18] There were also, without any doubt, lessons delivered by school-masters; now is the time to take a look at how they worked.

Education: public/private

All those who have discussed Spartan education have emphasized its public character, compulsory and identical for all, and, in view of the texts (especially, in the classical period, Xenophon and Plato), this opinion is incontrovertibly justified. But it is only valid for the aspect of education which these authors are talking about. The observation that education included another side, at least as important, necessarily leads us to pose the question whether this other side had the same public character.

The role of the family

There has been a general tendency to underestimate the part played in the Spartans' existence by their private life, which unfolded in the framework of the *oikos*. It is true that few texts speak of it, but there was such a thing nonetheless. When he paints the portrait of the 'timocratic man', which is largely inspired by Sparta, Plato underlines the importance of the private domain (*Republic* 8.548a): 'Such men will be eager for wealth, just as much as in oligarchies. In secret, they will fiercely worship gold and silver; they will have private treasure-chests, where they will hide them, and they will entrench themselves within the walls of their homes, as though in nests, where they will spend a great deal on their wife or on anything they want.' This portrait is echoed, perhaps deliberately, by a phrase in Dionysius of Halicarnassus (20, extract 13.2): 'As for what happens inside their houses, the Lacedaemonians neither worry about it nor keep watch over it; they consider the front door to be the frontier of individual liberty.' As Plato's text shows, this private life, which was highly valued, was consecrated to activities which we would call economic, but which equally had social aspects: management of wealth, contracts, arranging of marriages. The bringing up of children, especially that of boys, necessarily featured among these matters which the head of the *oikos* had in his charge.

Everyone recognizes, in any case, that until the age of seven, the age at which education proper began, the child's upbringing belonged exclusively to the family. The importance of this point should not be underestimated: at seven years old the foundation of the child's personality is already in place, and his future depends largely on what has happened during this period. After this age, we should not believe what can often be read, that the boy was 'taken away from his family'. It is impossible that he ceased to have contact with it, and to live within its bosom for an important part of his life. To be sure, as we have seen, he took his main meal outside the home, in his *syssition*; but what of the evenings and nights? He was not yet old enough for the 'barracks'. Plutarch, who tends rather to dramatize Spartan education, only speaks of communal sleeping for his 'older boys', above the age of twelve (*Lyc.* 16.13); since, throughout his account, he places a break in the boys' life at this age,[19] the implication is that, for him, before this they slept individually. As for Xenophon, he does not say anything about collective sleeping. The *paidonomos*, he says (2.2) 'assembles' (ἀθροίζειν) the boys, which seems rather to indicate that they came each morning from their homes,[20] and the pederastic relationship which he describes is inconceivable within a completely collective life. Likewise, the way in which Isocrates describes the practice of theft ('they send them') suggests that the main framework of the boys' life was the family.[21] I think that Plutarch, here as elsewhere, has dramatized and systematized reality. Sleeping out of doors is not an invention, but I think this only happened at certain points in life and for limited periods.

Some texts reflect an image of the Spartan family in which it is the mother who is considered responsible for the education of her children and its results: these are the apophthegms gathered together in the Plutarchan collection of *Sayings of Spartan Women*. Many of these texts present a mother and her son or sons, in a situation related to the ultimate test, war: departure or return. It is the mother who hands the young warrior his arms, who welcomes him after the combat, or buries him. These roles usually belong to the father; in the world of the *Sayings*, everything happens as if all the mothers of warriors were widows. It is the mother who judges the conduct of her son, whether congratulating him, rebuking him, or even punishing him (including capital punishment). She reminds him tirelessly that it is she who has brought him up, but not for herself, for the city, and that because of this she is responsible before the city for his conduct. In the Anonymous Saying 11 (*Mor.* 241d–e), where Pedaritos is supposed to have behaved badly on Chios, it is his mother Teleutia who, after conducting a veritable inquiry, writes to rebuke him. The idea that sons are the product of the mother, and of her alone, is clearly expressed in the Anonymous Saying 9 (*Mor.* 241d): 'When an Ionian woman was boasting of the luxury of one of her own robes,[22] a Spartan woman, showing her four sons, all perfectly educated (κοσμιώτατοι), said: "Here are the products of a noble woman."' Among the four sons there must be some who are more than seven years old, and perhaps even all of them are at least adolescents, for the results of their education to be capable of judgement: but nonetheless it is their mother who considers herself to be the only one responsible.

Perhaps Spartan females were in general strong women – even though some texts raise doubts;[23] but we should not take the sayings as reflections of reality, and it is clear that the *Sayings of Spartan Women* are strongly influenced by the myth of gynaecocracy. In the real Spartan society, it is certainly the father and not the mother who was considered to have the principal responsibility for the education of his sons. This is clearly demonstrated by the text, cited above (pp. 10–11), where Xenophon (*LP* 6.1–2) describes the right of punishment. The context of this passage is the partial communizing of certain material goods at Sparta: slaves, hunting dogs, horses, food. Unlike Plato (though there it is the ideal city which is in question)[24] and Plutarch,[25] Xenophon does not speak of a communization of children; what is shared amongst all fathers of families is simply the right, which becomes a duty, to punish children who misbehave. In all these passages, it is only fathers who are concerned; it is they who have authority.[26] It seems to me improbable that the Spartan father, as has too often been said with blind faith in Plutarch, should be uninterested in what was happening in his family, and in particular in the education of his son, who was destined to replace him in the city. I am convinced, on the contrary, that he passionately followed his son's performance in the education system, all the more so because the boys' progress was observed by the whole city and was not without consequence for the prestige of each *oikos*. Two inscriptions of the classical period can be adduced in support of this point of view. First, the dedication of Arexippos (*IG* 5.1.255, *A.O.* no. 1): he was victor in five boys' contests,[27] and his father – who alone could have commissioned and paid for this stele – wanted his victories to be proclaimed, and their memory preserved, by a monument 'which all can see'. Even better known is the dedication of Damonon (*IG* 5.1.213): after his own victories, equestrian and athletic, Damonon enumerates those of his son Enymakratidas, four of which were won in the *paides* category. This close association suggests that it was the father who trained the son, in order for him to be his successor in this area too, and that throughout his education he followed his progress and his exploits very closely.

So, the education of children involved, at the same time and *in close association*, both the city and the family. This is exactly what Xenophon says in relation to the *paidiskoi* (*LP* 3.3): Lycurgus 'contrived that not only the city representatives (τοὺς ἐκ δημοσίου), but also those responsible for each boy (τοὺς κηδομένους ἑκάστων: this clearly means his closest relatives) would see to it that he avoided bringing complete dishonour on himself in the city by cowardice.'

The problem of pedagogues

Xenophon seems to deny the existence of pedagogues at Sparta. Indeed, for him, on this point as on many others Lycurgus did the opposite to other Greeks (*LP* 2.1 and 2). As soon as children are of an age 'to understand what is said to them', other Greeks 'immediately submit them to pedagogues of servile status (εὐθὺς μὲν ἐπ' αὐτοῖς παιδαγωγοὺς θεράποντας ἐφιστᾶσιν, §1)'. Lycurgus, however, 'instead of allowing each privately to appoint slaves as pedagogues (ἀντὶ μὲν τοῦ ἰδίᾳ ἕκαστον παιδαγωγοὺς δούλους ἐφιστάναι)', placed the children under the authority of the *paidonomos* (§2). The sense appears clear. However, it seems difficult to imagine a Greek education system functioning without pedagogues, if only because someone would have been needed to take the children to their teachers every day and to the exercises organized by the city, in order to supervise and take care of them. It is thus tempting to speculate that, in his desire to set up a systematic opposition between the Spartans' behaviour and that of other Greeks, Xenophon has exaggerated the feature, and that in reality there was not necessarily such a sharp contradiction between *paidonomos* and pedagogues as he seems to express. What he might have meant is not that at Sparta there were no pedagogues at all, but that the only person really in charge and directing the education of the children was the *paidonomos*.

But this interpretation is categorically refuted by what Plato says. In his *Laws*, he presents pedagogues as an institution without which he could not conceive of a good education system: 'just as neither sheep nor any other kind of livestock can live without a shepherd, so children cannot do without pedagogues, nor slaves without masters' (7.808d). This claim may seem surprising, because at the end of the *Lysis* (223ab) a portrait is sketched of pedagogues which is scarcely flattering: they are drunk and speak execrable Greek. The text of the *Laws* shows that we should not take this portrait as condemning the institution; what Plato wants to demonstrate is that fathers too frequently appoint as pedagogues those of their slaves who are incapable of doing anything else.[28] If he considers pedagogues to be indispensable, it is not for the lowly material reasons I outlined above. The idea is the result of profound reflection on the nature of man and the function of education. Man's savagery is innate; it displays itself clearly in the behaviour of children left to themselves. The role of education is to tame this savagery, in order to allow humanity to develop in the man. This training is the work of pedagogues and teachers (7.808d–e; text cited with commentary above, pp. 58–9).

Moreover, one of the principal criticisms made of Sparta in the *Laws* is precisely that in this city *there are no pedagogues*: 'In your cities no one can be seen taking his own [son], snatching him away, all savage and furious, from his companions, in order to place him with a personal groom, calming him and taming him' (2.666e; above, p. 59). Since Spartan education is collective, the native savagery of the child is not tamed there. By the personal relationship (ἰδίᾳ is the keyword of the text) he establishes with the child, the pedagogue, whose sole task this is, imposes his authority on him and offers him a role-model. He represents the *private* element indispensable to any education.

Nevertheless, Plato is fully aware of the objection which Xenophon, in a manner which is perfectly clear for all its implicitness, makes to the institution of pedagogues: everywhere – except at Sparta – such an important and delicate mission is entrusted to slaves. Should pedagogy be a servile art? The matter obviously did not bother the ancients, who found it natural to entrust children to someone who could be truly said to *belong* to the family; it did not occur to them that this task should rather belong to the father. Plato, then, is not trying to refute the argument about servile status, a status which he himself emphasizes in the *Lysis* (208d). He confines himself to saying that a very strict system of supervision, in which all citizens participate, will keep the pedagogues in his city on the straight and narrow (7.808e–809a). This attitude shows how inescapable the institution of pedagogues is for him.

Must we then believe that during his education the Spartan boy had no servant who supervised and took care of him? I do not think so; but it was a young slave and not an adult who fulfilled this function. At least it is thus that, following various historians,[29] I propose to interpret the glosses we have relating to the word μόθων.[30] The glosses in question are those of Harpocration, Hesychius and the *Etymologicum Magnum*, and scholia on Aristophanes, *Knights* 635 and *Wealth* 279. As I have argued elsewhere,[31] I in fact consider that in order to understand these texts we should distinguish between those which concern the word μόθων and those which concern the word μόθαξ;[32] the realities which these two words signify are certainly not unrelated, but they are different.[33] Of these five texts, four present the same definition, the complete formulation of which can be found in Harpocration: 'the Laconians call *mothōnes* children who are brought up side by side with the free children' (μόθωνας δὲ καλοῦσι Λάκωνες τοὺς παρατρεφομένους τοῖς ἐλευθέροις παῖδας). Hesychius' gloss and the two scholia give summarized or abbreviated versions, which renders them occasionally unclear. The *Etymologicum Magnum*, for its part, supplies a completely different definition, 'a slave born in the house' (τὸν οἰκογενῆ δοῦλον); but servile status can be deduced in Harpocration from the opposition between the subjects defined and 'the free children'. From these texts, which thus can be combined, emerges a fairly clear picture of what a *mothōn* might have been. He was a slave; from birth, and who remained one, for no gloss indicates that his *mothōn* condition would have earned him enfranchisement. He was 'born in the house' and so belonged in principle to the category of domestic helots;[34] nevertheless, we cannot exclude the possibility that, in certain particularly wealthy families, there could also have been bought slaves. He was brought up 'side by side with' (παρατρεφόμενος) the son of the house. It is not said explicitly that he played a role in his education (or, more precisely, during his education), but this sense seems to me to be contained within παρατρεφόμενος, and the relationship of the word *mothōn* to its hypocoristic, the word *mothax*, which is itself associated with the *agōgē* by the two most explicit texts (Phylarchos and Aelian), confirms that this was indeed the case. Like Cantarelli, Bruni and Hodkinson, I think that the *mothōn* was brought up within the family, side by side with the young Spartiate, until the latter was seven, as a kind of foster brother;[35] and that then he accompanied him, as a little personal servant, throughout his entire education. However harsh and 'savage' this education may have been, it was not so to the extent of depriving boys of the service of a young slave.

Such was the institution which 'replaced' that of pedagogues at Sparta; but one can see that for the child it fulfilled only the function of 'footman', and not that of an adult capable not only of supervising him (something which a youth of the same, or almost the same, age could not really do anyway), but also, and primarily, of guiding and educating him. This is why Xenophon and Plato are entirely right to assert, one with praise, the other as a criticism, that Sparta was ignorant of the use of pedagogues.

How teaching worked

Among the questions posed by the intellectual and artistic education of young Spartiates, this is surely the most important, and it is at the same time one of the most serious and most difficult problems encountered by anyone who attempts to describe the Spartan education system. The most widely held opinion seems to be that basic lessons (*grammata*, *mousikē*, and even physical education too) happened in an entirely private context; but this is always presented in a very brief, affirmative or allusive manner, as though the matter went without saying (thus, for example, in Piérart 1974, 369 and 371). The opposite opinion is much rarer, but has found a weighty defender in Cartledge (2001, 85), who believes that lessons were given within the context of the *agōgē*; however, he too proceeds by affirmations. Real discussion only appears in Kennell (1995, 125–6), but it remains too much on the level of principle and is a little one-sided. What strikes me is not that opinions differ, but that, whichever one is expressed, it is done as though it were self-evident.

It is true that in order to have a discussion one needs some evidence. No reference to the subject is to be found, though, in sources of the classical period, nor even in Plutarch, the question not even being raised. However, I think we can take as a point of departure what Plato prescribes in his *Laws* (essentially 7.804c–d). In a general way, in fact, as we have already seen (above, p. 54), the words of the Athenian on education take Spartan reality largely into account; moreover, in this particular exposition, he seems to have it especially in mind: it is followed (from 804e) by a discussion of the education of girls, at the end of which, in 806a, Spartan practice in the matter is explicitly described and criticized. Reading Plato raises two precise problems, which can be posed in terms of the public/private opposition: that of premises and that of teachers.

The philosopher foresees that his ideal city will attend to 'the construction of gymnasia at the same time as public schools (οἰκοδομία…γυμνασίων ἅμα καὶ διδασκαλείων κοινῶν) in three locations in the centre of the city' (804c). There is nothing to prevent us thinking that at Sparta likewise lessons were given in public places. It is, however, probable that there was nothing compulsory about this. The situation which existed in the classical period had not been created at a stroke, but resulted from a long history; it is probable, then, that it presented a certain diversity, each case resulting from a particular development. Thus educational locations must often, as elsewhere (and as in Plato), have formed part of gymnasia, some of which might have been public, others private.

Plato is just as precise on the subject of teachers (804d). They are neither slaves, nor citizens, but resident foreigners (ξένους), 'metics' to use Athenian terminology. They are accommodated by the state in school buildings (ἐν τούτοις…οἰκοῦντας). They receive attractive salaries, which are paid to them by the city: this last, essential, point appears further on, in 813e (διδασκάλους τε εἶναι δεῖ κοινούς, ἀρνυμένους μισθὸν παρὰ τῆς πόλεως). They are recruited by the *epimelētēs* of education, who is also charged with supervising the lessons they teach (811d).

How did things happen at Sparta? As far as the teachers' salary is concerned, I do not really think it would have been paid by the city. On the one hand, the latter's budget was clearly rudimentary.[36] On the other, crucially, it seems that such a practice is not in reality attested anywhere in Greece. It is the case that in certain cities teachers are remunerated by the community from special funds, but this practice exists only in the hellenistic period;[37] moreover, this money is not taken from the state budget, but is supplied by foundations established by individuals, which places the practice in the realm of euergetism, rather than representing state control of education. The only possible example is a law attributed to Charondas, which Diodorus claims was applied in Thourioi:[38] teaching of letters there would be compulsory for all citizen children, and the teachers would be paid by the city (χορηγούσης τῆς πόλεως τοὺς μισθοὺς τοῖς διδασκάλοις); but the truth of this information is more than doubtful. Whatever the case, Diodorus specifies that such a measure had been 'neglected by earlier *nomothetai*', which naturally includes Lycurgus. Moreover, we might suppose that if a practice so contrary to the custom of other Greeks had flourished at Sparta, Xenophon would not have failed to mention it in support of his thesis.[39]

On the other hand, as far as the activities of the teachers are concerned, my opinion is that Spartan practice might have resembled that advocated by Plato. Indeed, I can hardly see the *paidonomos* failing to be interested in their recruitment, their conduct, and especially the content of their lessons. This is all the more probable if some of the teachers at least were foreigners, as in the *Laws*. This does not seem to me to be impossible. Of course, *Inst. Lac.* 4 (*Mor.* 237a), after repeating the formula of Plutarch, *Lyc.* 16.10, on the teaching of *grammata*, asserts: 'As for the other disciplines (παιδεύματα) they practised *xenēlasia* towards them, *xenēlasia* of ideas just as much as that of men'. But, on the one hand, this statement is so excessive (to the extent of contradicting Plutarch, *Lyc.* 19–21) that it loses any validity, and, on the other, the real sense of the phrase is not, as is generally believed, that the Spartans were supposed to have expelled very particularly all the bearers of *logoi*, teachers and public speakers, something which would be refuted by the facts we have (remember Hippias' declarations in the dialogue attributed to Plato). What the author (whoever he may be) means is that to the *xenēlasia* spoken of by all the Greeks, which was aimed at foreigners in general, should be added another, less well known one, that of *logoi* (the sense of which term seems to me best approached by the translation 'ideas'). To be conveying ideas which might appear dangerous, these 'lessons' would need to have been at a certain level: what is aimed at are the speeches of sophists and what occupied the position of higher education in Greece.

That foreigners might have been able to teach in Spartan schools seems to me likewise implied by the legend, fabricated in the classical period, which makes Tyrtaios not only an Athenian in origin,[40] but a school master summoned to Sparta.[41] These foreign teachers must have been the object of particular supervision, a concern not only of the *paidonomos* but also of the ephors. All in all, the Spartan *paidonomos*' supervision of teaching must have been closely comparable to that exercised by the *epimelētēs* in the *Laws*.

This leaves us face to face with the mystery of the organization of lessons at Sparta. The problem is not that of knowing whether the young Spartiate went to school, because it is evident that in one way or another he did: this can be seen in the degree of the city's literacy, and it is for this reason that I began this chapter with an examination of the results of basic education. The problem is knowing *what school*, that is knowing if lessons were, like the rest of the education system, public, compulsory and identical for all. Cartledge (2001, 85), thinks that *grammata*, *mousikē* and *gymnasia* were part and parcel of the rest of education, and thus that the school which taught them was a public school. However much of a minority opinion this may be, it has logic entirely on its side. Physical exercises, at the gymnasium and the palaestra, which neither Xenophon nor Plutarch mention, have obvious links with the training and the tests which these authors do describe, to the extent that we might almost say that the latter would be untenable without them. At the same time, they constituted the foundation of the future warrior's training, and made the youths fit enough to participate honourably in the *agōnes* organized by the city. Likewise, teaching of dance and choral singing, which was given within choirs by professionals, educated them to take a worthy part in public festivals, and constituted one of the essential elements of the citizen's training, as is shown by the place these disciplines hold in Plato's city. Moreover, dance, in some of its forms, was considered a preparation for war. As for poetry, it was closely linked with song and dance, and the texts of certain poets, of whom Tyrtaios is the best known, played a front-rank role in the moral and civic education of the young. It is thus obvious that *gymnasia* and *mousikē* should logically have been taught in the same way to all citizen sons. Things are apparently less clear in the case of *grammata*; one might argue that it was in the city's interest to have citizens capable of reading, writing and arithmetic, but it is open to doubt whether the Spartans would have been aware of the fact. In any case, we must not conclude that these lessons were left up to private initiative just because we are ignorant of how they functioned. Is it logical to maintain at the same time that Spartan education was a system organized by the state, compulsory and identical for all, and that the lessons which constituted a good proportion of it (they correspond to what was the entirety of education in most cities) presented exactly the opposite characteristics?

Such an argument is not lacking in force, and it would be convincing if one could believe that human institutions are governed by logic, and that Spartan education was the work of a Lycurgus. In reality, though, it was the product of a history, and could have combined elements of diverse, even contradictory, origins and nature. Logic would indeed mean that the lessons were organized by the state and identical for all, but this logic is not particular to Sparta: it is that of the Greek city in general, as can be seen clearly in Plato's *Laws*; and yet we know very well that in the classical period such lessons were everywhere privatized and fee-paying. What we are inquiring into is not what teaching *ought to have been* at Sparta, but what it actually was. On this point the Cretan parallel contributes nothing. Indeed, Ephoros (in Strabo 10.4.20) says only that 'the children learn their *grammata*', and this does not necessarily mean that this apprenticeship was public and compulsory: we could say the same thing of Athenian children. At Sparta, on the basis of the scene described by Plutarch (*Lyc.* 18.3–6), we might think that basic education in the different subjects was public and compulsory, because it was entrusted to the *eirēn* in charge of the group; but we can see clearly in this text firstly that it was really a matter of 'civic education' and secondly that, if the *eirēn* effectively played a very important pedagogic role, it was in the manner of a prefect rather than a master: tests, revision, practical exercises.

The idea of public teaching at Sparta comes up against a concrete problem, apparently limited, but which one soon realizes overrules all else: that of the teachers' salary. If, as is more than probable, for as we have seen it is the universal custom in classical Greece, it was paid not by the state but by the parents, we are obviously not talking about public schools. If Sparta had been a unique exception in this area, Xenophon would certainly have drawn on it for his argument; his silence makes me think that on this point matters there were just as they were everywhere else.

One solution which springs to mind would be to distinguish amongst the lessons some which might be the city's concern, and others which would be left to private initiative. *Gymnasia* on the one hand, song and dance on the other, are intimately linked to the development of the citizen and so belong to the first category, while *grammata*, poetry and perhaps oral expression too would be a matter for private teachers. But this route quickly turns out to be scarcely practicable. Why entrust 'laconism', which is one of the characteristics of Spartan identity, to private persons? Can poetry be separated from singing and dance? How would the two types of teaching be harmonized to make up a coherent educational programme? All in all, it would be better to suppose (without claiming any certainty) that only the aspect of education described by Xenophon was compulsory for all, the elementary-education aspect, despite its essential role in the formation of the citizen, being left to the initiative of families. This compels us to concede that, for example, the children were not all part of a choir, did not all attend a gymnasium; thus, however surprising this might appear in the city of the *homoioi*, that there was major inequality in terms of education. It is perhaps this situation which was the root of the Spartans' reputation for not being very interested in elementary education.

Economic aspects of education

A fragment of Phylarchos (81 F 43), cited by Athenaeus (6.271e–f), which gives a definition of the term *mothakes*, reports that at Sparta 'each of the children of citizen status takes, in accordance with what his means allow, either one or two *syntrophoi*, and some even more'. We shall return to the question of *mothakes* later; what demands our attention for the moment is just the expression 'in accordance with what his means allow', ὡς ἂν κατὰ τὰ ἴδια ἐκποιῶσιν. It implies, as a well known fact, not only that the education of a Spartan child had a cost, which is obvious, but that this cost was appreciable even for a well-to-do family, to the extent of limiting its possibilities in the practice of this form of patronage.

Was Spartan education costly? This is something which will surprise those who take Xenophon literally: does he not state that the boys went barefoot (*LP* 2.3), had very few clothes (2.4), and were meanly fed (2.5)? Yes, but it is probable that Xenophon is systematizing, and the majority of features which he enumerates are without real economic significance. We have Phylarchos' text to show that, without the help of rich families, a certain number of Spartiate boys would not have been able, for financial reasons, to benefit from the Lycurgan education. This aspect deserves examination. It has been very well treated by Kennell (1995, 133–4), which allows me to be brief. The preceding expositions have revealed two elements susceptible of being a significant financial burden: the contribution to the children's *syssition*[42] and the salary of teachers. We have no information as to what this might represent; let us say that for the *syssition* it must perhaps have been roughly the equivalent of half of what an adult contributed (minus the wine, naturally); this means that in total a child, especially an older child, would have cost appreciably more than half of what a grown man's own *syssition* cost him.

In this connection, Kennell (1995, 134 and n. 113) cites a passage of the *Cyropaedia* which helps us understand this problem, the relevance of which rests on the fact that the educational utopia described by Xenophon in that treatise borrows some of its features from Spartan reality. While in the *Lak. Pol.* the author, constrained by his apologetic aim, passes in complete silence over the economic aspect, in the case of the Persians he outlines it precisely. He explains that amongst them, in order to become a complete citizen, that is to have access to office and honours, it is necessary to have passed through the *ephēbeia*; and in order to be admitted as an ephebe, it is necessary to have attended 'the public school of justice' (τὰ κοινὰ τῆς δικαιοσύνης διδασκαλεῖα), where 'public teachers' (δημοσίοι διδάσκαλοι) teach. 'It is permitted to all Persians to send their children to the public school of justice. Those who can feed their children without them working (ἀργοῦντας) send them there; those who cannot, do not' (*Cyr.* 1.2.15). This is clear. There are obviously great differences from Sparta; this utopian education is, like that of the *Laws*, entirely state-controlled; but, like the Phylarchos passage, this text expresses, with particular clarity and insisting at length on its consequences, the idea of the cost of education as an insurmountable obstacle for the poor. Especially notable is the word ἀργοῦντας: what defines the poor is the inability to raise their children *without them working*. Of course, in ancient Greece working children are no cause for surprise; but can we accept this for Sparta? I shall not hazard an answer. What does appear not only possible but almost certain in this city is that, for a citizen on the brink of poverty, the additional cost entailed by the education (with its two aspects, physical training and elementary education, public and private) of a boy (and even more of several) would prove to be decisive for the family's destiny: if the father had managed, after a fashion, to maintain his citizen status, he was unable to finance the education of his son who, because of this, would never be a citizen. This is one of the causes of oliganthropy; it is to problems of this kind that the institution of *mothakes* was meant to bring the germ of a solution.[43] And, if he could only finance one of the two aspects of education, he would surely give priority to the city's training, giving up on the elementary-education aspect: firstly because he had of course to feed his son in any case, and contributing for his *syssition* was probably not much more expensive; secondly because it was the public education which gave access to citizen status. This could have reinforced the belief that the Spartans were not very interested in elementary education.

Notes

[1] *Agesilaos* 67, *Mor.* 213c = Leotychidas 3, *Mor.* 224d.

[2] Plutarch, *Lyc.* 20.8; cf. *Sayings of Kings and Generals*, *Mor.* 192b and *Spartan Sayings*, *Mor.* 217d and 231d.

[3] *Mor.* 221b.

[4] Cartledge 1978; Boring 1979. Whitley's 1997 article, especially 'Writing in ancient Sparta' (pp. 645–9), focuses on an issue which does not concern us here, i.e. the use of writing.

[5] Millender 2001, especially p. 149.

[6] *Pol.* 2.1272a30; cf. 1270a17–18. ἐξ ἁπάντων: 1270b25–6. Cf. Richer 1998a, 282–9: the ephors were representative of the entire Spartan *damos*.

[7] Cf. Birgalias 1999, 165–84; further bibliography can be found in David 1999. See also Powell 2001, 239–40.

[8] Aristotle fr. 611, 13 Rose. On the expression εὐθὺς ἐκ παίδων, cf. above, p. 111.

[9] The anecdote about the Samian ambassadors, at 3.46, is crystal clear on the subject; see also Anacharsis' speech at 4.77.

[10] Ion of Chios fr. 63 Snell; Thucydides 2.40.2 (implicitly) and 4.17.2; Plato, *Protagoras* 342d–e, *Laws* 1.641e (comparison between Sparta and Crete) and 4.721e; Aristotle fr. 611.13 Rose, cf. *Rhetoric* 2.1398b (ἥκιστα φιλόλογοι). On the *Protagoras* passage, see Richer's recent study (2001).

[11] Cf. above, p. 52, where we saw that this eulogy was absolutely serious.

[12] David 1999.

[13] David 1999, 120.

[14] In 18.5 he shows the *eirēn* making the children of his group do 'practical exercises' in 'laconism'.

[15] Poetry: Plutarch, *Lyc.* 21.1–2; for Homer, Plato, *Laws* 3.680c. Music: Plutarch, *Lyc.* 21.4–6 (Terpander and Pindar call the Spartans μουσικωτάτους); Athenaeus 14.632f (cited below). For dance, the main sources are Athenaeus and Pollux, but what Plato says about dance in the *Laws* refers largely to Sparta. Ion of Samos, author of the epigram on the monument of Lysander at Delphi (*c.* 400 BC) calls Sparta 'the country of fine choirs', καλλίχορομ πατρίδα, and Pratinas of Phlious (fr. 2 Bergk, *ap.* Athenaeus 14.632f), at the beginning of the 5th century, speaks of the Spartans as people who are mad about dance: 'the Laconian cicada, always ready for the dance'.

[16] Cf. Birgalias 1999, 193–219, with bibliography.

[17] Kennell 1995, 126.

[18] This is not the case for the earliest apprenticeships, which would have taken place before the boy had reached the age for being an *erōmenos*.

[19] On this break, cf. above, p. 24. I owe this point to Lévy.

[20] This was already de Coulanges' opinion: 1891, 73.

[21] Cf. above, p. 47.

[22] That is, made by her own hands; the anecdote opposes the 'products' of the two types of women.

[23] Ducat 1999a, 165–7.

[24] *Laws* 7.804d; above, p.54.

[25] *Lyc.* 15.14.

[26] Hence one cannot agree with Link's assertion (1994, 30) that the father's authority over his son ceased when he entered the *agōgē*.

[27] On this inscription, see below, pp. 210–12.

[28] The same is said in the *Alcibiades* (122b); but this dialogue is generally not considered to be by Plato.

[29] Cantarelli 1890, 465–84; cf. Bruni 1979, 21–31; Hodkinson 1997b, 50–2, and 2000, 336.

[30] These texts have recently been collected several times over (Lotze 1962; Toynbee 1969, 345 n. 3; Bommelaer 1977, 36–8), so it is unnecessary to cite them in full here.

[31] Ducat 1990, 166–8.

[32] Cantarelli and Hodkinson are the only scholars carefully to have made this distinction.

[33] On the *mothakes* and their relation to education, cf. below, pp. 151–3.

[34] On this category, cf. Ducat 1990, 54, and Hodkinson 1997, 50–2.

[35] Only wealthy families would possess enough helots for there to have been one who

was about the same age as (or, rather, slightly older than) the son.

[36] Aristotle, *Pol.* 2.1271b.

[37] Examples in Piérart 1974, 371 and n. 84.

[38] Diodorus 12.12.4; text cited and translated by Piérart 1974, 37.

[39] This is, I think, roughly Kennell's reasoning (1995, 125). On the other hand, his reference to Aristotle (*Pol.* 7.1338b) does not seem to me to be relevant, as this text refers rather to the Platonic theory of the four forms of virtue.

[40] A form of the legend attested in the 4th century; cf. above, p. 49.

[41] The *Suda*, s.v. Tyrtaios.

[42] Above, pp. 83–4; an aspect noted by Kennell 1995, 133.

[43] Only the germ, because the *mothax* did not automatically become a citizen, as we shall see. He had, by exceptional services rendered to the city, to redeem his original sin of poverty.

5

THE SOCIAL FUNCTION OF EDUCATION

I am acutely aware that, so far, I have not given a description of the Spartan system of education; we know too little about the subject even to imagine being able to do this successfully. All I was able to offer is a summary of the evidence and the problems, and we will have to be content with that while now proceeding to the next stage: examining the interpretations that have been put forward of this complex, and, in many respects, surprising, reality, and the manifold problems to be found in it. There are two types of interpretation. One of them seeks to explain the Spartan system of education in terms of its alleged aim – whether this be military (training warriors) or civic (turning boys into citizens). The other tries to account for it by reference to its origins, viewing the system as the ultimate expression of a set of initiation rites inherited from a supposedly remote past. I shall try to show that these modes of interpretation are not mutually exclusive, but are both 'true' in a way, and that they constitute approaches that can and should be combined. Following the practice of the ethnologist who, before doing anything else, listens to the explanations which the society he is studying gives of itself, I begin by setting out the interpretation on which the Greeks of the classical era were themselves unanimously agreed.

The military interpretation

The ancient Greeks were quite aware of the complexity of Spartan education. They knew that it contained contradictory elements, mixing order with disorder, discipline with savagery, a communal spirit with incentives for the individual to put himself first. Some of these characteristics, such as the incessant brawling of the *hēbōntes* or the obligation to steal, appeared bizarre and even shocking, but despite these difficulties, Greeks were intent on trying to understand it. Even when they were claiming to do no more than describe it, they knew quite well that, if it was to be intelligible, such a description had to be built on an interpretation that was already implicit. The explanatory model that conditioned their thinking was that of the training of a warrior. To say that it conditioned their thinking is justifiable, not only because, during the classical era, no one challenged it, but also because it was employed by all the authors considered in chapter 2. All, that is, except Aristophanes, an exception that is readily explained, however: he does not describe Spartan education but, rather, conjures up the ancient system of education in Athens – itself an ideal, in fact, of which certain elements were drawn from the actual system in Sparta.

The several allusions Thucydides makes to the *paideia* of the Athenians' enemy reveal that, at the time of his writing, the military interpretation is already the accepted one. In the opinion of Archidamos (1.84.3), Spartan discipline (*to eukosmon*) is the product of this education. 'So,' he says, 'our discipline makes us brave as warriors and prudent as men.' To the Athenians, who are going to war without having made any special provision for it, Pericles (2.39.1–2) draws the contrast with their enemies ('they'), 'who', he says, 'only attain courage at the price of harsh training from early boyhood'.

Criticism of the warlike purpose of Spartan education, implicit in Pericles' speech, becomes, in Isocrates' *Panathenaicus*, an explicit argument on which the author lays considerable stress. In his view, the Spartans actually inculcate in their children that urge to conquer and dominate which is their hallmark:

> By training, they instil in their young an attitude whereby they aim to act not for the benefit of other men, but so as to do as much harm as possible to the rest of the Greeks (§210).

As for the orator Lycurgus, he draws attention to the role played, in this cultivation of military virtues, by the poetry of Tyrtaios (*Against Leocrates*, 106) .

In the cases of Plato and Aristotle, contemplation of the Spartan education system obviously takes on another dimension, but not once is the military interpretation examined afresh; it continues to be accepted as a fact. Their analysis bears on the consequences that ensue, and these do Sparta no service. The education system thus becomes one of the principal chapters of a radical criticism. For Plato, it is only one aspect of a constant that is present in Spartan institutions as a whole, and which, for simplicity's sake, I shall christen 'militarism'. In the *Laws*, the Athenian charges both Megillos and Kleinias with this:

> What both of you required of a good lawgiver was that all the institutions he devised be geared to waging war (3.688a).

> Your institutions are those of a military camp rather than of a community of townspeople (2.666e).

Because of the role it plays throughout society, the education system is, at one and the same time, a privileged field for cultivating this 'militarization' and an essential cause of it. By contrast, what Plato wants for each child in his city is 'an education that would make of him not simply a good soldier, but someone capable of running a state and towns' (2.666 e). He does not argue with the necessity of being prepared for war, nor with the notion that courage is a virtue; but courage is merely one among four types of virtue, and Spartan education, by being directed solely toward preparation for war, loses its point, even in the field that is its speciality; for a man schooled in every form of virtue would be superior to the Spartans in that sphere too; 'A man like that, as we said at first, would be a better warrior than those envisaged by Tyrtaios' (2.667a).

Is there a connection between the 'savagery' of Spartan education, which comes under scrutiny immediately after the phrase, cited above, in which Sparta is compared to a barracks, and its bellicose ends? Plato does not spell it out as such, but the juxtaposition invites argument along those lines. One result of bringing up boys collectively, in permanent groups (the metaphor of a herd of colts recurs throughout the analysis), is that their natural wildness remains untamed; that could only work if each of them was taken in hand by his own groom (the pedagogue). It is no accident, then, that the Spartans raise their children in this way, so that, by preserving all their aggressiveness, they turn them into ferocious fighters. Of course, he does not say as much, perhaps because he has anticipated the objection that the aggression of the hoplite bears no comparison with that of a young boy; but he leaves it to be inferred.

Aristotle is only following Plato when he asserts, as he does on several occasions, that the sole function of Spartan education is to act as a preparation for war (*Pol.* 2.1271b1–6; 7.1324b3–9; 1333b5–23; 8.1338b9–38). At 1333b11–21 he pokes fun at those who rave about the Spartan approach, and there must have been many who did, because, after naming a certain Thibron, about whom nothing certain is known, he adds 'and all those who have discussed the institutions of Sparta', amongst whom he most probably includes Xenophon. Like Isocrates, he levels the accusation that this system cultivates the violent mentality and the desire for domination which, while allowing the city to become wealthy for a while, brought it, in the end, to catastrophe. He insists – at greater length than does Plato – on this savage tendency, and, in so doing, is the first to formulate it as a concept (*to thēriōdes*); he does not see it as the result of collective upbringing, but as a goal the Spartans willingly pursue in order to increase the effectiveness of their warriors.

I take Xenophon as a separate case. It is not that he had misgivings about the warlike objective of the education system; like everyone else, he takes it as read. But, on the one hand, he makes novel use of it, while, on the other, he sometimes uses expressions which indicate that he did not regard preparation for war as their only aim, and in this respect he shows himself to be, perhaps, more clear-sighted than his contemporaries.

In its conventional form the military interpretation is not explicitly set out in the *Lak. Pol.* It is only mentioned in a passage of the *Hellenica*, as part of the speech delivered in 369 by Prokles of Phlious: 'It is in their earliest boyhood that they (the Spartans) begin training for war on land' (7.1.8).

While the *Lak. Pol.* contains no definitive assertion of it, chapter 2 describes certain specific aspects of the education system, otherwise obscure, that become intelligible provided their true purpose is a military one – something the author is content merely to hint at. When, at §2, Spartan boys are trained to go barefoot, it is because in that way they learn to move about with speed and confidence over mountainous terrain; this acquirement may, of course, stand them in good stead when hunting, but one strongly suspects that it is really aimed at warfare. When, at §4, they are compelled to wear only one kind of garment throughout the year, it is, says Xenophon, so that they may be 'better prepared to endure cold and heat alike'; but this process of toughening-up only makes sense if its objective is to fit them for the rugged life of the warrior, who cannot carry his entire wardrobe around with him. At §5, their being accustomed to simple food, or even, sometimes, no food at all, can only be aimed at adapting them to life on campaign, where, by the nature of the circumstances, they might have to go without food all day, while still expending – if they want to stay alive – all the energy they can summon. The expression ἀσιτήσαντας ἐπιπονῆσαι evokes, by means of juxtaposition, two fundamental realities of military life: the *sitos*, the daily ration, and the *ponos*, the 'exertion' of being at war. Only one thing remains to complete this picture of the soldier's day – the business of sleeping; this would be the moment to recount, as Plutarch does (*Lyc.* 16.13–14), how the boys make their beds out of reeds; but Xenophon does not mention it, perhaps because this custom did not yet exist in his time. A similar use of vocabulary to imply that the system of education is like a course of military training recurs in chapter 3: Lycurgus imposed on the *paidiskoi* certain πόνους (§2); to shirk them is tantamount to desertion (φύγοι §3), and that denotes cowardice (ἀποδειλιάσαντες).

Of all the exercises required of the Spartan boy, the most difficult to account for must surely be that of stealing. It is not Xenophon's method to make a bald assertion that this was a part of training for war; that would scarcely be a convincing way to go about it. Rather, he causes it to emerge, by analysing the qualities that stealing both calls for and encourages (§7). The language employed conveys the warlike character of these qualities: knowing how to keep awake by night (ἀγρυπνεῖν: the job of the sentry), and, by day, 'to be wily and to stay alert' (ἀπατᾶν καὶ ἐνεδρεύειν). Carrying out a theft is likened to a military operation, for the success of which the leader must know how 'to post his scouts' (κατασκόπους ἑτοιμάζειν); it is, then, a schooling in initiative and leadership. In this way, through the entire length of §§3–7 and §9, Xenophon negotiates a challenging undertaking very neatly. Instead of seeking to enforce a military interpretation on the exercise of stealing, he creates, in a way, a situation in which it is to be the reader who, guided by the language, reaches this conclusion for himself. Another characteristic which makes this account plausible is that it is not just an abstraction. Beneath the surface of his discourse we can detect those personal experiences of waging war in difficult conditions which the author himself gained during the retreat of the Ten Thousand. Moving swiftly and stealthily through mountainous country, enduring cold and hunger, leading raids – he knew just what these meant. That this is not pure conjecture on my part is evident from the conversation, joking in its manner but serious in its purpose, in which Xenophon says to Cheirisophos that a raid such as the one he is planning will be easy for a man like him, who had spent his childhood learning how to steal (*Anabasis* 4.6.14–15).

The credibility of Xenophon's image of the military model of Spartan education, far from being diminished, is actually reinforced by the fact that, in the same breath, he hints at another objective – the moulding of the citizen. He does it through his choice of adjectives for defining the transformation this education effects in Spartan boys. They become εὐπειθέστεροι (2.14), ἐγκρατέστεροι (ibid.), αἰδημονέστεροι (2.10 and 14). Obedience and self-control are indeed soldierly qualities, but they are every bit as much the qualities of a citizen, especially a citizen of Sparta. As for *aidōs*, which seems to be the most important of these qualities, since it appears twice, it is one of the major values (albeit difficult – for us, at least – to define) of Spartan society.[1] These qualities are present here only in the form of allusions, but these become clear when one thinks back to chapter 8, which might reasonably be entitled 'On Obedience'. There, the verb πείθεσθαι recurs time and again (§§1, 2, 3, 5), and in contexts that are purely civil, with the exception of §3, where a single phrase lists all the situations in which authority is wielded: τὸ πείθεσθαι μέγιστον ἀγαθὸν εἶναι καὶ ἐν πόλει καὶ ἐν στρατίᾳ καὶ ἐν οἴκῳ, ('obedience is the paramount quality, whether it be in the city, on campaign, or in the household'). Because he is conducting a eulogy of Spartan education, rather than employing it as a tool for an inclusive critical survey, Xenophon is the only author of the classical era to state unequivocally that its aim was to produce not only warriors but citizens.

The military interpretation is certainly well-founded; that does not mean that it has to be 'true': it would serve no purpose to frame the problem in these terms because that would merely lead to the observation, on the one hand, that while there was some truth in the interpretation there was error in it as well,[2] and, on the other, that it is very far from taking account of the complex whole that was Spartan education. When I describe it as well-founded, I mean that it is supported by the observation, made by all Greeks in the classical era, that this system of education enabled the young Spartan to acquire the qualities which, at that period, made a good warrior.[3]

What are these qualities? Firstly – and this seems to have been the order in which they were ranked by the ancient Greeks themselves – physical strength, and, especially, endurance. For the Greek soldier on campaign, almost all his exertions were expended on the march – 95% sweat, let us say, to 5% actual bloodshed. There is no point in his being courageous in battle if he cannot sustain this physical effort. He must endure the extreme discomfort that goes with military life: uncertain lines of supply, scant protection against the elements, sleeping rough. Next – as in any army – comes discipline, that is to say, both unquestioning obedience to orders, and self-control. Yet another quality, one especially necessary in hoplite warfare, is a sense of joint responsibility; the hoplite must forego personal displays of courage, and devote all his energies to the effective operating of his unit. Finally, there are the moral qualities: gallantry, loyalty to the city, a sense of honour.

These qualities are, according to the sources, the very ones instilled in the young Spartan by his compulsory education. Its keynote was physical training, directed principally at promoting hardihood. Xenophon stresses this point constantly, whether it be in the case of the *paides* (chapter 2) or that of the *paidiskoi* (πλείστους πόνους, 3.2), and Plato assigns to Megillos a speech on the subject (*Laws* 1.633b) which opens with the words: 'The systematic training we undergo in the endurance of pain', (τὸ περὶ τὰς καρτερήσεις τῶν ἀλγηδόνων πολὺ παρ' ἡμῖν γιγνόμενον).

Immediately afterwards, Megillos mentions 'the collective bouts of unarmed combat' (ἐν ταῖς πρὸς ἀλλήλοις ταῖς χερσὶ μάχαις). Whereas Xenophon only refers to the single combat in which the *hēbōntes* engaged each other (a completely different affair), this phrase of Plato's seems to indicate that collective fights, which, according to Plutarch (*Lyc.* 16.9; 17.4), were common amongst boys of all ages, already existed in the classical era; it was quite natural to see in these a form of military training. It is, no doubt, the emphasis placed on physical training that generated the opinion, widely held throughout Greece, that the Spartans paid little attention to study; the aspect of their education that cultivated endurance was the one that earned them admiration in the Stoa.

The second quality of the warrior, discipline, together with self-control, also appears to have been a crucial objective of Spartan education. As Lévy remarked,[4] this aspect of education was reinforced by the fact that the boy was not placed under the authority of one of his father's slaves, but under that of leaders (*paidonomos*, *eirenes*) who were, in relation to him, the representatives of the city, as indeed, any citizen could be, no matter who he was. Whether in the case of the *paides* or that of the *paidiskoi*, we see Xenophon laying stress on their obedience and their rigorous discipline.

With regard to the third quality, a sense of joint responsibility, no other city took as much care as did Sparta to accustom its young to communal living, in close contact with groups of comrades, age-classes, or smaller bands. Being the same for all, the state education developed in them the sense of belonging to a fellowship. It was natural to think that it was from this that there sprang the exceptional degree of cohesion and the skill in tactical manoeuvre (Xenophon, *LP* 13.5) of the Spartan phalanx.

As for the moral and ideological aspect, it was omnipresent to such an extent that the tendency to present Spartan education as a kind of indoctrination is all too common. From his earliest years the Spartan boy was taught, both in principle and in practice, to place loyalty to the city above every other consideration. As Plutarch admirably shows (*Lyc.* 21.1–2), the poetry he learnt, and the songs, reiterated to him without let-up how he ought to conduct himself as a Spartan warrior, what glory was earned by those who died in battle and what vilification was meted out to the 'tremblers'. The code of honour governing the city genuinely became part of the framework of his personality.

A military purpose could even be attributed to the pederastic relationship. Xenophon states this, not in the *Lak. Pol.*, but in a passage of the *Symposium* (8.35), where Socrates asserts that love causes the *eromenoi* to fight gallantly so as to bring honour to their *erastai*, despite the fact that the battle order of a Spartan army precluded their fighting side by side. Similarly, an author of the second century BC – Sosikrates, cited by Athenaeus (13.561e; 461 F 7 Jacoby) – records that 'before going into battle, the Lacedaemonians offer sacrifice to Eros, in the belief that their security depended on the bond of affection (φιλία) uniting the combatants'.[5]

These observations alone must naturally have led the Greeks to explain Spartan education in terms of military training. Equally, other considerations have contributed to winning general acceptance for this interpretation. In the fourth century, the role Tyrtaios' poems played in the schooling of Spartan boys was well recognized outside Sparta. Plato devotes to the most famous of them, fragment 12 (West), on 'true virtue', a lengthy critical commentary (*Laws* 1.628a–30d), while the orator Lycurgus, after attributing to the poet the organization of education in Sparta (above, p. 49), himself cites fragment 10. From the fact that the poet came across as a war-poet it was easy to conclude that this system of education was genuinely warlike. But one would certainly not have regarded this interpretation as having reached this point on its own without the aid of a hard fact, one which, before 371, no one would have dared to challenge: the superiority of the Spartans over all other Greeks in hoplite battle. And it is there, in a more general sense, that the theory of Spartan 'militarism' had its origins. A good reason had to be found to account for this excellence. It was already there, supplied by Thucydides: training from earliest boyhood.

Even if, as appears to be the case, they corresponded with what the Spartans themselves believed, opinions current among Greeks in the fourth century in no way constitute proof that Spartan education *really* was, in the main, a course of military training. Well-founded as this explanation may seem, it is neverthelesss no more than a theoretical system developed in the course of the fifth century to account for a reality already in existence. There are several arguments, moreover, that may be mounted against it.

The first is methodological. The idea that an assemblage as complex (not to say disparate) as the Spartan education system could have been conceived, at a given moment, with a precise aim in view, is hard to accept. The ancient Greeks did not have this problem, of course, since they could attribute the devising of the system to a lawgiver, thus explaining its apparent coherence. We, for our part, know that this system is in fact the product of a long history, and that it did not owe its character to a single will and intelligence but, rather, to a series of material influences acting on it throughout the period of its existence. It may be that, in the course of this history, a moment arose when the Spartan state decided to take over what there was in the way of education for boys, and impose some order on it, and that, at this juncture, it defined an objective; it is of this kind of 'crystallization' that Finley was thinking when he spoke about the 'sixth-century revolution'. But, even if that is how it occurred (which is far from certain), such an objective could only have been to 'train the young' *in a general way*, not to train them solely for war. The notion of an ultimate objective that was purely warlike assumes the prior existence of the myth of Spartan 'militarism'.

The second objection rests on the palpable gap that separates exercises prescribed for young boys from the reality of war as waged by Sparta and other Greek cities. There is nothing new in this argument. As early as 1913 Jeanmaire was making the point, when discussing the Crypteia, that the Spartan warrior had nothing of a 'bush-crawler' about him, and this observation has often been reiterated since, notably by Vidal-Naquet.[6] The young Spartan seems to have been prepared for a species of war fought almost on his own, a war of ambushes in mountain and forest, a sort of Anabasis, rather than for ordered, conventional confrontations, on level ground, between two phalanges in heavy armour. There is nothing in common between the unarmed bouts of two teams of boys, and hoplite combat. However, this line of reasoning, while basically justified, has its limits. For one thing, it is a theoretical simplification to imagine all Greek warfare, even in the sixth and fifth centuries, in the shape of set-piece engagements. Only the great battles generally conform to this description – and the great battles are rare. As becomes perfectly clear from a reading of Xenophon's *Hellenica*, the strategic activity of the campaigning year actually consisted of marches and small-scale operations: skirmishes, pursuits, raids and 'recces', often in uneven or wooded terrain.

Besides, could a man *really* prepare himself for hoplite battle? Its very nature precluded the staging of simulated combat, unless one half of the army were to be set against the other, fighting with actual weapons. The same applies to all battles and to all wars; no exercise, however realistic, can even approach the reality of the battlefield – something that defies all imagination, all description. This, it seems, is already the sentiment Tyrtaios is seeking to convey about the reality of war. One prepares as best one can, by trying to give soldiers good physical training, and by inculcating in them some basic principles. As I see it, it is in this respect that Spartan education was most successful. It rendered young men capable of sustaining the efforts of a normal campaign and of conducting themselves effectively in the small-scale operations that were its staple; but as for the set battle, that was something that could only be learnt in the field, and for which the preparation would be more moral than technical in nature.

Bearing these facts in mind, I think there still remains an element of validity in the initial argument. Is there any real point in forcing young boys only to wear one garment throughout the year simply so that, when they grow up, they can endure the heat and the cold? In keeping them on short commons so that, later, they will live on army rations without grumbling? In compelling them to steal so that they know how to pull off a raid? It seems to me that there exists an unbridgeable gulf between what is presented to us as a course of military training and the practical reality for which it is supposedly designed. It is as though the relationship between the two things was more symbolic than actual. Spartan education seems to *mimic*, rather than actually to be, a training for war. Its character is too savage, whereas, for an army, no matter what kind of action it engages in, the absolute requirement is for discipline and self-control.

The third objection is that, if the avowed end of Spartan education was to subject all young boys to an identical course of training, it was, as we shall soon see, aimed just as much at selecting, from amongst them, an elite. One might say that an army also needs an elite; but what the Spartans were seeking to identify and single out had nothing specifically military about it; it was, rather, an elite of the citizen body. This remark demonstrates that if

Spartan education existed with an objective in view, that objective was necessarily greater in scope than preparation for war alone: it could only have been training for the role of the citizen.

The moulding of the citizen

War is only one of the activities of the citizen. An education that was merely a preparation for that would indeed deserve the criticism which Plato and Aristotle levelled at Sparta, namely, that she cultivated only one of the constituents of virtue. Any city that followed this absurd course of behaviour would lay itself open to serious errors of judgement, to the point where it risked failing to function at all. Despite what Pericles insinuates in Thucydides (2.40.2), history does not portray the Spartan citizen as a passive one; he was obliged, perhaps to an even greater extent than was the Athenian, to play an active part in public affairs. If he wanted to be involved in directing these affairs, he would have had to gain the understanding and qualities necessary for discharging the functions of ephor or member of the Gerousia, just as he would for the numerous other offices, magistracies or missions, including military ones. If he was unwilling, or unable, to do this, he had still to be, at the very least, capable of playing his proper part in the decision-making that concerned the whole community, and, when it came to the election of officials, to know how to choose those who would act, or think, in the best way for the city. Also, one can explain in terms of the need to train future citizens for their responsibilities all the principal hallmarks of Spartan education: its obligatory character, the fact that it was organized by the city, its collective nature, and the fact that, while it was identical for all, even so one of its chief functions was to select an elite.

Obligation: education and citizenship

This probably did not work as a direct and explicit obligation; in my opinion, a citizen who omitted to enter his son for state education (insofar as that was conceivable) would not have been viewed as having committed a misdemeanour and thus as having incurred a penalty. There was no need for obligation of this kind, and the constraints of social pressure were far more effective. It was actually the boy who was penalized, because unless he participated in this education, he could not become a citizen; it was this that created an obligation. The only ones to be exempt from state education were those sons of kings who were intended to succeed their fathers; the evidence for this is found only in Plutarch (*Agesilaos* 1.4), but it is widely accepted.[7] It is also accepted, and in my opinion rightly, that the rule whereby obtaining citizenship was conditional upon completing the course of education was already in force by the classical era; however, it is worth noting that obligation, in this guise of necessary condition, is only mentioned in texts postdating this period: two texts presenting two cases that are, moreover, different in character.

The earlier of these is a passage about the *agōgē*, written by Teles and cited by Stobaeus, 40.8:[8]

> τὸν δὲ μὴ ἐμμείναντα, κἂν ἐξ αὐτοῦ τοῦ βασιλέως, εἰς τοὺς Εἵλωτας ἀποστέλλουσι, καὶ τῆς πολιτείας ὁ τοιοῦτος οὐ μετέχει.

> anyone who has not completed it, even if he is son to the king himself, is consigned to the ranks of the helots, and such a man is excluded from citizenship.

In view of its obvious oratorical nature, this text should only be used with caution. The phrase in its entirety (I have only quoted the second part of it here) rests on an opposition, manifestly contrived, between one term and another, the statement that a person who completes the *agōgē* becomes a citizen and even more, whilst the one who fails to complete it becomes a non-citizen and even less. Here it is not the allusion to the kings' sons that creates the real problem; a situation like that could well arise, because those of them who were not destined to succeed were in fact subject to the public education system (as was the case with Agesilaos). What does derive from pure rhetoric is the notion of being reduced to slavery; no other source says anything of the kind, nor do we know of anyone who ever *became* a helot.[9] The circumstance envisaged by Teles seems to be that of failure by withdrawal (τὸν μὴ ἐμμείναντα); we shall revisit this question later.

The other text is an apophthegm, one we have already encountered.[10] In about 330 BC the ephor Eteokles refuses to send Spartiate boys to Antipater as hostages 'so that they should not be deprived of their education and thus fail to reap the benefit of the ancestral *agōgē*; for then they would not even be citizens' (Plutarch *Ap. Lac.*, Anon. 54, *Mor.* 235e). 'Not even...citizens' (οὐδὲ πολῖται γὰρ ἂν εἴσαν) is a surprising phrase; it seems to imply that it is because they would not have pursued their education *at all* (this clearly being the circumstance he envisaged) that they would be treated thus, and hence that there existed lighter penalties in cases less serious than this. We shall come back to this question, too.

We should accept, then, that one could not become a citizen without first having completed the education organized by the state. The converse proposition makes the connection between education and citizenship even more obvious. This is what we find expressed in the first part of Teles' statement cited above:

> τὸν μὲν μετασχόντα τῆς ἀγωγῆς καὶ ἐμμείναντα, κἂν ξένος κἂν ἐξ Εἵλωτος, ὁμοίως τοῖς ἀρίστοις τιμῶσι,

> anyone who has taken part in the *agōgē* and has completed it, whether he be a foreigner or the son of a helot, him they honour in the same way as the best.

Here, again, the style is marked by oratorical emphasis. Furthermore, the assertion that it was possible for the sons of helots to participate in state education suggests that, here, *mothax* and *mothōn* have been confused; it is, no doubt, this (intentional?) confusion that explains the vagueness of the final expression: not only do they become citizens (something inferred from the second part of the statement) but they receive (in reality, they may receive) substantial honours; in fact, as we shall find, some of the greatest men of Sparta during the classical era were *mothakes*.

Another text, *Inst. Lac.* 22, seems to have the same content as this first part of Teles' statement, and is, perhaps, an adaptation of it. It runs as follows:

> ἔνιοι δ' ἔφασαν ὅτι καὶ τῶν ξένων ὃς ἂν ὑπομείνῃ τὴν τοιαύτην ἄσκησιν τῆς πολιτείας κατὰ τὸ βούλημα τοῦ Λυκούργου μετεῖχε τῆς ἀρχῆθεν διατεταγμένης μοίρας· πωλεῖν δ' οὐκ ἐξῆν.

This paragraph balances the preceding one, which deals with those who 'did not complete' τὴν τῶν παίδων ἀγωγήν; hence the expression τὴν τοιαύτην ἄσκησιν. The overall structure is thus the inverse of that encountered in Teles' text. ἄσκησις τῆς πολιτείας does not convey any true sense; in translation it would read something like 'the practice of citizenship', but the system of education cannot be described in that way; the reading 'schooling for citizenship' would, obviously, come closer, but this would mean forcing the sense of ἄσκησις. Thus it is preferable to make τῆς πολιτείας the complement of μετεῖχε, which is all the more attractive since μετέχειν τῆς πολιτείας is by far the most natural phrase to convey the idea of full rights in the city. From this we should infer the existence of a lacuna after μετεῖχε.[11] This lacuna could be filled by a simple καί, but another part of the passage, πωλεῖν δ' οὐκ ἐξῆν, makes this solution impracticable, and, in fact, shows that after μετεῖχε the author had embarked on a different topic, namely the system of ownership.[12] The lacuna is thus rather long, and what follows μετεῖχε actually belongs to another paragraph, which could be called 22a. So §22 may be translated thus:

> Some said that, in accordance with Lycurgus' purpose, anyone, even a foreigner, who endured such training, was admitted to citizenship.

The opening formula, ἔνιοι δ' ἔφασαν, suggests that the author considered this opinion rather extreme. He had good cause; as in the case of Teles' text, it held that successful completion of the course of education automatically conferred citizenship.

To put the case like this is to distort it considerably. The fact of the matter is that certain boys who were not sons of citizens were allowed to participate in Spartan education. Of these, we know of two types, called, respectively, *mothakes* and *trophimoi*.

On the subject of *mothakes* there are two principal sources, which may, by and large, be taken together except for one important respect in which they contradict each other.[13] The principal text is that of Phylarchos, an excellent witness on the realities of Spartan life,[14] 81 F 43 Jacoby (ap. Athenaeus 6.271e–f):

> εἰσὶ δ᾽ οἱ μόθακες σύντροφοι τῶν Λακεδαιμονίων. ἕκαστος γὰρ τῶν πολιτικῶν παίδων, ὡς ἂν κατὰ τὰ ἴδια ἐκποιῶσιν, οἱ μὲν ἕνα, οἱ δὲ δύο, τινὲς δὲ πλείους ποιοῦνται συντρόφους αὑτῶν. εἰσὶν οὖν οἱ μόθακες ἐλεύθεροι μέν, οὐ μὴν Λακεδαιμόνιοί γε, μετέχουσι δὲ τῆς παιδείας πάσης. τούτων ἕνα φασὶ γένεσθαι καὶ Λύσανδρον τὸν καταναυμαχήσαντα τοὺς Ἀθηναίους, πολίτην γενόμενον δι᾽ ἀνδραγαθίαν.

> the *mothakes* are *syntrophoi* (brothers-by-upbringing) of the Lacedaemonians. In fact, each boy of citizen status takes, according to his means, one or perhaps two *syntrophoi*, possibly even more. So, *mothakes* are free, yet without being Lacedaemonians, and they participate in the entire course of education. They say that even Lysander was one of these, he who defeated the Athenians at sea, after having been made a citizen in recognition of his bravery.

Not only does Phylarchos define the *mothakes* but he also describes the mechanism that produces them. Throughout the text, the term 'Lacedaemonians', as the first occurrence of it clearly demonstrates, is to be read (as it so often is) as 'Spartans'. As I have already made clear,[15] I take the view that when Phylarchos speaks of free *mothakes*, he means that their condition is free, that is to say, free by birth;[16] it seems to me that that becomes obvious the moment a distinction is drawn between *mothakes* and *mothōnes*. They are not foreigners, because for foreigners there was, as we shall see, a different designation; nor are they Perioikoi, who, at Sparta, had the same legal status as foreigners. These boys, then, could belong to two categories: as sons of citizens unable to pay for their education; or as sons of Inferiors, that is to say, in this context, a category of children born into families who had lost their citizen status through poverty.[17] In fact, a remarkable feature of this text is the attention paid to economic realities; we have already noticed this regarding the cost of education,[18] which, as Phylarchos says, limited the possibilities even for well-to-do families. 'Patronage' is, I think, a more appropriate term than 'adoption' or 'fosterage' to describe the mechanism that creates *mothakes*, since the boy remained a member of his own family. This patronage made state education (and there is no reason why this should not also apply to the private one), accessible to the sons of Inferiors when this would otherwise be denied them on account of their status, and to the two categories of boys listed above who would otherwise be denied it on account of their poverty.

The *mothax* is probably integrated into the same age-class as his 'brother-by-upbringing' and remains with him through the entire process. Phylarchos' insistence on the fact that 'he takes part in the *whole* course of education' probably stems from a desire to underline the importance of the advantage thus obtained, but, since the tone here is informative rather than rhetorical, I am inclined to think that his wording also implied that, occasionally, boys of other categories (and this, as we shall see, could be the case for *trophimoi*) might only have been eligible for part of the course of education.

The other text on the subject of *mothakes*, a passage of Aelian (*VH* 12.43), is less clear-cut, but it describes a mechanism that is substantially the same.

> Καλλικρατίδας γε μὴν καὶ Γύλιππος καὶ Λύσανδρος ἐν Λακεδαίμονι μόθακες ἐκαλοῦντο. ὄνομα δὲ ἦν ἄρα τοῦτο τοῖς τῶν εὐπόρων <συντρόφοις>, οὓς συνεσέπεμπον αὐτοῖς οἱ πατέρες συναγωνιουμένους ἐν τοῖς γυμνασίοις. ὁ δὲ συγχωρήσας τοῦτο Λυκοῦργος τοῖς ἐμμείνασι τῇ τῶν παίδων ἀγωγῇ πολιτείας Λακωνικῆς μεταλάγχανει,

> Kallikratidas, Gylippos, and Lysander were called *mothakes* in Lacedaemon. It was the name given to the *syntrophoi* of rich boys, whom their fathers sent to compete against them in the gymnasium. Lycurgus, who (first) allowed this, admits those of them who have completed the boys' *agōgē* to Laconian citizenship.

This description of the process is a little confused, partly, perhaps, because of the poor state of the text (the word *syntrophoi* is restored), but Phylarchos' text allows us to grasp the meaning; that Aelian seems to conceive of the *agōgē* solely as a course of physical training is an error of little consequence. Aelian has certainly drawn on Phylarchos, then, but there are certain differences. The first is that Aelian groups Gylippos and Kallikratidas with Lysander. It may seem surprising that one of the most distinguished of the generals and the two principal admirals in the Peloponnesian War should have been *mothakes*, but, after all, it is possible, and in the cases of Lysander and Gylippos there are arguments to support this.[19] The other difference is important for our purpose, because it brings into play the link between completing the education and obtaining the full rights of the city. For Aelian, the one is followed by the other mechanically; as with Teles and *Inst. Lac.* 22, he takes the extreme stance that, even for those who did not belong by birth to the citizen body, it was enough to have followed the course of education to the very end, to qualify automatically for citizenship. What Phylarchos says is quite different: that, thanks to the the patronage of a wealthy family, Lysander had been able to pursue the course of education; but that this had not been enough for him to gain citizenship; he had to earn that by his bravery.[20]

What, then, really happened? For the sons of citizens who were only prevented by a lack of funds from pursuing their education, there was no problem. Intervention on the part of the 'patron' family was limited to re-establishing the normal course of events for them, and they became citizens automatically. For all that, this does not make Aelian right, because the whole of his text is, patently, written from the perspective of a *liberty* granted (συγχωρήσας), which would not make sense if he was intending to speak of young men fulfilling the condition fundamental to their birth. As for boys born to fathers who had lost their citizen status, the idea of an automatic reintegration strikes me as impossible to accept, because, in fact, this constitutes a grant of citizenship, which normally implies a vote in the Assembly; yet that is precisely what Phylarchos says of Lysander. To have pursued the state education to its completion was a necessary condition for becoming a citizen, but it was not by itself sufficient qualification; there were other conditions to be met (by birth, or by grant).

Trophimoi. Certain foreigners could enter their sons for Spartan education. The texts mention three specific cases, Xenophon, Phocion, and Pyrrhos. The information about Xenophon's sons goes back to Diokles, a first-century BC author of *Lives of the Philosophers*, cited by Diogenes Laertius, 2.54:

> Meanwhile, as the Athenians had voted (in 370/69) to send an expedition to assist the Lacedaemonians, he despatched his sons to Athens so that they could participate in it. They had actually been educated there, in Sparta, as Diokles records in his *Lives of the Philosophers*.

Plutarch, *Agesilaos* 20, 2, supplies the detail that it was at Agesilaos' invitation that Xenophon had decided to send Gryllos and Diodorus to Sparta. This information is very widely accepted, but whether justifiably is less certain. In fact, if Xenophon did send his sons to Sparta, it can only have been during the period when he himself was resident at Skillous, since, when he was installed there, they must have been roughly of an age to begin their education. Yet, when he recalls, in the *Anabasis* (5.3.10), the annual festival of Artemis at Skillous, Xenophon indicates that his sons took part in it, which suggests that they were living there with him. On this, Higgins[21] puts forward other reasons for doubt, which hinge on the reliability of Diogenes Laertius' source, Diokles. Moreover, had Xenophon's sons been educated in Sparta, would he have sent them to fight in the Athenian army? This act shows that he viewed them as true Athenians.So the education of Xenophon's sons at Sparta could well be no more than a legend, born, along with others, out of the prominence accorded to Spartan education in the *Lak. Pol.*

In the case of Phocion, we know too little to have precise and clearly defined doubts about the historicity of the episode. Having become a celebrity after his victory in the race for *apobatai* at the Panathenaic Games, his son Phokos led a dissolute life.

> Being desirous that the young man might make a complete break with this way of life, he sent him to Lacedaemon and to the company of young men who were completing what is known as the *agōgē*. (Plutarch, *Phocion* 20.4)

There is still less to say about Pyrrhos, seeing that the only thing he did was, at best, a not very serious intention declared in a propaganda speech, and at worst, a mockery. When he invaded the Peloponnese in 274,

> he declared that he had come to liberate the cities subject to Antigonos, and, by Zeus, to send, unless he were prevented, his youngest sons to Sparta to be brought up according to Laconian customs, so that in this way they might possess something over and above what all the other kings had. (Plutarch, *Pyrrhos* 26.21)

Although, as we can see, these texts may be a long way from constituting genuine documentation, they do allow us to draw certain conclusions about the manner in which, according to opinion among fouth-century Greeks, this education proceeded for foreign boys in Sparta. It is obvious that only personages of the highest rank could have contemplated sending their children there. The case of Xenophon, if it is authentic, confirms something which seems equally obvious at first glance, namely that such personages had to be invited by a Spartan citizen with whom they had a relationship of friendship and hospitality; that citizen's family became the guest family for the child. The motives of these fathers appear to have varied widely. For Xenophon they would be essentially ideological, but, as Hodkinson has pointed out,[22] there was more to it than that; he was in exile, his situation dependent on the circumstances of the Spartans, he had to secure his sons' future, and, lastly, Agesilaos' invitation had something of the command about it (ἐκέλευε); all of this meant that he had little choice. Phocion seems more like the father in a bourgeois comedy who is at his wits' end about his son and is contemplating some stern institution, an establishment of the English type, where he could be sent for correction. The texts reveal yet another thing, which is unquestionably true. Phocion's son was clearly no longer a child. Since foreign children, as a rule, did not come with the aim of obtaining Spartan citizenship (the case of Xenophon being, perhaps, an exception), it was apparently possible for them, and this was doubtless what happened most of the time, to follow only part of the *cursus* of Spartan education, preferably, it seems, the part which concerned Xenophon's *paidiskoi* and which was, according to him, the severest of all, a real *school for good behaviour*;[23] thus Plutarch describes Phokos now as *meirakion*, now as *neaniskos*. It is perhaps for this reason that Phylarchos says of the *mothakes* that *they* used to complete the *whole* course.

A passage very often cited from the *Hellenica* (5.3.9) gives an idea of the position of these young foreigners in Spartan society. Xenophon describes the expedition against Olynthos which Agesipolis mounted in 381.

> πολλοὶ δὲ αὐτῷ καὶ τῶν περιοίκων ἐθελονταὶ καλοὶ κἀγαθοὶ ἠκολούθουν καὶ ξένοι τῶν τροφίμων καλουμένων καὶ νόθοι τῶν Σπαρτιατῶν, μάλα εὐειδεῖς καὶ τῶν ἐν τῇ πόλει καλῶν οὐκ ἄπειροι,

> Accompanying him were well-born Perioikoi, who came as volunteers, foreigners belonging to the class known as *trophimoi*, and bastard sons of Spartan citizens, young men of excellent appearance and not unacquainted with the 'good things' the city had to offer.

Trophimoi ('foster-children') is, then, the name given in Sparta to foreign children who were pursuing, or completing, their education there.[24] The fact that a collective term was coined for them shows (what the other texts did not reveal) that they were numerous enough to constitute a genuine social category, and to deserve mention in a text describing the personnel involved in an expedition. This name is significant in itself; it indicates that these youths were received into a Spartan family, of which they became temporary members by a kind of quasi-adoption (which, more so than in the case of *mothakes*, may be likened to 'fosterage'); they were subject to the 'foster-father's' authority. Unlike the *mothax*, the *trophimos* seems not (or, at least, not necessarily) to have had a 'brother-by-upbringing'.[25] As Hodkinson has shown,[26] some of the *trophimoi* could well have been the sons of Perioikoi, and, to me, it even seems natural to suppose that this applied to most of them. Their presence on the expedition shows that certain *trophimoi* were of military age, some as *hēbōntes*, and others perhaps because, from personal choice made in response to particular circumstances (a family in exile, for instance), they remained in Sparta after having fully completed their education. One element in this choice could have been the fact that, as the final sentence of the passage from Xenophon indicates,[27] they were well thought of in the city; this is logical, since they were living examples of that web of powerful connections which great Spartan families were able to weave with families of similar status in other cities. Here, they seem to be members of Agesipolis's 'staff', since that is how I would interpret αὐτῷ…ἠκολούθουν. But they remained *xenoi*, and they therefore had this in common with the *mothakes*, sons of Inferiors, that even a completed education did not automatically qualify them for the rank of Spartan citizen.

Having thus defined the relationship between education and citizenship, a relationship which, as we have seen, was strong but by no means automatic, we now approach the issue from the other angle, by looking at the problem of *failure*. Anyone studying a system of education must inevitably come to devote some attention to this: whether it exists, how it is defined, what proportion of pupils suffer it, what are its consequences. It goes without saying that discussion of failure in the context of Spartan education could not be applied to boys who, by virtue of their personal status or as a result of particular circumstances, had had no access to that education. Hence, neither the children of Inferiors nor those whose fathers cannot finance their education unless they are 'patronized' by a wealthy family, can be regarded as failures.[28] The same is true of those called to mind as potential examples by Eteokles' apophthegm; the word he uses, ἀτευκτήσαντες, clearly indicates that in this case it is the circumstances that would deny them access to education.

The words used in the texts to express the notions of success and failure are compounds of μένειν: either ἐμμένειν (Teles: τὸν…ἐμμείναντα, τὸν μὴ ἐμμείναντα; Aelian: τοῖς ἐμμείνασι), or ὑπομένειν (*Inst. Lac.* 21, ὃς ἂν μὴ ὑπομείνῃ; 22, ὃς ἂν ὑπομείνῃ); the boy who fails is one who does not 'persevere with' , does not 'endure', his education. These terms show that the failure in question is portrayed as desertion. That such desertion would have caused citizenship to be withheld, as Teles and Aelian say, seems to be the inescapable conclusion.

Nevertheless, there are two texts that seem to present the matter differently. One of them is of particular importance, because it is a passage from Xenophon's *Lak. Pol.* (3.3): there, the issue concerns the tests laid down for the *paidiskoi*:

> ἐπιθεὶς δὲ καὶ εἴ τις ταῦτα φύγοι, μηδενὸς ἔτι τῶν καλῶν τυγχάνειν, ἐποίσε μὴ μόνον τοὺς ἐκ δημοσίου ἀλλὰ καὶ τοὺς κηδομένους ἑκάστων ἐπιμελείσθαι ὡς μὴ ἀποδειλιάσαντες ἀδόκιμοι παντάπασιν ἐν τῇ πόλει γένοιντο,
>
> In prescribing also that anyone who shirked these obligations would have no further share in the 'good things', he contrived that not only the city representatives but also those responsible for each boy would see to it that he avoided bringing complete dishonour on himself in the city by cowardice.

This text is enigmatic. What penalties has Xenophon in mind when he uses the expressions 'no further share in the "good things"' and 'bringing complete dishonour on himself'? Exclusion from citizenship? That is not what he is saying; on the contrary, it seems that he is resorting to these vague expressions *precisely so as not to speak of* such exclusion, for which specific terms existed anyway. Amongst these vague expressions, one which we have already encountered – *ta kala* – is, for us, the most significant, certainly, but also the most mysterious. In this text the issue is that of dishonour, degradation, but not of being deprived of the rank of citizen. Yet, is it not precisely such deprivation that constitutes the ultimate dishonour, as its very name – *atimia* – indicates?

This passage from *Lak. Pol.* is very similar to another, where the issue is explicitly that of loss of the status of *homoios* (10.7):

> εἰ δέ τις ἀποδειλιάσειε τοῦ τὰ νόμιμα διαπονεῖσθαι, τοῦτον ἐκεῖνος ἀπέδειξε μηδὲ νομίζεσθαι ἔτι τῶν ὁμοίων εἶναι,
>
> (Lycurgus) stipulated that if anyone should shrink from the effort required of him by the laws, he should no longer be reckoned one of the *homoioi*.

On the one hand it is fair to say that the similarity between these two texts lies chiefly in the terms used to express the offence (ἀποδειλιάσειε/ἀποδειλιάσαντες; διαπονεῖσθαι, cf. πλεῖστοι πόνοι); this is only natural, since the offences are comparable and both are likened to cowardice in the field, the ultimate gold standard, for which the penalty is also a form of *atimia*, the one suffered by the 'tremblers'. By contrast, though, there is a major difference between these two types of culprit: on the one hand, full-grown men who already belong to the *homoioi* (hence ἔτι); on the other, adolescents[29] on whom it would be hard, it seems, to inflict a penalty that would categorically deprive them of a future so early in their lives. Nevertheless, the education itself is likely to have been one of those *kala* of which, according to Xenophon, the offending *paidiskos* would be deprived; how not to think that such a penalty would also debar him from citizenship?

A chance of escape from this *impasse* might lie in looking at the offence that attracts this punishment. Here, we are not dealing with desertion, plain and simple, which was the issue in the texts previously examined. We might define it by saying that, in the case of the *paidiskos* referred to by Xenophon, his behaviour was judged by those in charge of education as being equivalent to a 'flight' (εἰ…φύγοι) in front of the obligations imposed by the law. Clearly, this definition does not solve the problem of the nature of the punishment, because the 'flight' in question may be considered, depending on the circumstances, either as an irremediable shortcoming, entailing a definitive penalty, or as a weakness for which amends could be made. Besides, we know that, even for the 'tremblers', the punishment was not necessarily definitive.

The other text, unfortunately, does nothing to dispel the obscurity. This one comes from *Inst. Lac.* 21: τῶν πολιτῶν ὃς ἂν μὴ ὑπομείνῃ τὴν τῶν παίδων ἀγωγὴν οὐ μετεῖχε τῶν τῆς πόλεως δικαίων, ('a citizen who gave up on the boys' *agōgē* did not enjoy civic rights').

The terms defining the sanction, τὰ τῆς πόλεως δικαία, have puzzled commentators; saying, as Lévy does (1997, 155), that it is 'rather unusual' is putting it mildly. It could be considered a clumsy way of referring to citizenship; thus might a Roman put it who knew little Greek and thought it a way of translating *ius civitatis*. The fact that nos. 21 and 22 together form a unit would confirm that the topic here is indeed the *politeia*, since the very next passage seems to state that a person who did endure the *agōgē* attained citizenship. On the other hand, a ready-made phrase is available for expressing citizenship, the very one that seems to have been used in no. 22, whereas the author of no. 21 gives the impression, just as Xenophon does, that *he took care not to say* that the penalty consisted of exclusion from the *politeia*.[30] We can press the comparison with Xenophon's statement on the erring *paidiskos* further: perhaps, when he says τὰ τῆς πόλεως δικαία, the author of *Inst. Lac.* 21 intended a 'translation' of the term *ta kala*, which had become unintelligible, the paragraph thus constituting a kind of paraphrased précis of *Lak. Pol.* 3.3. What he says could actually be glossed 'he had no share in what was due from the city to each man', that is, he did not have a share of *timē* equal to that of other citizens.

This interpretation, which may seem reasonable, is, unfortunately, contradicted by the terms used, in the passage, to convey the offence. Let us leave aside the incongruity of using τῶν πολιτῶν to refer to those who pursued the education, even though it confirms that we are dealing with an oddly-worded text. The offender is defined as 'one who gave up on the *agōgē*', an expression that, as we have seen, corresponds to failure through desertion, which carried with it the withholding of citizenship. This kind of failure is very different from that evoked by Xenophon.

Since *Inst. Lac.* 21 remains unresolved, we must return to Xenophon, according to whom someone displaying a serious lack of aptitude in the course of his education was denied not citizenship but 'good things'. We must assume, then, that this boy was not *excluded* from education[31] but was able to go on with it, and that once he had completed it he became a citizen, certainly, but a citizen of a lower order. That such a category should exist may be surprising, but a study of the 'tremblers' reveals that there were men in Sparta who, while being, in one sense, citizens, suffered a variety of restrictions, and, just as Xenophon says of the inadequate *paidiskoi*, lived in a condition wholly devoid of honour. Below the rank of full citizens, the so-called *homoioi*, there would thus have been inferior citizens, branded, as a result of misdemeanour, by *atimia*, a withdrawal of *timē* and, at the same time, an exclusion from certain prerogatives, the scope of which could have been highly variable.[32] This is not another instance of the hierarchism peculiar to Sparta; it is the nature of citizenship itself among the Greeks, and the very widespread existence of different kinds of *atimia*, whereby, between the man who is a full citizen and the one who, albeit free, is no citizen at all, all kinds of intermediate conditions can exist; it was a situation that presented Aristotle with an almost insoluble problem when he came to defining citizenship.

Failure could, therefore, take several forms: refusal to submit to the course of education, giving up on the way, definitive exclusion, 'severe reprimand' entailing, for the one who persevered despite everything, access to an inferior kind of citizenship. It remains for us to enquire into its frequency: on the answer to this depends, in no small measure, the image of Spartan education. Kennell presents failure, in the form of exclusion, as common currency, and paints an appalling scene of selections operating throughout the course of education.[33] The truth is that we do not know of a *single* case of *failure* in the true sense of the word. It would have been suicidal for the Spartan state, which, at the period concerning us, was suffering so serious a lack of citizens, to set the bar too high. My view is rather that the threat of a penalty involving a type, complete or partial, of failure, was largely theoretical. This is why the texts dealing with this subject are opaque, when they are not contradictory (which is why the above discussion of them might often have appeared somewhat Byzantine), and why Xenophon, in particular, expresses himself in a style that is vague and rhetorical. What he says on the subject resembles less an exact procedure, frequently applied, than a precept connected with the Lycurgan *corpus* and instilled into boys who had reached the age of serious affairs. The actual norm was rather that, except in case of accident, the group of young Spartans embarking on their education should emerge, complete, at the end, to swell the ranks of the citizen body.

Education: the business of the city

The *paidonomos* is simultaneously the head of the state 'education service', and the personification of the educational system as a whole. The fact that a magistrate should be the living embodiment of the city in the eyes of the young, and that it should be his prerogative to exercise, in its name, authority over them, clearly shows the care taken by the state to keep a firm hand on them, and, itself, to organize the training of future citizens.

The *paidonomos* is even one of the most important magistrates in Sparta, according to Xenophon, who states that he is 'a citizen chosen from among those who hold the principal magistracies' (*LP* 2.2), using, when he does so, language which suggests that such citizens constituted a separate class. It is remarkable that, despite their importance, the functions he exercised should devolve on a single man rather than a college. That is due, no doubt, to the fact that his role, however crucial it may be, does not call for genuine political *power*, which would need the checks that collegiality imposes. Obviously, the *paidonomos* was assisted in his task. Xenophon mentions the 'whip-bearers' (*mastigophoroi*), drawn from the *hēbōntes*, who used to accompany him. I think that, while they could, when the occasion arose, intervene so as to maintain order, or mete out the punishments ordained by the *paidonomos*, their role was primarily that of an escort (like the lictors in Rome) who emphasized the exalted rank of this personage and symbolized the authoritarian and repressive face of education. The *paidonomos* also had (and it may be that we would see this as the most important thing) 'pedagogic' assistants, in the persons of those of the *eirenes* who had been selected to command a 'troop'; in addition, any citizen could consider himself an assistant to the *paidonomos* and, as such, could take a hand where education was concerned. In fact, Xenophon reverses the order of these details: when he is explaining who could stand in for the *paidonomos*, the first ones he names are 'any citizen who happened to be there' (2.10 and 11; apparently, there was always someone); which demonstrates that, here, he is not viewing the question from the educational standpoint (it is obvious that the *eirenes* played a more important educational role than any citizen, whoever he might be), but from the political (in this hierarchy, the citizen, whoever he may be, clearly ranks far above an *eirēn*).[34]

There are, in other cities, magistrates comparable with the *paidonomos* of Sparta. Kennell (1995, 120–1) cites, in this respect, the *agōnothetai*, magistrates responsible for organizing certain competitions, who, like the *paidonomos*, had an escort of *mastigophoroi* or *rhabdoukhoi* ('staff-bearers'), who symbolized their authority. In fact, what the comparison emphasizes more than anything else is the original nature of the *paidonomos*, whose functions were not confined to a few contests, nor even to all those in which the young competed, but who directed the entire sphere of education – system and personnel together. According to Ephoros (70 F 149 *ap*. Strabo 10.4.20) there were *paidonomoi* 'in Crete', but their status was very different: the Cretan *paidonomos* appears not as a state official, but as a member of the *syssition* charged with directing and supervising the boys who ate in company with the men and served them.

The *paidonomos* was not the only magistrate whose business was with the young. The ephors would also be actively involved, though only at the level of the *hēbōntes*: they punished those who failed to obey the adults (Xenophon, *LP* 4.6) and, according to Agatharchides (86 F 10 Jacoby), used regularly to inspect the *neoi*. Such interventions did not constitute a check on the powers of the *paidonomos*, but were derived, as we have seen (above, p. 105), from the ambiguous status of the *hēbōntes*, which lay somewhere between *paides* and full citizens.[35] This raises afresh the question of the 'other face' of education, namely teaching: was this also directed by the *paidonomos*? In fact, its working seems to have been essentially private in character. One might assume that both the recruitment of teachers and the content of their teaching were regulated by the city, but, given that here it was the teachers, not the pupils, whom the city was concerned with supervising, it seems to me that this task must, rather, have devolved upon the ephors.

What we now call *supervision* (Xenophon, for his part, talks of authority: ἔρημοι ἄρχοντος, *LP* 2.10, and 11) – supervision of every single moment, as Xenophon states in the same passages – is one of the principal characteristics of Spartan education. Obviously, a form of it exists in other Greek states, but it is wholly private. At Sparta, it is public and is exercised by the entire city. It is primarily, of course, the job of the *paidonomos* and those of the *eirenes* who commanded a 'troop'. According to Plutarch (*Lyc.* 18.7), these *eirenes* were themselves frequently inspected, in the course of their duties, by 'older men' (*presbyteroi*; in my opinion – and here I am in complete agreement with Lupi – this term, in Plutarch's scheme, did not necessarily refer to old men but to 'real' adults, 'fathers', over thirty years of age) and by 'magistrates' (*archontes*), who were probably the ephors. What Plutarch is describing resembles a genuine system of 'inspections': the visiting officials attended, without saying anything, the schooling session and the administering of punishments, then waited for the boys to return to their homes before making their comments to the *eirēn*. On this procedure, which points to an astonishing similarity between the Spartan state system and our own public systems of education, Plutarch is, admittedly, our only source, but I see no *a priori* reason to reject his account.

We come back to Xenophon for the most remarkable feature of the authority exercised over the boys, the way in which it could, to a great extent, be delegated. Firstly, each father not only could, but was obliged to, give orders to any boy, no matter whom, and punish him if he caught him making a mistake (*LP* 6.1–2). This prerogative was reserved to fathers, because the exercising of it depended on the reciprocity involved, which Xenophon presents as the necessary condition. But the disseminating of authority went further still: any citizen, says Xenophon – without mentioning, here, any requirement for that citizen to have a son of his own – could involve himself in the educational system, and 'give the boys whatever orders he wanted, and hand out punishments' (*LP* 2.10). This right is a powerful practical demonstration of the notion that education was indeed the business of the city, in the person of its citizens. As Birgalias (1999, 307–8) most ably expressed it, it shows that all Spartans felt themselves involved in the education of every boy and personally bound to take an active part in this process of constantly renewing a city which nevertheless stayed the same. Xenophon's account implies, moreover, that the education took place under the very eyes of the citizens, and this, too, is what Plutarch says: 'When they had no other assignment, they would supervise the boys and teach them something useful' (*Lyc.* 24.1).[36]

Reading Plutarch one even gains the impression that, for numerous Spartans, the educational system functioned like a continuously recurring *spectacle* – one of many offered by the city to its citizens (cf. Powell 1989). I do not know whether things went quite as far as that (though why should they not?), but what is certain is that the activity of supervising simultaneously served another purpose: through observing the boys, the citizens were gathering information, about their characters and abilities, which thus became incorporated in the collective memory, so enabling them to pick out the best.

The education of the young was so much the business of the entire city that even the feminine sex seems to have played a part in it. Once again, this is information found only in Plutarch (*Lyc.* 14.5–6), but, in my view, it can be retained because it accords so well with the classical Spartan mentality. In this passage, Plutarch describes certain sacred ceremonies which take the form of a spectacle (θέα). These ceremonies were particularly solemn, and the spectacle was particularly popular, since 'the kings and the Gerousia were in attendance together with the ordinary citizens'. It is in full view of the entire city, then, that the young girls performed songs they had composed themselves, in which the boys (doubtless those of their own age) were either praised or censured. As a form of mockery (σκώμματα) it represented a Laconian counterpart, as it were, of one of the functions of Attic comedy. As a preserve of females, this peculiar 'prizegiving', to which I shall return later, manifestly supports the statement that education took place under the gaze of the *whole* city. All citizens, including even the most important, felt involved in its progress and its results. So the conventional term 'supervision' offers too narrow a description, and conjures a slightly distorted, and over-repressive, image of something that was also an object of interest and a focus of participation for everyone. It was almost a civic duty, because *what they were really supervising was not the boys so much as the education itself*, checking that its progress was just as it should be.

A logical consequence of unremitting supervision is that it should give rise to frequent *punishment*. Reading Xenophon (and Plutarch writes in exactly the same vein), one gains the impression that, in the case of Spartan education, punishments were, in fact, both numerous and severe (*LP* 2.2, 8, 10; 6.2). He constantly makes the connection between wielding command and meting out punishment; for him, these are the two complementary expressions of authority. Most of the time, punishment means beating; the constant recourse to corporal punishment, which might almost prompt the conclusion that the boys were, in a sense, treated like slaves (cf. Plutarch *Lyc.* 17.4, ὑπηρέταις χρῆται) is, moreover, by no means a Spartan speciality. Its commonest form seems to have been a whipping: in 2.2, the punishments inflicted by the *paidonomos* are strictly associated with the presence of the *mastigophoroi*; we encounter the whip again at Orthia. Yet the Greek whip was a formidable instrument, more akin to a bull whip than to a cat-o'-nine-tails;[37] compared with that, the mysterious[38] thumb-biting by the *eirēn*, described by Plutarch (*Lyc.* 18.5), seems no more than a comic figure from folklore. However, I am not sure that what Xenophon says about punishment should be taken literally. It is probable that his purpose of presenting an *apologia* leads him to exaggerate the severity of Spartan punishments: in fact, for him, as for all his contemporaries, a good education meant a severe education, and severity was measured by the number of lashes. The effectiveness of the supervision meant that in Sparta it was certainly more difficult than anywhere else for a boy to make a mistake without being caught, but, as I see it, we have not a single serious reason for thinking that physical punishments there were unusually harsh.

Drakontios must constitute a separate case, since his is not a true instance of child punishment. Xenophon, who calls him a 'Spartan', relates (*Anabasis* 4.8.25) that 'in childhood he had been exiled from Sparta for having unintentionally killed another boy with a *xyēlē*', (ἔφυγε παῖς ὢν οἴκοθεν, παῖδα ἄκων κατακάνων ξυήλῃ πατάξας).[39] In Xenophon's scheme, *pais* signifies a child under 14 years of age. It may be astonishing to picture so young a boy condemned to exile, though admittedly it was for an exceptional offence; for, even without the intention of killing, he had deliberately struck his fellow with his weapon. In fact, though, φεύγειν can just as well mean 'to go into exile' as 'to be exiled'; in this instance it comes to very nearly the same thing, because, in view of his age, Drakontios probably did not come before a tribunal, and it is his father who took the decision, reasoning that in all respects it would be better for his son to leave Sparta. Also, this being a case of unintentional killing, the decision was more religious (to ward off pollution) than penal in character.

In other cities (as Xenophon would say) the chastising of children was a private matter, reserved to the father of a family. In Sparta, since education was the business of the city, the right to punish was extended to many; here we meet, once again, the hierarchy we found in the sphere of 'supervision'. The child was punished by his father for offences committed within the home and, where his father had learnt of them, for those committed beyond it. The same passage of Xenophon (*LP* 6.1–2) shows that he could also be punished by any other father; with punishment on these terms we have already moved onto the level of the city, if, following Aristotle's analysis, the city is viewed as a community of families. The *erastēs* was considered responsible for his *erōmenos*, which implies that he was able to punish him; but in carrying out this task he was himself supervised by the authorities. The same went for the *eirēn* in respect of his troop. Finally, of course, the city magistrates (the *paidonomos*, Xenophon, *LP* 2.2, and perhaps also 8 – the case of a boy caught stealing; and, where the offenders were *hēbōntes*, the ephors, who fined them because they were adult, *LP* 4.6) had, to the highest degree, both the right and the duty to impose punishment. But what best substantiates the notion that education was the concern of the whole city is the fact that, as with 'supervision', the right/duty to punish was extended to all citizens, as Xenophon (*LP* 2.10) and Plutarch (*Lyc.* 17.1) record. This is why Plato (*Laws* 7.804d), and then Plutarch (*Lyc.* 15.14) are justified in saying that in Sparta the boys were truly 'the common property of the city' (κοινοὺς τῆς πόλεως, Plutarch; cf. above, p. 54).

Having been educated by the city, the young Spartan, naturally, *belonged* to the city. The purpose of the education was not so much to frame his personality as an individual, as to produce a disciplined member of the civic community. Paramount among the values it instilled in him was, as Herodotos says, obedience to the laws; this obedience was not only a military virtue, but the civic virtue *par excellence*. And in this, Sparta was doing no more than putting into practice the ideal of Greek cities in general, the ideal reflected, for example, by the famous prosopopoeia of the Laws in the *Crito*. It is probable, moreover, that the education of young Spartans afforded them a genuine schooling in the laws of the city. A recent study by Ruzé[40] draws attention to the practice, attested in a number of cities, of setting the laws to music to make them easier to learn and commit to memory,[41] while the same study also suggests that, rather than the texts of the laws themselves, it was the prologues (προοίμια), less technical and more akin to precepts, that were sung in this way.[42] A text like the 'Great Rhetra', if indeed it is genuine, could have been transmitted like this; that would explain its 'poetic' style and the assonances that give it its rhythm. It is to this context that we should assign a practice recorded in the *Souda*, in the entry on Dikaiarchos: the Spartans decided, one day, that the *Constitution of the Lacedaemonians* which this disciple of Aristotle's had composed should be read once a year, in the ephors' office, to the youths of the class of *hēbōntes* (τοὺς τὴν ἡβητικὴν ἔχοντας ἡλικίαν, a phrase borrowed from Xenophon); this practice, according to the entry, had lasted 'for a long time'.[43] In my view, this reading did not replace the study of the laws, but rounded it off; the Spartans judged that with this treatise (which probably dwelt on the precepts of Lycurgus and on the Spartan way of life rather than on the laws in the strict sense) they were at last in possession of a text that gave of their city the image they desired.

The pederastic relationship

This was considered by all Greeks of the classical era to possess an important educational value. Pushing this argument to its limit, the Spartans made it a constituent of the course of education the city caused its young to pursue.

Xenophon clearly states that the pederastic relationship was part of the education: ἐστὶ γάρ τι καὶ τοῦτο πρὸς παιδείαν ('for this also contributes to education'), he says, when he starts to explain the point (*LP* 2.12). He then takes this further, reporting the opinion attributed to Lycurgus that, provided it was conducted with propriety, the pederastic relationship was 'the most excellent form of education', καλλίστην παιδείαν (2.13). The adjective *kallistē* indicates that it was a training of the whole personality, including from the moral standpoint, an initiation into virtue; the same idea is developed in the two *Symposia*, that of Plato and that of Xenophon, which on some subjects seems to be discussing Plato's. It forms part of the basis of the speech justifying pederasty.[44] In order that it could be presented as a means of training the intellect and attaining high moral standards, all trace of the physical aspect of it had first to be removed; Plato does this (in absolute terms) and so does Xenophon (for Sparta). Conversely, if, in the fourth century, somebody wants to criticize, not pederasty in itself (no one does that), but the way it is practised in this or that city, he has to say that physical love is, there, tolerated, not to say encouraged; this is what Plato (*Symposium* 182b) and Xenophon (*LP* 2.12; *Symposium* 8.35) say of the Boeotians and the Eleans. This preliminary point concerning the physical aspect is a formidable obstacle, and we have seen that Xenophon did not make the best job of negotiating it; his logic leads him to present the pairing of the lovers in a purely intellectual and ethical light, which is scarcely convincing.

For all that, we need not dismiss as fiction everything he says about the worth of the pederastic relationship and the essential part it played in the educational process. Leaving aside, for the moment, the other problems pertaining to pederasty in Sparta, I shall confine myself to the topic that concerns me here: the analysis of how this relationship contributed to the moulding of a Spartan citizen. It began to take effect at an age when the boy was about to finish, or even when he had to all intents and purposes finished, the basic stage of schooling, and we may regard this as the moment when the *erastēs* took over the role of the *didaskaloi*. In the course of so intimate and enduring a relationship[45] there would evolve a full and reciprocal exchange of experiences and knowledge; it is quite conceivable that when it ended the *erōmenos* would know almost as much as his *erastēs*, of both oral and written expression, of reckoning, of every aspect of *mousikē*. This instruction differed from what the boy had been receiving so far, in that it no longer took place within a collective framework but was instead sustained by means of a personal relationship.[46] It is obvious that this educational relationship was not confined to scholarly 'subjects', and that the lover shared with his beloved his experience of life in general: so, from then onward, the younger male had access, admittedly indirect, but nonetheless personal, to the adult world, and began to witness how the life of the city was conducted.[47] That is not all. Xenophon depicts (*LP* 3.5) the *paidiskoi*, in some cases, being present at men's mess-table: this probably occurred when the *erastēs* introduced the young boy to his *syssition*.[48] Thus the pederastic relationship afforded the boy his first direct contact with what constituted the basic structure of citizen life. This brought in its wake a decisive broadening of the boy's horizons and the first break with the world of childhood. We can also assume that, as Birgalias suggests (1999, 244), the relationship was equally fulfilling for the *erastēs*, in that it placed him in a position of responsibility and made him exert every effort to avoid disappointing the boy he loved.

When he describes the forming of the pair, Xenophon presents it as a wholly private affair: 'When a man of the right disposition was seized with admiration for a boy's character and did his utmost to make him a blameless friend and live with him...' (*LP* 2.13). Plutarch strikes a similar note, while apparently also saying that this was what happened to every boy: 'When they (the boys) reached this age (12 years), young men of excellent reputation became their *erastai* and spent their time with them' (*Lyc.* 17.1).[49] The pederastic relationship appears to develop from the meeting of two individuals and from their mutual sympathy. For all that, it is not presented as a relationship of equals: almost always it is the elder who takes the initiative and, apparently, does the choosing; but occasionally the converse situation would arise, when an *erōmenos* with several suitors declared his preference for one of them. Nothing is said about the *erastēs* paying 'court', as he would most probably have done, to the object of his choice, in Sparta just as elsewhere.[50] Nor is anything said – though this is readily understandable – about the role which the families of the two protagonists might have played in this pairing, at least when those families were prominent ones. Clearly, the texts give this lovers' encounter an idealized, almost other-worldly, image, in which the information has been filtered, and from which all reference to the realities, social no less than emotional, is banished. Indeed, the speech in defence of pederastic love was not only expected to exclude any physical aspect, but had also to set the relationship exclusively under a banner of excellence.

In real life, pederasty was not only an affair between two people; it operated as an institution within the state institution that was the education system. Xenophon suggests it himself, when he records that Lycurgus approved of it, and wholeheartedly, even; that amounts to considering it as a norm. Another text shows the city magistrates keeping an eye on how it functioned; this is a passage from Aelian (*VH* 3.10), who records some of the features of this surveillance, while ascribing it to the ephors. He brings together texts of different kinds: in the present tense, universally applicable 'laws' (punishment of the *erastēs* if his *erōmenos* made an error, and, at 3.12, the repression of physical love); in the aorist, two anecdotes. A document like this obviously cannot be accepted without some scrutiny. The anecdotes, in which there is very little personal detail, and the edifying nature of which leaps out of the page, lack any secure historical basis. The authenticity of the alleged 'laws' is more than doubtful, and one might wonder whether the behaviour they envisage could have attracted penalties such as fines. But, for us, what is crucial about this passage is the ideology it expresses: that the pederastic relationship contributes to the moral progress of the pair (anecdote 2), the reason why its establishment should be based on ethical criteria (anecdote 1); physical relations are totally forbidden. This is exactly the ideology found in Xenophon.

The first anecdote displays the vigilance exercised by the magistrates over the forming of a pair:

> One day, one of those boys who were in the public eye made it plain that he preferred a rich *erastēs* to one who, albeit of excellent character, was poor; they fined him, thereby, apparently, punishing love of money by exacting money.

In this case, it is the *erōmenos* who is in a position to choose between several suitors; this comes of his being no ordinary boy. Such situations were well known in Athens and certainly also existed in Sparta for young boys who possessed some oustanding personal or (more probably) social, quality. Plutarch also touches on it (*Lyc.* 18.9), but does so when relating that, instead of entering into competition over a boy, the suitors shared his favours between them – a masculine counterpart of female polyandry?

The second anecdote depicts the pederastic relationship as obligatory, but in a rather unexpected way, for the *erastēs* – a recalcitrant *erastēs* being the subject of the tale.

> They also fined another person, a most worthy man, who refused to offer his love to any of the well-bred young boys, for the reason that although he excelled he did not love anyone. In fact it is plain that he would have caused his beloved to become like him, and might have done the same to another as well.

This anecdote appears to me to be adapted from an apophthegm, since the structure characteristic of this genre is found in the narrative: the account of certain behaviour at the beginning of the action; the central event, namely the penalty inflicted by the ephors; the key 'saying' ('because although he excelled he did not love anyone'), which is, as ever, the answer to the question 'Why?' put, implicitly in this case, to the ephors; and a comment from the author, explaining the 'saying'. An apophthegm like this could have been composed at any time, perhaps in the third century, but it is related to the same speech in praise of Spartan pederastic practices as that of Xenophon. This speech cannot depict the pederastic relationship as anything other than the forming of an attachment, from mutual choice, by two beings of sound character; but the reality that shows through, every time, is clearly that of a liaison that forms one stage in an obligatory *cursus* of education.

Obligatory: this is an important word, and, before uttering it, it would be as well to take a closer look at it. Certainly, since the pederastic relationship formed part of a course of education that was obligatory and identical for all, it is logical to conclude that it, too, was mandatory for every boy. But reality is not always bound by the rules of syllogism, and we also have to take account of the way in which Xenophon and Plutarch describe the forming of a pair. That it should have stemmed from a choice – usually made by the *erastēs* – implies that some boys may have been left without a lover. That is the more plausible in that this is what used to happen in Crete: Ephoros' account (in Strabo 10.4.21) even shows that, since the young boys who were the targets of 'kidnapping' (known as *parastathentes*; for that is how it was done) enjoyed exceptional honours for life and bore the enviable title *kleinoi* ('glorious'), they formed a tiny minority.[51] I think it more likely that in classical Sparta, where society ran on more egalitarian lines, it was those who were left who formed the minority; but it is highly probable that there *were* some. This prompts two questions. The first concerns the criteria governing choice. The texts mention only physical and moral qualities, but I am persuaded that – as in Crete, from what Ephoros says – social criteria (thoroughly analysed by Cartledge, 2001, 103–5), played at least as important a role. A boy from a prominent family obviously had greater opportunities to attract suitors than one from an ordinary background. The second question relates to the possible consequences of 'failure'. In Crete, so Ephoros records, these only damaged a boy's prospects when he was 'of good appearance and illustrious birth'; but this was in a society where the elected ones were few. Since the situation in Sparta was probably different, the fear, there, might be that failing to be chosen as someone's *erōmenos* could constitute a pretty poor start in life.

A collective education

Nowadays, education in its various forms has a pronounced collective character, and specialists underline the importance of what they call socialization in developing a child's personality so that, in the future, he may become integrated into society with ease. In Sparta, this feature was particularly important. We can assume that the aspect of education concerned with imparting basic skills was collective, since, while certain boys from rich families could have had teacher-pedagogues, rather like private tutors (although this is not attested), certainly most young Spartans regularly attended schools where the teaching was conducted in classes. The other aspect of education functioned within the contexts of age-class and 'troop'. The way in which Xenophon presents the *paidiskoi* gives grounds for thinking that they were allowed more individual expression in their lives than were the *paides*, but that this was to prepare them for entry to new social groups, such as the adult messes. This scope for individuality was, naturally, even greater for the *hēbōntes*. Those admitted to the ranks of the *hippeis* encountered there a new model of collective living but one that did not act as a permanent bond;[52] as for those who failed to attain this rank, one has the impression that they carried on with their lives and tried to salvage their 'careers' individually, each man for himself.

If Spartan education is of so collective a character, it is because it is designed to prepare the young for an equally collective civic life. Certainly, the Spartan citizen's life was not inherently so to the extent that Xenophon and, particularly, Plutarch would have us believe; he engaged in economic activity (albeit only the management of his inheritance), he had a personal life, a family life, matters about which little is said but which must still have existed. Having said that, more of his life was spent in collective settings than in any other city: the gymnasium, mess dinners, discussions in the *leschē* and in the Agora, combined with political and military activity, took up a great deal of his time. Thus, the collective nature of this education, rather than crushing the personality of the young, had the effect of preparing them for the kind of life awaiting them as citizens, and did it so well that, in the course of their lives, they had no sense that they had surrendered their individuality, but, on the contrary, felt they were doing the very thing they had been made for.

The educative importance of the pederastic relationship hinges on the fact that, in a life which, when the boy was not with his family, was spent entirely in groups, it introduced another dimension, that of a mutual personal relationship with an adult who was, even so, still young.

An egalitarian education?

To the extent that it was a state institution, education was the same for everyone. Rich children, poor children, sons from prominent families, sons from ordinary ones, were mixed together in age-classes and 'troops', even if it is likely that the performance of boys from important families was followed with closer attention and attracted more comment than that of ordinary ones. The fact that punishment was not inflicted solely by fathers, but, rather, by anyone taking a part in education, by all fathers, and, in the final analysis, by all citizens, meant that all the boys saw the same 'justice' being applied without the least possibility of anyone's being privileged.

The aim of this egalitarian treatment was, obviously, to create citizens who were all 'alike'. Between Spartan citizens there existed every conceivable form of inequality, but they were able to call themselves 'alike' because they had all been educated to lead the same kind of life (*diaita*). This is what Thucydides, with great precision, says, in a frequently cited passage (1.6.4): 'The Lacedaemonians were the first to adopt simple clothing, as we all do nowadays; and, generally speaking, the rich pursued, as far as possible, equality with ordinary people in their manner of living' (ἰσοδίαιτοι μάλιστα). The author gives the specific example of clothing; it is, actually, the first thing someone visiting Sparta might notice. This is a point on which Xenophon also insists, in his account of Spartan education: the boys, we read, could only wear one kind of garment throughout the year (*LP* 2.4). Xenophon explains that this is intended to harden the boys against cold and heat; but it could also be viewed as an egalitarian measure, since without it the rich would be able to flaunt their superiority by providing their sons with a wardrobe appropriate to each season, something the poor could not do. The key-word in Thucydides' text – and in the Spartan conception of equality – is *isodiaitoi*, a compound of *diaita*. This term generally refers to 'way of life', but, with Hippocrates, it acquired a special usage to convey the idea of 'diet'. Now, the dietary restrictions imposed on boys is a subject on which Xenophon speaks at length. Chiefly he stresses the fact that they were kept on short commons, but we have seen that this could only have been effective within the framework of communal meals, where the rations brought by each one were all pooled. Thus the boys were used to sharing their food, exactly as happened within the *syssition*, practising strict equality in what was, in antiquity, a fundamental domain of life.

But we should not forget that what we have just said only holds good for the public and communal part of education as a whole. The 'instructive' element, which was almost the same as what constituted the whole of education in Athens, was conducted privately, and depended on the decisions, and the means, of each family. It must, therefore, have been very variable and far from equal. Ancient authors refer only to the system organized by the state, but, in real terms, a boy's education would have been the product of both kinds, and might have differed markedly from what we believe about Spartan education. This is the kind of reflection one cannot help engaging in when faced with actual evidence (as a lawyer would say) like Damonon's dedication (*IG* 5.1.213). What might Enymakratidas' education have been like? Obviously his father brought him up (since we really *can* say that he brought him up) to follow in his footsteps in the active pursuit of athletics, and in racing horses and, later, chariots. He took his son with him, or sent him off to take part in contests held in distant sanctuaries. How could these activities be reconciled with the demands – extreme, by all accounts – imposed by state education? Should we assume that, in the case of the very rich, some degree of compromise was possible? Damonon's career itself prompts an enquiry into equestrian skills. Nowhere is it mentioned that training in this field formed part of the state education. But when we consider the assignments entrusted to the *hippeis* (such as those found in Xenophon's account of the crushing of Cinadon's conspiracy; this was not, according to Xenophon himself, an unusual case, the alleged mission entrusted to Cinadon having been preceded by several others), we find that they involved the ability – and no slight ability – to ride a horse. From this it follows that any *hēbōn* who was (by implication) a candidate for selection as *hippeus* must have learnt to ride, which in turn suggests that his family would have owned horses.[53] This example testifies to the inequality that really did exist both in education and in access to public office.

Competition and the choosing of an elite

While Spartan education was (in part) uniform, and while its intended aim was to ensure that future citizens were as 'alike' as possible, it also had the function, if not of definitively detaching off an elite, at least of setting in motion a long-term process of selection. There is nothing at all contradictory in this: a group might all be given the same course of training, but if the people giving it are also looking out for those whose responses display the greatest physical, intellectual, and moral promise, that is by no means abnormal.

As early as 1968 Finley had underlined the importance of competition in Spartan education (p. 147) as also in Spartan society (pp. 151–3). Where it affects education, this topic has been explored as much by Hodkinson (1983, pp. 248–9) as it has by Cartledge (1987, pp. 27–9), which means that I need only touch on it here. Xenophon speaks of the 'enduring glory' earned by whoever won the cheese-stealing contest at the altar of Orthia (*LP* 2.9), and indicates that it was 'the cleverest of the *eirenes*' who was appointed as captain of a 'troop'. Plutarch is more explicit about the younger age-group: it was 'the most intelligent and the most courageous in combat' whom the boys under twelve took as their leader (*Lyc.* 16.8); he then repeats (17.2) what Xenophon recorded about the *eirenes*. From his description (16.9) of how the adults urged boys to fight each other and then 'observed' how they went about it, it becomes clear that their purpose was to spot who had the greatest aptitude for this kind of activity. The evidence does not amount to much, especially if one decides to confine oneself to the testimonies of the classical era; I have no doubt, however, neither of the reality of the competition, nor of the fact that the constant 'supervision' of the boys had for its main aim to pick out the best of them. Sparta saw itself as the very model of 'government by the best', which was necessarily, and almost by definition, the best form of government; to remain viable over a long period, this system is based on the assumption that it really should be the best people who attained positions of responsibility (the obvious problem being to discover what was meant by 'the best'). Xenophon confirms this, indirectly, in his account of the trial of Sphodrias in 378: Agesilaos' argument in favour of acquitting him (reported by Etymokles in the course of conversation, *Hell.* 5.4.32) is that 'it would be difficult to put to death a man of this calibre, who, as *pais*, *paidiskos*, and *hēbōn*, always conducted himself well and honourably'. This remark shows that the achievements of the young, throughout the three principal stages of their education, were, tacitly, being noted and remembered, if not by society as a whole, at least by those in official positions, and that, to a great extent, they determined an individual's future. It is not an exaggeration to claim that it was on account of his achievements that Sphodrias became the friend of king Kleombrotos (and his son Kleonymos, the *erōmenos* of Archidamos, son of Agesilaos, and himself a future king) and was appointed as harmost in Thespiai; it is certain that he owed it to them that he escaped his sentence.[54] Did his educational achievements allow a Spartan of modest background to attract notice enough to offset his social handicap and give him access, one day, to important office, as Cartledge asserts?[55] It was at least theoretically possible, but I know of no unequivocal example of it.[56] After all, even in democratic Athens, self-made men were rather rare.

If Xenophon does not say much about competition amongst the *paides* and *paidiskoi*, everything changes when he comes to the *hēbōntes*: in his account of them (*LP* 4) he actually talks of nothing else. Among the numerous selection procedures undergone by this age-group[57] he paid special attention to the one for the *hippeis*, because this was the driving competitive force among the *hēbōntes*; not without reason, since the other selections only chose a handful of them, whereas there were 300 *hippeis* to be chosen every time: so each *hēbōn* might reckon he stood a good chance, with the result that the whole class seethed with competitiveness, from top to bottom. The clear impression we have gained (cf. above, pp. 18–19 and p. 103) is that this competition was carried on in the worst possible manner; that what Xenophon called the 'struggle for virtue' consisted, in reality, of dozens of personal clashes in which no holds, not even espionage or denunciation, were barred; that *eris* became *stasis*; and that this free-for-all was a most bizarre way of producing disciplined and self-controlled citizens.

There is, moreover, in the story of 'Pedaritos' Smile', an ancient criticism, implied but nonetheless robust, of this kind of competition; three versions of the story survive, two in the form of apophthegms, and the third, a simple narrative.[58] Pedaritos explained that, if he smiled when he learnt that he had not been selected as *hippeus*, it was because he was delighted that the city possessed 300 citizens who were better than he. By his conduct, Pedaritos challenges the Lycurgan norm, which intended that the selection be contested, and he triumphs over it: to consider as enemies both those who have been chosen in preference to you and those who made that choice, could only be good because that was what Lycurgus approved; but to accept the decision, or better still, to rejoice for the sake of the city, and thus to show that one has placed Sparta's interest above everything else, is an incomparably superior response. The lesson we learn from this anecdote is that there is clear evidence of a gap, not to say a contradiction, between the customary norm and what ought to be the conduct of the perfect citizen. Yet, to produce the perfect citizen is the avowed objective of Lycurgus' laws: the author of this apophthegm, whoever he was, has succeeded very neatly in bringing these laws into direct conflict between themselves.

One could certainly say, by way of justifying how the *hēbōntes* went about competing with each other, that it was an extremely efficient method of supervision; it is clear that if a *hēbōn*, had he been selected, or, even, rejected as *hippeus* (since Xenophon, *LP* 4.4, is careful to specify that supervision was reciprocal), did something reprehensible, or showed evidence of an unpleasant attitude, there would always be some enemy there to notice the fact and denounce him to the authorities; to that extent it is fair to say that each *hēbōn* lived 'in the midst of his enemies', as it were. But, attractive though this might be for the security of the state, such an objective is not enough to explain the strange forms these rivalries took. I see two possible approaches to trying to uncover an educational purpose in them.

The first is to follow Xenophon in every detail. He depicts the institution of the *hippeis* (including the *hippagretai*) as a sort of 'joke' institution, the sole function of which was to serve as a stake in a competition that would, in fact, be the only objective. There seems to be an element of truth in this, because, although the *hippagretai* were appointed by the ephors, they still belonged to the *hēbōntes* class, who were, as we have seen, potential citizens only; as such, their nomination manifestly did not invest them with the kind of authority that put them beyond the reach of any challenge to their selection. It is quite obvious that 'reject' *hēbōntes* could not have blamed the 'real' city magistrates as they blamed the *hippagretai*. As for the *hippeis*, they had, after all, only been nominated by one of their friends. The logic of the system decreed that they submit annually to a process of reselection (and this is confirmed by the 'saying' of Pedaritos); so the 'reject' would pick one of them as his target and then seek to create some obstacle to that man's reselection, so that he himself might take his place. Thus, for the *hēbōntes*, each year constituted a sort of stage: a stage of holding responsibility, both for the *hippeis*, who had to show themselves worthy of their title if they were to be reselected, and, to an even greater extent, for the *hippagretai*, before whom there opened up, if all went according to plan, a promising political career; and for the 'rejects' a stage of contesting the selection, a whole year in which to demonstrate that they were better than those who had been selected in preference to them.

The obvious objection to this interpretation is that it is only tenable as long as one stays within the confines of Xenophon's text. As soon as one quits it, then it becomes clear that the *hippeis* were nothing like a 'joke' institution. On the one hand, to be *hippeus* was quite genuinely an honour and offered palpable benefit: it allowed one to fight in an elite unit, alongside the king, where one was better protected and could more easily be noticed (especially *by* the king) than if one fought in the front rank of the phalanx. At the same time, it was the first step towards a real 'career'. On the other hand, the corps of *hippeis* played an important role in the administration of public affairs, especially when a serious crisis arose, since it was a 'strike force' always at the disposal of the authorities, that is to say, the ephors: the case of Cinadon provides a notable example of this.

The second approach is even more hazardous. It consists of assuming that, long before the time of Chairman Mao, the Spartans had discovered the educational virtues of rebelliousness, and its political advantages, when exercised within certain limits, and had grasped that young men were of the age where such instruction could be applied. According to this model the role of the Red Guard belonged not to the *hippeis* but to their rivals. The *hippeis* symbolized authority, established order, directives from on high, everything, therefore, that had to be challenged; Lycurgus was a very fair equivalent of Chairman Mao.[59] The Spartans had taken measures to ensure that, with adult supervision, competitive behaviour should be channelled and contained, confined as it was to personal confrontations.

The obvious objection here is that Communist China and Sparta are not really comparable at all. The 'reject' was not fighting for an idea or a political trend, he was fighting for himself, something in which it is hard to find anything of educational value.

So, neither of these approaches offers any explanation, in terms of education, for the different ways in which the *hēbōntes* went about competing with each other. Nonetheless, they all have something in common, and it may be that this was the lesson Xenophon was aiming to impart: the idea that had to be inculcated in the young was that, in Spartan politics, nothing is ever definitively gained or definitively lost. A citizen who, in a given year, is not elected to office should not consider this a failure past recovery. It is up to him, if he can, to prove in the eyes of the city that, in the future, he will deserve to be chosen; the very life of Pedaritos is an illustration of this lesson. This is the law of a 'timocratic' regime, this is what the doctrine of 'government by the best' implies. To ascertain whether this ideal was borne out in reality is another question altogether.

Unquestionably, the view of Spartan education as a course of training with an exclusively military purpose dominates the sources to the point where, for us, it represents the standard thinking on the subject in antiquity. It arose because of certain elements in that education and because it was, at the same time, a convenient explanation for Spartan military superiority. But it is chiefly a view held by men contemplating Sparta from the outside. Certainly, Xenophon, who was better acquainted with the city from within, was very much of this opinion, both as to the whole and as to details, but we have noticed (above, p. 143) how some of his discussions also testify to a broader view of the objective of Spartan education, one whereby he saw it as a training for citizenship. Slight as may be our penetration of this society's inner workings (something a study of its education, despite immense and inevitable gaps, does to some extent facilitate), it is demonstrable that there, as in all Greek cities, military service represented only a part of the citizen's activity, and that it would be at once absurd and impossible to train the soldier without training the citizen.

Notes

1 Cf. Cairns 1993 and Richer 1999.

2 Plato is mistaken when he makes the collective nature of Spartan education responsible for the 'savagery' which, according to him, condemned it to defeat (Aristotle, for his part, makes no such error). For an education system to be effective and balanced, there comes a point where the child must be absolutely integrated into a group; and no one would say that seven would be too young for this to be feasible. The interpretation Xenophon offers of practices such as going barefoot, having scanty clothing and food, and, above all, stealing, however neatly he puts it, cannot be accepted by us as 'true'.

3 On this point I agree entirely with Lévy 1997, 156–9, but not when he seems to deduce from it that this interpretation is 'true'.

4 Lévy 1997, 156.

5 On this passage, cf. Buffière 1980, 27; Cartledge 2001, 101 and n. 59, 210; Parker 1989, 166, n. 22.

6 Vidal-Naquet 1981, 162.

7 See, for example, Cartledge 1987, 23–4; Kennell 1995, 133; Lévy 1997, 155.

8 Cf. above, p. 63.

9 Lévy 1997, 155, n. 22, takes the text literally and sees in it 'an allusion to a particular fact'. In my own view, that seems to contradict the very nature of helotism (as I perceive it at least).

10 On this text and its actual date, cf. above, p. 69.

11 As early as 1891, Bases recognized a lacuna at this point; likewise Fuhrmann 1988, n. 6, 240, who, otherwise, reads τὰς…διατεταγμένας μοίρας.

[12] See the analysis by Hodkinson 2000, 88–90.

[13] See finally Hodkinson 1997, 55–62, summarized in Hodkinson 2000, 354–6. I refer to his article for his demonstration (p. 56–8) that this social category existed as early as the classical era. Obviously, I do not accept the argument taken from Kennell's thesis that Spartan education was broken off in the 3rd century; on the other hand, the fact that all the examples cited in the texts date back to the end of the 5th seems to me an essential clue.

[14] Cf. Powell 1999, 406.

[15] Ducat 1990, 166–8, with previous bibliography.

[16] Paradiso (1991, 47–9) returns to the traditional theory of a servile origin; her arguments are refuted by Hodkinson 1997, 59.

[17] In this same sense, Hodkinson 1997, 59–60.

[18] Above, p. 134.

[19] Cf. Furuyama 1991, 11–14, and Hodkinson 1997, 58, summarized in Hodkinson 2000, 355–6.

[20] In a manner that strikes me as a little arbitrary, Hodkinson, 1997, 61 (but not 2000, 355–6) rejects Phylarchos' version as a fiction designed to emphasize the fact that Lysander owed his rise to merit alone. I think one can credit Phylarchos with more reliability than that.

[21] Higgins 1997, 160, n. 46; see also Humble 2004, who, however, concludes positively.

[22] Hodkinson 1997, 64.

[23] Above, p. 15.

[24] A detailed study of the *trophimoi* as a social category may be found in Hodkinson 1997, 62–5, with the main points of which I agree.

[25] On this point, cf. Hodkinson 1997, 63.

[26] Cf. Hodkinson 1997, 65 and n. 41. There are, however, two points on which I cannot agree with him. (a) The partitive τῶν τροφίμων does not signify that there were several classes of *trophimoi*, but merely that certain members of Agesipolis' entourage were *xenoi* belonging to the class of *trophimoi*. (b) I think that the *trophimoi* in question are also there as volunteers, since I do not see how young men of the status of *xenoi* could be subject to military discipline (the case of Athenian metics is entirely different).

[27] For I think that the laudatory description 'young men of excellent appearance, etc.' applies not only to the *nothoi*, but also to the *trophimoi*. The Perioikoi have, in fact, already received their own laudatory description, and it would be astonishing if the *trophimoi* alone were left without one – especially if Xenophon's sons were amongst them.

[28] As Kennell does (1995, 133–4); they are the only cases of 'failure' he was able to cite, together with the very unusual case of Drakontios, who had been exiled when still a child for having killed one of his comrades, and so is not an example of true failure either (Xenophon *Anabasis* 4.8.25; on this episode, see further, p. 213).

[29] That this statement is included in the chapter on the *paidiskoi* shows that, as far as Xenophon knew, it was out of the question for those whom he calls *paides* to suffer so heavy a penalty.

[30] In the same vein, Lévy 1997, 155: 'an expression...which suggests that Plutarch was unwilling to go as far as saying that they were utterly deprived of citizenship'. The translation by Fuhrmann, 1988, 'they had no rights to the justice of the city' is, in any

case, unacceptable.

[31] This exclusion may have been imposed, but doubtless only in cases of exceptionally serious misdemeanour: we drew attention, above (n. 28), to the case of Drakontios; this also poses a problem, for it raises the question of how he could have become a 'Spartan', as he is designated by Xenophon.

[32] To the same effect, Lévy 1997, 155: 'Adolescents who dodged the rigours of Spartiate education have no share in honours (τὰ καλά), meaning that they would only be inferior citizens, unable to hold office'.

[33] Kennell 1995, 134: 'But ability was severely tested, too, and at every stage the members were thinned out, so that only the 'crème de la crème' could attain the reward of honour and privilege that was their due as full citizens'. Likewise, Link 1994, 29 and 83, believes in the existence of genuine selection through education.

[34] This is an application of the concept of the 'generational society' (Lupi 2000).

[35] Likewise, the ephors kept their eye on the working of the pederastic relationship (above, pp. 166–8), which was logical, since it was the adult member who was considered answerable for the couple.

[36] For intervention by adults in educational activities, cf. also *Lyc.* 16.9 and 17.1; *Inst. Lac.* 8 and, perhaps, 38.

[37] Cf. Ducat 1995, 364–6.

[38] Cf. Den Boer 1954, 274–81.

[39] On this episode, above, n. 28 and 31, and below, p. 213.

[40] Cf. Ruzé 2001.

[41] In Crete: Ephoros (*ap.* Strabo 10.4.20), where τὰς ἐκ τῶν νόμων ᾠδας should be read as 'songs derived from the laws' rather than 'stipulated by the laws'; at Sparta: Clement of Alexandria (*Strom.* 1.16.78.5) records that Terpander would have set the laws to music; Plato makes provision for something similar in his Ideal State (*Laws* 2.659d–e). Cf. Powell 1994, 307.

[42] On the study and reciting of *prooimia*, cf. Stobaeus, *Flor.* 2.24 (the laws of Charondas). Plato draws a clear distinction between the prologues and the laws themselves (*Laws* 9.854c; 870a).

[43] Some historians, like Tigerstedt (1965, 586, n. 651) and Kennell (1995, 19), have estimated, but for different reasons, that this practice would only have been instituted during the Roman era. Like Lévy (1997, 154, n. 16), whose argument strikes me as wholly convincing (cf. Hodkinson 2000, 36 and n. 19), I think the measure was adopted as early as the 4th–3rd century. An inscription, of Roman date, referring to the role of 'reader', ἀναγνωστής, is worth noting (Steinhauer 1998, 433–4, no. 4).

[44] Cf. the chapter in Marrou 1948, 'De la pédérastie comme éducation' ('On pederasty as education'), 61–73; see also Patzer 1982 and Percy 1996.

[45] It began when the boy was about 12 and, in my opinion, normally lasted – in Sparta as elsewhere – only until he became an ephebe; cf. above, pp. 107–8.

[46] There are some very sound comments on this subject in Birgalias 1999, 243.

[47] On this kind of access to city affairs, cf. the bibliography in Birgalias 1999, n. 79, 251.

[48] Cf. above, p. 93.

[49] Of the two possible translations offered by Cartledge 2001, 96 and n. 24, 208, frankly I prefer the second. To me, the other one does not even seem possible, in that the partitive genitive τῶν εὐδοκίμων νέων depends on ἐράσται not on τοῖς τηλικούτοις;

besides which, the term νέοι is not applicable to boys of twelve.

[50] Stibbe (1976, no. 1, 7) has published a Laconian cup fragment depicting just such a scene.

[51] Brelich 1969, 199.

[52] In the account of Cinadon's conspiracy (*Hell.* 3.3.9), the ephors tell Cinadon to find the eldest of the *hippagretai* who would put at his disposal 'six or seven of those who happen to be there'.

[53] On the level of prosperity that this suggests, see Hodkinson 2000, 312–16.

[54] This analysis of the case of Sphodrias is the classic one by Cartledge (2001, 104–5).

[55] Cartledge 1987, 27.

[56] The case of Lysander, cited by Cartledge, is hardly convincing, since he was a Heraclid through his father Aristokritos (Cartledge 1987, 28).

[57] Cf. above, p. 103.

[58] Plutarch, *Ap. Lac.*, Paidaretos 3, *Mor.* 231b; *Reg. Imp. Ap.*, of Paidaretos, *Mor.* 191f; *Lyc.* 25.6. Cf. Ducat 2002, 14–19.

[59] My comparison is, of course, purely 'illustrative'; I am not unaware of the reality behind the image the Cultural Revolution gave of itself.

6

EDUCATION AND INITIATION

The initiatory model

Alongside the 'historical' interpretation, which attempts to understand Spartan education by putting it back into the context of the city, there exists an 'anthropological' (its adversaries would say 'a-historical') interpretation, which appeals to comparison with other societies; the neutral formula 'alongside' can correspond to relationships either of concurrence or of complementarity. This interpretation sets out to shed light on (not necessarily to explain) the Spartan education system by comparing it with one of the most widespread practices in 'primitive' societies all over the world, initiations, which are sometimes called tribal in order to distinguish them from other types of initiation, such as those which precede entry into secret societies, brotherhoods, or groups practising mystery cults. Very briefly, initiation can be defined as a collection of rituals carried out by the community, or in its name by a few 'representatives', in order to effect a transformation in the young which qualifies them to enter its bosom as full members.

This end is clearly the essential point of the definition; but it is common to initiation and to every kind of education. However, we should not imagine that in the history of humanity education succeeded initiation and replaced it as its 'secular' form: in one form or another education exists in all societies, which means that in those which practise initiation (for there are 'primitive' societies which do not) the two function side by side. It is even frequently the case that some 'lessons' are given within the framework of initiation: hunting, fishing, agriculture (or the culture of a particular vegetable like the yam), group myths and traditions, songs, dances, etc. What makes the difference is the character of the whole process, ritual on the one hand, pedagogic on the other, and this character is not always obvious.

Attempting to shed light on Spartan education by means of ethnological comparisons is not a recent idea, linked to the fashion for 'human sciences'. To my knowledge, the first to have had it is the Jesuit priest J.F. Lafitau, who, having lived in Canada from 1712 to 1717, in 1724 published his *Moeurs des sauvages amériquains comparées aux moeurs des premiers temps* (*Customs of the American Savages Compared to Customs of the Earliest Times*).[1] His sound knowledge of the ancient texts allowed him to compare with the 'savage' world not only the Greeks 'of the earliest times', but also those of the classical period. Amongst the American Indians he knew, in particular the Algonquins, Hurons and Iroquois, the initiation rituals, which are spectacular, attracted his attention, and he compared them with the Spartan and Cretan education systems (II, 1–70); the flagellation at Orthia's altar figures largely in his study. Much later, ethnological comparisons played a role in Wide's fundamental study of Spartan religion, *Lakonische Kulte* (1893). Next comes Bethe's great article on the significance of 'Dorian' pederasty (Bethe 1907). In 1912 another great article, that of Nilsson (Nilsson 1912), pays close attention to comparison between Spartan education and initiations. On one particular and important point, the Crypteia, Jeanmaire in 1913 presents an interpretation entirely based on ethnographic parallels. The comparatist trend then develops with, notably, the works of Ferguson, Jeanmaire and Krauth.

General characteristics

The culmination of comparison between Spartan education and initiation is Brelich's book (Brelich 1969), which remains the reference work on the subject. The procedure which is followed in this bears witness to a rigorous approach which is slightly lacking in the earlier studies. In a very full Introduction (which extends to p. 112), the author, having defined the concept of initiation and given an account of its general characteristics, undertakes, on the basis of vast ethnographic documentation, to draw up a kind of portrait type of it. He is keen to determine the *age* at which it takes place, extremely variable but with an average around adolescence (p. 28), then the periodicity of the ceremonies (pp. 28–9). What formally characterizes initiation right away is that it most often happens in the course of a period of *segregation*. This can be spatial (outside the settlement or on its margins, pp. 29–30), and be accompanied by the *isolation* of initiands (p. 30), who have then to keep *secret* the rites in which they have participated. It can also consist of a *particular way of life*, which reinforces the marginal character of their situation (dietary regime, dress, particular language or silence, p. 31); to this can be added suspension or reversal of social norms, which will be analysed below. It is during this period of material and/or symbolic separation that the transformation of individuals is effected, at the end of which they can be integrated into the collective.

The methods of this transformation are very numerous: 'maltreatment' (pp. 31–2: *diet*; submission *to heat and to cold*; *sleep deprivation*; the making of various *marks and wounds*, often of a sexual nature, accompanied by suffering which is often voluntarily increased; *tests of resistance to pain*, which can go as far as torture, and of which one of the most common forms is *flagellation*); 'lessons' given during the seclusion (pp. 32–3); *fake death* followed by rebirth, symbolizing and dramatizing the change of status (pp. 33–4); collective or individual *combats*, between initiands or setting them against the recently-initiated (p. 35); *deviant sexual practices*, which can go as far as *orgies* where every norm is suspended, or imposition of *homosexual relations* (p. 35); other *suspensions or inversions of the norm*, initiands for example having the right, as well as the obligation, to engage in all kinds of *theft* and plundering (pp. 35–6); *intervention of supernatural beings* (pp. 36–7: the 'supreme being', when there is one, the 'common ancestor', the 'first man', the totemic figure, 'spirits of the forest' or of ancestors, the 'master of animals'); *intervention of members of the community*, who exercise a close 'surveillance' of the process of initiation (it might be a case of all the adults, or of a more specialized personnel: chief, elders, sorcerers, recent initiates, who often play the role of 'guardians' of initiands, sometimes on an individual basis). To complete this picture it only remains for the author to examine the *leaving rituals* (pp. 38–9: these are the ceremonies marking the end of the isolation and the integration of the new initiates into the collective), the case of *initiations by stages, by degrees or by ranks* (pp. 39–40), the role of *age classes* (pp. 40–1), and *female initiations* (pp. 41–4).

The territory having thus been duly marked out, the next stage stands out clearly. It consists of a close examination of the facts available about Spartan education, in order to make apparent the features which it has in common with 'primitive' initiations ('Iniziazioni spartane', pp. 113–207). This analytical and enumerative method is rigorously subordinated to its aim, which is to show that Spartan education is nothing other than an initiation which only underwent the adaptations made necessary by the fact that it operated in the bosom of a political society and not an archaic population. Spartan education is thus envisaged not as it really was, that is a system which was both coherent and dynamic, where every element derives part of its meaning from the place it occupies in the whole (cf. the previous chapter), but, as it were, in detached pieces. Another inconvenience of this approach is that it takes into consideration only the similarities, instead of being concerned also with the possible significance of differences, whether it is a matter of features of initiation which are absent from Spartan education or vice versa.

That said, we shall pursue the analysis as Brelich did, reviewing the features of Spartan education which seemed to him to replicate features of 'primitive' initiations; but we shall do so in a critical fashion, because, on the one hand, he is clearly trying to demonstrate a thesis (which is not our case at all), and, on the other, his vision of Spartan education is absolutely global (as it was at the period when he was writing) and employs texts of very diverse nature and date. We should note first that most of the general characteristics of Spartan education, as have been analysed in the previous chapter, have parallels in initiation. The latter is *compulsory*: society imposes initiation on all young boys, because it considers it indispensable to its perpetuation to 'normalize' them. Initiation is compulsory in exactly the same way as education is at Sparta, in the sense that anyone who does not submit to it, or reveals himself unable to endure the tests it includes, does not become a member of the community: he is treated as a 'child' or a 'little girl', he cannot marry, nor own property, etc. Cases are, moreover, rare, and most often confined to the feeble-minded: this might constitute confirmation that failures would likewise have been rare at Sparta. Initiation is *organized by the whole community*, even if there are often people who have a particular responsibility for it; the community supervises its course closely, and the initiands are always surrounded. *Pederasty* is part of it as at Sparta, and seems to have an institutional character. The *collective character* is equally present, with the important reservation that individual initiations also exist (we shall have cause to discuss these in relation to the Crypteia); when initiation is collective, it is as completely so as the part of Spartan education which is the state's concern. Finally, the process of initiation is *the same for all*, which is logical, since its aim is to subjugate everyone to the same norm. There is only one of the major features of Spartan education which is absent from initiation, and this is *competition* between individuals. This is because they are different kinds of societies: archaic societies seek homogeneity, and have no need to select elites. We can see from this that if Spartan society used the structure supplied by initiation, it adapted it to its own model, that of 'government of the best'.

Duration

Variations between societies are considerable. Most often initiation is basically confined to the period of segregation, which is generally fairly short (from a few days to a few months), but can also last for several years. Brelich believes that the duration of Spartan education (23 years in total, including the probationary period corresponding to the age of *hēbōntes*) is not without parallel in 'primitive' societies. It is true that, in some, initiation begins very early, at 6–9 years, 5–8 years, or even 3 years old (p. 57 n. 20), and that in others it ends very late, at 30 or even 40 years old (n. 21); but these figures do not indicate a duration, because they do not apply to the same societies. To my knowledge, the only initiations which are comparable to Spartan education in duration are those which belong to the category of initiation by stages. Spartan education cannot be assimilated to this type, because it includes interruptions between the stages (for example, amongst the Kwoma of New Guinea, there are four 'cycles' of five years). I do not believe that any initiations exist of 23 years' *continuous* duration as at Sparta. It seems to me that, by this very duration, Spartan education shows precisely that it is not (that it is no longer?) an initiation; its contents demand more time, because they are not simply a collection of rites which it is necessary and sufficient to accomplish, but a process of training.

Age classes

Age classes are one of the most widespread structures in human societies, both geographically speaking and in terms of types of society: they can be found amongst both hunter-gatherers and pastoral and agricultural societies. The first element of comparison is that in some societies, especially African ones, they are 'functional' and serve in the recruitment of the army, the members of each class making up a 'party' of warriors. Their relationship to initiation is not clear. There are societies where age classes exist from birth; the period of initiation, then, fits into a framework which seems to predate it. There are others, distinctly more numerous, where age classes are defined in relation to an important moment of initiation, like circumcision; they thus seem subordinated to the initiation. We might ask ourselves to which of these two types the Spartan system is most closely connected, but a fundamental question must first be posed: are the age classes which exist at Sparta of the same type as those which function in societies with initiation? Indeed, we have already seen (pp. 71–2) that what exists at Sparta is a system of annual groups which begin at birth and continue up until the end of military obligation, since they serve in the recruitment of the army and its deployment on the ground. I am not sure that we can really talk of age classes in this case. That the young should be arranged in annual groups is an extremely commonplace situation, which can be found in societies very different from those which the ethnographers study. To my thinking, we cannot talk of 'true' age classes at Sparta except for the period when these groups have names, always the same, the order of which indicates a hierarchy. The name of, say, *rhōbidas*, which every boy of this age bears, although in a sense common, is applied to each individually, his identity defined by it for a year, and it situates him precisely in society; it is part of his being. These names, as we have seen, emphasize the irremediably puerile status of the young males: it is a mark of segregation, and they are treated as 'babies' like initiands in some societies. This character, which gives the Spartan age classes the air of 'true' age classes, only exists, to our knowledge, during the period from 14 to 20 years of age, which seems to confirm their relationship to the idea of initiation. Spartan education thus appears as the transposition of an initiation by degrees, the names showing that each year a new stage is passed; this is not an initiation by ranks, because everyone is supposed to pass all the stages.[2]

Segregation

Segregation is one of the most widespread and characteristic features of initiation. For a period of which the duration, as we have seen, varies greatly from society to society, the initiands are withdrawn from their habitual environment and taken to live collectively in a place apart from the settlement, under the direction and supervision of a certain number of adults. This place can be simply on the edge of the settlement (a hut on the edge of the village, for example); but it is often much further removed, isolated, and presents characteristics which make it the opposite of the space where men usually live. This might be an ambiguous environment, like the edge of water (sea, lake, river, marsh), but the most typical case is that of the forest, a wild space where one meets both fierce animals and 'spirits'. Either the young men have to manage by themselves for food, or the community provides it (for example the mothers cook for them and bring them food). The period passed in these conditions is the most important part of the initiation, and often constitutes the whole of it. It is at this moment that the performance of certain rites, and in some cases the assimilation of certain 'teachings', produces in the young men the 'transformation' which will allow them to become full members of the collective.

Segregation, then, is not only a moment and a characteristic of initiation, it is its framework par excellence, and almost its necessary condition. We have to note that it is difficult to find a trace of it in the Spartan education system. It is true that some texts (much later than the classical period) evoke something like it. Thus Justin gives the impression of viewing Spartan education as a kind of 'primitive' initiation: 'Lycurgus prescribed that the children, once pubescent, should be taken not to the public square but into the countryside (*non in Forum sed in agrum deduci*), in order to pass their first years not in luxury but in suffering and hard work. He decided that they would not have beds to sleep on, that they would live without eating gruel, and that they would not return to town until they had become men' (3.3.6). The allusion to the *deductio in Forum* does not clarify matters, because this does not happen at the start of adolescence, but in connection with the taking up of the *toga virilis*; doubtless we should see in this a mere literary effect, without real significance. What is certain is that Justin (= Pompeius Trogus) conceived Spartan education as happening, at least from the age of 14, outside the city; this is confirmed by his description of Lucanian education, of which he says at the beginning that it 'conforms to the laws of Lycurgus': it happened from childhood in the woods, the children had neither clothes nor bedding, and fed themselves on milk and the products of their hunting (23.1). This indeed is similar to what he says about Sparta. The picture is thus coherent, but it would better fit the Crypteia than the education system: there has perhaps been some confusion here.[3] It agrees neither with Xenophon's account, which shows the children living constantly or nearly so under the watch of the whole city, nor with the other texts susceptible of making reference to a period of 'retreat'; this throws serious doubt on its documentary value.

Amongst these other texts figures first the gloss of Photius on the word συνέφηβος. This does not supply any certain information. The Spartans and the Eleans, it says, 'separate' ephebes from children at the age of 15 or 16 and 'prepare them apart (καθ' ἑαυτούς) to become men'; these formulae could suit a segregation, but they apply just as well to a simple institutional differentiation, the phenomenon described being just the commonplace one of the *ephēbeia*. More interesting is the passage where Plutarch depicts what I have called the boys' 'camping'. When they have reached their twelfth year, he says, 'they sleep together, by *agelai* and by *ilai*, on *stibades* which they have made themselves', with reeds gathered on the banks of the Eurotas (*Lyc.* 16.13). To read this passage in isolation, we might imagine that for Plutarch the boys of this age always lived like this, but what follows shows that this was not the case: meetings with adults and the formation of pederastic couples (17.1); frequenting of gymnasia (*ibid.*); supervision by all citizens (*ibid.*); meals with the *eirēn* 'in the house' (κατ' οἶκον, 17.4); thefts committed in the men's *syssitia* (17.5). It is clear that, as in Xenophon, the boys' life is represented as happening for the most part in an urban environment. Certainly the term *stibas* is characteristic of improvised bedding, in the open air; but it still is not necessary for it to have taken place in the depths of the woods, and I wonder if in reading Plutarch we have not allowed ourselves to be influenced by the images which Justin conveys.

So, these texts are not only 'late' but also ambiguous. The most interesting is perhaps Hesychius' gloss on the Laconian term φούαξιρ· ἡ ἐπὶ τῆς χώρας σωμασκία τῶν μελλόντων μαστιγοῦσθαι, that is to say, according to the usual interpretation, 'physical training, in the countryside, of those who are going to be whipped'. The formulation shows that the author of the gloss is thinking of the flagellation of the Roman period, but we shall see later (pp. 254–5) that it may also and primarily concern the ritual of the classical period. If it is incontrovertibly a question of a kind of retreat, this has a precise and limited aim, preparation for a religious ceremony. Moreover, I am not persuaded that this retreat really happened 'in the countryside'. That would rather be expressed ἐν τῇ χώρᾳ, or, more clearly, ἐπ' ἀγροῦ. ἐπὶ τῆς χώρας seems to me more probably to indicate 'on the spot': in writing these words, the author of the gloss was thinking of the rest of his phrase, and the training would take place in the same spot where the ceremony was going to happen, that is in the sanctuary of Orthia. This is sufficiently on the margin of the urban space also to have accommodated the 'camping' described by Plutarch, and sufficiently near the Eurotas for the boys to be able to go and gather on its banks the reeds for their *stibades*.

All we can say for certain on the subject, for the classical period, is that when Xenophon, in a very vague manner, evokes the boys' training to walk barefoot on sloping ground, this can hardly be happening in the city; but we know nothing of the organization of these sorties, nor if there was organization. The Crypteia certainly includes a setting apart (particularly radical, with complete prohibition of communication), but it differs from initiatory segregation on several important points: instead of being surrounded like initiands, the Crypteians are left to themselves and perhaps even solitary; the Crypteia takes place after initiation proper, during the probationary phase of the *hēbōntes*; and above all, it only concerns a few chosen individuals.

We must agree, then, that, in the picture of education during the classical period, the segregation aspect is completely elusive, if we take the word only in its spatial sense; at the most it seems that there were phases of 'retreat'. It was moreover materially impossible for the whole education to take place during a period of segregation; firstly, of course, because of its length, and also because one of its major characteristics is that it happens in front of the whole city and with the participation of all.[4] The absence of segregation is all the more significant because, in the picture of initiation, it is, as we have seen, much more than just one feature amongst others. Nonetheless, this does not mean that the theme of segregation is totally absent from Spartan education. The setting apart could in fact have been realized by other means than spatial segregation: by imposing a particular way of life on the initiands,[5] notably in the areas of diet, clothing and communication with other members of the community.

Diet

Brelich (70, n. 58) notes that it is rare for some form of dietary taboo not to appear in an initiation; what calls Sparta in particular to mind is that the prohibition of certain food stuffs, or the imposition of certain others, is explained by those concerned as a means of encouraging or controlling the growth of the young: Xenophon (*LP* 2.5–6) and Plutarch (*Lyc.* 17.7–8) say exactly this. There is, however, an important difference: at Sparta it is not a matter of prohibiting or prescribing for the children this food or that, which would contribute to giving them a way of life apart, but of imposing on them a kind of diet. This custom belongs to the 'maltreatment' rather than to segregation; it is also the case in societies where children are forbidden the best foods (for example, in the Fiji islands, the best variety of yam and fresh-water fish) and given the most mediocre.

The rubric of diet is not confined to foodstuffs alone; it also includes the manner in which the food is taken. In Crete, according to Ephoros (fr. 149, in Strabo 10.4.20), children belonging to the category of 'little ones' would eat seated on the ground, while waiting on the men and on themselves. At Sparta, Plutarch's description of the *eirēn*'s meal (*Lyc.* 17.4–18.7) gives the impression that it happened in the same way, and that they would eat in a corner while serving the *eirēn*, who would himself be reclining. The significance of this mode of behaviour is clearly explained by Plutarch: they play the role of the *eirēn*'s 'servants', and the word which means 'servant', ὑπηρέτης, is also one of the terms commonly used to designate slaves. By this method of feeding themselves, the young Spartans are almost put outside the civic community; this is an element of what Vernant (1989) calls their 'shame'.

Dress

In archaic societies, it is frequent for initiands to wear special clothing, which denotes their position on the edge of society. For example, if the usual custom is to be clothed, they are naked; if the custom is to be naked (or nearly), their body is painted. The young Spartans did not go naked, except on the occasion of certain festivals and gymnastic exercises; we shall return to this in connection with the Gymnopaidiai. But we can say that the clothing which was imposed on them (the existence of a rule on the subject being significant in itself) was in a way special. The role that this kind of custom plays in initiations leads us back to what the texts say on the subject. Plutarch declares that after the age of 12 the boys wore nothing but a *himation*, a single one for the year, without a tunic underneath (*Lyc.* 16.12). As we have seen (above, p. 7), Xenophon does not say this, but just that the children only had the right to one *himation* for the entire year (*LP* 2.4). To me this means 'a single kind of *himation*', and they had the right to change it; but it is possible that poor children effectively wore *the same* cloak all year. In their case, in might therefore also have been as dirty and patched as that of the 'tremblers' in the portrait painted by Plutarch (*Agesilaos* 30.4), and so have constituted, as for them, special clothing. The matter was evidently less clear-cut for the children who had the means to change. It is clear that in the case in point the essential thing was the symbol, and that the same kind of *himation* worn in every season was thought of as a uniform denoting belonging to a category, if not inferior, at least marginal.[6]

The Cretan parallel confirms this view. Ephoros (fr. 149, in Strabo 10.4.20) depicts the young children ἐν φαύλοις τριβωνίοις, φοροῦντες καὶ χειμῶνος καὶ θέρους τὰ αὐτά, 'in poor cloaks; they wear the same ones winter and summer'. Not only is usage on this point the same on both sides, but the authors present it in the same way. Indeed, Xenophon's interpretation of the single cloak is that it trains the young to bear heat and cold. It is not explicitly formulated by Ephoros, but his reference to the seasons shows that this is what he too had in mind; heat and cold are mentioned, moreover, at §16. It is possible that this is his personal interpretation, but it is also possible that it had been the common one among the Cretans.

What clearly demonstrates that the children's dress functioned as a kind of uniform symbolizing their status is the importance accorded to the moment when they abandoned it in order to put on another. In some cities this moment was solemnized by a festival: we know of the Endymatia at Argos, the Periblemaia at Lyttos and the Ekdysia at Phaistos. It is no surprise that this custom should be especially alive on Crete. The famous oath of Dreros (end of the third century) was taken by youths on leaving the *agela*. The inscription calls them ἀγελάοι πανάζωστοι (A 1.10), 'members of an *agela*, completely naked': what they wore was considered as non-clothing, they were naked as babies. Further on (C 1.12–14) the text says that if the Kosmos (chief magistrate) does not make those who will leave the *agela* take the oath, he must be referred to the Council; the formula is τὰν ἀγέλαν τοὺς τόκα ἐγδυομένους, as it might be, literally, 'those who will then undress the *agela*': there is a complete equivalence between dress and status. Passage from one status to the next is envisaged, in different cities, in two opposing ways: if at Dreros one takes off the old costume, at Malla one puts on the new, [τὰν ἀγέ]λαν τὰν τόκα ἐσδυομέναν; we find this duality again in the names of festivals, Ekdysia at Phaistos and Endymatia at Argos. At Sparta, we have no document of this kind; apparently the act of 'abandoning the cloak' was not solemnized there. The significance of the child's dress as symbol of a marginal status there was blurred to the point of no longer being conscious. It had been eliminated to the advantage of the interpretation transmitted by Xenophon, that of the single cloak as 'maltreatment', as a test intended to toughen.

The explanation, presented above (p. 170) of this custom by a will for equality seems to be ruled out by the fact that it is also found in Cretan cities, which are not particularly egalitarian. I think, however, that in a sense it remains 'true', and that we have here an example of the difference between explanation by cause and interpretation by effect. The children's dress is a structural given, and its 'cause' is that, in initiations, it is necessary to symbolize the marginal status of the initiands in a strong manner. But if the custom endures in a society which is no longer an archaic society, it can at the same time be interpreted differently (here as a test) and have different effects (here an effect of equalization). All this is 'true', but at different levels.

I shall add to this development some remarks concerning the body. First, *anypodēsia*, that is the practice of going barefoot. Xenophon (*LP* 2.3), followed by Plutarch (*Lyc.* 16.11), talks as if this was the children's habitual dress, and gives the custom the usual military explanation (which implies that for him it did not conform with current usage). The practice, in a society where the norm is to wear shoes, of going barefoot, is just as significant as that of going naked in a society where the custom is to be clothed. Like complete nudity, *anypodēsia* can have a religious significance.[7] It also symbolizes an attitude of humility and submission, which explains how it might belong to the world of initiations too; we shall return to this in connection with the Crypteia (p. 299). The second aspect of the state of the body is dirtiness. Plutarch is the only author to mention this feature (*Lyc.* 16.12), which he presents as a test: we shall return to this subject below (p. 191). And finally, hairstyle. Societies where the initiands are distinguished by the state of their hair are innumerable, and there are some initiations where it plays a central role (Brelich 1969, 71–2 n. 59). Two solutions are possible: either the initiands wear their hair long and cut it when they become adults, or, on the contrary, as we have seen at Sparta (pp. 109–11), they must have short hair.

Silence

According to Brelich (1969, 71 n. 58), the prohibition of talking (or of talking loudly) features among numerous taboos imposed on initiands during their segregation. Thus, among the Mandja of Ubangui silence was the rule during their two months of segregation. There is no real parallel at Sparta, where the boys were probably rather noisy, but we can legitimately evoke, as does Brelich,[8] in this connection the behaviour of the *paidiskoi* outside and at the men's *syssition*, as described by Xenophon (*LP.* 3.4–5). As David has remarked,[9] this behaviour adds to verbal silence what one might call corporal silence: for it is their entire body which, by its attitude, the position of the hands, the eyes, expresses silence. By this extreme reserve, the young boys demonstrate that they do not consider themselves worthy to communicate with their hosts, and show to what extent they have internalized their segregation. Furthermore, Xenophon compares this attitude to that of young virgins; initiands, meanwhile, may frequently be qualified as 'girls'.

We must not, however, exaggerate the extent of this parallel. Firstly, it only concerns the *paidiskoi*, whose discipline is presented by the author as much more severe than that of the children; and they are in a particular circumstance which is extremely important for them. In the street and in front of the men gathered for dinner, it is in fact a real *test* they are undergoing. They are expected to conduct themselves as perfectly educated boys , and we have seen (p. 15) that this stereotype was far from particular to Sparta. Moreover, as David (1999) has argued very well, it is in a general way, and not just for the young, that silence is commanded at Sparta. It is considered as a proof of self-control and self-effacement, of the capacity to merge into the group. It is equally a natural complement of laconism: words have more impact and are more efficacious if they stand out against a background of silence, and only silence allows one to prepare a response which will hit the mark (above, pp. 122–3). These reservations stated, however, I would tend to think that, as we have already noted in connection with the age classes, the condition of the *paidiskoi* is, in the whole of the Spartan education system, that which lends itself most to comparison with initiations.

Secrecy

Secrecy is a completely different thing from silence. The obligation placed not only upon initiands but also upon the initiated to keep secret the rites which they have accomplished or undergone is one of the most characteristic elements of initiations. Brelich (p. 125–5) tried to find traces of it at Sparta, but, in my opinion, without success. He cites the state secret of which Thucydides speaks (5.68), and the secrecy imposed on members of the *syssition* concerning everything which is said there (Plutarch, *Lyc.* 12.4). It is a fact that the Spartans were thought of as experts in secrecy, in particular of defence-secrecy, and that the *xenēlasiai* were explained thus. But we have here, to some extent, one of the elements of the image, not to say the myth, of Sparta; and, insofar as it corresponds to a reality, this secrecy is precisely secrecy *in the exercise of power*, which was always opposed to the 'transparency' of democracy. I see nothing in common between this kind of secrecy and initiatory secrecy, which is the prohibition of revealing what happened during initiation. Nothing of the sort could have existed in the Spartan education system, which took place in an entirely public manner.

Tests

We have finished with segregation in its various forms, spatial and symbolic. Among the methods employed to 'transform' the youths, there is one which is hugely represented at Sparta, the 'maltreatments' or 'tests'. It appears that in this city *everything which has to do with education tends to take the form of a 'test'*. We have just seen this in connection with the behaviour of the *paidiskoi*. We have seen another example with regard to food: alimentary taboos are not imposed on the children, but a partial starvation diet is. There are examples of starvation diet in 'primitive' initiations (Brelich 1969, 73 n. 64), but it is most often a case of total starvation, so of short duration (five days, for example); in other cases, the initiands have to content themselves with certain types of food, for example raw. The arrangements concerning dress may also take the form of a test: according to Xenophon, their aim was to accustom the boys to bear heat and cold. Such tests do in fact exist in initiations (Brelich 1969, 73 n. 64), but they are presented differently: taking prolonged baths in very cold water, sleeping on the ground during the night, standing very close to a hot fire, etc. Apart from the interpretation given by Plato (*Laws* 1.633c) of the Gymnopaidiai, nothing of this kind exists at Sparta; but it is perhaps the idea which lies behind the explanations given of the single cloak. We have mentioned another test in connection with the state of the body: dirtiness. Plutarch (*Lyc.* 16.12) states that the children were dirty (αὐχμηροὶ τὰ σώματα), and that, except for certain specified days, they had to do without baths and rub-downs. If this was the case, we might consider this custom as aiming to make the youths lead a kind of life apart: the same thing went for the 'tremblers', according again to Plutarch (*Agesilaos* 30.4). On this point, Xenophon says nothing, but Aristophanes partially confirms and at the same time leads us to correct Plutarch's statement (above, p. 37). The old education does not deny baths in general, but only *hot* baths, considered as softening. So Spartan children were not necessarily dirty, but in order to be clean they had to bear the test of cold water. The last example that I shall give of the tendency of Spartan education to turn everything into a test is *anypodēsia*. Xenophon explains it as a military training, intended to accustom the children to walk on uneven terrain; but this kind of walking 'on a rocky and steep path', τραχείας ὁδοῦ καὶ ἀνάκτους, reappears in Ephoros' account (he uses this expression) of Cretan education (in Strabo 10.4.16), in a context which is indeed that of a test: living rough, heat and cold, blows and fighting.[10]

Let us now come to the maltreatments proper, which sometimes go as far as torture. In initiations they can take several forms. One consists of voluntarily increasing the suffering caused in any case by the making of physical marks, which are very frequent in initiations: circumcision, incision of the penis, extraction of teeth, scarifications, tatoos; in this case, only part of the pain is gratuitous. In the other form, pain is sought for its own sake. Flagellation is by far the most widespread of these 'tortures'; its effects can be augmented by the use of stinging plants or thorny woods. Biting is fairly frequent; in Australia the head would be bitten through to the bone. The pulling out of clumps of body- and head-hair is also practised. A particularly elaborate form consists in applying to a sensitive part of the body, the stomach for example, a kind of small cage into which ants or wasps are introduced. Certain Guyanan Indians used to combine flagellation, depilation and the ant-cage.

Those concerned provide various justifications for these 'tortures'. The most common consists in making them tests of resistance to pain: the initiate must prove his virility by enduring the maltreatments without showing his suffering. Where a process which draws blood is concerned, for example incisions in sexual organs, it will be said that the end sought is to rid the subject of his feminine blood, that which he has from his mother, so that he can definitively leave sexual indecision behind. Equally numerous are cases where the blood-drawing maltreatments (circumcision, flagellation) are interpreted as a momentary death (Brelich 1969, 80 n. 85).

At Sparta, some mysterious details connected with education seem to me susceptible of gaining sense when they are put back into the context of initiatory 'maltreatments'. I shall begin with the biting of the thumb by the *eirēn* (Plutarch, *Lyc.* 18.5). This curious treatment, naturally presented as a punishment, has been the object of a study by Den Boer[11] who gives the impression of not quite succeeding in his explanation. Admittedly, Plutarch is the only source, which means that we cannot be sure of the antiquity of the custom; but it must be said that one can hardly see Xenophon explaining details of this kind. Is the thumb a substitute for the penis? the biting a substitute for, if not the removal of, a mutilation of the same kind as those that we see in initiations? Perhaps this is the direction in which we should look. The second detail to bring in here is the famous anecdote of the fox-cub, of which there are two versions, one very summary in the form of an anecdote (Plutarch, *Lyc.* 18.1), the other in the more explicit form of an apophthegm (Plutarch, *Spartan Sayings* Anon. 35, *Mor.* 234a–b). For the ancient Greeks, despite what has been said about it, the anecdote as such was perfectly coherent and logical. Of course, the fox, even a young one, is usually not edible: this shows simply that, as far as the author was concerned, the children sometimes stole things other than food; this is why the apophthegmatic version states that they would steal 'everything that they could'. This is not a wild animal, but a young fox tamed as an animal companion: in the apophthegmatic version, its owners are in search of it (whence the drama). The problem is to find out if *for us* there is another meaning hidden in the depths of the text. Two paths seem possible. The first has already been partially explored.[12] It takes as its point of departure the Laconian word for fox, φοῦα, from which are derived the substantive φούαξις, which means, as we have seen (p. 185), training with a view to flagellation, and the verb φουάδδειν, to follow this training, literally 'to do the fox' (all according to Hesychius). We end up, then, with flagellation: there is indeed a troubling resemblance between the torture inflicted on the young boy by the fox and the bite of the whip. Furthermore, the fox is the symbol of cunning; now, says Xenophon (*LP* 2.7), he who wishes to steal must 'use cunning and lie in ambush', ἀπατᾶν καὶ ἐνεδρεύειν, and this certainly also holds true for the classical period's stealing of cheeses amidst flagellation. There is more: according to Pausanias, one of the two discoverers of Orthia's *xoanon* was called Alopekos, the 'fox' in common Greek. We are thus obstinately led back to the ritual at Orthia's altar and to flagellation; but, in the anecdote, it is a real death which is met.

The other path is the form of torture which the young boy endures. Here he is confined with the fox, a prisoner under his cloak; not by constraint, but by his feeling of honour. This situation strangely ressembles that of children suffering the agony caused by insects fixed to their side by a cage. Like the initiates of Amazonia, he must hide his suffering, and he succeeds; he triumphs through the test. This anecdote, then, is not lacking in meaning; significance is, on the contrary, superabundant.

On tests of resistance to pain, Xenophon is fairly discreet, and this makes sense: before the fashion for Stoic ideas, it was better for a defender of Sparta not to insist on the cruel and even savage aspects of the education system. He mentions just the suffering which has necessarily to be endured by those who participate in the ritual at Orthia's altar. On this point, the fundamental text is Plato's *Laws* (1.633b). Megillos is giving a veritable lecture on the 'inventions' of the Spartan lawgiver with a view to preparation for war; he has already mentioned the communal meals, gymnastic exercises amd hunting. 'Furthermore and fourthly,' he continues, 'I would like to try to talk about the systematic training in bearing suffering which is pursued amongst us', τὸ περὶ τὰς καρτερήσεις τῶν ἀλγηδόνων πολὺ παρ' ἡμῖν γιγνόμενον. This introduction announces a systematic development, and Megillos reviews four *karterēseis*: the 'collective bare-handed fights'; 'some seizures executed in the midst of a hail of blows which rain down every time', a formula in which we can recognize the ritual at Orthia's altar in its classical-period form; then come two notes, equally allusive but a little more explicit, one on the Crypteia, the other on the Gymnopaidiai. This is what for Plato, via Megillos, constituted the essentials of the tests of resistance to suffering at Sparta. Leaving the fights, Gymnopaidiai and Crypteia for later, we shall only concern ourselves here with the ritual at Orthia's altar, often called flagellation.

This ritual will be described and studied further on, in the chapter on religion; the only question to be examined here is the following: in the form which it took in the classical period, was it a flagellation? Brelich's answer is resolutely positive: he recognizes both forms of the ritual and distinguishes them perfectly (133–5), but he considers that the first form deserves to be qualified as flagellation too. To begin with, this affirmation seems a little arbitrary, but he justifies it further on (192), by the fact that the struggle which takes place near the altar is not really a fight, since it opposes unarmed adolescents to men equipped with sticks or whips. I doubt that this is sufficient grounds for us to speak of flagellation. In his study of 'the identity of the young Spartan', Vernant (1989) has a comparable standpoint. He too clearly recognizes the difference between the two forms of the ritual, but he seems to consider that of the Roman period as the more authentic;[13] thereafter, no longer distinguishing between the two forms, he speaks only of 'flagellation' (200), of the 'flogging received' (209). This is no more than the end-point of a very old tradition. From Lafitau to the present, it is always the more recent form which has been compared to 'primitive' rituals and interpreted as an archaic rite, either of expiation, or of purification, or of fertility, or of initiation.[14] The equivocation is well demonstrated by the fact that Brelich combines with the classical-period ritual the *aition* reported by Pausanias, which, quite evidently, belongs to the recent form, since it implies that the altar is spattered with blood. This allows him to discover in Spartan education the theme of 'death and rebirth', so widespread in initiations, which is otherwise completely absent; this, on the grounds that flagellation is often considered as a kind of death – although even that of the Roman period is always presented only as a competition in resistance to pain.

In reality, the question is delicate and demands reflection. In the first place, I would say that between the ancient form of the ritual and flagellation there are such great differences that the name is not suitable. Firstly, the youths have an active attitude, whereas a flagellation can only be suffered; further, in this game, it is they who are the assailants, the whip-bearers playing the role of guardians of the altar. Second difference: while in the flagellation of the Roman period one had to receive the greatest possible number of blows, in the classical ritual it matters to receive the least possible, while taking as many cheeses as possible.

But reflection finds itself here at a watershed. In order to practise the game well (the ritual takes the form of a game), it is indispensable thoroughly to understand its principle. Here, the principle is clearly not to avoid blows, but to take the most cheeses possible. The advice which concludes Xenophon's short development on this competition (*LP* 2.9) is that the strategy of a serious competitor must, as a matter of priority, be centred on the taking of the cheeses, which is the condition of victory. He considers that receiving blows is inevitable in any case ('a suffering of short duration'). Plato too, despite his brevity, insists on the blows necessarily received: 'in the midst of a hail of blows which rain down every time' (*Laws* 1.633b). It is this which makes the ancient form, too, a test of resistance to pain. The importance thus accorded to the blows received leads us to ask if, after all, they might not be the essential part of the ritual, and if the form which it took, that of a theft from an altar, might not be a scenario designed to stage and to justify what, at bottom, was effectively a flagellation. We shall leave it there for the moment; it is not until after having studied the classical ritual in detail, in all its constituents, that we shall be able to propose a valid answer.

Teaching

It is frequently the case that during their initiation the youths receive something which is closely related to teaching. Sometimes this is sufficiently varied to constitute a real programme. Brelich (76 n. 73) cites the case of the Korogo of New Guinea, where singing, dancing, ethics, discipline, games, mythical traditions, magic, practice of sacred musical instruments, and tree-clearing technique are combined. Of all these lessons, it is that of dance which is the most widespread in the world and the most developed, and there are often particular dances for initiation. It is possible that at Sparta apprenticeship in dance had had a separate place in the education system and had belonged to the part which was obligatory and identical for all. It is impossible to avoid comparison with the case of an archaic people amongst whom dance has become an endurance test (Brelich 1969, 75 n. 71): in order to progress to the next stage of initiation, the youths had to succeed in dancing for a whole day without any break.

Supervision

Among the major characteristic features of the Spartan education system is what we have called 'supervision', a word which translates into reality the fact that education was the concern not only of relatives and specialized personnel, but also of the community as a whole. This is equally a feature of 'primitive' initiations (Brelich 1969, 37–8, with nn. 117–25). In societies with reduced numbers, all the initiates, that is most often all the adult males, and sometimes the women too, take an active part in the initiation of the young. In more populous societies, it is the more special responsibility of particular adults or particular groups: the relatives of the young boy, the Elders, and, for some specific acts, 'technicians' like sorcerers or blacksmiths; but these men act in every case as 'representatives' of the community. Sometimes the initiators form a coherent and hierarchical body, with a chief at its head (Brelich 1969, 92–3 n. 124). Spartan organization is similar to this type, but the form it took was determined by the fact that it functioned in the bosom of a city (thus the *paidonomos* is a magistrate). Another comparison seems more relevant: it is that which concerns the role of the newly-initiated, those who have just left their initiation or who have been out for a few years. They often play the role of auxiliaries at the command of the chief, the Elders or the specialists, teach the initiands on a day-to-day basis how they should behave in every circumstance, see to their food: all this closely evokes the role of the *eirenes*, and, as far as discipline is concerned, that of the whip-bearers, which Xenophon (*LP* 2.2) says was taken by some of the *hēbōntes*. It is often the case that the newly-initiated serve as 'guardians' to the initiands, and there can be as many as one 'guardian' to every initiand (Brelich 1969, 93 n. 125): here we might think rather of the *erastēs*. This participation in the initiation of the young is often a condition which the newly-initiated have to fulfil in order to clear the last stage, allowing them to become a complete member of the community of men; the ambiguous condition of the *hēbōntes* finds a parallel here.

Even if everyone takes part, the transformation of children into adults is a task at once too important for the survival of the community, and too complex, to be operated by human forces alone. This is why initiations are often placed under the patronage of one or several supernatural powers, which are guarantees of their efficacity. These can have very diverse characters; one of them is conventionally called 'Lord', or, when its nature is feminine, 'Mistress of animals', an expression borrowed from Homer (*Iliad* 21.470). This power, often partially or entirely theriomorphic, reigns over the wild world where the initiation takes place and from which the initiands have to be wrested (Brelich 1969, 88 n. 111 and 132 n. 49). At Sparta it is Orthia, a local divinity later assimilated to Artemis. A 'divinity of the margins', in Vernant's apt phrase, mistress of both savage nature and the growth of the young, she patronizes the change of state constituted by adolescence and directed by education. The localization of her sanctuary, in an ambiguous place, both a 'suburb' (Strabo) on the edge of the urban space and a marshy river bank, between earth and water, suits her perfectly, as it suits the initiation of the young. Brelich has remarked (1969, 174–7) that all the elements of her cult that we know about have a connection with this initiation, as if it was her sole function in the city.

Pederasty

Three points remain which demand a slightly longer development. First, pederasty. Lafitau was the first to compare Greek pederasty with the practice of homosexual relationships during initiation amongst 'savage' peoples, in this case the Hurons and the Iroquois. The idea that it is of initiatory origin is today largely accepted. It is indeed frequently the case in archaic societies[15] that homosexual relationships are imposed on the initiands; 'imposed' is, moreover, the appropriate term since in these relationships they practically always (only one exception is noted) play the passive or 'feminine' role. Brelich (1969, 84–5 n. 100) briefly cites some examples; in his now classic study of Spartan pederasty,[16] Cartledge gives a short account of three peoples (of which two were already cited by Brelich), the Aranda of central Australia, the Keraki of Papua New Guinea and the Marind-Anim of New Guinea, this last society presenting particularly spectacular ressemblances to the Spartans. To these examples Ogden has added that of the Sambia of New Guinea,[17] to which we shall return later. In numerous cases it is the newly-initiated or recent initiates who play the active role; among the Aranda, for example, the couple thus formed during initiation can last for several years. In other cases (so that of the Marind-Anim), the youth's partner is a mature man, who, in the initiation, becomes his 'father' by delegation. In the great majority of cases a full homosexual relationship is in question, including anal copulation, or, much more rarely, fellation (such is the custom amongst the Sambia). But societies are also known (Brelich cites some in the New Hebrides) where the 'father' has to content himself with para-sexual contacts. In general, those concerned justify these practices by claiming that they are good for the youth's growth and his passage to adulthood. As for the ethnologists, they have offered numerous interpretations: sexual education forming part of the 'teaching' given during initiation; behaviour showing that the initiand has not yet left behind sexual indifferentiation and remains at least in part a 'woman'; acquisition of the qualities necessary for a man by means of the sexual act; inversion of the norm, a characteristic of initiations (the homosexual act sometimes happens in the course of 'orgies'). In other words, the significance of this practice appears complex.

The resemblance to Greek pederasty in general, and to Spartan in particular, is clear. At Sparta, too, the pederastic relationship is integrated into the initiatory-educational process, which gives it an almost institutional character. The fact that, in initiations, the physical aspect is most often present leads us back to the issue of the nature of Spartan pederasty. This question is as old in the western tradition as interest in Sparta, but it is with Bethe's article (Bethe 1907) that it took a scientific turn (some perhaps would say pseudo-scientific). Using the ethnographic parallels he had available, he tried to show that the origins of Spartan pederasty, as of homosexual relationships in archaic societies, can be found in the idea of a transmission from the initiated to the initiand, by means of sperm, of the physical and warrior qualities of the adult; thus, that the essential of the matter was anal coitus. Basing his argument on the case of Sambia, Ogden has taken up this interpretation again, replacing coitus with fellation. This way of looking at things has not convinced everyone, and the debate about the physical or non-physical character of Spartan pederasty remains open.

This situation results from the fact that the ancient sources on this point do not allow us to reach a conclusion. If we keep to the sources of the classical period (the others, in any case, being dependant on these), we can almost say that they are disqualified right away. Indeed, on Sparta at this period no one is truly neutral. Knowing that a strong prejudice against physical homosexuality was widespread amongst Greek 'intellectuals' (especially Athenians) from the second half of the fifth century on, we can immediately understand why Sparta's adversaries claim that sodomy was the rule there, and that her defenders, like Xenophon, maintain that pederastic relationships there were of an irreproachable chastity. Add to this that the theme was a source of jokes for the comic poets, who make up a good part of the classical sources on the subject,[18] and that Sparta's adversaries had every interest in tacitly conflating pederastic relationships with the practice of true homosexuality, between adults, which was certainly quite common in this city, at least amongst the elite.

An exception must be made for Plato, whose declarations on the nature of Spartan pederasty are sufficiently nuanced to merit examination. In the *Symposium* (182ac), he puts in Pausanias' mouth a speech on the subject of pederasty in which 'some cities' are opposed to Athens and Sparta taken together, and this opposition is the following. In these cities, he says, the custom in the matter is clear and unequivocal, whether, as in Ionia 'and elswhere', pederasty is entirely condemned, or on the other hand, as in Elis and Boeotia, it is allowed without any restriction, including physical relations. At Athens and Sparta, for Pausanias, the *nomos* is, on the contrary, *poikilos*: nuanced, complex, almost contradictory. The problem is that, though he goes on to explain in what respect Athenian custom is *poikilos*, he does not do so for Sparta. Whether this is an oversight, or is due to the fact that the matter appeared self-evident to him, I do not know; in any case, we are thus reduced to conjectures. The most plausible is that of Cartledge:[19] Spartan custom might be 'complex' because, as Xenophon explains, although pederasty is not only allowed but made official, and, from the fact that it is placed under the patronage of Lycurgus, practically compulsory, all physical relations are absolutely forbidden.

It is true that the text of this passage of the *Symposium* has often been corrected in such a way as to place Sparta on the same side as Boeotia and Elis. Following Dover, Nafissi and Cartledge, I think that such a correction must be rejected. Not only is it arbitrary, but it is ignorant of the existence in Greek thought of a kind of tradition opposing either Sparta and Athens together, or Sparta alone, to the couple, always identical, made up of Boeotia (or Thebes) and Elis, in that it is only in these latter cities or regions that the physical relationship is allowed.[20] If some have corrected the text, it is only to reconcile it with the passages of the *Laws* where Sparta is condemned for having encouraged physical relations between men, which Plato considers as 'against nature' (above, p. 60); but this contradiction can be explained. Cartledge has proposed two alternative solutions: either that the two texts are not talking about the same thing, that which is presented as chaste in the *Symposium* being pederasty and that which is condemned in the *Laws* being homosexual liaisons between adults; or that Sparta is approved in the *Symposium* for the theoretical rule she has imposed, and blamed in the *Laws* for not (or no longer) respecting it. I shall add that it is also possible that Plato had changed his mind: when he wrote the *Symposium*, he believed in the chaste pederasty described by Xenophon, while at the end of his life he no longer had any illusions on the subject.[21]

I shall propose that we give some consideration to another text, despite Cartledge's opposing opinion;[22] it is a phrase of Cicero: 'The Lacedaemonians, who, in the area of the love of free young people, permit everything except coitus (*praeter stuprum*), erect a very weak barrier around the one thing which they forbid: indeed, they authorize kissing and sleeping together, on condition that a cloak separates the lovers' (*Republic* 4.4). I do not maintain that Cicero's words express the truth, but they seem to me to extend and clarify what Xenophon says. In any case, this text is interesting in making us aware of the fact that we are posing the problem badly when we discuss the 'physical' or 'non-physical' character of the pederastic relationship. In this kind of liaison, there is *always* and necessarily a physical side. The Greeks knew this very well, as what one might call 'the quarrel of the kisses' between Plato and Aristotle shows. In the *Republic* (3.403bc), Plato sets the following rule: 'That the *erastēs* should not kiss, keep company with or touch his beloved except in the way a father would his son; that it should be with a view to good, and with the reservation of having obtained his consent'. In the *Politics* (2.1262a32–7), Aristotle provides lively criticism of such liberties, remarking that in reality 'between a father and his son or between brothers they would be extremely improper'. Aristotle thus rejects this pederasty; but when in the classical period someone asserts, as does Xenophon, that the pederastic relationship at Sparta is chaste, this does not mean that every physical aspect is excluded from it, but only the sexual act.[23] Cicero says exactly this.

Here, then, we find ourselves led back to Bethe's thesis. What was the rule on this point at Sparta? Some texts assert that the pederastic relationship excluded all copulation, others say or suggest, without specific reference to education, that physical homosexuality was widely practised there. Do we have any other elements of information? I am aware of three, which are all debatable. Brelich accords great importance to the rock-cut inscriptions of Thera, which are indeed unambiguous, while considering that if they make it probable that in the archaic period Spartan pederasty included sexual relations, it is possible to follow Xenophon and believe that things were not the same in the classical period; to which it should be added that documents from Thera do not count as proof for Spartan realities. Bethe, and then Ogden, have argued from certain Spartan terms relating to the pederastic relationship[24] in favour of the practice, the one of sodomy, the other of fellation. This is to forget that, when it comes to interpreting Greek terms, no ethnographic comparison is able to take the place of proof. In reality, it seems to me, neither the verbs ἐμπνεῖν/ἐμπνεῖσθαι (Xenophon, Plutarch), εἰσπνεῖν (Aelian), nor the noun of agent εἰσπνήλας/εἴσπνηλος (Callimachus, Theocritus), have any assured sexual connotation. The two verbs simply mean 'to blow (into)', whence 'to blow in spirit, to inspire', which can in no way disquiet even the most rigid moralist. The third piece of evidence is iconographic and dates from the middle of the sixth century; it is a cup representing an anal copulation which has been interpreted sometimes as heterosexual, sometimes as homosexual.[25] Like Powell, I think that homosexual relations are in question; but, on the one hand, ceramic images are quite a different thing from a reproduction of reality, then the context seems to be that of a religious ceremony, and finally the *erōmenos* is visibly an adult: this is not, therefore, a scene of pederasty.

Neither the texts nor the other sources, then, impose a solution. I am personally very sensitive to the argument which emphasizes the eminently apologetic and rhetorical character of Xenophon's account of pederasty at Sparta, and which notes, as did Cicero, how unlikely it is that, in the progressive moves which make up the strategy of every amorous conquest, the rule of chastity was really respected; this is why I am tempted to approve the way in which Cartledge presents Spartan love. I cannot, however, categorically reject Nafissi's argument,[26] which reckons that if Spartan society had decided to impose a limit, whatever it may have been, on pederastic love, it possessed the means to ensure it was respected; but why would it have decided this?

The points of contact between the pederasty practised at Sparta and the behaviours which form part of many 'primitive' initiations are sufficiently numerous and precise to render its initiatory origin likely; a very widespread opinion, in fact, since the eighteenth century. There are, however, some contrary opinions, of which one merits particular consideration, because it is that of an eminent specialist in Greek love, Sir Kenneth Dover. Noting that pederastic love does not appear in a definite way either in literature or in vase-painting before the end of the seventh century, he concludes that this practice was only accepted and developed in Greek societies from this period on.[27] This observation means, according to him, that Greek pederasty should be imagined, not as the heritage of a distant past, but as a construction built by Greek civilization in the course of its evolution. The observation itself is difficult to challenge, inasmuch as the development and the quasi-institutionalization of pederasty maintains obvious links with two other major aspects of Greek civilization in the seventh century, the athletic life and the *symposion*. But the conclusion is not so constraining as it appears. On the one hand, indeed, pederasty could have existed in a 'subterranean' form, without then being developed to the point of finding a place amongst the themes of artistic expression. On the other, as is only natural, Dover considers pederasty in isolation, as a form of homosexual relationship, while at Sparta it is an integral part of education and must be envisaged in this ensemble. Finally, like every element of the Spartan education system, it can be initiatory in origin without necessarily dating back to an extremely distant past.

Let us note, to end with, that some historians are not satisfied with an explanation, admittedly a little vague, of pederasty (Greek in general and Spartan in particular) in terms of initiation. Some have wanted to be more precise, talking about Indo-European origins;[28] this hypothesis is hardly convincing, because initiatory pederasty is universally attested, and that which took place at Sparta resembles that of the Marind-Anim as much as that of German or Scandinavian tribes. Others have preferred to see in it a feature characteristic of warrior societies,[29] but this interpretation is tied to a representation of the community of Spartiates as a military brotherhood which is at least simplistic.

Stealing

Of everything which Spartan education imposed on children, stealing is what ancient writers had the most difficulty explaining, and the same goes for us. We saw above that Xenophon, who had recourse on this point as on all the others to a military explanation, despite the undeniable skill he deploys, did not really succeed in being convincing. It is, then, for the understanding of this practice that ethnographic comparisons should show themselves most useful. Though not standard, stealing is well attested in initiations. Most often it is a case of the stealing of food. Some examples, especially African ones, can be found in Brelich's work (1969, 85 nn. 101–3): stealing of small livestock among the Bambara, of sugar-canes among the Kamba. Among the Monumbo of New Guinea, the initiands, during their long segregation beside the sea, steal in the plantations. On the island of Bougainville, where they are set apart in the forest, they frighten women with the noise of a rhombus and seize what they were carrying. The interpretation given by those concerned, especially in the case of a warrior people like the Masai, is, as in Xenophon, preparation for war. For ethnologists, the explanation is delicate, because the possible significance of the custom can vary according to the nature of the objects stolen. When it is food, the theft can be considered as a test (especially if the children caught in the act are punished), but it can also be explained as forming part of the same ensemble as alimentary taboos. When it is livestock, it could signify that the initiands are assimilated to beasts of prey. Some think that in thus playing tricks on the adults, they behave like spirits of the forest. It is also possible to seek an interpretation which would be valid whatever the object of the theft, that is by an inversion of the social norm, as being a material representation of the kind of life apart led by the initiands: this would explain why they must steal without being authorized to do so; but this way of looking at things does not take into account the preponderance of cases of theft of food, which suggests the existence of a link between the two things. Ethnographic comparisons, then, cannot bring us to an understanding of the significance of stealing at Sparta; their interest is primarily in reducing its strangeness.

We can also contribute to this result by considering in detail the modalities of theft at Sparta and the way in which it is represented.[30] It seems to me, indeed, that the image which Xenophon gives is partially determined by two other completely Spartan realities. The most apparent, because it is mentioned by him immediately afterwards, is the ritual at Orthia's altar. It is a ritual of theft; a theft of food (cheeses); the act is at the same time imposed and forbidden, and certainly entrains an identical sanction, the whip. The resemblance is such that if the *Lak. Pol.* was our only source on children's stealing at Sparta, we might ask ourselves if the ritual at Orthia's sanctuary was not the sole reality underlying this representation; but other texts, a conversation in the *Anabasis* (4.6.14) and the passage of Isocrates which was presented in chapter 2 (pp. 46–7), show that the practice of theft in Spartan education was indeed a reality in the fourth century.

The other Spartan custom which Xenophon's expression invites us to compare with the stealing is the Crypteia:[31] in connection with the thief's strategy, the words καὶ νυκτὸς ἀγρυπνεῖν καὶ καθ' ἡμέραν ἀπατᾶν καὶ ἐνεδρεύειν καὶ κατασκόπους ἑτοιμάζειν (*LP* 2.7) evoke fairly closely, with the opposition of day and night, Aristotle's description of the Crypteia (below, p. 285). We might even ask ourselves if Xenophon, who does not mention the Crypteia anywhere, is not amalgamating the two things, but I do not believe this to be the case; the ressemblances were in reality itself, and the child thief like the Crypteian had to remain unnoticed.

We can also diminish the strangeness of the stealing by noting its association with a well-known activity held in particularly high esteem at Sparta, hunting. We have seen this in reading Isocrates: when Spartan parents whose children had gone out stealing were asked where they were, they would reply that they were hunting. My opinion is that this was not simply a means of dressing up reality to save face, but that there existed in Spartan thought a real homology between the childrens' stealing and hunting. This way of looking at things was, moreover, common amongst the Greeks in general, as Schnapp (1997, 138–40) has noted. Plato, in particular, insists on this point in the *Laws*: for him, stealing is a variety of hunting (7.823b), and hunting is similar to stealing at nature's expense (823e).

At Sparta, this comparison is all the more justified because stealing was for the children a means of ameliorating the ordinary fare of their meals (which, we are told, had great need of it) in exactly the same way as hunting was the means for even poor citizens to bring an 'extra'[32] to the communal meal. According to Plutarch, this supplementary contribution of the children had two sources (*Lyc.* 17.5). One was the *syssitia* of the men, where they went to steal food. In Crete, the children ate at the men's communal meal, although apart and while providing service; at Sparta, then, this type of theft could be considered as a roundabout way of associating the children with the men's food,[33] but that would presuppose a sort of tacit connivance which does not seem to have existed at all. The other source of stolen food was made up of the gardens situated around the town, where the children would go to pilfer whatever they could, fruit, vegetables, poultry and other farmyard animals; it is primarily of this that Isocrates seems to be thinking. We almost get the impression that the space where gardens, orchards and hen-houses were to be found was thus a hunting ground for the children just as, in the hunt, wild spaces belonging to the community were the hunting ground of the men.[34] Assimilating stealing to a form of hunting has the effect of normalizing it.

In archaic societies, moreover, hunting is frequently one of the 'subjects' taught to initiands during the segregation phase, even among peoples who are no longer hunting peoples (Brelich 1969, 77 n.75 cites some African examples, like the Bambara and the Ngindo), which suggests that it too belongs to the 'original model'. In Crete, according to Ephoros (in Strabo 10.4.20), it was one of the principal occupations of the adolescents. At Sparta, Isocrates is the only one to speak of it, but it is possible that the contest called *katthēratorion* in the Roman period was the transposition and survival of a teaching of hunting during education. This teaching probably no longer existed in the time of Xenophon, who only speaks of hunting (with great praise) in connection with adults (*LP* 4.7); everything is as if it had been 'replaced' in the classical period by the practice of theft, which demands the same qualities of astuteness and patience.

The third limit on the strangeness of the stealing: its exercise seems to have been the object of a kind of regulation. First, it has been possible to maintain that there was a 'time' for stealing. This is what the Anonymous *Spartan Saying* 35 (*Mor.* 234a) seems to say: 'When it was the time (ἐπεὶ παρῆν ὁ καιρός) when custom decreed that the free children should steal whatever they could...' Kennell (1995, 122–3) was right to draw attention to this text,[35] but his interpretation is more problematic than he says. The apophthegm does not agree with Xenophon's presentation, in which the stealing was permanent; Isocrates claims it was even everyday. Is this just a matter of exaggerations? When talking about a custom of the classical period, should we prefer an apophthegm, whose Stoic coloration Hodkinson (2000, 204) has rightly noted, to fourth-century texts? It is not necessary, however, completely to reject the apophthegm, because καιρός can indicate the 'season' of life, so age. Kennell supports his vision of the children's theft as reserved for particular occasions like festivals with the argument that, if it had been permanent, either it would have been intolerable for Spartan society, or it would have been of a pure form, with the adults letting it take its course. The two terms of this false dilemma should both be rejected: the first, because, as Hodkinson says (2000, 205), these larcenies were of little consequence, and the second because the texts, which are unanimous on this point, leave no doubt about the harsh reality of the punishments received by those who were caught. Relating the stealing to particular festivals and deducing therefrom that it had a religious character is pure speculation. The existence of this first limitation is thus more than dubious.

The same does not go for the other, which is clearly explained by Xenophon: the children did not have the 'right' to steal everything.[36] In the *Lak. Pol.* (2.6), the practice of stealing as Lycurgus 'permitted' it is limited to 'certain things which would appease their hunger'. In the *Anabasis* (4.6.14), he (as author and speaker at the same time) underlines both its limitation and its quasi-legal character: '[Amongst you] it is not shameful but fine to steal everything which the law does not forbid' (ὅσα μὴ κωλύει νόμος); the law, or rather custom. We should note the negative formulation, which translates the difficulty of imagining permission for an act which was nonetheless punished. The two texts complete each other: what custom thus 'does not forbid' to be stolen is food. On this point, too, the anecdote of the fox-cub is in conflict with Xenophon, in saying that the children used to steal 'whatever they could'. In fact, this presentation of reality is rendered necessary by the story itself, and thus does not even need to be discussed.

This limitation contributes very effectively to contextualizing the strangeness of the children's stealing, on the one hand by legitimating it, up to a point, by hunger, to the extent that we might think of asking ourselves if the aim of this diet was not to push the children to steal (but this alimentary regime itself, as we have seen, also has parallels in initiations, and the relating of hunger and stealing may very well be nothing but a rationalization by the classical authors); on the other, in that this appropriation of food can be compared to a Spartan custom which was, itself, absolutely regular and legal. Xenophon explains this in the chapter (*LP* 6) which he consecrates to communal practices at Sparta. Among the private goods which each Spartan is obliged to make available, to any of his fellow citizens who demands use of it, feature the provisions which are to be found in country cottages (6.4). In the case of the children's stealing, it is thus as though the products of the gardens, the orchards and the hen-houses (which were situated in the vicinity of country cottages) were likewise, up to a point, offered to anyone who knew how to take them without being caught. What this specification ressembles most is the strange prescription in Plato's *Laws* (8.845e) which we have studied in chapter 2 (p. 57). The making available there concerns the fruit of the orchards; it is accompanied by a ritualized theft ('to pick on the quiet'), as is also the resistance, strictly codified, of the owner. This clause in the *Laws* resembles a synthesis of the two Spartan customs which are the making available of provisions and children's stealing.

Carried out according to the rules, then, this theft is not forbidden; it is even obligatory. It is, however, punished ('with numerous blows', says Xenophon); the punishment is doubtless inflicted by the injured owners, but the father, we know, could repeat it. This custom might appear absurd, but Xenophon explains its logic very well: the child, he says, is not punished for having stolen, but for having let himself be caught, so 'for having stolen badly' (ὡς κακῶς κλεπτόντας). This might appear sophistic, but it clearly signifies that, like numerous other elements of education, stealing was considered as a test in Sparta; the blows were a sanction against failure. As for 'success', it demanded, in the first place, that one did not let oneself get caught; but the anecdote of the fox-cub shows that the business did not end there, and that it might happen that the owners, if they really cared about the object which had been stolen from them, might investigate, in which case the child had to prove his capacity to confront an interrogation. As in all tests, success could bring a certain renown; this is what Isocrates says (not without rhetorical amplification), and there is no reason to doubt it. This presupposes that the thefts (not ordinary thefts of food, but those which were in some way remarkable) did not remain unknown for long, but were subsequently claimed by their authors. Thus, the children's stealing ceases to be a strange custom contrary to the most elementary social ethics and becomes a test amongst so many others.

Without totally removing the strangeness of the children's stealing, all these specifications combine to normalize it and integrate it into Spartan life and mentality, and thereby to render it not only acceptable but commendable. This integration results from the multiplicity of referents: the ritual at Orthia's altar, the Crypteia, hunting, the communal meals with their 'surplus', the communal practices concerning the utilization of provisions, the rivalry for excellence, the tests. It is the most demonstrative example one could give of the way in which a practice belonging in origin to the world of 'primitive' initiations could be framed, remodelled and re-imagined in order to be integrated into preparation for the life of the citizen and Spartan life in general.

The case of theft is all the more exemplary in that, by its nature, this behaviour does not seem capable in any way of being used in the context of an educational system. In order better to understand how this was possible, we must turn to an ethnology which is no longer of archaic populations, but that of childhood.[37] As it was practised by Spartan children, in a manner which, as we have seen, obeyed certain norms, stealing necessarily created a very strong solidarity in the heart of the 'bands' which were formed for this end. These 'bands' had their own hierarchy: a leader conceived and directed the operation, executors helped him to carry it out (Xenophon). One would like to know, firstly, if these groups were stable (this is what usually happens), and for how long; and also whether command was monopolized by a single child (this is what emerges in bands of children created spontaneously), or if there was a rotation aiming to re-establish equality between the participants (a feature which would almost certainly betray the intervention of a norm imposed by adults). In parallel with the hierarchy existed a technical division of functions: in addition to the leader, there were watchers (Xenophon) and simple executors.

Thus conceived, theft had the pedagogic value of a game; only, it was a *serious* game, in the sense that it was not purely childish, but also implicated the world of adults. It is interesting to work out this implication. (a) It was not an autonomous game 'invented' spontaneously by the children; it was imposed on them, with all its rules, by the adults. (b) It was an imitation of a sort of perpetual war (night and day, says Xenophon) between some children (the thieves) and some adults (their victims). It was not a head-on war, but a war made up of ambushes (ἐνεδρεύειν, Xenophon), of espionage and ruses (ἀπατᾶν), which compensated for the disparity of strength and status. The military vocabulary employed by Xenophon, then, is not only a convenient proceeding aiming to support his justification of stealing by a hypothetical military aim; it corresponds also to reality, the stealing being conducted in the manner of guerrilla warfare. Once the theft had been accomplished, the child had in addition to confront its consequences: as the anecdote of the fox-cub shows, to bring home a victory was not to win the war. (c) While spontaneous children's games happen in principle apart from adults, here the exploits of the young boys were regarded by the whole city, which distributed praise and blame, and accorded to the best a kind of glory. Far from being pure exaggeration, what Isocrates says on the subject turns out to be perfectly logical and is probably true. (d) The punishments inflicted by the adults on those who let themselves get caught (physical punishments and, worst of all, dishonour) introduced into the game an element of risk which valorized it, playing in a way the role of an official sanction, which again reinforced the solidarity of the band of children.

It was, then, a serious game, because it was taken seriously not only by the children (which is always the case), but also by the adults, and this serious side augmented its powers of integration and socialization. But, at the same time, the permanent intervention of adults, logical in an inclusive society like that of Sparta, made the game less than natural: a game controlled by adults is no longer free and is thus no longer really a game. Everything is as if the Spartans, having perfectly understood the pedagogic value of the children's stealing, had wanted to regulate it in accordance with their adult conceptions, which could hardly fail to denaturalize it. However this may be, it is evident that thus understood the children's stealing practised at Sparta has practically nothing in common with those we encounter in some initiations. The only relation which remains is what I shall call the initial impulsion: I mean that, without the presence, in reality or only in the spirit, of the model of initiations, the Spartans would certainly never have thought of making stealing into an important element of their educational system.

Brutality

I shall finish with what we may call, in the absence of a better term, brutality. Some elements of Spartan education involve a form of human relationship which we might be tempted to call violence. We think first of the harshness of the education system, as much in the humiliations and the 'maltreatments' which the children have to endure (heat and cold, privation of food, dirtiness, even flagellation) as in the punishments which were inflicted upon them. Doubtless the latter were probably no more severe than elsewhere (even though at Sparta the whip seems to have come readily to hand), but the fact that the version of education which is known to us via the texts is organized by the city gives this violence the appearance of a state violence, the symbol of which is the whip-bearers who accompany the *paidonomos*, and which is all the more shocking because it is exercised against children. There are, moreover, cases where these punishments might appear particularly unjust, for example when a child is punished for having stolen, after he has been expressly ordered to do so: Xenophon's justification does not work well on the ethical level, and one cannot escape the impression that this is not a punishment but pure violence. It is also possible to say that, insofar as this education prepares for war, not during a short *ephēbeia* period but from the youngest age, it is an education for violence. But what is perhaps most serious, it is an education *by* violence, that is the children and the young people are obliged to lead a life where relationships between individuals are marked by violence. This is what Aristotle seems to have meant to denounce by his use of the term 'savagery' (*thēriōdes*), thus showing that at least some Greeks (in fact, I believe, all Greeks, but in a more or less clear manner) were aware of this reality. Nonetheless, the concept of violence as we use it today is, I think, too ill-defined and too emotionally charged to apply in this context. This is why I prefer to employ the term 'brutality' to indicate the particular coloration that the norm imposed on relationships between the young, and which resulted to a great extent, as Xenophon's chapter on the *hēbōntes* very clearly shows, from the permanent competition which was maintained amongst them.

In comparative studies, in particular that of Brelich, there is no heading 'brutality' (which is perhaps significant in itself); what comes closest is the heading 'combats'. It is indeed frequently the case in initiations that combats, not simulated but regulated and carried out without real arms, are organized between troops of children or youths (Brelich 1969, 35 and 82–3 nn. 94–7); they may oppose either initiands against each other, or initiands against the newly-initiated. The 'model' supplied by ethnology is, then, that of regulated combats which oppose groups. We can compare three kinds of confrontation at Sparta.

First, ritual combats. The only known example is the Platanistas combat.[38] This can properly be called ritual because, according to Pausanias' account (3.14.8–10), which is by far the most complete source, it was preceeded by two sacrifices, to Enyalios and to Achilles. The problem is that it is not absolutely certain that this combat already existed in the classical period. On the one hand, none of the authors who mentions it is earlier than the first century BC; on the other, Kennell has noted in Pausanias' description of the place of combat some features which seem to him characteristic of the hellenistic period at the earliest: the presence of statues of Lycurgus and Herakles, as well as the role played by Achilles; the fact that the place is presented as an artificial landscape, architecturally composed, which has been compared to the 'maritime theatre' of Hadrian's villa at Tibur. Each of these points could be debated; it seems to me, for example, that nothing in Pausanias' text makes this vision of a completely artificial place compelling, and that there is nothing impossible about statues of Herakles and Lycurgus at Sparta in the fourth century. But this is not the essential point. It is obvious that Pausanias could only describe the place in the form it had at the time of his visit, and that this place could, and indeed must, have undergone important modifications in the course of the centuries; 'recent' elements, if there were any, do not in any way tell against the possibility of the high antiquity of the combat itself.[39] In fact, besides the way in which the combat took place, elements like the sacrifice of a young dog and the duel of boars used as a portent have an archaic appearance, and the theme of combat in a place surrounded by water, water into which it was convenient to throw one's adversary, seem very ancient. Nonetheless, everyone knows that nothing resembles the very archaic so much as the archaizing, and it is precisely this ritual's accumulation of apparently very primitive elements, combined almost wantonly, which may arouse scepticism.

The second type is regulated combats, more or less imitating war (but without arms), fought on fixed dates, by troops of children; this is what best corresponds to the 'model' of initiations. We should note carefully that Xenophon mentions absolutely nothing of the sort; we only find it in Plutarch.[40] On the other hand, Ephoros (in Strabo 10.4.20) describes in precise detail combats of this kind which took place among Cretan children, both 'little ones' ('they fight one against another, either between members of the same *syssition* or between *syssitia*') and 'older boys' ('on some fixed days, they engage in combat, *agelē* against *agelē*, to the sound of the flute and the lyre and rythmically, as one does in war too; they even strike blows against each other, either with bare hands or also by means of arms not made of iron'). Did such battles exist at Sparta? The Cretan parallel obviously does not lay down a particular answer, and Plutarch could have transposed to Sparta what happened on Crete; but it seems to me that Plato attests something of this sort when, in the *Laws* (1.633b), he gives Megillos, in his account of the 'endurance tests' organized in the city with a view to war, a passing allusion to 'collective bare-hand combats' (ἔν τε ταῖς πρὸς ἀλλήλοις ταῖς χερσὶ μάχαις). The use of the article and of the plural seems to indicate that it was a frequent and organized practice, and to exclude the possibility that the allusion refers to an annual ritual combat like that of the Platanistas.

It must be admitted that, as far as both ritual combats and regular combats are concerned, the results of this enquiry are particularly uncertain, and that their very existence is nebulous from our point of view; in any case, it does not seem that they would have been organized in a systematic fashion as on Crete, where they constituted a real imitation of war, as Ephoros emphasizes. On the other hand, Xenophon describes in precise detail a third form, individual combats, but resulting from a collective norm, which opposed the *hēbōntes* against one another (*LP* 4.6). I have already emphasized several times (pp. 18–19, 102–3, 172–4) the extent to which these perpetual confrontations, presented by Xenophon as the manifestation, desired by Lycurgus, of a healthy rivalry, profitable for the city, appear in reality as negative for those concerned and dangerous for the collective, which makes it difficult to explain them as the training of future citizens. Here I shall place the accent on another remarkable aspect of these confrontations, their exclusively physical character. We could very well understand why a young man who had been excluded at the selection of the *hippeis* might seek to denounce the weaknesses of the one who had been preferred to him, and might do his best to show himself the better person with a view to the next selection. But why is it necessary for him to enter into a fist-fight? There is no logical, pedagogic or political explanation for this; it is necessary for there to be combats because they are part of the 'model' of initiations. Indeed, it happens quite often in archaic societies that the newly-initiated are considered to be dangerous, because initiation is supposed to have filled them with an excessive charge of energy. Some of these societies judge that this is a fact which needs to be accommodated, and that they must allow the young men to expend this energy in committing depredations and damage and aggression against the person (and often against women). Others, on the contrary, channel it by organizing combats, either amongst the newly-initiated or between them and the initiands. The behaviour of the inhabitants of the island of Nauru, in the south of the Marshall Islands, recounted by Brelich (1969, 83 n. 96 *bis*), very much ressembles that of the Spartans: after initiation, the young men passed the years preceding their marriage (which marked their true entry into the category of men) in challenging each other on every occasion to single combat, which was carried out as a fist-fight. It is this almost primitive atmosphere of physical violence, characteristic of Spartan education in general, which I mean by the term 'brutality'.

A precise object constitutes the symbol of this brutality: the sickle, which seems to have been the companion of the young Spartiate during his education. The most abundant and spectacular documentation of this object is a series of 135 stelai, of which the majority have been found, in widely varying states of preservation, in the sanctuary of Artemis Orthia.[41] They bear dedications made to the goddess by the victors in the contests of children in the context of her cult; they consecrate to her the prize which they have received, a sickle,[42] which was embedded in the stele itself. The tools have generally disappeared, but one of them is preserved (dedication of Leonteus, second century AD; *AO* no. 7; it is made of iron); as for the others, one can, when the state of the stele permits, clearly trace their form in that of their casing. These forms are very variable, between extremes constituted by the offering of Arexippos (fourth century BC), where the object, elongated and very curved at the extremity, might seem rather to deserve the name 'bill-hook' or 'pruning-hook', and by that of Leonteus, where, with its wide and regularly curved blade, the name sickle is appropriate. It is, however, always the same object, with the same function, and it is indeed a sickle that the texts call it: in two forms, δρέπανον and δρεπάνη, the name appears in three dedications (*AO* nos. 4, 8 and 9).[43]

Only one of these stelai belongs to the classical period, thereby justifying detailed treatment here: that of Arexippos (*AO*, no. 1; *IG* 5.1.255). It has always been dated to the fourth century, and even, by some (Wilamowitz, followed by Woodward), to the beginning of that century. I think that today it would be placed rather towards 350, but no matter. It bears the casings of five sickles; the (metrical) text is as follows:[44]

> ϝωρθείαι τάδ' Ἀρ[ή]ξιππος νικῶν ἀνέσηκε
> ἐν συνόδοις πα[ί]δων πᾶhιν hορῆν φανερά.

Despite its simplicity, this poses a problem of meaning. It is possible to make ἐν συνόδοις παίδων depend on πᾶhιν hορῆν φανερά and translate, with Kennell (1995, 126), 'Victorious Arexippos dedicated these to Orthia, manifest for all in the gatherings of boys'. It is also possible to make this expression depend on νικῶν, indicating the gathering of participants in the competitions won by the dedicant; this is what Hodkinson does (1999, 178 n. 4), who speaks of 'multiple victories in the "gatherings of boys"'. The second interpretation has the advantage of not leaving νικῶν without a determinant, but the first seems to me better to correspond to the flow of the text and to the division of the lines: the second expresses the idea, very common in inscriptions from the fourth century on, of publicity, or of glory if you prefer, and ἐν συνόδοις πα[ί]δων specifies and completes πᾶhιν.

This document is particularly remarkable for its chronological isolation. There is no earlier sickle dedication, and, to find another afterwards, we have to wait at least two centuries, with that of Xenokles (*AO* no. 2). It is also unusual in the number of sickles which it once exhibited, five, corresponding to as many victories. The texts tell us of triple and quadruple victors, and, as far as actual sickles are concerned, the stele which bears the most after that of Arexippos only has three (Xenokles' stele). It is not impossible that there is a connection between this exceptional number of sickles and the chronological isolation of the document. I do not mean to speak of its isolation with regard to those which follow: this problem (is the gap which separates *AO* no. 1 and no. 2 just the result of chance in finds? or should we, on the contrary, think of an interruption and see in Xenokles' stele evidence of a new beginning? in this case, is the latter related to the transformation of the ritual at Orthia's altar?) will concern those studying Spartan education in the hellenistic period, if there are such people one day. What interests me is what happened previously. It is possible that there had been other stelai, now disappeared, before that of Arexippos; but it is also possible that this really was the first, and that the dedications made earlier had taken the common form of a simple deposition of the sickles in the sanctuary. The later documentation confirms that to win five victories in the *paidikoi agōnes* was truly an extraordinary performance. So it is possible that the author of this feat (or rather his father) had the idea of celebrating it with an offering of an absolutely new type, where the showing-off of the sickle takes a spectacular form: it is exactly this, I think, which the formula πᾶhιν hορῆν φανερά should mean.

What competitions had Arexippos won? The later stelai, which range from the second century BC to the third century AD,[45] show the existence of five competitions, called *katthēratorion*, *mōa*, *keloia*, *eubalkēs* and *deros*.[46] Would Arexippos have won these five competitions? We can neither assert this nor even propose the hypothesis, for there is no evidence that they had existed, or had all existed, or had had these names, in the classical period. Moreover, it is not necessarily the case, and in fact is improbable, that Arexippos would have won these five victories in the same year: his dedication, like that of Xenokles, which consecrates three prizes all won in the competition called *moa*, and thus in three different years, must have had (as also Damonon's dedication) a recapitulative value, and have come, for example, at the end of his 'career', when he left the category of *paides* or of *paidiskoi*. It seems to me in any case very unlikely that the theft of cheeses from Orthia's altar featured among these contests, because the inscriptions show that the victors in the Orthia event (at least in the form it had taken in the Roman period) did not dedicate sickles (because the sickle was not the prize), but statues.

The wording of Arexippos' dedication likewise shows the very particular character, from a functional point of view, of stelai of this type. The usual function of a stele concerning a dedication is to be the bearer of a text which assures the dedication's publicity: to which deity, by whom, in what circumstances. These elements are indeed all present and correct here, and we are not in a position to say that the text which transmits them was not considered important by its author: it is carefully inscribed and set off in a kind of 'panel', and it has been composed with very particular care, since a professional poet has been called in to do so. Nonetheless, it is clear that the important thing in this case is not the written text, but the sickles. Their display is the principal function of the stele (τάδε… φανερά); the text is just a commentary on the objects shown.

Let us, then, return to the sickles. Of course the question has already been asked: why sickles? That is, not 'why dedicate sickles?', for the answer is obvious: because they are the prizes won by the victors; but 'why were these prizes sickles?' Such prizes are at first sight very strange. There is no connection to be found between these objects, whatever their use may have been, and the competitions which they crowned, and which, according to what we know about them in the Roman period, appear to relate to *mousikē* (song, dance, mime). The only explanation which Kron (1998, 203) finds is the agrarian character of the cult of Orthia; but this is nowhere attested, and the context of these competitions is the education of children. We must, then, look in another direction, by asking ourselves what these sickles would have represented for the boys of Sparta.

A few texts allow us to get some idea – texts which bring us back to 'brutality'. I only cite the first for the record, for it is very imprecise, but it will put us in the right area: it is the woman's *Saying* (Plutarch, Gyrtias 1, *Mor.* 240e) in which we see Akrotatos[47] brought home as though dead, after receiving numerous blows in the course of a combat between children (ἔκ τινος τῶν παίδων μάχης πολλὰς πληγὰς λαβόντα); we are not in a position to assert that the wounds he is supposed to have received (the anecdote itself is suspect for many reasons) were inflicted on him by sickles. Another apophthegm, however, is more significant: this is the Anonymous *Spartan Saying* 34 (*Mor.* 233f–234a), which begins thus: 'Two children were fighting with each other, and one of the two wounded the other fatally with the blow of a sickle (δρεπάνῳ)'; after this the words of the dying boy show that it was a true duel. A fact reported by Xenophon shows that fatal accidents of this kind really happened in the classical period. In the *Anabasis* (4.8.25), he recounts that, on arriving in Colchis, the Greeks organized a gymnastic competition for which they chose as *agōnothetēs* 'the Spartan Drakontios, who, when he was a child, had been exiled from Sparta for having involuntarily killed another child with the blow of a *xyēlē*.' The ξυήλη λακωνική has already appeared in the *Anabasis* (4.7.15), where it serves as a parallel in the description of a kind of long knife carried by the Chalybes. In the *Cyropaedia*, the word *xyēlē* means, in accordance with its etymology, an instrument for polishing wood (the shafts of lances, 6.2.32). These occurrences allow us to envisage it as a long blade, pointed and with a cutting edge, curved at its end, and susceptible of many uses, which corresponds very well to the form of the sickles in the stelai of Arexippos and Xenokles. There is hardly any doubt, then, that it is with what the inscriptions call a 'sickle' that Drakontios had killed his young fellow.

It emerges from these texts that the sickle was an instrument that the young Spartiate had with him at least frequently.[48] It would have been used to cut wood (especially for making fires for meals, Plutarch, *Lyc.* 17.4) and for working it. It is probably what Plutarch is thinking of when he says (*Lyc.* 16.13) that the children used to cut reeds beside the Eurotas 'without using iron', ἄνευ σιδήρου. Of course, the children were not the only ones to use sickles; they were a common instrument at Sparta, as shown by their presence (πολλὰ δὲ δρέπανα) in the list which Cinadon draws up of tools abundantly available which could serve as weapons.[49] But they were considered as typical of children's equipment, and constituted their special weapon: a weapon with which, because of its curved form, it was difficult, but not, as we have seen, impossible to deliver mortal blows. Such a use was, of course, formally forbidden, and Drakontios was severely punished (which, in the case of a child, poses some problems, as does the fact that Xenophon qualifies him as a 'Spartiate'). In order to train citizens, from their youngest age, to bear arms at all times,[50] the Spartan state chose to run a risk: the fierceness of competition and the heat of the combats would indeed have rendered accidents almost inevitable. From now on we shall better understand why Xenophon insists so strongly on the need to exercise a close and constant surveillance over the children (*LP* 2.10–11).

It is not only on the material level that the sickle was associated with Spartan children. A peasant's tool, it could serve as a weapon, but it was, in Greek eyes, a weapon characterizing primitive periods or barbarian societies:[51] a weapon which is at the opposite pole from the instruments, entirely functional and highly specialized, which equipped the true warrior, the hoplite. It was thus entirely suitable to become the symbol of the ambiguous and marginal status of the children. Examination of Greek myths where it plays a central role (Kronos and Ouranos, Perseus and Medusa, Herakles at Lerna) can even lead us to see it as the typical weapon of young men in the process of initiation. This association, at once real and symbolic, with children explains why it was given as a prize to victors in the children's contests.

That Spartan education comprised teachings made it an education like others, and in addition it was also an excellent training for the job of citizen; but it took place in an atmosphere of physical brutality and near-savagery. The Greeks of the classical period clearly perceived this, and they were all in agreement in explaining this surprising feature by the desire to create warriors capable of bearing anything. The philosophers – characteristically – thought further. As we have seen (p. 59), Plato criticized this brutality vigorously: he considered it to be innate in man, but reproached Spartan education, because it was collective, for not sufficiently repressing it. Aristotle was more radical (pp. 63–4): because it was preoccupied solely with military efficiency, Spartan education, according to him, voluntarily created and systematically developed 'savagery' in the child. The vivacity of this attack shows that he had been struck, much more than his predecessors, by the atmosphere of brutality which reigned in this education.[52] Even if this brutality ultimately originates in the combats between youths which are included in numerous initiations, it goes infinitely further, to the point of giving an impression of voluntary violence which archaic societies do not give to the same degree in this area. We should see here the consequence of a behaviour which hardly exists in these societies, the organization by adults of a permanent and fierce competition amongst the young.

Conclusion

Before attempting to establish a conclusion from the comparison between Spartan education and 'primitive' initiations, we must pose some problems of method. The first and the most obvious concerns the ethnological evidence which has been used above. I am very aware of its limitations. I have confined myself to taking up what Brelich collected, and which is thus earlier than 1969; in fact, in his bibliography, many important titles go back to the beginning of the twentieth century, and few references are more recent than 1955.[53] I have never had either the intention or the capacity to devote myself to personal research in this area, and I have only meant to re-trace the road followed by Brelich, while keeping a critical eye on its course. Initiations are so widespread in archaic societies that to put together an up-to-date synthesis on the subject would, I believe, be a whole life's work.[54] Nonetheless, I do not think that this flaw invalidates our main conclusions. On the one hand, for my purpose as for Brelich's, an overview, although necessarily imperfect, was sufficient. On the other, what has evolved in the meantime is not so much the facts, which had already been collected in abundance before the end of the nineteenth century, as the way in which ethnologists look at them[55] – inasfar as one can distinguish between these two realities. It is the collection of facts which was important to me, and I have generally abstained (except in some cases, *exempli causa*) from reporting the ethnologists' interpretations, and above all from reasoning on their basis. As for distortions introduced by the observation itself, I have not felt qualified to remedy them.

The second problem is more fundamental for my argument: is it legitimate to base a historical study on a comparison between two types of societies as different as archaic societies and a political society like that of Sparta? This preliminary was raised by Finley,[56] who contested, not the value of the comparison in itself, but the choice of its point of application on the Spartan side. It should be applied, in Finley's view, to a distant indeterminate period when initiation rites were a living reality. It can inform us about that period, but not about the classical period, when initiation rites only survived in fossilized fragments, reused and 're-functionalized' in an institution endowed with a totally different meaning. This remark made an impression, and it has been repeated by some of the best Sparta experts;[57] others subsequently have submitted it to a close re-examination and have found it less well founded than it at first appears.[58] As Lupi has observed, it rests on presuppositions which he qualifies as being both evolutionist (fossilized survivals) and functionalist (the 're-functionalization' of these survivals enacted at the time of the 'sixth-century revolution', a concept itself taken up from Ehrenberg). Today it is no longer possible to believe that an abyss separates archaic societies and political societies. We know that traditional societies, too, evolve and react to their surroundings; as for classical Greek societies, they are in many ways, particularly in their social institutions and value-system, traditional societies. On the other hand we can assert, even before drawing up a detailed conclusion, that, at Sparta, where initiations are concerned we are not dealing with fragmentary survivals, but, as Brelich said, with a complete system which *became* the classical education system. We find in it the *structure*, that is to say not only numerous isolated elements, but above all the way in which they are organized one in relation to another, including at the level of representations and interpretations provided by those involved. This structure remains efficient because it conserves its *function*, to tranform the children into complete members of the community. That the latter had changed in nature, which is true to a certain extent, does not change the function in its principle. There had not, then, been a 're-functionalization': even where, as at Athens for young girls, only fragments of initiation rites survive, now integrated into the cults of particular deities, the function endures.

The third problem is that of the right use of comparisons with a view to understanding Spartan education. Two extremes should be avoided. One consists in assuming a pedagogic aim wherever possible, and in reserving ethnological comparison for the residue of the cases, for example stealing and the 'maltreatments'. Convenient in appearance, this method would in reality be absurd. Indeed, having recourse to comparison, even if only to clarify a single aspect, amounts to recognizing its validity in principle, which means that it cannot be denied for other aspects without arbitrariness. The other extreme would consist in believing that comparison can explain everything. In fact, it cannot properly speaking *explain* anything; it is not designed for that. We must not expect the comparative method, when applied to Spartan education ('they made the children do *x because* that was part of the process of initiation'), to substitute for explanation by aim, the pedagogic interpretation ('they made the children do *x in order to train* them for *y*'). 'Primitive' initiations can be an interpretative model, but they are not the reason for Spartan education. This reason is the historic process which brought it into existence; unfortunately, we have no real information about this process, and to speculate on this point would be to go beyond the scope of this research. All that comparison allows us to do is to pose questions and to seek to give a meaning to behaviours which at first sight seem to be meaningless.

Let us now come to a conclusion on comparison. Some features of initiations can be found without much modification in Spartan education: 'supervision' exercised by all the adults, pederasty, restrictions on diet and clothing, stealing. It is true that this last only plays a marginal role in initiations, but I suspect that its importance at Sparta was exaggerated by the discussions of which it was the object in the fourth century. In all, the great number of points where comparison brings meaning shows that, as far as initiations are concerned, Sparta's situation, as Brelich often emphasized, was very different from what one meets in other known Greek cities, with the exception of Crete. There are cities where some customs manifest the presence of the initiation model, but the initiatory elements are reduced to the state of isolated fragments which have served as material and have been integrated into new ensembles, either in myths or in cults, in the form of festivals where youth is involved, especially girls: this is the case at Athens.

This phenomenon, as we shall see in chapter 8, can be observed at Sparta too; but what has been the object of the present chapter is something else. The system of initiations survives there in the form of structure; a structure which was not only incorporated into the state's educational system, but made up its essential basis and explains, as we stated at the beginning of the chapter, its principal characteristics. This structure has likewise preserved its purpose, and between education and initiation there are, from this point of view, only differences of means.

Another, more fundamental, continuity reinforces the impression that a complete system of initiation can be found in Spartan education: it is that of the internal logic which, in both cases, gives the whole its coherence. It is not a pedagogic logic: there is no preoccupation with discovering the most suitable means of teaching and educating; but it is, nonetheless, a logic. We can even, to begin with, distinguish between two logics which work together. The first is the *logic of the test*, which consists of putting youths into difficult or painful situations, or of forcing them into deviant behaviours: insufficient food and clothing, fierce combats, stealing, homosexual relations. The other logic has already been identified, but in rites of passage in general. It is the *logic of inversion*, which means that, in order to make a human being pass from one status to another, from one state to another, he is made to traverse an intermediary phase, during which he is compelled to be the opposite of what he must become. This means that, in order to complete the integration of a young man into the community of adults, he is made to pass through a phase where the opposite of integration is pushed to an extreme, and where his behaviour is the opposite of what it will have to be when he becomes a responsible citizen, respectful of the laws and self-controlled.[59] It is easy to see that all the examples given above of the logic of the test are just as much examples of the logic of inversion. This is obviously not by chance; it stems from the fact that *it is precisely inversion which constitutes the test*. The test is not to make an effort to become a good citizen, it is to bear, for this end, being forced for a period to do exactly the opposite.

This does not mean that I am adopting Brelich's conclusion, that Spartan education was only an education in appearance, and that in reality it can only be understood as a complete ritual of initiation. Brelich was only able to come to this conviction because he was keen to catalogue the similarities and continuities, without noting also the absences, the modifications, the innovations. Thus, there is in the Spartan education system an essential feature which does not appear, or at least not with the same intensity, not with the same systematic aspect, in initiations: the principle of permanent competition. Its existence can be explained by the nature of Spartan political society, which lives according to the system of government of the best. It is this elite which, from childhood, Spartans seek to pick out and to train; it is this ideology of the good form of *eris* ('competition') which they seek to inculcate.

On the other hand, some typical features of initiations are lacking in Spartan education, and this absence is all the more significant because they are really essential features. Thus, despite what Brelich was able to say on the subject, we find no serious trace of the secrecy which characterizes every type of initiation (not just that of the young). Also lacking is the phase of physical segregation, which is generally the central moment of the initiatory process. These two absences have the same cause, which is that the Spartans chose that the process of their education should be entirely public. It happens before the eyes of all, and any citizen who wants to can participate. They thus took to its conclusion the, eminently logical, principle which demands that an operation on which the survival of the city depends, in fidelity to the model which she has chosen for herself, should be everyone's business. The norm, resulting from the logic of inversion, according to which the initiands have to lead a life apart, is certainly also in force at Sparta, but it is realized by means other than physical isolation. The young have a particular way of life, and internalize a kind of state of psychological reclusion, as Xenophon's description of the behaviour of the *paidiskoi* shows. This is how the reconciliation works between the demands of the two models, that of 'tribal' initiations and that of the training of a member of a political society.

It is not so much these two symmetrical absences (that of competition from the initiations, and that of secrecy and segregation from Spartan education) in themselves which are significant, for it goes without saying that each particular initiation does not necessarily (and even necessarily does not) include *all* the features of the theoretical model; what is significant is that they clearly result from the fact that, in Spartan education, the dominant model is that of the city. The same goes for several features which are certainly taken from initiations, but with differences which show their adaptation to the model of the training of the citizen. Thus we have seen that the duration of Spartan education had no real parallel in initiations. This divergence can be explained by the difference of programme: to train citizens takes more time than to carry out a few rituals. The age classes become the rational and efficient structuring principle of the group of citizen-soldiers, from birth to the age of 60. On top of this annual structure is superimposed, as Lupi (2000) has shown, another structure which also functions in some archaic societies, the 'generational' structure, which in the city distinguishes sons, fathers and Elders, and which explains, among other things, the ambiguous position of the *hēbōntes*. As far as the boys' food is concerned, we do not find at Sparta the taboos characteristic of initiations, but a partial diet, which has been put into a logical relationship with the obligation to steal. There is no special clothing for the young, but their dress is uniform and severely regulated, whence a kind of 'clothing diet'. The 'maltreatments', so typical of initiations, become at Sparta tests to overcome, and this theme of the test is dominant throughout the education system. As for tortures, only traces of these survive, which take the form either of religious rites (the ritual at Orthia's altar is, as we shall see further on, a variation on the theme of flagellation), or of punishments of a pseudo-pedagogic character (the biting of the thumb in Plutarch). For combats similar to those which numerous archaic societies organize among the initiands or between them and the newly-initiated, we have no certain evidence, and the confrontations of the *hēbōntes* are individual; but we can be sure that the brutality which characterizes them is in fact present throughout the education system. Homosexual relations imposed on the young men, often during the phase of segregation, have become a stable pederastic relationship, which seems indeed to play a real educational role. But it is doubtless the case of the stealing which allows us to witness in most detail the society's creation of an ideological structure, the object of which is in a way to 'civilize' a practice inherited from initiations, by weaving multiple links between this apparently deviant and potentially dangerous conduct and other perfectly permitted behaviours.

These transformations, these adaptations, these subtle shifts of accent, show how far Brelich was both right and wrong. It is entirely true that the initiatory features in Spartan education are not fragmentary and fossilized survivals, but make up a living structure[60] which evolved to the rhythm of the city's history. But he was wrong not to say (though this would not have gone against the main thrust of his ideas) that this system of initiations had been used, adapted and interpreted in accordance with the needs and values of the city in the course of its development, and had for this reason changed in nature. In the classical period, Spartan education is not an initiation, but a training for the job of citizen. It is a remarkable example of an educational system inside which is present, alive and close enough to be perfectly recognizable, the package of initiation rites on which it had been modelled, with the modifications which its change of nature imposed.

Notes

1 On Lafitau's work, see Vidal-Naquet 1981, 177–81.

2 On the terminology, see the references given by Cartledge 2001, 208 n. 23.

3 In the same vein, see Birgalias 1999, 75.

4 This integrally 'public' character can indeed be found in some initiations (Brelich 1969, 68 n. 54), but in Sparta's case it is better explained by the model of the city.

5 In the same vein, cf. Kennell 1995, 124: 'Their segregation was for the most part symbolic, not physical'. He adduces (123–4) the *anypodēsia*; the diet; the clothing; the sleeping on *stibades* in Plutarch (which he accepts for the classical period because it

features also in the *Inst. Lac.* 6).

[6] Along the same lines, Kennell 1995, 123.

[7] Cf. the examples cited by Kennell 1995, 208–9 n.7. To these we can add the Selloi, servants of the cult of Zeus at Dodona.

[8] Brelich 1969, 125, who, however, omits to distinguish this silence from the secrecy of initiation.

[9] David 1999, 119.

[10] Cf. Nikolaos of Damascus, 90 F 103: 'climbing mountains barefoot'.

[11] Den Boer 1954, 274–81.

[12] Cartledge 2001 (on the case in point, 1992), 86; Kennell 1995, 122. Cf. Ducat 2004.

[13] For instance (Vernant 1989, 199): 'As it is thus described [by *Inst. Lac.* 40], the ceremony has taken on an unequivocal significance': this implies that the ancient form was not a pure and simple flagellation.

[14] There is a long list of references in Birgalias 1999, 135–6 and notes.

[15] On this frequency, and the impossibility, for numerous reasons, of our putting a figure on it, cf. Cartledge 2001, 99 and n.46.

[16] Cartledge 2001, 100–1.

[17] Ogden 1996, 140–7.

[18] See the references in Cartledge 2001, 207 n.16. Cf. Harvey 1994.

[19] Cartledge 2001, 95.

[20] The texts are the following, in what is only a possible chronological order: Xenophon, *LP* 2.11; Plato, *Symposium loc. cit.*; Xenophon, *Symposium* 8.35; 'Plutarch', *On the Education of Children, Mor.* 11e (where it is clear that the author has read Plato's *Symposium* in the same text as our manuscripts).

[21] After all, there is a development of ideas in Xenophon himself, since, having maintained at the beginning of the *Lak. Pol.* that Sparta owed her power to her fidelity to the laws of Lycurgus, he states in chapter 14 that she no longer respects them.

[22] Cartledge 2001, 209 n.33.

[23] For discussion of the 'penetration criterion', see most recently Davidson 2001.

[24] This vocabulary is gathered in Cartledge 2001, 208 n.18, and studied in detail by Ogden 1996, 144–7.

[25] Powell 1998a, 130–3 and fig. 4; discussion in Cartledge 2001, 98 and 209 n.36.

[26] Nafissi 1991, 187–9.

[27] Dover 1978, 194–6; Dover 1988.

[28] Sergent 1986.

[29] This is the thesis of Jeanmaire 1939, followed by Marrou 1948; cf. Ogden 1996.

[30] Hodkinson (2000, 201–5) has gathered and commented on the sources for theft by children; my point of view is a little different, but I largely share his conclusions. Cf. Ducat 2003.

[31] As noted by Birgalias 1999, 125 n.56.

[32] On the *epaiklon*, see Hodkinson 2000, 356–7.

[33] Den Boer (1954, 262) thinks that this aspect of the stealing shows that its aim was that the children should appropriate the men's strength. This explanation appears rather improbable today.

[34] Xenophon, *Cynegeticus* 12.7, implies that, in a comparable fashion, the youths only practised hunting in the vicinity of the town.

[35] As does Link 1994, 32, who seems to believe in seasonal stealing.

[36] Cf. MacDowell 1986, 59.

[37] The account which follows is based on the study of children's games conducted by Delalande 2002.

[38] In the absence of a real monograph on the subject, the documentation can be found in Kennell 1995, 55–9.

[39] This possibility is anyway admitted by Kennell himself (1995, 111: 'substantial renovation').

[40] Among the 'little ones', *Lyc.* 16.8 and especially 9; among the 'older boys', 17.4, ἐν ταῖς μάχαις, and 18.8, ἐν τῷ μάχεσθαι.

[41] *Artemis Orthia* nos. 1–135. For more details, see Kron 1998, 201–8.

[42] That these were prizes is strongly suggested by the dedication of Arexippos (*AO* no. 1) and is explicitly stated in those of Timokrates (*AO* no. 4, τόδ' ἄεθλον) and of Leonteus (no. 7, τάδ' ἔπαθλα λαβών).

[43] I do not, then, have to consider the other, very varied, interpretations which have been proposed of these objects; Kron's study provides an overview.

[44] Cf. Hansen 1989, 229–30 no. 821.

[45] On these dates, cf. Kennell 1995, 28.

[46] On these contests, cf. Kennell 1995, 51–5.

[47] Is this the son of Cleomenes II or of Areus? Fuhrmann (1938, 347 n.7) thinks it is the son of Areus; but the similarity between this anecdote and that which Diodorus (19.70.5) recounts inclines me towards the son of Cleomenes.

[48] Some documents indicate that he would have carried it not at the belt (he probably did not have one), but attached to a strap slung across the shoulder and over the chest: there are archaic mirror handles representing young girls wearing such a strap to which is fixed, amongst other objects, a miniature sickle (Kron 1998, figs. 16–18).

[49] Xenophon, *Hell.* 3.3.7.

[50] When we study the Crypteia, we shall have to ask ourselves if the *encheiridia* which, according to Aristotle, cited by Plutarch (*Lyc.* 28.3), were the only arms of the Crypteians, could have been sickles; the two words are associated by Herodotos (7.92 and 93).

[51] Herodotos makes it the typical weapon of the Lycians (7.92) and especially the Carians (5.112; 7.93).

[52] This is something which was well appreciated by Vernant, whose argument about the savagery of Spartan education (1989, 206) is basically a commentary on Aristotle's word *thēriōdes*.

[53] Cf. the remarks of Lupi 2002, 311–12.

[54] Lupi (2002, 312) notes some recent studies of age-classes (Stewart, Bernardi) and male homosexuality (Herdt).

[55] We know, for example, that, especially in Africa, some initiation rituals which look completely archaic have been reactivated and reconstructed, like other social structures, in an effort on the part of traditional societies to preserve their identity in the face of colonization (bibliography in Kennell 1995, 144–5; cf. Lupi 2002, 311).

[56] Finley 1972.

[57] Cf. Cartledge 2001 (article published in 1981), 99 and 101; Nafissi 1991, 196–7.

[58] Kennell 1995, 143–6; Lupi 2000, 20–4; Lupi 2002, 310.

[59] It is Vernant's 1989 study which gives the most detailed demonstration of this logic

at work in Spartan education.

[60] It is not necessarily the case that, as Brelich believes, this initiatory ritual dates back to a distant prehistory; I tend to believe that it was put in place by the human community whose evolution gave birth to the city of Sparta.

7

THE EDUCATION OF GIRLS

The education of girls in Sparta is an even more difficult subject of study than that of boys. Clearly, the sources are more scarce, particularly for the classical era; they are also so fragmentary that, in order to have anything at all to discuss, we often have no choice but to include material from a much later period, albeit knowing quite well that, without a shred of doubt, girls' education, like that of boys, has most certainly had a history. The distortion generated by the 'Spartan legend' presents another obstacle, one more hazardous than in any other field. It is readily understandable that, in an exclusively male literature such as that pertaining to the Spartan tradition, as soon as the subject of women is raised, fantasy springs up everywhere. The mythology of the Spartan woman is, therefore, particularly rich. Three themes may be detected in it. The first, and doubtless the most important, is the liberty allegedly allowed to women in Spartan society. There is reality lurking behind this myth, for it seems to be true that women were more often involved in civic life here than was the case elsewhere.[1] This alleged 'liberty' clearly took a sexual form: combined, in the minds of other Greeks, with the sexual appetite attributed to the female nature, it led inevitably, in their view, to licentiousness. We meet this theme of liberty-therefore-licentiousness again when we come to consider young girls, since it is in their education that its origins were thought to lie. Combined with the thirst for power and the desire to dominate, which Greek thinking also ascribed to women, this liberty engenders female power, the gynecocracy which the Greeks thought so often they could detect in Sparta. This aspect of the myth is not applicable to young girls, who as yet have no man they can dominate; on the other hand, when we consider young girls, we encounter a third theme, that of the 'beauty' attributed to Spartan women. It is this beauty that turns men's heads and allows women to satisfy both their sexual appetite (hence the licentiousness) and, at the same time, their desire to dominate (hence the gynecocracy). Even for those who confine their study to young girls, these accepted ideas, which combine to form a genuine system, could well be blurring the available information, time and again.

It would be desirable to know, before embarking on a description of it, whether the girls' education, like the boys', was organized by the state, obligatory and identical for all – whether there existed, as was said formerly, a female *agōgē*; but I do not think we should begin by addressing these difficult questions. It is better first to gather the evidence so that, in the process, we may collect the components of an answer, if such a thing exists.

'Civic' education

Girls' education, like that of the boys, allowed for an element of tuition. They (or, more probably, some of them) studied what are conventionally called *grammata*: reading, writing, and reckoning. Of this aspect of female education, it is safe to say that we know nothing. We are particularly in the dark as to the circumstances in which it took place; it was probably in a family setting rather than in 'classes' organized by teachers. My view is that, in the upper levels of Spartan society, it was usual to give young girls this kind of tuition. I shall rely less on epigraphical evidence for female 'literacy', which does not, on its own, amount to proof, and which Cartledge [2] has shown to be ambiguous in character, than on two female apophthegms (Anon. 10–11, Plut. *Mor.* 241d–e) which show women of good family (principally the second of them, Teleutia) writing letters to their sons. I certainly do not claim that these stories are true, but they show that at the period – unfortunately impossible to determine – when they were devised, it was regarded as normal for a woman of the upper class to be able to read and write.

When it comes to the teaching of *mousikē* (music, dancing, singing, and thus poetry) we have a slightly clearer view of how it was conducted. Using the text of Alcman, Calame has built up a picture of the way in which it may have been done at the end of the seventh century; things must have altered very little by the classical era. For young girls, the context for their education in these subjects is the chorus.[3] This is led by a *chorēgos*, chosen from among the oldest girls in the group; but the principal teacher is the professional poet. His responsibilities lie not only in the spheres of dancing and singing; also, it is he who composes the verses which, when set to music, dictate the movements and songs of the chorus. Alcman's text does not allow us to answer the question that immediately springs to mind: is the chorus a public or a private institution? Was it obligatory for all young Spartan girls to participate in a chorus, or was it a privilege reserved for the few? Who paid the poet? Was it the city or the families of those taking part? All these questions are connected, and we have no answers to them. The most commonly held opinion is that in Sparta the chorus was organized by the city, but this is by no means proven; the answer one gives depends essentially on the image one has of Sparta. A passage from Plato's *Laws*, in which physical education is also discussed, is sometimes taken to indicate the public nature of the chorus, but, as we will discover later, this interpretation is not necessarily the only one possible. So, for now, we must leave the question open.

What is certain is that the teaching of *mousikē* to young girls was unanimously considered a matter of importance to the city; if it was not actually public, it was certainly conducted under the eye of the authorities. Its aims were actually threefold. To start with, it had, naturally, to prepare young girls in such a way that the choruses in which they performed could worthily play their proper part in festivals and contests; the importance of this will be demonstrated in the following chapter. Next, and it is perhaps this that mattered most to society, it was to instil in them, through the medium of the verses composed by the poet, the values held dear by the city, and to make the assimilating of these the permanent focus of competition among them. Lastly, it should turn them into accomplished young girls, the 'beautiful girls' (and, as we shall discover, their physical education also contributes to this) whom every young citizen might wish to take as his legitimate spouse, to beget, and raise, future citizens for Sparta. The results seem to have been at least the equivalent of those to be found in other cities. Sparta was especially famous for its choruses of dancers, and, in Plato's *Protagoras* (342d), Socrates asserts that in Sparta and Crete 'it is not only the men who pride themselves on their education (ἐπὶ παιδεύσει), but the women as well'.

Something that is implicit in any course of instruction is that the understanding and accomplishments acquired will be tested. It was the entire city, assembled for festivals, contests, and processions, who acted as jury. On these occasions, the young girls' choruses were displayed before the public and were set to compete with each other. Plutarch, who records the fact, specifies that in certain processions the girls (probably the very young ones, to judge from bronze statuettes representing them) paraded nude. Each member of the civic community could thus assess the results of the girls' education. But (still drawing on Plutarch, who is our only source for this), in certain circumstances they played a much more important role and, in a way, took an active part in the education of the boys. In fact, says Plutarch,

> there were even occasions when they heaped blame, as appropriate, on boys who had misbehaved, by hurling ridicule at each one, while, conversely, they would address praises, in songs of their own composing, to those who deserved them, thus exciting in the young men a sense of ambition and a lively desire for honours. In fact, anyone who had been praised for his manliness and had become a celebrity among the girls went off priding himself on their admiration, while the barbs of their jokes and ridicule stung as sharply as a severe reprimand, since the kings and the Gerontes attended the spectacle along with the other citizens. (*Lyc.* 14.5–6)

I do not know what source Plutarch used (perhaps Sosibios), but it seems to be reliable, and the description is sufficiently detailed for us to learn some interesting lessons from it. For him, this ceremony (which may, perhaps, have been annual) took place as one in the series of religious festivals (ἱερά) where young girls danced and sang nude (γυμνὰς…ὀρχεῖσθαι καὶ ᾄδειν), in the presence, and under the gaze, of young men (τῶν νέων παρόντων καὶ θεωμένων); in fact that is what is stated in the final phrase of §4, while the beginning of §7, 'the nudity of young girls…', shows that this is the subject of the entire discussion, even if that may seem rather astonishing for the ceremony in question. On the girls' mode of expression, the text seems to point to a difference between the sarcastic remarks (σκώμματα) and the admiring ones (ἐγκώμια). Only the latter are uttered μετ' ᾠδῆς πεποιημένα (which suggests that they were composed as little odes); that seems to imply that the former took a less elaborate form (perhaps in prose, without the accompaniment of song). We cannot determine with any precision how old the participants were: if the girls are always called *parthenoi* (which indicates nothing precise), the boys are designated, in turn, *koroi*, *neoi* (§4) and *neaniskoi* (§5). I would be inclined to think that, in Xenophon's terminology, these are not *hēbōntes*, since I have trouble imagining warriors, even young ones, allowing themselves to be targets for the sarcasm of young girls; I think, rather, that they are *paidiskoi*. Plutarch's use of the imperfect indicates that the ceremony he is describing belonged – at the time of his writing – to the past. In fact, the presence of the kings provides proof that this was going on before the end of the third century, and there is nothing to suggest that it had not already been celebrated in the classical era. One last detail: to describe the young men who are 'glorified' by the girls, the text uses the adjective *kleinoi*. The fact that this term should likewise be used (admittedly in a completely different context, since it concerns relationships of a homosexual, rather than a heterosexual, nature, but still in an educational setting and with a value no less laudatory) in some Cretan cities (above, p. 168) prompts the question of whether it was also a 'technical' term in Sparta.

So then, even if education for males and females constituted two separate worlds, there was still a relationship between them. The custom recorded by Plutarch shows that the girls were perfectly well acquainted with the behaviour and activities of the boys (those of their own age?), and that they took note of each one's achievements. They were almost the first to witness them: this is a reminder that, as we have already seen (pp. 161–2), the education of the young was, in some respects, a spectacle for the whole city, which meant that their compliments or jibes were intelligible to everyone. One could readily suppose that the boys, in their turn, were studying the girls, though no doubt their appraisals were conditioned by somewhat different criteria. Logically, that brings us to the possibility that there were mixed activities, a question to which we shall return. Criticism, which often took the form of mockery, was regarded, in Sparta, as a potent educational tool: it instructed the person to whom it was applied, by pointing out his shortcomings and instilling in him a sense of humility, but it also instructed the author of the criticism, who had to exercise judgement and develop a habit of expression that was witty and to the point (*Lyc.* 12.6–7; cf. 18.3–5 and 19.1). Young girls were, likewise, tutored in this aspect of 'Laconism'. They did not voice their criticisms in the privacy of the *syssition* or in conversation in the *leschē*, as the men did; on the contrary, the author insists on the eminently *public* nature of these ceremonies, which we can safely say were attended by the whole city. To see young girls devoting themselves to this exercise even constituted a spectacle (Plutarch uses the word θέα), richly coloured and particularly enjoyable. The young girls' praises were not framed in ordinary language but sung in the form of poetic texts which they had composed themselves, doubtless under the direction of the poet; this highly formalized mode of expression gave the ceremony an aspect of solemnity.

In this exercise, of which the satirical aspect echoes one of the functions of Attic comedy, the young girls were not simply looked at, but also, certainly, judged, as much for the pertinence of their remarks as for the manner of their making them. Their judge was the assembled city, who used this occasion (among others) to make sure that the girls were receiving an education worthy of daughters of Sparta. Moreover, the role they were required to play on this occasion was a preparation for one of those they were to play in the city once they were adults and the wives of citizens: that of a kind of 'chorus' (in the theatrical sense) who constantly observed and evaluated the behaviour of the men, essentially in the form of a speech intended for public consumption: the apophthegm. Apophthegms reveal the woman as the haughty and passionate guardian of a code which the men espouse in principle but do not always respect. Hence, the ceremony described by Plutarch seems like the crowning moment of the truly 'civic' education these girls received.

Physical education

The feature which the ancient world was unanimous in considering the most characteristic and most original of the education of Spartan girls is that it included an element of physical training. The oldest account we have of their education, that of Critias (D.-K. 81 F 32), insists most particularly on this point. How, he wonders in this fragment of his *Lakedaimonion Politeia*, can the city provide itself with the most robust children possible? To do that, he says in answer, not only must the men exercise their bodies, but the women must do so as well: 'That the mother of the child to be born should strengthen her body and practice physical exercises (γυμνάζοιτο)'. Some commentators have imagined that what Critias meant by this was to prescribe physical exercises for pregnant women, but this was obviously not his meaning: the phrase 'the mother of a child to be born' has a general significance and applies to all young girls insofar as they are future mothers.[4] Hence he roundly approves of this Spartan custom.

The physical aspect of girls' education in Sparta is a commonplace in the classical era. Most of the authors refer to it, as Critias does, in glowing terms: Xenophon, certainly (*LP* 1.4), and also Plato (*Laws* 7.806b), who takes over this Spartan custom for his own scheme, and regrets that their practice of it is not even more thorough-going. On the other hand, Euripides, in his *Andromache* (ll. 595–601), puts into Peleus' mouth a violent diatribe against this practice. The portrait of Lampito, in *Lysistrata* (ll. 77–83), where Aristophanes emphasizes her superb physical fitness, again takes up this theme with admiration (albeit not without humour), but adds the striking peculiarity that the woman concerned is married, a situation by no means free of problems, if the text is taken literally. Lampito tells everyone that she does gymnastic exercises (γυμνάδδομαι): should we take this to mean that she frequents a gymnasium? And if so, is it a female gymnasium? But the example she gives of her exercises, the *bibasis*, was liable to be practised anywhere, not just in a specific place, and Lampito could have been doing her training at home. In any case, we should not forget that she is a character of comedy, and that Aristophanes' world is not the real one.

What gymnastic activities was a Spartan girl supposed to pursue?[5] Xenophon divides them into two categories: running races, and 'trials of strength' (*LP* 1.4: δρόμου καὶ ἰσχύος…ἀγῶνας πρὸς ἀλλήλας), of whose nature he supplies no further detail. His wording shows that these activities were not only the focus of training but also the constituents of official contests, according to the usual practice of Greeks in matters of athletics. I shall deal later with the races, which I notice Xenophon treats separately; but what were these exercises in 'physical strength', which are themselves, *a priori*, surprising? Plutarch (*Lyc.* 14.3 = *Ap. Lac.* Lycurgus 12, *Mor.* 227d) gives the following list: wrestling, discus, and javelin, in addition to racing; all the components of the pentathlon, then, except jumping. After some discussion, Arrigoni (1985, 90) accepts this list, but does so chiefly by a kind of 'begging the question', namely that in Sparta, female athletics existed as an imitation of male. My approach will be a more cautious one. Apart from Plutarch, the only other author to mention the throwing events is Propertius (Book 3, elegy 14), who credits the Spartan woman (since his subject is the married woman, not the young girl) with a great mass of physical activities, some of which are more than surprising: wrestling, ball games, bowling the hoop, the pancratium, the cestus, the discus, equestrian skills, swordplay (note that the javelin is not included); she is at once an all-round athlete and a warrior. The poet clearly does not expect his reader to take this picture as the description of some actual situation. He likes to draw the contrast between the Roman woman, shut in and watched over by her husband, and the imaginary woman of a virtual Sparta, who, living out of doors and being as active as a man, would thereby be more accessible to her suitors. The accumulation of exercises in physical strength ascribed to this woman, and the contrast between this formidable assemblage and the goal actually pursued – sexual freedom – show that the poet is not being serious. Plutarch remains, therefore, the only one to maintain that Spartan girls threw the discus and the javelin. Not one artistic representation supports this claim. Plato (*Laws* 7.806a–b) reasons that it would be desirable for women to participate in the defence of the city, first by shooting arrows and hurling javelins, and also even, 'like Athene', wielding spear and shield, and thus that they should be trained in these disciplines; but he makes it clear that this is not what happens in Sparta, where 'they take no part at all in training for war', which seems to me to exclude, for the classical era, the practice of hurling the javelin.[6]

Thus the sole remaining exercise in 'physical strength' is wrestling. In the classical era it is mentioned in only one text, but one that carries some weight: that tirade of Peleus', in Euripides' *Andromache*, which I have already mentioned (ll. 596–601). 'In Sparta, the young girls...frequent the race tracks and the *palaistrai*, mingling with young men there, something I should not be able to tolerate' (δρόμους παλαίστρας τ' οὐκ ἀνασχετούς ἐμοι | κοινὰς ἔχουσι). Consequent upon the very nature of the athletics practised there, implying, as it does, close physical contact, the *palaistrai* seem to arouse a special sense of outrage in Peleus. It is probable that the authors who, afterwards, alluded to wrestling in relation to Spartan girls, did no more than reproduce what they read in Euripides. Firstly, there is an anonymous Latin poet (probably Accius), cited by Cicero (*Tusculan Disputations* 2.15.36); according to the text, the *palaistra* is one of the places most eagerly frequented by Spartan girls. Lucian, for his part (*Dial. Deor.* 20.14), conjures an image of Helen 'practically nude, and engaged in a bout of wrestling'.

One might perhaps have doubted whether the Euripidean Peleus' claims should be taken seriously had it not been for the existence of a little series of four bronze statuettes[7] from the second half of the the sixth century, which represent female wrestlers and of which the model is probably of Spartan origin. They are:

1. Athens, NM 7703, from Aegina. Mirror handle. Arrigoni, pl. 9. The girl is standing on a tortoise.

2. New York, MMA 41.11.5 (Rodgers Fund). Provenance unknown. Mirror handle (Scanlon) or vase handle (Arrigoni). Scanlon, fig. 12, 3.
3. Trento, Museo Provinciale d'Arte 3061. Provenance unknown. Vase handle. Arrigoni, pl. 10a; Scanlon, fig. 12, 4a–b.
4. Olympia B 3004, from Olympia. Vase handle. Arrigoni, pl. 10b.

In every case, the figure represented is that of a young girl, conforming in all respects to the canons of Nabokov, with slight, high-set breasts, and a slim but sturdy body. This physique is typically that of Spartan female statuettes. The only garment worn by the girl are some sort of triangular drawers (διάζωμα), which enable us to identify her, with confidence, as a wrestler. This is actually the appearance given, in vase representations, to Atalanta, the archetype of the female wrestler as well as of the female runner. Of the four published examples, only no. 4 is really likely to be of Laconian manufacture; it is also the best in terms of technique and style.[8] No. 1 is also quite sophisticated and, in my view, shows a clear Corinthian influence. Nos. 2 and 3 are no doubt adaptations, manufactured in Magna Graecia. I think that here we are dealing with a genre, of Laconian origin and representing a typically Laconian subject, which enjoyed a certain popularity in the Greek world, the strangeness of the figure represented being enough to explain, at a stroke, both the success of this genre and the limits of that success. The conclusion to be drawn from all this is that the 'trials of strength' to which Xenophon alludes were, most probably, contests in wrestling.[9]

Another female physical activity, typical of Sparta, may be viewed as calling for 'physical strength', but it is not usually included in the conventional gymnastic catalogue: this is a particular form of jumping known as *bibasis*. The lexicographer Pollux, and the physician Antyllos, cited by Oribasius, provide us with a reasonably accurate idea of what it was. Pollux 4.102:

> The *bibasis* was also a kind of Laconian dance; contests in this were organized not only for boys but also for young girls. They had to leap while drawing their feet back close to their buttocks. A count was kept of the leaps, whence arose the epigram about a girl leaper...' (this follows, below).

Oribasius, *Coll. Med.* 6.31:

> To these (the single jump and the progressive jump) may be added the jump tapping the buttocks, formerly practised by Laconian women. It is a leap during which the legs are bent so that the heels come into contact with the buttocks; the kicks are performed thus: now with one leg after the other, now with both together.

This exercise was sufficiently well-known during the classical era to constitute one of the features typical of the Spartan woman's demeanour. This is how

Lampito claims to keep fit: 'I exercise and practise the buttock-tapping jump' (γυμνάδδομαι καὶ ποτὶ πυγὰν ἅλλομαι), *Lysistrata*, ll. 82.[10] Pollux's notice shows that girls also devoted themselves to this sport. It, too, mentions the organization of contests for it, and cites, on the subject, an epigram[11] about a girl or young woman having set a new record (πλεῖστα δὴ τᾶν πήποκα) of one thousand leaps. It is probable that in the classical era only the young girls took part in such contests, since it is hard to visualise married women of that period exhibiting themselves in this way.

A privileged pursuit: racing

There is good reason to believe that racing had a special importance and played a particular part in the education of Spartan girls. As early as the end of the seventh century Alcman's *Partheneion* evokes a race that threw members of the chorus into turmoil, particularly Agido and Hegesichora (ll. 58–9, though the theme is heralded by the equestrian metaphors beginning at ll. 45–9).[12] Other texts describe races taking place in a more formal setting. There was a race, probably held each year, during the festivals of Dionysos, which is mentioned by Pausanias, 3.13.7:

> Opposite this, one comes to a precinct known as Kolona, and the temple of Dionysos Kolonatas. Nearby there is the sanctuary of the hero who guided Dionysos on his way to Sparta. Before sacrificing to the god, the Daughters of Dionysos and of Leukippos sacrifice to this hero. Other women who are also known as Daughters of Dionysos, and of whom there are eleven, hold a race in which they compete (τὰς δ' ἄλλας ἕνδεκα, ἃς καὶ Διονυσιάδας ὀνομάζουσι, ταύταις δρόμου προτιθέασιν ἀγῶνα).

It is Hesychius who states that these are young girls: 'Dionysiades: young girls in Sparta, who compete in a running race at the Dionysia' (Διονυσιάδες· ἐν Σπάρτῃ παρθένοι αἱ ἐν τοῖς Διονυσίοις δρόμον ἀγωνιζόμεναι). Likewise, the Daughters of Dionysos – twelve of them, this time – are mentioned in an inscription, of the Imperial period, referring to a race organized by the *Biduoi* (*SEG* XI, 1954, no. 610). So it is clear that this concerns a race organized by and taking place in the city, as is usual, as part of a cult;[13] the surprising thing about it is the number – more surprising still if (or when) there were eleven of them, and in any case astonishingly small – of the participants. Why so few? How were they selected? Did they perform other rituals besides this race? We just do not know.

We are even less well acquainted with another race, known only from a notice of Hesychius': ἐν Δριώνας· δρόμος παρθένων ἐν Λακεδαίμονι, '*en Drionas*: a race (or race track) for young Lacedaemonian girls';[14] because of the similarity between the names, it is generally held that this race was run in honour of local divinities (male, θεοί), the Driodones, who are also mentioned by Hesychius and about whom nothing whatever is known. This connection presents a problem, however. As Arrigoni has remarked, *en* (= Attic *eis*) *Drionas* resembles, more than anything else, a toponym which should mean 'near the bushes' or something to that effect;[15] in which case Hesychius' word *dromos* would refer not to a race but to a track, reserved for the use of young girls.

The third race known from the texts is almost as mysterious. In Theocritus' *Epithalamium of Helen*, the chorus declaims (ll. 22–5):

> Of us – young girls all aged alike, who, oiled like the men, run on the same track, beside the Baths of the Eurotas – who are four times sixty in number, the female flower of the city, yet every one would be found wanting, compared with Helen.

On several aspects of this text, the debate is still open. Who are these 240 girls? The text states that they are of the same age (and very likely of the same age as Helen, who, before her marriage, must have belonged to this group), but this number, although it could not have corresponded to the total of young girls, still clearly exceeds that of one year-group and comes closer, rather, to two; so the term συνομάλικες denotes not a year-class but an age-category. Are we dealing, then, with two complete year-groups? Should we not, rather, envisage a *selection* made from a much broader age range (like that of the *paidiskoi* among the boys)? What would be the criterion for making such a selection? Is the phrase 'four times sixty' merely a poetic device to express this high number, 240, or is it intended as a reference to the structure of the group? And if so, what *was* this structure? Was it based on years? Or on social groupings, the *ōbai* for instance (although without Amyklai)? Did the 240 girls compete in a single race (though that would obviously involve quite a crowd), or should we think in terms of an event that evolved in a series of heats? All these unanswered questions bear witness to the depth of our ignorance about everything to do with the way girls' education was organized. So I shall have to leave them like that, and confine myself to a recapitulation of what seems probable. On a track (since the use of the word *dromos*, further on at l. 39, indicates that this is how it should be interpreted) situated along the Eurotas, near a spot on the river known as 'the Baths', doubtless because there was a pool there,[16] (not, therefore, *the Dromos* to which Pausanias draws our attention, which was situated in the Agora or its immediate vicinity) a race was held, somehow or other bringing into competition 240 young girls, probably selected, all of roughly the same age, and who ran the race nude. This race was closely connected with the divine Helen. In the poem, the girls, having run the race, weave a garland which they will hang from a plane tree known as 'Helen's Tree'; as far as we can make out, this is to honour the memory of their chorus leader, who has left the group to get married, and the passage, in all probability, records the *aition* of a ceremony which, in the historical period, formed part of the cult of Helen.

Racing, like wrestling, is a physical activity, but it has markedly different characteristics. When practised by young girls it seems at first glance to be a 'natural' pursuit: all children run spontaneously, girls as much as boys; so there is nothing extraordinary in the fact that this activity is continued into puberty. Conversely, it is surprising to find girls wrestling, and the adolescent body shape does not lend itself well to this activity – which may lead us to think of it as having been borrowed from the male scheme of athletics. All the same, it would be a mistake to believe that racing is a purely natural pastime. It is subject to rules, and thereby shows its cultural face. Its importance in the sphere of initiation is strongly indicative of this cultural character.[17] For boys, this importance is particularly evident in Crete: terms like *dromeus* and *apodromos* show that racing was perceived as the test above all others that would qualify a young man as a member of the civic community. For girls, in Sparta, the initiatory value of racing, that is, its capacity to transform a young girl into a spouse for a citizen, a future mother of citizens, is apparent as much in Alcman's verse, with the competition between Agido and Hegesichora, as in that of Theocritus, with the race he depicts in the *Epithalamium of Helen*.

Sparta did not have the monopoly on female racing. Most of the instances of whose existence we are aware are only attested for the Imperial period, notably those that formed part of the great panhellenic games. In the classical era, we know that they existed in Athens in the context of the cult of Artemis. A verse attributed to Sappho mentions one of her pupils, Hero, who was especially swift-footed. The best-known and most famous of female races in antiquity was that of the *Heraia* at Olympia, described by Pausanias (5.16.2–3):

> Every four years the Sixteen Women weave a *peplos* for Hera and organize a contest called the *Heraia*. It consists of a race for young girls not all of the same age: first to run are the youngest, then those who are older, and finally the eldest. This is how they run: with hair flying, the *chitōn* caught up a little above the knee, and the right shoulder bare to the breast. This competition also takes place in the stadium at Olympia, but for this race the distance is reduced by about a sixth. The winner is awarded an olive crown and part of the sacrificed heifer; she also has the right to dedicate, in the temple, a statue bearing her name.

Is it appropriate to picture the young girls' races in Sparta as having been modelled on this competition, which itself seems like the counterpart of male contests (with *agōnothetēs*, age-categories, internal regulation, and prizes)?

Like Arrigoni, I think not: neither the Dionysia, with just eleven (or twelve) participants, nor the vast race pictured by Theocritus, seem to correspond to the Olympic model.

The case against the education of girls in Sparta: 'indecency'

The education of Spartan girls was, like that of the boys, a perennial subject for discussion in the Greek world. When Aristotle embarks on his critical assessment of Spartan conventions concerning women, the word he applies to them is 'indecency' (ἀπρέπειάν τινα…τῆς πολιτείας, *Pol.* 2.1270a13). The attenuating effect of τινά shows that this is a metaphor, and that Aristotle is thinking, at the same time, of the loose living of Spartan women, to which he has actually referred at the beginning of the discussion (1269b22–3). So the starting point of his whole account of women, itself ostensibly of a strictly political and economic tenor, is the classic theme of licence-bred-of-liberty. Now, the tirade of Peleus in Euripides' *Andromache* clearly shows that, for most Greeks of the classical era, the cause of Spartan women's unbridled behaviour – which was, according to them, notorious – was to be sought in the education they had received; essentially, indeed, in their physical education:

> Albeit she might want to, a young maiden would not know how to behave properly in Sparta, where girls mingle with young men and, abandoning their homes and with thighs exposed and skirts hitched-up, frequent the race tracks and *palaistrai*, something I should not be able to tolerate. Is it any wonder that you do not produce decorous wives? (ll. 595–601)

Admittedly, this text is a furious polemic and as such should be treated with caution; but it certainly reflects an opinion widely held in Athens around 420–410. In it, two specific elements are identified as being responsible for 'indecency': the mingling of the sexes, and 'nudity'.

We may well question whether physical education really was mixed. After this period, this theme does not reappear until Philostratus refers to it, and then only in a very unobtrusive way, in the form of a participle συγγυμναζόμενος, '(one) who trains with'.[18] As for Euripides, what exactly does he mean? His method is clear: the use of suggestive language. Some even think that, according to him, promiscuity went as far as allowing boys and girls to wrestle together (i.e. 'boy against girl').[19] Such a practice would be astonishing, but it is attested on Chios, although, since it is one of Athenaeus' Deipnosophists who reports the fact, the period in question is indeterminate.[20] Euripides would certainly not have been upset that such an interpretation should have been placed on Peleus' remark, but, for that matter, he would have been quite able to defend himself on this score, saying that he did not necessarily mean that wrestling in Sparta was mixed. In fact, his description of the behaviour of young girls shows that what he actually has in mind is racing. For all that, we cannot claim that he states categorically that there was mixed racing in Sparta: the expressions ξὺν νέοισι (l. 597) and κοινάς (l. 600) may indicate that boys and girls frequented the same athletic amenities, but one after the other, not simultaneously; this is reasonable, since the two sexes pursued both racing and wrestling. Euripides is, then, equivocating deliberately. Even if, as I believe, physical training in Sparta was not mixed,[21] he still cannot be accused of telling lies. In the interests of a clear conscience here, let us go back to our old friend Xenophon; when he raises the subject (*LP* 1.4), he gets rid of any idea that the practice was mixed when he states that, in accordance with Lycurgus' precepts, young girls engaged in contests of racing and strength (= wrestling) 'with each other', πρὸς ἀλλήλας.

There are degrees of nudity, as there are degrees of mingling of the sexes. Complete nudity was standard in the sphere of male athletics; moreover, it was made out to be a Spartan 'invention'. Where young girls are concerned, the only text that depicts them completely nude when engaged in physical exercise is the passage where Theocritus describes the race of the 240 maidens. Apart from that, nudity is only attested for certain festivals and processions; although Plutarch is the only one to mention it (*Lyc.* 14.4 = *Ap. Lac.*, Lycurgus 13, *Mor.* 227e), there is no particular reason to doubt him. In any case, the nudity to which he refers was not connected with physical activity; its importance was religious, and this is also how it should be interpreted when it comes to the race of the 240. This solid fact did not prevent some Greeks from claiming, in an inaccurate and malevolent context, that the Spartans had the bizarre habit of displaying their girls nude for anyone who wanted to see. [22]

What the majority of Sparta's enemies objected to, starting with Euripides' Peleus, was not the girls' complete nudity but, rather, what they wore for athletics, a special tunic, shortened, and light enough for racing. Garments like this also existed outside Sparta; as we have seen, Pausanias describes one example in his notice about the Olympic *Heraia*: 'the *chitōn* caught up a little above the knee, and the right shoulder bare to the breast' (5.16.12). This short *chitōn* was also considered typical dress for Spartan girls. In the *Comparison of the Lives of Lycurgus and Numa* (3.7), Plutarch describes it thus: 'a tunic of which the lower parts of the sides were not sewn together, so that it would fall open, thus totally exposing their thighs when they walked'; the description is echoed by the lexicographer Pollux, who calls it 'a split *chitōn*'.[23] In the same passage, Plutarch cites a term used by a sixth-century poet, Ibycus of Rhegium, who called Spartan girls 'thigh-flashers' (*phainomērides*), clearly in a tone of reproof, and three verses of Sophocles (Nauck², 788) which describe

Hermione thus scantily clad. Although these fail to mention the (striking) detail of the bared breast, one might be tempted to think that the garment described by Pausanias, and that attributed to young Spartan girls, are one and the same thing, and that it is legitimate to complete one description by reference to the other. But the statuettes we have of female runners conflict with this; and in fact, far from resolving the problem, they complicate it further.

The complete statuettes of this type, which date from the middle, or the second half, of the sixth century, are three in number.

1. London, BM 208, from Prizren (in present-day Kosovo); Arrigoni, pl. 3.
2. Athens, NM, Karapanos Collection 24, from Dodona; Arrigoni, pl. 2.
3. Palermo, MN 8265, provenance unknown but most probably Southern Italy; Arrigoni, pl. 5.

The find spots (of which the significance is entirely relative, given the small size of the series) do not point particularly to Sparta; even so, the fact that northern Greece predominates is a reminder of the well-known relationship between Laconia and Dodona (Hodkinson 2000, 296–7, with nn. 46–7). The style affords us no firm indication: the origin of no. 3 probably lies in Magna Graecia; no. 2, which is often considered Laconian, seems to me rather to have Corinthian affinities. No. 1, with its long-limbed and fluid model, is the one that could most easily have been manufactured in Sparta. As for the garment, there is no escaping the fact that it is different for each example. No. 1 corresponds exactly with Pausanias' description (short *chitōn*, with right breast exposed), which has allowed a number of commentators to identify this representation as that of a competitor in the Olympic *Heraia*.[24] No. 2 wears a very short *chitōn* (reaching only to mid-thigh), the collar level with the throat. Female runner no. 3 could scarcely provoke the wrath of Peleus; she is dressed in a mid-length *peplos* (practically mid-calf-length), a piece of which is draped round her shoulders to form a sort of bolero. None of these garments is split; hence, none of them corresponds precisely with what Plutarch and Pollux describe as having been the usual dress of a Laconian female runner.

It was an easy game for enemies of Sparta to pose as defenders of lofty morals, and, by giving the impression that they believed Spartan girls always dressed like this, to make ironic comments about them or to denounce them as 'thigh-flashers'. If they are to be believed, the Spartans displayed their maidens far more than was proper. Peleus' diatribe reveals the kind of ideology that lies behind this criticism. In it, he connects the wearing of indecent clothes, and the promiscuity between the sexes that goes hand in hand with it, with (and this is undoubtedly the most serious criticism) playing truant from the family home (ἐξερημοῦσαι δόμους). As a rule, the young girl belongs – as in the majority of traditional civilizations – in the most intimate circle of the private domain. By causing her to 'go out', by allowing her to show herself to the world, dressed so that she is almost falling out of her clothes, the Spartans, in a way, turn her into a public spectacle, who is exhibited, hence offered, to the first comer. Matters go even further, and Peleus has no inhibitions about saying so: if your daughter is licentious, how could your wife not be so as well? So, for Sparta's critics, it is the young girls' education that bore primary responsibility for the licence-bred-of-liberty which, in their view, characterized the conduct of women in that city.

In defence of female education in Sparta

To make the case for the nudity of Spartan girls was not exactly the easiest task. Elements of a justifying argument, undoubtedly taken from earlier authors, may, however, be found in Plutarch. Actually, they appear contradictory. The first argument lies in recognizing that, while indecency – that is, erotic incitement – did indeed exist, the motive for allowing this was a good one, namely that it should promote an awareness of marriage: 'Then there were also ways of inducing them to marry: I mean the processions, the nudity, and the contests, at which the young men were the spectators' (*Lyc.* 15.1); this theme reappears, in a lighter vein, in an apophthegm (*Ap. Lac.*, Charillos 2, *Mor.* 323c). This argument dates back to the classical era: Plato, to whom Plutarch makes explicit reference in this passage of his *Life of Lycurgus*, envisaged an identical purpose in the mixed physical training he organized in his ideal city (*Rep.* 5.458d). The other argument consists in denying the indecency and maintaining that only people of ill-will can detect it in the Spartans' conduct: 'There was nothing shameful in the nudity of young girls, since it went hand in hand with modesty, and was free of intemperance' (*Lyc.* 14.7: αἰδοῦς μὲν παρούσης, ἀκρασίας δ' ἀπούσης). Paradoxically, despite the patently idealized image it reflects, this mode of justification is, perhaps, the closer to reality of the two. On the one hand, the context of these 'exhibitions' is, in fact, always religious: processions, festivals, contests; in these circumstances, restrained behaviour is absolutely the order of the day. On the other hand, as the end of Plutarch's sentence accurately emphasizes ('the female sex derived a noble pride from the thought that it had an equal share of merit and honours'), these ceremonies brought out the public aspect of the girls' education, and launched their participation in the life of the city.

But semi-nudity in athletics was merely a consequence of the fact that young girls engaged in physical activity. So it is chiefly this activity that had to be justified. Why did Spartan girls practise wrestling and running? Why did Lampito train? Would the ultimate purpose have been warfare?

Surely not.[25] The notion that the Spartan woman was trained for a warlike purpose only appears in late sources, and never in a really positive manner. It makes a very fleeting appearance in the verses (probably by Accius) cited by Cicero (above, p. 229), where it is only suggested by the word *militia*; Propertius (3.14) paints a totally unrealistic portrait of the Spartan woman as an Amazon; the Plutarchan apophthegm, Lycurgus 12, *Mor.* 227c, does indeed speak of preparation for a possible war, but this part of the sentence merely echoes the Platonic ideal expressed in the *Laws* 7.806b. This passage of Plato's shows that in the classical era there was never any question that Spartan women actually took part in warfare. It took one historical episode, the Theban invasion of 369, to demonstrate to the whole of Greece that they were quite incapable of doing any such thing.[26]

The warlike purpose was excluded, then. Was it so that women might become accomplished athletes and carry off victories at the great panhellenic games? It is obvious that it was not; apart from the *Heraia*, female contests of this kind only come into existence in the Imperial era. Spartan women did win Olympic victories in the fourth century, but only in chariot racing, and then only as the owners of the stables concerned. During the classical era, the pursuit of competitive athletics remains a male preserve. Highly implausible, too, is the explanation that athletic activity for girls was designed to make them physically strong as mistresses of the household, so that they would have no trouble carrying out the most arduous of domestic tasks. This theory only appears in the writings of Philostratus, who combines it with the classic explanation we shall encounter later on, that of *teknopoiia*:

> Lycurgus ordained that young girls should perform physical exercises and undergo training to race in public, obviously to ensure that, thanks to the bodily strength they would have acquired, they would rear healthy babies and produce the best children; in effect, when they took up residence in their husbands' homes, they would not baulk at carrying water or grinding grain, because they would have been trained to it from their earliest years. (*Gymn.* 27)

But, one might ask, if the Spartan girl pursues sporting activities, if Lampito, a married woman, continues to train, why should it not be, quite simply, so that the one might become beautiful and the other remain so? From remote antiquity the beauty of Spartan women was proverbial. In the *Odyssey*, Sparta is referred to as the city 'of beautiful women' (Σπάρτην ἐς καλλιγύναικα, 13.412). One poetic text, which, after a long history in the course of which it certainly knew several transformations, ultimately appeared as a Delphic oracle given to the people of Aigion (or, in some versions, Megara), and which, in its original version (the first three verses), dates back, perhaps, to the seventh century, draws up a catalogue of the things in which the different regions of Greece excel: Sparta is singled out (l. 2) for its women.[27] So Lampito corresponds to that image of the Spartan woman commonly held by the Greeks of the classical era. At the same time she helps us to gain a better understanding of what the term 'beauty' means in this instance; for, the criteria by which this is judged vary considerably according to the period and the culture. Of course, there is grace and allure, and, obviously, the reputation of the Spartan woman owed something to the person of Helen. But it is not such things as these that Lysistrata accentuates when she paints her portrait of Lampito (ll. 79–81). She celebrates her complexion, a clear sign of health, and, above all, her strength ('you would strangle a bull', l. 81; an allusion to the practice of wrestling). The exaggeration raises a laugh, certainly, but the remark agrees perfectly with the image of the Spartan woman.

There is a slightly different orientation in the pseudo-oracle for the people of Aigion. The Spartan woman appears in the first part of the list (introduced by μέν), which also includes the Pelasgian plain and the Thessalian cavalry (or Thracian, in one alternative version), the second part being devoted to warriors, to *andres*. The contrast between these two parts cannot be better characterized than by reference to Dumezil's categories: the one concerns the third function, the other the second. The physical strength and sparkling health of the Spartan woman are the object of so many compliments only because they would have guaranteed her capacity to bear strong, beautiful children. This is how we have to read Kleonike's admiration for Lampito's breasts. She praises chiefly their size and firmness (and feels them, l. 84). In her estimation, they are not so much a trump to be played in the seduction of men (although they *are* that, of course, especially in the context of the women's 'plot') as baby-feeding machines.[28] What is quite clear is that Lampito's body, for all its athletic capabilities, is in no sense masculinized. It exemplifies the type of beauty which, it was believed, the Spartan girls' education – thanks to its physical component – was sure to give them.

These considerations on the subject of 'beauty' bring us to what was, in the classical world, by far the most common argument justifying female education in Sparta: procreation, or, to adopt, as Napolitano has done,[29] the Greek term – more vivid and more precise (since it envisages the process as a kind of *technē*) – *teknopoiia*, 'the manufacture of children'. This argument may take two forms, both of which are in keeping with the level of medical science at the time. In the classical era the opinion is that, by a sort of inheritance of acquired characteristics, the physical qualities both parents will have gained from their training would automatically be transmitted to the child. It is Critias who, first of the surviving sources, expresses this idea, at the beginning of his *Lakedaimonion Politeia*:

> I begin with the conception of the man. How can he be born with the best of physical health and strength? Thus: if the man who begets him practises

> physical exercises, eats solidly, and trains his body, and if the woman who is to bear him strengthens her body and exercises it. (fr. 32 D.-K.)

It is easy to recognize in this passage the Hippocratic idea that a balance between diet and exercise will result in good health. Xenophon contents himself with outlining a simplified form of Critias' notion:

> Judging that the most important business of a free woman was *teknopoiia*, he (Lycurgus) began by establishing a regime of physical exercise for the female, as well as for the male, sex; then he set up contests for them, in running and physical strength, under the same conditions as those for men, in the belief that if both sexes were vigorous then their offspring would be more sturdy. (*LP* 1.4)

Plutarch's version is less simplistic:

> He directed that young girls should train their bodies by running, wrestling, hurling the discus and javelin. He thought that their children's development would be improved if, as embryos, they took vigorous root in vigorous bodies, and that the women themselves would be well conditioned to undergo labour and would cope easily and successfully with the pain it entails. (*Lyc.* 14.3)

He thus distinguishes two points at which a woman's physical training makes its benefit felt most: her pregnancy and her confinement.

In accordance with Greek opinion of the time, the woman is here considered merely as the soil that nourishes the embryo; the stronger and more healthy its source of support, the better will be its development. On the subject of confinement, Loraux[30] has remarked that, to describe the courage of women in this situation, Plutarch used vocabulary (ὑπομένουσαι, ἀγωνίζοιντο) carrying warlike connotations and evoking, in particular, the 'steadfastness' that characterizes the hoplite. More generally, she has shown, in the same study, that confinement is viewed by the Greeks as a *ponos*, a mixture of toil and suffering, which could be considered the female equivalent of what constitutes the warrior's *ponos* for the male. The similarity goes even further, since, in both cases, an exceptional service is being rendered to the city;[31] in both cases, their lives are at stake; both actions require comparable qualities of endurance and self-discipline. Her confinement is thus a test for the woman, on a par with that of combat for the man, and one whereby she gives the supreme proof of her *aretē* by bringing to birth future warriors, or future mothers of warriors, for the city. If it is only men who can wage war, it is only women who can bring those men into the world. This 'monopoly' is expressed in crystal-clear fashion by an apophthegm attributed to Gorgo, and of which several variants exist.[32] To the question (one which is, sometimes, only implied) 'Why is it that you Laconian women are the only ones who command men?', Gorgo replies: 'Because we are the only ones who give birth to men'. 'Only', *monai*: in Sparta, the word expresses division, yes, and, to a certain extent, contrast, but it also expresses the complementarity of the sexes, whose co-operation alone can ensure the city's survival. It is in terms of the need to prepare the woman for this function, as the man is prepared for his, that the form of girls' education in Sparta could best be explained and justified.

Female education and male education

Historians who have studied the question generally claim to have gained the impression that close parallels existed between female and male education in Sparta. As early as 1908, Nilsson presented the clearest account of this theory: in his view, young girls were compelled to undergo a genuine *agōgē*, which, in its development and its stages, was comparable to that of the boys. Very little is known about how girls' education functioned, but some details seem to support this point of view: the practice of certain physical exercises, entailing total or partial nudity, as it did for boys;[35] the competitive spirit which, patently (to judge from, for example, Alcman's *Partheneion*), existed among the girls as much as the boys; there may also have been homosexual relationships, whether between younger and older girls, within the choruses, or, on the lines of male convention, between young girls and adult women (if, at least, we are prepared to trust the information transmitted by Plutarch, *Lyc.* 18.9, although on that subject we might entertain doubts precisely because of its inherent parallelism). This parallelism, if it existed, could have been part of the structure, and have dated back to the origins (possibly initiatory, since female initiations did exist), of the education system; but the predominant view is to see the female education system as having been developed *in imitation* of the boys'. It is this 'copy' theory which it is rather astonishing to find Brelich accepting (1969, 160), although he asserts elsewhere (pp. 41–3) that female initiations, far from being pale, more recent copies of the male, are something else altogether.

If the education of girls in Sparta was copied from that of boys, one would have to acknowledge that the copy was only a very partial one. Many of the characteristic features of male education are absent, or, if present, take a different form. There are no age-categories: the texts mention only *parthenoi*, without indicating the age at which they began their education, particularly their admission to the ranks of a chorus (as for when it ended, obviously this was, as a general rule, with marriage, our model for this being the *Epithalamium of Helen*). Certainly, there existed no annual system of age-classes; nevertheless, the adjective *synomalikes* used by Theocritus suggests an awareness, on the part of the girls, that they belonged to the same 'generation'. They would not have undergone tests of endurance, or 'harsh treatment' (with regard to clothing or diet, for instance), and were not compelled to steal; yet they were obliged to devote themselves to physical activities, which may, in a sense, be considered as tests. There is some truth in all of this, which is why Vidal-Naquet[34] is able to assert that 'this copy is not a perfect one', and that 'the young Spartan girl was, in the full sense, a "garçon manqué"', the emphasis being placed on the adjective.

It is not my intention to demonstrate that this 'copy' theory is mistaken, only that another point of view is possible. We should ask whether the education of girls does in fact display the same characteristics as that of boys. Question one: was it collective? It has often been claimed that *agelai* existed for girls as well as for boys. But, in the first place, as Kennell has shown (above, p. 78), *agela* was probably not the term used in the classical era to designate boys' 'troops'. Moreover, in the case of girls, the only text that might be cited in support of this claim is a brief fragment of Pindar's (112 Snell), Λάκαινα παρθένων ἀγέλα. In poetic language, however, the word *agela* may be used to designate any team of young girls, who are thus, by implication, compared with, say, a troop of fillies,[35] and there is no certainty that, in the case of Pindar, the term refers to some 'institution'. It is quite true that the boys' 'troop' does have its female counterpart, namely, the chorus; but, on the one hand, the role it fulfils is not the equivalent one, since there are also boys' choruses, and, on the other, the chorus of young girls is in no way peculiar to Sparta; it occurs everywhere as the collective setting for training in *mousikē*. It would be meaningless, then, to present the young girls' chorus in Sparta as a 'copy' of the boys' 'troop'.

Question 2: was female education, like that of boys (or, to be more precise, like that element of their education that was not scholastic instruction; it is obvious that, for girls also, this element, the only detectable one, is all we are discussing at the moment), compulsory and organized by the state, and therefore identical for all? Just to pose this decisive question is almost enough to demonstrate that it is impossible to answer. Let us start with the aspect of obligation. If this is neither necessary nor likely in the case of choruses, since it is more than probable that not all the young girls in the city were called on to sing and dance at festivals, it would seem, by contrast, logical in the case of physical activities, because they were supposed to be favourable for childbirth, and because every young girl was destined, as a rule, for marriage and motherhood. But this line of argument would only be valid if *teknopoiia* was *genuinely* the reason behind physical activities. In reality, as we have observed, it was only at the period when Greek medicine began to expand that *teknopoiia* was advanced as an explanation to justify what was a far older practice. The only text one might have been able to cite in support of the claim that it was obligatory seems to me to prove nothing. Plato, *Laws* 7.806a: 'Should we prescribe the intermediate regime, that of the Spartans, obliging young girls to participate as much in physical activity as in *mousikē*, in the course of their daily lives…' (ζῆν δεῖν…κόρας μὲν…γυμνασίων μετοίκους οὔσας ἅμα καὶ μουσικῆς…). The sentence does not necessarily mean that in Sparta all the girls have to practise gymnastics and *mousikē* at the same time, but it can (and, to my mind, should) signify simply that all those who practise the one should also practise the other. This text by no means excludes the possibility that only certain girls, daughters of the best families, were able to take part both in a chorus and in physical exercises.

This brings us to the principal question: was it the state that organized and took charge of the education of young girls? This is the view expressed, though not without reservations, by Cartledge (2001, 113–14): 'Spartan girls were also given some form of public education'. I can find nothing to support this statement, and the idea of a female education organized and paid for by the state in an actual Greek city is so surprising that it might be better to refrain from advancing it without proof. If male education, and only one element of it at that, was taken over by the city, and was identical for all, it is because its purpose was to form citizens and warriors who would all be 'alike'. Such an aim could not apply in the case of girls. It strikes me as natural, in the circumstances, to regard their access to education as having been unequal, as it was in other cities.

Nothing is proven, then; neither that female education was structured on the same lines as male, nor that it was merely a later copy of it. It seems to me more probable that girls' education, having acquired a specific form (the chorus and the privileged pursuit of running), was a reality independent of, and just as ancient as, that of boys. That does not preclude the possibility that, over the centuries, it was subject to the other's influence. It even seems natural, the Spartan value-system being, as it was, essentially male. Nevertheless, this influence only shows itself clearly in one respect, the addition of wrestling to running, among the physical activities of young girls.

The education of girls as initiation

Female initiations exist in archaic societies; Brelich (1969, 41–3) has analysed their principal features, maintaining, and certainly with good reason, that they are not later imitations of the male. Insofar as they are initiations, they have the same ultimate purpose, that of turning children into fully formed members of society, and, broadly speaking, they conform to the same model; hence, it is natural that similarities should exist between the two. But they also have specific features of their own. Women are members of the community but they have their own particular functions, for which it makes sense to prepare them. Furthermore, female development is punctuated by physiological changes that are immediately noticeable; so, initiation very often begins simultaneously with the first periods and terminates with marriage. A third feature peculiar to female initiation is the frequency of individual initiations; these are sometimes difficult to distinguish from simple rites of puberty or marriage, but what marks them out as different is the fact that they affect the community as a whole (even in the case of individual initiations), whereas rites of puberty and marriage are private.

Having said that, most of the major elements characteristic of male initiation also occur in the female variety: there is a phase of segregation, though with the difference that it takes place in a hut rather than in the wild; there is the involvement of female guardians and tutors who, during this period of retreat, impart 'lessons', some of which are of the same kind as those given to boys (songs, dancing, the recounting of myths), while others are specific to the female condition (notably those dealing with sexuality and motherhood). Secrecy, over all or some of these 'lessons' (especially the things revealed), has to be preserved. There are no 'tortures', in the strict sense, but the inflicting of marks or mutilations, in particular those of a sexual nature, is frequent. The existence of rites and festivals of re-emergence, celebrated by the assembled community, is quite often attested.

Calame considers that, in Sparta, the phase of segregation was represented by the participation of girls' choruses in festivals and ceremonies held in frontier sanctuaries, and was thus located at the boundaries not only of the habitat but even of the territory of the Spartans: the sanctuaries of Artemis Limnatis and Artemis Karyatis.[36] In both cases, the songs and dances performed by these choruses were the most important and significant of the whole festival. According to the same author,[37] the festival of Hyakinthia, which is discussed in the next chapter, may have embodied the rite of re-emergence. Although this interpretation trips up over certain details (participation in both these festivals was reserved for certain girls only, and the initiatory character of the Hyakinthia could be contested), on the whole it may appear all the more probable, in that, in Greece generally, it is only thus that evidence for initiation survives, as dispersed fragments reinterpreted in the context of certain religious festivals and myths. All the same, Calame seems to me to be showing undue optimism when he considers that he has hereby reconstructed a genuine cycle of female initiations in Sparta. In particular, I think it inappropriate, as much in the case of girls as in that of boys, to pour energies into searching the field of education for evidence of physical segregation. This setting apart of the young is shaped, rather, by a particular way of life. For girls, some aspects of this way of life remained in their original setting, which became that of education, but they are far more rare and difficult to detect than is the case for boys. This applies to nudity: we have observed, when considering male initiations, that a particular mode of dress (or physical state) could be laid down for initiands; the nudity, in certain specific circumstances, of Spartan girls, which other Greeks found so surprising, might be understood in this way. The 'lessons' imparted to the chorus are similar in nature to some of those given to initiands during their period of retreat. In everything that happens, then, it is as though the role of the chorus, in the education of Spartan girls, was the same as that of the period of retreat in 'tribal' initiations. Inside the group who make up the chorus, Alcman's poems allow us a glimpse of the bonds of affection uniting younger girls with more senior members, and this homosexual relationship, which itself also has a tutelary function, is as much a part of their education as is the case with its male counterpart. There is no incontrovertible evidence for actual age-classes similar to those of the boys, but the notion of 'generation' is there, and it is possible to detect a resemblance between the situation reflected in the *Epithalamium of Helen* and a practice observed by certain peoples in the Solomon Islands, where girls of the same age form a group around the chieftain's daughter, until the day of her marriage. Lastly, if running is the most traditional and most typical of exercises for young girls, it is perhaps on account of its initiatory value, which some explain in terms of the trance-like state which it induces.[38]

The ancient Greeks were powerfully aware of the originality of female education in Sparta compared with that of other cities, but most often (with some exceptions, such as Euripides and Plato), in their desire either to praise or to censure it, they did not bother to say in what this originality consisted. They placed the accent on physical exercise, because this is territory in which it was easy for Sparta's enemies to mobilize orthodox opinion, and in which, therefore, her supporters had to defend her. But physical exercises represent only one among several aspects of this originality. The essence of it lay in the fact that, instead of being brought up wholly within the family, with the prospect of a life spent sequestered in the *gynaikeion*, fulfilling 'economic' functions, the Spartan girl was educated, during an important part of her life, 'outside' (Euripides was highly sensitive to this trait, which he regarded as 'desertion': ἐξερημοῦσαι δόμους), and it was this that prepared her to fulfil, as a woman, her role in the open, public, spaces of the city.

Notes

1 This is the subject of my article, Ducat 1998.

2 Cartledge 2001, n. 54, p. 216; female dedications are, as elsewhere, few in number.

3 Calame 1977, I, 386–410. Cf. Ingalls 2000.

4 In a passage in which he follows Critias closely, Xenophon (*LP* 1.3) uses the word *korai*.

[5] This subject has been studied on several occasions, relatively recently: Arrigoni 1985, Scanlon 1988, Angeli-Bernardini 1988.

[6] To the same effect, Napolitano 1987, 138.

[7] Scanlon draws attention to a fifth, unpublished (1988, 204, no. 24).

[8] This is, perhaps, the explanation for the low date (the beginning of the 5th century) assigned to it (mistakenly, in my opinion) by Arrigoni.

[9] When he raises (*Laws* 8.833d) the subject of exercises in physical strength (τὰ κατ' ἰσχύν), Plato cites 'wrestling and things of that kind'.

[10] Antyllos' notice seems to draw on this verse for its definition of the *bibasis* (the name of which it does not supply, moreover – any more than does Aristophanes) as τὸ πρὸς πυγὴν ἅλλεσθαι.

[11] Preger 1891, 107, no. 134.

[12] See Calame's commentary, 1977 II, 67–72.

[13] Why a running race for Dionysos? On this question, which does not actually concern us here, see Arrigoni's hypotheses (1985, 77–84).

[14] On this entry, cf. Arrigoni 1985, 74.

[15] Names containing -ών typically designate a place where something, usually a plant, grows in abundance. τὸ δριός means 'bush'.

[16] The young girls may have bathed there after the race. I think that it is bathing of just this kind, rather than a mythological subject, that was represented on a cup (now lost) by the Hunt Painter (Stibbe 1972, no. 209, Pipili 1987, no. 95): three young girls bathing in the Eurotas. In antiquity, this was a classic erotic theme, to judge from the epigram by Rufinus, *Anth. Pal.* 5.60; cf. Cameron 1981.

[17] On the initiatory value of female racing, cf. Serwint 1993, 419; on racing as a central element of initiation in Macedonia, cf. Hatzopoulos 1994.

[18] *De Gymn.* 27, εἰ δὲ καὶ νέῳ καὶ συγγυμναζομένῳ συζυγείη, 'if, besides, she marries a young man who even practises gymnastics with her'.

[19] Thus, Cartledge 2001, 114 and n. 43.

[20] Athenaeus 13.566e: 'On the island of Chios, it is quite delightful to stroll round the gymnasia and along the tracks, and to watch young men wrestling (προσπαλαίοντας) with young girls'. Here, too, the erotic connotation is obvious.

[21] Likewise, Napolitano 1985, 22–3, and Arrigoni 1985, 70–4, 86–7.

[22] Plutarch, *Ap. Lac.*, Charillos 2, *Mor.* 232c: τὰς κόρας ἀνακαλύπτους…εἰς τοὔμφανες ἄγουσι. Athenaeus 13.566e: ἐπαινεῖται καὶ τῶν Σπαρτιατῶν τὸ ἔθος τὸ γυμνοῦν τὰς παρθένους τοῖς ξένοις.

[23] Pollux 7.54–5: 'They also gave this name to the *chitōniskos* worn by young girls, which, since the edges of the garment were left unstitched to a certain length above the hem, allowed their thighs to be exposed; this was chiefly the case among girls in Sparta, which is why they were known as "thigh-flashers".'

[24] On this costume, cf. Serwint 1993.

[25] On this subject I take the liberty of referring to an earlier study of mine (Ducat 1999a). Cf. also Powell 2004.

[26] See Aristotle's stern comment, *Pol.* 2.1269b34–9.

[27] Parke and Wormell (1956, 82–3, no. 1) consider it authentic, a view challenged, with good reason, by Fontenrose 1978, 276–8, no. Q 26.

[28] To the same effect, cf. Christien 1997, 55.

[29] Napolitano 1985.

[30] Loraux 1989, 29–53, especially n. 6.
[31] As Loraux puts it: 'Men give their lives, women their sons'.
[32] *Lyc.* 14.8; *Lacaen. Ap.*, Gorgo 5, *Mor.* 240e; *Ap. Lac.*, Lycurgus 13, *Mor.* 227e.
[33] Xenophon, *LP* 1.4, states that Lycurgus instituted girls' contests modelled on those of the boys.
[34] Vidal-Naquet 1981, 206.
[35] In the same vein, Brelich 1969, 158, n. 139.
[36] Calame 1977 I, 253–64 (Artemis Limnatis) and 264–76 (Artemis Karyatis).
[37] pp. 305–23.
[38] Arrigoni 1985, 81. On the initiatory value of running, cf. above, p. 233. On certain points (the level of female instruction, and the practice of riding and of weaving), one might complete the present chapter by consulting the one Pomeroy has devoted to education, in her recent work of synthesis on Spartan women (Pomeroy 2002, 3–32).

8

EDUCATION AND RELIGION

During their period of education, young Spartiates were required to take part in certain state festivals. The role they played in these festivals amounted to a major element in their upbringing. In most cases, other sections of the population also took part, along with the young. But in one particular festival the young were alone; with this we begin.

Artemis Orthia and Spartan boys

The most important divinity for the education of boys was Artemis Orthia, or rather simply 'Orthia'.[1] (The latter was the name used in the classical period, as at Xenophon *LP* 2.9.) Our evidence allows us to perceive only two aspects of the goddess's role in education. On the one hand there were various contests involving the boys, the prizes of which were the sickles mentioned earlier. All the evidence on these contests derives from long after the classical period,[2] with one exception: the stele of Arexippos, which dates from the fourth century (above, pp. 210–12). This stele makes clear that the contests existed at the time, but tells us nothing of what they involved, how many they were, or what they were called. It is probable, but no more, that their names were the same as those evidenced at a later period.[3] We are left, then, with the other aspect of the goddess's role in education: a ritual, itself involving a contest, which was widely known in the Imperial period under the titles 'the whipping' (διαμαστίγωσις) and 'the festival of whips' (ἑορτὴν Λακωνικὴν τὰς μάστιγας, Libanios) but which is also recorded in the classical period in a very different form, by two highly elliptical texts.[4]

The ritual

Xenophon writes (*LP* 2.9):

> Moreover, deeming that it would be a fine thing to snatch as many cheeses as possible at Orthia's shrine, he enjoined upon others to whip those who did the snatching (καὶ ὡς πλείστους δὴ ἁρπάσαι τυροὺς παρ' Ὀρθίας καλὸν θεὶς μαστιγοῦν τούτους ἄλλοις ἐπέταξε); in doing this he also intended to show that brief suffering can lead to enduring glory. Further, this advertises the principle

> that, where speed of action is essential, anyone who acts timidly gains nothing but instead brings on himself the greatest trouble.

This passage is far from descriptive. It is part of a context which aims to explain and justify the role of compulsory theft in the Spartan education system, and in particular to solve the paradox that children are ordered to steal but then are punished when caught doing so. For Xenophon, the religious quality of the ritual is proof that this strange custom is justified; the ritual acts as a paradigm of childhood theft at Sparta. In the work to which Xenophon is writing a response, there may have been a genuine description. Quite what happened in the course of the ritual cannot be reconstructed from Xenophon's passage, taken on its own. One might suppose, for example, that there were two stages to the process: that first there was a contest of cheese-stealing in the sanctuary, with the winner being the person who stole the most, and that afterwards there was a collective 'punishment'. Such would seem best to suit the expression which Xenophon uses in place of a description, but it would not apply so well to the comment which follows.

Xenophon draws two lessons from the ritual. The first is ethical and educational, to do with suffering and fame. Suffering is what makes fame possible, and this can only apply if the theft of cheeses and the whipping happened simultaneously. The second lesson is described in the same gravely didactic tone, but in reality is very different. It is a piece of technical advice and could apply almost as well to coaching for sport as to a military context. For young people to be taught to play a game well, they must above all be imbued with the spirit of the game. Thus in football everything follows from the principle, so simple to express but so difficult to apply, of scoring as many goals as possible while conceding as few as possible. Similarly in this case, Xenophon makes clear the basic principle of the ritual-cum-game: to get as many cheeses as possible while being hit as little as possible. But – and herein is the lesson – unlike football, the two elements applying to the ritual are not on the same level. Victory here depends only on the number of cheeses taken. Avoiding the whip does matter, because the participant needs to remain in a fit state to continue the contest. But to avoid being hit is only secondary. So, Xenophon concludes, the point is not to retreat but rather to have a firmly aggressive strategy. The person who only thinks of self-protection (ὁ βλακεύων) not only i[illegible]variably loses (ἐλάχιστα μὲν ὠφελεῖται) but in addition, because of h[illegible] f determination and spirit, is hit most often (πλεῖστα δὲ πράγματα [illegible] On this ritual-cum-game, Xenophon's comments reveal more than [illegible] But we are only able to understand his meaning because other [illegible] an idea of what in reality went on.

Plato *Laws* 1.633b reads thus:

> Fourthly, I should like also to speak of the systematic training in the endurance of pain, which is undergone in our own community, consisting both in group fights with bare knuckles and also in the process of certain acts of theft which take place amid a constant hail of blows (καὶ ἐν ἁρπαγαῖς τισι διὰ πολλῶν πληγῶν ἑκαστότε γιγνομένων).

This amounts to even less of a description than the Xenophon passage. It is in fact a mere allusion, with no indication even that it concerned a religious rite, let alone the cheeses. Indeed, throughout this account of Spartan techniques of preparation for war Megillos talks so elliptically and obscurely (as here with ἐν ἁρπαγαῖς τισι) that only the initiated could understand. This no doubt was intentional on Plato's part. Megillos is obliged to give a defence of his city, which the Athenian speaker has accused of educating its citizens only for war. But this involves speaking of matters which seem to Megillos to involve a need for censorship, to protect military secrets.[5] He says nothing to suggest that the thefts in question took place in the sanctuary of Orthia, and that young boys were involved; for all he says, we might be dealing with a contest like the ones he had mentioned just previously. So is the traditional approach, which is to explain this passage by reference to the passage of Xenophon, really justified? Is this not to approach the obscure by way of the more obscure? The only strong point in favour of the comparison is the recurrence of the word for snatching: ἁρπάσαι, ἁρπαγαῖς. As we shall see, words from this root mean something different from κλέπτειν and its cognates. They mean rather the appropriation by trickery, not simply through force but through alertness, of food left as offerings in a sanctuary and often on an altar. However, there are many cases where ἁρπάζειν acts as a mere synonym of κλέπτειν. What unites our two texts and allows a limited reconstruction of the process in question, is that they share a resemblance to the ritual which took place in much later times in the sanctuary of Orthia, on which there are numerous sources from the Roman period: from the late Republic (Cicero) and above all from the Principate.

This ritual from Roman times need not be analysed here.[6] It has obvious differences from that mentioned by Xenophon and Plato, sketchy though their testimony is. The ritual in Roman times was properly a whipping, and was called as much. The cheeses and the theft no longer exist. The young people have to go around the altar, or to lean against it: on this the sources vary. And in doing so they present their backs to be whipped. The winner is the person who endures for longest. The ritual in classical times seems not to have been a whipping for the sake of it: it is a theft of cheeses in the sanctuary, opposed by guards armed with whips. Are the two rituals sufficiently similar for us to be able to treat the later one as a development of the former? Recent studies show that they were.[7] We can, then, use our knowledge of the later ritual to help us understand the earlier one.

Also relevant here is a passage of Plutarch (*Aristides* 17.10), describing an incident reportedly involving the regent Pausanias during the preparations for the battle of Plataia:

> Some writers say that, just as Pausanias was conducting sacrifice and prayer a short distance in front of the ranks, a troup of Lydians suddenly descended on him, snatching and scattering (ἄφνω προσπεσόντας ἁρπάζειν καὶ διαρρίπτειν) all the material for the sacrifice. Pausanias and the men with him, having no weapons, used sticks and whips to hit the Lydians. Which is why to this day, in imitation (μίμημα) of this attack, at Sparta the ephebes are hit at the altar and this is followed by the procession of the Lydians.

This 'account' is very obviously an *aition*, indeed it is presented as such; its purpose, to be precise, is to explain the existence of the whipping and the name of the procession which followed. On the whipping, the story reflects the complexity of Plutarch's own historical situation. He writes 'to this day', and so must mean the ceremony existing in the Roman period when he lived. But the anecdote as it stands does not fit with the idea of young men undergoing the whipping passively. What it describes is theft from the altar, with the thieves being beaten with sticks and whips by people defending the altar. And this is exactly the structure of the ritual in the classical period. So it was the classical ritual for which the *aition* originally provided an explanation. Additionally, the setting of the story, which is essential for its meaning (involving Pausanias, the battle of Plataia and the Lydians), exists to explain the name of the procession.[8] Which shows that the procession too existed in the classical period.

We can now attempt a description of the ritual at Orthia's shrine to which Xenophon and Plutarch refer. The initial setting consists of cheeses which have been placed as offerings in the shrine, probably on the altar. The action consists of boys each snatching as much as they can, while other participants do their best to prevent them by hitting them with whips. There is an element of paradox in all this: those who are whipped are not victims but the exact opposite, attackers, while those doing the whipping are not torturers but the defenders of the shrine. This is reflected in the *aition*: the young Spartiates taking part in the ritual stand for enemies, indeed barbarians which is even worse: people with no respect for Greek religion. There could be no better illustration of the fact that young people, at moments in their initiation or education, could be regarded as alien to the community – to any community.

Even when summarized in this schematic way, the ritual as described raises various questions. Were we justified in saying 'on the altar'? Might not the cheeses have been on a table for offerings (τραπέζα)? Indeed. But an altar is likelier, on the assumption of a certain continuity between the ritual in its two forms. In the later form everything centred on the altar, which had to be sprinkled with the boys' blood. In one way or another, this element – blood on the altar – was presumably present in the earlier form of the ritual.

How old were the 'attackers'? This is an important question: to what stage of the adolescents' upbringing did the ritual belong? We have only a single, inconclusive clue: the way our sources suggest the age of those who underwent the whipping in the Roman period. They are described as παῖδες in Nicolaos of Damascus and in Plutarch *Inst. Lac.*, and as ἔφηβοι in Plutarch *Lycurgus* and in Pausanias. In Latin they are *pueri* in Cicero, *adulescentes* for Hyginus and Servius and *iuvenis* in a scholion on Horace. Are we justified in assuming something similar for the classical period? If only for a physiological reason – namely, that the boys must have been fairly well developed – it seems likely that they belonged to the age-group which Xenophon calls *paidiskoi*, as he makes clear that they had to undergo 'various tests'. How many were these boys? How did the competition proceed? It is hard to see how an entire year-group, which in the fifth century may have amounted to at least 120 youths, could have competed in this test simultaneously. Are we to imagine several 'heats', or had the competitors gone through some form of selection? We cannot say.

Who were the 'defenders'? These, I believe, were from the *hēbōntes*. Their relation to the 'attackers', whom they are submitting to a test, is one of 'superiority', and that must refer to the age-hierarchy. We recall what took place during the initiation rites, the fights between the young; in the present case the role of those with whips is typical of the newly-initiated. And if indeed they are *hēbōntes*, one inevitably thinks of the 'whip-bearers' (μαστιγοφόροι) who assisted the *paidonomos* and who, according to Xenophon (*LP* 2.2), were chosen from among the *hēbōntes*. Admittedly, the two roles are very different, but they could have been performed by the same individuals.[9]

Moving now beyond the schematic description, other questions arise. Why cheeses? At best only a partial explanation may be suggested. In general, cheese is well suited for a sacrifice to divinity since it is a foodstuff of complete religious purity.[10] Seeking a more specific link with Artemis, Den Boer pointed to a fragment of Alcman which portrays Artemis as making cheese from the milk of a lioness.[11] Is this the *aition* of offering cheeses to the goddess? What does seem certain is that cheeses were used in the ritual not because they were particularly suitable to be stolen by the young but because they were a sacrificial item typical of Orthia.

The winner of the contest was the one who succeeded in getting the most cheeses; we are not told whether he had to get them in a single go, or whether he could have as many goes as he wished. In any case, the fact that it took the form of a contest is an important aspect of the ritual. Ranking the contestants by the number of cheeses seized need not be an original feature; this element may have been introduced into the ritual at the period when the agonistic model became widepread in Greece, the seventh century. Only from the Roman Imperial period do we have evidence for the title 'winner at the altar', βωμονίκας. Was this title used as early as the classical period? It may be significant here that in the Imperial period βωμονίκας was a formal title, conferred for life, as several honorific decrees show.[12] It was thus highly prestigious. Now, this corresponds exactly with words of Xenophon: his phrase 'enduring fame' (πολὺν χρόνον εὐδοκιμοῦντα) shows that, even if the title itself did not yet exist (as it may quite well have done), the reality already did.

Was there a period of preparation for the solemn occasion? The question arises from the gloss of Hesychius (above, pp. 185–6): φούαξιρ· ἡ ἐπὶ τῆς χώρας σωμασκία τῶν μελλόντων μαστιγοῦσθαι, '*phouaxir* (= *phouaxis*): the physical training in the countryside (or "on the spot"), of those preparing to undergo the whipping'. At first sight it seems that the ritual of the classical period cannot be meant here. The expression 'undergo the whipping' undoubtedly refers to the ritual as it was in the Roman period. And the term φούαξιρ itself, with its rhotacism, inevitably recalls the archaizing vocabulary found in ephebic inscriptions from Sparta of the Imperial period. On the other hand: apart from the rhotacism, which may be a late addition, there is no reason why the word φούαξις should not have been of great antiquity. The phrase used for those who underwent whipping may result simply from the fact that the original source of this definition was itself written in the Roman period, and represented things as they were then. The word φούαξις is cognate with φοῦα, again a Laconian term given by Hesychius (perhaps, indeed, from the same source) and meaning 'fox'. It seems, then, that there was something fox-like about the period of preparation, which involved 'acting the fox' (φουάδδειν, once more found in Hesychius). Now, it is hard to see any connection between the fox, or rather its traditional image as trickster, and the ritual as it was in its later form – where all that was involved was passively enduring the lash. But with the earlier form of the ritual, the theft of cheeses, there is a very obvious connection. The fox is above all an accomplished thief; a master of cunning, this animal could teach boys the tricks they needed to penetrate the defensive screen. The fox is also a model of clear-thinking and of opportunism, energetically carrying out a preconceived plan. And, as Xenophon says (*LP* 2.9, see above, p. 250), these are all qualities essential for success in this type of 'sport'. The term φούαξις, the meaning of which is complex and goes beyond mere cunning, fits so well with the ritual in its early form that it was very likely coined to apply to it, and was subsequently applied to the later ritual for reasons of tradition. Additionally, if – as I have suggested[13] – the phrase ἐπὶ τῆς χώρας means 'on the spot', our image of the theft of cheeses is enhanced. The ritual in that case was preceded by a period of withdrawal into the sanctuary itself (the site of which was, we should recall, near the edge of the town); during this period 'trainers' prepared the boys physically and psychologically[14] for the ordeal of stealing while being hit. In any case, there was preparation of this sort, even if rather it took place 'in the countryside'.

Finally, there is the 'procession of the Lydians'. In the passage from the *Aristides* (17.10) where he gives the *aition* of the ritual (the ritual of the classical period, that is), Plutarch makes a close connection, both logical and chronological, between the ritual and the procession – the latter being known to us only from this passage. It has been convincingly argued by Diels that the same people as had stolen the cheeses and undergone the whipping were those who formed the procession, and were called 'Lydians' for the occasion.[15] It makes sense that after coming through the ordeal of whipping they should be presented to the whole community in this way. But why the name 'Lydians'?

Our scant information hardly allows an answer. Only some outline speculations are possible. One such has been supplied by brief remarks of Graf.[16] His starting point is a series of texts concerning the origins of pastoral poetry.[17] Diomedes, the author of one such, after giving the version of these origins which involves Syracuse, adds : 'It is believed that some [of these country-folk] reached as far as Italy, Lydia and Egypt; they were called Lydiasts and Bucolists.' The text seems to mean that bucolic rituals existed elsewhere than at Syracuse, and that the performers in some places were known as Lydiasts (and Lydians?), perhaps because of their clothing. Acccordingly, it may be that at Sparta boys who had just undergone the ordeal processed across the town, dressed in the style of bucolists, possibly masked (masks of Orthia?), while singing and dancing to hymns in honour of Artemis, a goddess known to be the addressee of bucolism. But this may be too fanciful. It may be better to avoid the somewhat fragile and elaborate theory involving bucolism, and to settle instead for the idea that the boys made the procession in girls' long dresses.

Such inversion of gender is, as we have seen, common in initiation rites – indeed, in rites of passage generally. Later, when the original meaning of this transvestism was forgotten, the clothing could have been interpreted as oriental, and as Lydian in particular – Lydia being the symbol par excellence of luxury and effeminacy attributed to eastern peoples.[18] So, just when the boys had proved their courage and their manhood, they were exposed to the greatest humiliation: being likened to girls. Inversion of this kind may seem paradoxical, but it is frequently found in initiation rites. Perhaps it was through incomprehension of such a mentality, at a time when the procession had taken on a celebratory tone, possibly as early as the classical period, that the name 'Lydians' was felt to need explanation, in terms of an event wholly creditable in nature and belonging to the Persian Wars. Such is the *aition* given by Plutarch.

Comparisons

There are two festivals from other cities which seem comparable with the Spartan ritual. The first, called Kotyttia, is recorded only in a gloss on a proverb:

> ἁρπαγὰ Κοτυττίοις· Κοτύττια ἑορτή τίς ἐστι Σικελική, ἐν ᾗ περί τινας κλάδους ἐξάπτοντες πόπανα καὶ ἀκρόδρυα ἐπέτραπον ἁρπάζειν,
>
> Seizing at the Kotyttia: the Kotyttia was a Sicilian festival, during which cakes and nuts were hung from certain branches and people were ordered to go and seize them.[19]

According to Strabo (10.3.16), Kotytto was a divinity of Thracian origin who also had a cult at Corinth. From Sicily the Kotyttia are so far only attested in the 'sacred law' of Selinus (*REG* 108, *Bull. Epigr.* 1995, no. 692). The likely scenario is as follows: the cakes and nuts, offerings to the goddess, were hung from trees growing in the sanctuary, like the biscuits shown on the 'Lenaia vases', and certain individuals were required to go and snatch them. Such a reconstruction depends mainly on the words ἁρπαγά and ἁρπάζειν, but these words do now increasingly appear to have a clear sense of snatching sacred objects. Who the thieves were in this case, and whether there were defenders, we cannot tell.

On the second festival we are better informed. It took place in the shrine of Artemis on Samos. No description of it survives, but one can be constructed from the *aition* of the ritual given by Herodotos (3.48):

> Periandros, son of Kypselos, had sent to Sardis, to Alyattes, three hundred young Corcyraeans, the sons of leading citizens, to be castrated. The Corinthians who were taking these young people landed at Samos. The Samians then learned the whole story, and why they were being taken to Sardis. First they instructed the boys to take up position as suppliants at the sanctuary of Artemis. Then they opposed all attempts to remove the suppliants from the sanctuary. And, since the Corinthians were preventing the boys from getting any food, the Samians invented a festival which to this day they celebrate in the same manner. For as long as the boys remained in place as suppliants, at nightfall the Samians

> organized choirs of girls and young men and, as these choirs performed, they began the custom of bringing cakes of sesame and honey, so that the Corcyraean children could snatch them (ἁρπάζοντες) and be fed.

By connecting this text with the passages of Xenophon and Plato relating to the theft of cheeses at Sparta,[20] I have suggested a reconstruction of the Samian ritual as follows: the festival took place at night, in the sanctuary of Artemis. A choir made up of both sexes, boys and girls, brought on trays the cakes which were laid as offerings either on the altar, or on an offering-table. A group of Samian boys, acting the role of the Corcyraeans, had to snatch these offerings, while a second group, composed of young men (the 'new-initiates'), 'the Corinthians', tried to prevent them by hitting them with whips. Thus we should have, as at Sparta, a ritual of opposed theft at an altar.

The above reconstruction has been criticized by Bonnechère.[21] He argues, not that the reconstruction is necessarily wrong, but that a different one accords better with the evidence of Herodotos. He correctly points out that Herodotos nowhere mentions explicitly a battle around the altar, and concludes that normal method requires us to suppose that the 'Corcyraeans' got hold of the sacred food without any opposition. He locates the ritual as a whole in a religious and mythical context quite different from theft at the altar. In his view, it belongs with stories in which adolescents, of either sex, who find themselves seriously threatened, through trickery find refuge in a shrine where (by a variation of the reclusion familiar in initiation rites) they are shut in for a time, before being rescued for good. Among the examples given by Bonnechère, the most relevant are the myth and ritual surrounding the Locrian virgins sent to Troy, and the story of the Heraclidae in Attica. These interesting considerations add significantly to our understanding of the ritual on Samos. However, I trust that my main argument is still valid.

Herodotos' account does indeed make no explicit mention of any brawling around the altar. But the atmosphere of the episode, arising from the contacts between Corinthians and Corcyraeans, is throughout marked by violence, the violence which the former employ against the latter and, worse still, the violence which they threaten to employ. In the section of the episode which concerns us here, violence occurs at the point where the Corinthians 'cut off the young Corcyraeans from all food' (σιτίων τοὺς παῖδας ἐργόντων τῶν Κορινθίων): this could only have been achieved by the use of force. It is hard to imagine that this violence would have been stopped by the fact that the food in question was in the form of offerings to the goddess, especially since the Corinthians could have posed as guardians of the altar or of the offering-table who sought to prevent sacrilege. I believe that the verb ἁρπάζειν clearly marks the reaction of the young Corcyraeans to this violence. It is no accident that this word recurs regularly in the texts we have assembled. [22] It describes the action of someone getting possession of something through stealth and speed where someone else has set himself to prevent it; without such opposition there can surely be no 'seizure'.

The context of ritual and myth assigned by Bonnechère to the Samian ritual does indeed seem to apply to part of the *aition*, but not to the ritual itself. An *aition* is never an exact copy of the relevant ritual. Its function, rather, is to explain the ritual by recounting 'the first time'. It thus has to begin by setting out in narrative form what we might call 'the initial situation': namely, what had happened *previously* to bring about an event which, by repetition, has hardened into a ritual. In the case of the Samian ritual, the account of the initial situation is particularly detailed and persuasive, because of being so well integrated into history (the Corinthian tyranny, the conflict between Corinth and Corcyra, the reign of Alyattes in Lydia, the existence of eunuchs in the East, and the position that Samos had at the crossroads of all this); the genius of Herodotos as storyteller also plays a part. Into this *logos* on 'what happened previously' come the themes to which Bonnechère refers: the young Corcyraeans must indeed have managed, somehow or other, to escape from their guards so as to find refuge in the sanctuary. But this element is not explicit in the story; all that is needed, in the story, to make the thing happen is for the Samians to advise the young Corcyraeans to do it. Why has this element been suppressed? Quite simply because *it did not form part of the ritual*. What marks the beginning of the section which applies jointly to the *aition* and to the ritual is the phrase 'the Samians created a festival which they still celebrate today in the same way'. It follows that the ritual could not have been focused, as Bonnechère suggests it was, on the rescue of the children through their entry into the sanctuary. Rather, it focused on the way in which they were fed: this took the form of a 'divine meal' which was brought into the sanctuary and which they then had to get hold of by theft.

Did the boys, however, have to fight for the food? Given that Herodotos' wording suggests that violence was involved throughout the episode, it would be strangely dull if there was no violence in the ritual itself. Every festival is also a spectacle; could this festival have amounted only to the following: the choir of boys and girls bringing cakes and laying them out, and the young 'Corcyraeans' then taking and eating them peacefully? What role would then be left for the group which represented the Corinthians? Would they remain idly in the background, or even simply be absent? If so, we should have one of the three main groups in the *aition* left with no role in the ritual. This, then, is why I believe that there was a combat around the altar. Admittedly, this is no more than a hypothesis. Even without it, however, there was undeniably a theft in the shrine of food which had been dedicated. It seems, accordingly, entirely correct to make the familiar link between the ritual on Samos and the theft of cheeses at the shrine of Orthia.

From *bōmolochia* to whipping

The above comparisons show us that the Spartan ritual was not the only one of its kind, but they do not on their own explain its existence. What was the point of this theft, so insisted upon and yet so stoutly resisted, of offerings placed on the altar? And why the whipping?

Theft at an altar of food placed thereon, performed by boys and sometimes under a hail of blows, is a well-known phenomenon from the ancient Greek world: it was called *bōmolochia* (βωμολοχία). It is the subject of a pioneering study by Frontisi-Ducroux, which deals with all the meanings of the term, literal and metaphorical.[23] It is the literal usage that concerns us here. βωμολοχία is a compound, made up of the words for 'altar', βωμός, and for 'ambush', λόχος. The military metaphor is especially relevant because in some cases a combat results around the altar. But the word refers to a stage in the proceedings which precedes the theft itself: it refers to the thieves' waiting and watching for a suitable moment.

Bōmolochia was not always accompanied by violence. In some cases it did not even take the form of theft. Definitions given by ancient lexicographers (Harpocration, the *Souda*, the *Etymologicum Magnum*) and by scholia (on Ar. *Clouds* 910) show that the word can denote a form of begging. Harpocration writes, s.v. βωμολοχεύεσθαι: 'The word βωμολόχοι was mainly applied to people who sat at the base of an altar when sacrifices were taking place, and who begged with much flattery.' From this in part derived the metaphorical sense. Those who begged thus were adults, socially marginal, from the lowest elements of the community. They cringed at the foot of an altar, in a posture which was almost that of a suppliant. Their activity consisted entirely of pestering humbly for food while flattering the person conducting the sacrifice. And it was probably one of the commonest forms of begging in antiquity.

Bōmolochia as theft was quite different. The sources present it as a form of behaviour practised only by children – understandably; an adult doing it would have risked his life. Its commonest form seems to have been '*bōmolochia* with jokes': to distract the cooks (μάγειροι) who prepared the sacrifice, the children chatted, played tricks, made jokes and clowned about. Then, once they saw an opportunity to get some food without being caught, they seized their chance. We find one example of this behaviour in the mid-classical period, at ll. 417–20 of the *Knights* of Aristophanes, where the Sausage Seller mentions thefts of this type which he had committed as a child. But scholia on Aristophanes *Clouds* (l. 910), and *Knights* (l. 901) reveal that there was also a more direct, and more brutal, form of theft at the altar. In this, the children did not bother with trickery but stole the offerings of food blatantly, at the cost of being hit several times before being able to run off. There were also cases where the process was begun 'with jokes', only to turn into straightforward theft when the cooks proved too vigilant. Every case of children's *bōmolochia* involved the risk, for those taking part, of being hit. The choice of strategy, with or without jokes, depended above all on how many attackers there were; to embark on a *bōmolochia* as straightforward theft, an organized gang was needed.

So close is the similarity between the latter form of *bōmolochia* and the Spartan ritual as to leave no doubt: the special qualities of the ritual, indeed its outlandishness, were due to the fact that it was modelled on these real forms of children's behaviour which were universally familiar in Greece. Also, the *aition* given in Plutarch, in which the Lydians openly attack Pausanias and his companions in order to 'sabotage' the sacrifice, before being driven off by sticks and whips, itself closely resembles *bōmolochia* in the form of simple theft.

We have yet to explain why the Spartan ritual was copied in this way from *bōmolochia*. Although the latter was centred on an altar where a sacrifice was taking place, it should not be taken as itself in any way a ritual, or ritualized behaviour. The sources all point one way: this was a real and always deviant practice, which, when it involved theft, was performed only by children. The role of the altar was simply as a source of food. How, then, did this deviant and actively prohibited behaviour come to serve as model for a ritual, and a ritual which was, moreover, one of the high points of 'civic' education for Spartan boys? The problem is complicated by the compulsion placed on boys to steal (above, pp. 46 and 201–7). This latter theft may perhaps be seen as a generalized form (limited to Sparta) of a practice which, in other states, was only happening near an altar. The fact remains that the ritual at the shrine of Orthia was imitated from *bōmolochia*. How did this come about?

The only plausible answer involves the question we formulated earlier (pp. 193–4), and left unanswered: was the Spartan ritual in the classical period already intended to be a flagellation? Given its likeness to *bōmolochia*, the inevitable answer seems 'Yes'. It seems that the model for initiations which was used in constructing the Spartan education system required that some whipping be included. Everything points to the idea that, when this whipping took the form of a festival conducted around the altar of Orthia, the Spartans' way of giving sense and unity to the occasion was to present it as if it were an 'imitation' of a real-life children's activity; in this 'imitation', the hitting was 'explained' as the consequence of theft from the altar.

Girls and boys in the festivals of Apollo

Our information on the various festivals across Laconia in which Spartan girls and boys took part is very uneven. In many cases we know more about the *aitia* and the myths surrounding a festival than we do about what actually took place. This is true of the above-mentioned festivals of Artemis Limnatis and Artemis Karyatis, in which choirs of *parthenoi* had the leading role. As for the boys, we have an inscription from the very late fifth or early fourth century to give us an idea of how boys might travel quite widely in Laconia to take part in competitions. This is the dedication made by Damonon.[24] Enymakratidas, the son of Damonon, while in the *paides* won four victories on the same day: three in foot-races (the stadion, double stadion and the 'long race') and one on horseback. This was at the Parparonia, which took place at a sanctuary in the Thyreatis. Damonon himself, in his own time as *pais*, had won two victories in the foot race (the stadion and double stadion) in three sanctuaries quite distant from Sparta: those of Parparos, of Apollo Lithesios at Cape Malea, and of Apollo Maleatas, which was most probably on Mt. Parnon, north-east of Geronthrai. In Sparta itself he had won the same two events during the festival of Poseidon Gaiaochos, and one event (the stadion) at the festival of Athena (Athena Poliouchos, no doubt). Now, the sheer number of these victories made them untypical, as Damonon the author of the inscription proudly points out. That Enymakratidas, while a child, took part in competitions over a wide area arose from the fact that his father was both a passionate sportsman – a sprinter in his youth who later converted to chariot racing and racing on horseback – who had trained his son in the same activities, and also was rich enough to bear the expenses involved. Very likely the same thing had happened to Damonon in his own childhood. These pursuits, which were both religious and (above all) sporting in character, were a private matter, depending on family; they were in no way part of the state education, which was compulsory and the same for all.

They suggest that in the classical period the private aspect of education, for which the father was chiefly responsible, was much more important than is usually claimed.[25] Damonon and Enymakratidas were certainly not an isolated case, and probably Spartan girls (or, rather, some Spartan girls) were not the only young people to take part in festivals at sanctuaries remote from Sparta. So these religious and competitive activities caused young people (or, rather, some young people) to travel across the state's territory from one end to the other, a process which (albeit in a very different form) is a typical element of Greek *ephēbeia*.

However, our evidence requires us to concentrate mainly on three festivals of Apollo which took place at, or very near, Sparta itself.[26]

The Hyakinthia

These were among the most important Spartan festivals and among the best-known, even outside Sparta. They were celebrated annually, though there is no consensus as to the time of year; they focused mainly, but not exclusively, on the sanctuary of Apollo and Hyakinthos at Amyklai, 5 km south of Sparta. The festival is referred to from the time of Herodotos (9.7.11) and Thucydides (5.23.4–5) to that of Philostratus (*Lives of the Sophists* 2.12.3) and Pausanias (3.19.1–5). There are also references in hellenistic writers (Polemo, Polykrates) cited by Athenaeus (4.138e–139f). This was a festival which belonged to the whole community. First, of course, it included the Amyklaians, as Xenophon makes clear (*Hell.* 4.5.11): 'the Amyklaians are accustomed to go home to sing the paian at the Hyakinthia', even when they are away on a military expedition. Indeed all the Spartiates took part, from the kings downwards. According to Xenophon again, while commanding an expedition against Argos Agesilaos returned to Sparta to take part in the festival and to sing the paian as an ordinary member of the choir (*Agesilaos* 3.17). The festival was a major occasion of state: Thucydides (5.23.4–5) writes that it was at the time of the festival that the treaty of 421 was renewed annually. Every section of the community took part, and not only the male citizens. The women did so; Euripides' *Helen* 1469–73 mentions the all-night festival at which the women – married women, since Helen is said to be able to join them – danced in honour of Hyakinthos. Two inscriptions from the second century AD carry the claims of women to have been ἀρχηὶς καὶ θεωρὸς τοῦ σεμνοτάτου ἀγῶνος τῶν Ὑακινθίων (*IG* 5.1.586–7). Even slaves took part; Polykrates (ap. Athenaeus 4.139f) writes that they were invited by their masters to take part in the sacred meal. Finally, there were the foreigners who came to Sparta in numbers, it seems, to see this spectacular festival. And, as we shall see, in addition to all these social groups the young also took part.

This complex festival had various aspects. Its two parts were utterly different in tone. The first stage, which according to Polykrates lasted a day and a half, featured a sacrifice of the heroic type (ἐναγισμός, in Pausanias' word) in honour of Hyakinthos. The atmosphere was that of religious mourning for the dead hero, and there was a ban on certain kinds of food, on wearing wreaths and on singing the paian. But then came the stage sacred to Apollo: a happy, colourful festival, with processions, sacrifices (θυσίαι) and a banquet (κοπίς). It contained a succession of strikingly-varied episodes: the singing of the paian by the men, which Xenophon represents as the most important ceremony of all; the dancing of the women by night; the (probable) bringing of the god's *chitōn* from Sparta, where it had been woven, to Amyklai; the displaying of the breastplate of Timomakhos, and then the final banquet. To all this the activities of the young were additional; evidently these were no more than was the young people's due, as an essential part of the community.

Information on the young people's role comes from Polykrates (588 F 1), quoted by Athenaeus (4.139d–f):

> Halfway through the three days a varied spectacle begins, amid a striking and joyful gathering of people. Boys wearing a high-belted *chitōn* play the lyre and sing to the accompaniment of a flute; while running the plectrum over all the strings, they sing in honour of the god to an anapaestic rhythm and at a high pitch. Other boys ride across the theatre on horses which are equipped with finery. Numerous choirs of *neaniskoi* enter and sing local verses; dancers join them and perform figures in an old-fashioned style, to the accompaniment of flute and song. The girls appear, some of them riding on expensively-decorated *kannathra*, while others parade in a procession on two-horse racing-chariots. The whole city is filled with the excitement and happiness of the festival.

These activities listed by Polykrates belong to three categories of young people. The activities of the *paides* take various forms. The Greek word should probably be taken in the sense given it by the glosses, and not in Xenophon's sense. These, then, are the 'big boys', what Xenophon calls the *paidiskoi*. Some of them acted as musicians, singing while accompanying themselves on the lyre (in a way which for us recalls rock guitarists) and while being accompanied by the flute. Pettersson (1992, 21) reckons that what they sing is in fact the paian, which according to Xenophon was the centrepiece of the festival. Although the rhythm of the paian was indeed lively and anapaestic, as Polykrates says, this idea seems unacceptable. It was the men who sang the paian, as we can see from the two settings in which Xenophon mentions it. And the belt which the boys wore high (ἀνεζωσμένοις) is the mark of people who want to wear a long garment while staying free to move unimpeded, like charioteers and certain dancers (cf. the Motya statue). Their every action is, like their way of playing the lyre, marked by excitement and virtuosity. The activity of other boys is purely physical: they ride across the theatre in all directions, on horseback. The reference to the theatre appears to show that at this stage (at some point during the second day) the festival is taking place in the town – for Amyklai seems not to have had a theatre. The last sentence of the passage quoted ('The whole city is filled...') seems to confirm this. All this supplements our information on two aspects of boys' education. First, on musical education (in the modern sense of 'music'): our passage shows that it reached quite a high level, and involved in particular a mastery of instruments; contrast Aristotle (above, pp. 61–2), who states the opposite. Second, the art of riding: to ride around in numbers inside a theatre where others are also present is the achievement of skilled horsemen. It is unlikely that all the *paides* performed these activities. Indeed, this is certain in the case of the horsemanship, which was open only to the wealthiest. As for learning a musical instrument, when Aristotle says that it had no place in Spartan education, he was probably thinking of public, compulsory education. In fact it had its place, like equestrian skill, in the private sphere of education. Thus the *paides* mentioned here must have belonged to a social elite.

Next it was the turn of the *neaniskoi* to enter (εἰσέρχονται); probably, here too, the theatre is meant. Their activities were purely musical. By *neaniskoi* Polykrates probably meant the same people that Xenophon calls *hēbōntes*,[27] though perhaps only the youngest of them. They were arranged into choirs, some of which sang traditional songs, and others performed traditional dances.

Finally, Polykrates describes the role of the *parthenoi*. Only equestrian activities are mentioned. This is strange, but understandable, because it gives them great prominence: the girls, in fact, are parading. Some of them process in special wagons, *kannathra* (κάνναθρα), the 'carriagework' of which was made out of plaited bulrushes (κάνης) or reeds (κάννα), in the form of animals or of imaginary beasts.[28] Plutarch says that these wagons processed through the streets of the town. So we have left the theatre; a passage of Xenophon (*Ages.* 8.7) makes clear that the wagons transported the girls as far as Amyklai. This parade took place along the 'Hyakinthian Way'. It resembled a modern carnival parade with floats – likewise carrying pretty girls. Other *parthenoi* had a still more surprising role; they competed in a procession of wagons drawn each by two animals (ἐφ' ἁμίλλαις ἁρμάτων ἐζευγμένων). Since the text does not state that these animals were horses, we should assume – following predominant Greek practice – that they were mules. In the above-quoted passage of the *Agesilaos*, Xenophon writes that the daughter of this king was taken to Amyklai in a *kannathron* belonging to the community. The context, of praise for Agesilaos' modest life-style, shows that these 'public wagons' were used for carrying those girls whose families could not afford their own *kannathron*. However, it probably was not the case that every poor girl was made able to take part in the parade; this was expected only of those girls whose father held an important office, such as that of ephor. As for racing chariots and their teams of animals, there is no evidence that any such were publicly owned; ownership of them was, even more than of *kannathra*, a badge of great wealth (Hodkinson 2000, 315). The Hyakinthia was clearly a good advertisement and helpful for marriage-making. Although the public wagons provided a compensatory mechanism, girls took part in this festival on a far from equal basis.

Thus young people, boys and girls, had a major role in this festival. Indeed, on the second day they were the stars. But the festival did not belong only to them; it belonged – like the Panathenaia for the Athenians – to the whole city assembled. And every element of the city took turns to play a role. For this reason it seems wrong to see this, with Pettersson, as a moment of initiation of the young. He argues mainly from the way the festival was structured. He sees the first phase, the time of mourning, as marking the end of the status which the initiants had possessed until then. The second phase is the recognition of their integration as adults into society. Two other points he sees as supporting his case. First, the character of Hyakinthos. But, as Pettersson himself shows, the character in question is ambivalent: there is Hyakinthos the adolescent, as portrayed on Attic vases around the turn of the sixth–fifth centuries and in Euripides, and Hyakinthos with a beard, as in the sculpture on the 'throne' of Apollo. Each of these two figures may be interpreted in terms of an initiation. The young Hyakinthos may be the model adolescent, as Jeanmaire stated. And the mature Hyakinthos may be seen as an ancestor of the Spartan community. However, the impression left by such arguments is that almost any detail taken in isolation can be pressed into service as evidence of initiation. Pettersson also cites the displaying of Timomachos' cuirass, as symbolizing the entry of the initiates into the category of hoplites. But, so far as we know, the cuirass in question was displayed to everyone; Timomachos was a warrior who served as a model to all men. The festival undoubtedly is structured as a *rite de passage*, but a *rite de passage* is not necessarily an initiation ritual. Far preferable seems the theory of Brelich (1969, 143): that the Hyakinthia are a new-year festival (whence the importance of the argument about its timing), and that they enact a renewal of the whole community. This theory gives an economical explanation of several elements: the presentation to the god of a new *chitōn* brought from the city; the inversion of roles as master invites slave to eat with him, and the noisy, cheerful proceedings of the young people in Sparta and on the road to Amyklai.

The Gymnopaidiai

Though in antiquity one of the best-known of Sparta's festivals, and in later times the one best remembered in Western civilization, we have no description of the Gymnopaidiai to compare with Polykrates' account of the Hyakinthia. The sources are fragmentary; they date from different periods and are highly problematic. And previous scholarship has been more concerned to explain this festival than to determine what exactly happened during the course of it.[29] Thus to understand the part played in the festival by young people, we need to go back to the texts which may reveal what happened in the course of the event.

The Gymnopaidiai were without question one of Sparta's main festivals. Pausanias says as much: 'if there is one festival which the Spartans celebrate with their heart and soul, it is the Gymnopaidiai' (3.11.9). This was already the case in the classical period, as is clear from an episode of the Peloponnesian War recounted by Thucydides (5.82.1–3): with the Gymnopaidiai to look forward to, the Spartans were strongly averse to marching out to Argos to help the oligarchs there who were engaged in an uprising. The Gymnopaidiai, like the Hyakinthia, attracted many people from outside Spartan territory, and in this case too from the classical period onwards. Xenophon states that the wealthy Lichas (fifth century) was renowned for his hospitality to the non-Spartans who stayed in the town during the festival (*Mem.* 1.2.61),[30] and Plutarch writes that for this occasion the town was 'full of foreigners' (*Ages.* 29.3). The festival in which the Spartans made their boys play a prominent role was, then, important and famous. The event was dedicated to Apollo: we are told this by Pausanias, who goes on to state that near the spot where the choral singing took place there stood the statues of Apollo Pythaeus, Artemis and Leto (3.11.9).[31] Both elements of the name 'Gymnopaidiai' (γυμνοπαιδίαι) are ambiguous; consequent misunderstandings affected the tradition in Antiquity. To begin with the element -παιδία: this is almost certainly not derived from παῖς (child), as von Gaertringen realized,[32] but is related to the verb παίζειν meaning 'to play' and also 'to dance'. The latter sense is attested in Homer and, epigraphically, from the Late Geometric period (on an oinochoe from Dipylon). The point was misleading even in Antiquity; a mistaken interpretation of the name caused some sources to exaggerate the role of children in the festival, at the expense of other age-groups. As for the element γυμνο-: no one disputes that it refers to 'nudity', but how is that idea to be understood? The word can indeed mean nudity in the familiar sense, but it can also – especially in the archaic and classical periods – mean being unarmed: in that case, we should have a dance without arms.

The location

Pausanias is precise on where the Gymnopaidiai took place:

> In their *agora* the Spartans have statues of Apollo Pythaeus, Artemis and Leto. This whole area is called 'the dancing ground' (χορός) because there, during the Gymnopaidiai…the ephebes perform in choirs in honour of Apollo. (3.11.9)

This information is repeated by Hesychius and by the gloss in Bekker 1, p. 32. The question of location seems, then, to have been settled from the outset, and all the more so because a position at the heart of the *agora* is eminently suitable; also, as venue a simple 'dancing ground' has a convincingly archaic air. We can imagine it as a paved area, circular in outline, like the one which has been found at Argos (though the latter is not earlier than the fourth century). However, the site of the Gymnopaidiai is portrayed quite differently in sources from the classical period. Herodotos (6.67) tells of a piece of verbal aggression directed during the festival by Leotychidas against Damaratos *c.* 490–485, after which the latter leaves 'the theatre' (ἐκ τοῦ θεήτρου).[33] The same word 'theatre' is found again in Plutarch's *Life of Agesilaos* (29.3), concerning the defeat at Leuktra: 'It was the Gymnopaidiai, and the choirs were competing in the theatre.' With these words Plutarch is simply taking over and clarifying the expression used by Xenophon (*Hell.* 6.4.16), the source which he follows closely for this episode. Xenophon there wrote that, when the news of the defeat reached Sparta, 'it was the last day of the Gymnopaidiai, and the men's choir was inside (ἔνδον ὄντος)', and likewise further on, 'they did not make them go out' (οὐκ ἐξήγαγον). Could such language have been used if the location was a dancing ground in the *agora*? Similarly the description of the Gymnopaidiai by Sosibios suggests a theatre rather than an area of the *agora*:[34] he says in effect that one choir is in front and another on the left. This implies an area with a definite structure and orientation, one which has a front and a rear, and would hardly suit a circular dancing ground. Kennell may seem, then, to be correct in saying that the site of the Gymnopaidiai must have changed by the Roman imperial era; that having formerly been celebrated in the theatre, it was later held on the *choros*.

However, there is an inescapable paradox in such a theory. In the age of Augustus a magnificent theatre of marble was built at Sparta. If the festival of the Gymnopaidiai did move, one would have expected it to do so in the opposite direction, *into* the theatre – especially given the number of visitors who poured into Sparta for the festival, in greater and greater numbers as the centuries passed.[35] On the other hand, can we be sure that there was a theatre at Sparta from, let us not say 490, but even from Herodotos' time onwards? Polykrates' description of the Hyakinthia implies that a theatre existed in the late hellenistic period. One solution to the problem would be to assume that what Pausanias called the *choros* was, in the classical period, called the 'theatre'. This would have the advantage of not ascribing a change of site to a festival as venerable as the Gymnopaidiai. The building of a real theatre, whenever that occurred, would have caused the former name to be dropped. The idea of a space with definite orientation, which emerges from Sosibios, is in fact compatible with a simple *choros*. All that is needed is for the *choros*, rather than having been a perfect circle, to have been – as at Argos – next to a portico or a rear wall. The *choros* would then not have been a space lacking orientation, and 'theatre' would be an understandable name for it. It is also possible that the statues mentioned by Pausanias supplied the points of reference for orienting the *choros*. That would explain why Pausanias wrote that 'the whole place is called *choros*' and thus implied that the name was used not just of the dancing ground but of something larger, of which the dancing-ground was the centre. This in turn would mean that the word ἔνδον in Xenophon did not mean exactly 'inside' but, as we would say, 'on stage'.

The Gymnopaidiai were not a mere display by various teams who sang and danced, but rather took the form of a competition. This is made clear by certain words of Xenophon: the ephors 'allowed the team [which was on stage] to go on with the competition' (διαγωνίζεσθαι, *Hell.* 6.4.16). Plutarch, here following Xenophon, likewise says that 'the choruses were taking part in the competition' (*Ages.* 29.3). But who were the competitors? To that complex question we now turn.

Boys' choirs

Our sources from the classical and hellenistic periods, Xenophon and Sosibios, suggest that other age groups in addition to the *paides* took part. But, with the exception of Plutarch (who is a special case), sources from the Roman Imperial period mention only ephebes or *paides*. The most important of these is Pausanias, who writes: 'The ephebes perform celebratory choruses...' (3.11.9). The others speak of *paides*: these are a gloss in Bekker I, pp. 32 and 234, and the *Etymologicum Magnum*, s.v. Γυμνοπαιδία. This difference in terminology poses no problem; it shows simply that the *paides* in question were 'big boys', *paidiskoi*. Kennell infers (1995, 68–9) that the competition had changed its form and that by the time of Pausanias (who here, as Kennell observes, uses the present tense) the only competitors were choruses of *paides*, or – more precisely – of ephebes. The Gymnopaidiai would thus have been absorbed into the *ephēbeia* and reduced to no more than a competition between ephebes. This is quite possible, and on this period one is ready to defer to Kennell's expertise. It would, however, be very surprising if so famous a festival had been allowed to degenerate in this way. Admittedly, Plutarch for one always writes of the festival in the past tense. But that fact is not on its own decisive. And we have to allow for the possibility that the very name of the festival, Gymnopaidiai, could have caused Pausanias to connect it exclusively with 'children'.

The trichoria

A type of Spartan choir now known as the *trichoria* is mentioned, or indeed described, by several texts. Its name is taken from Pollux (4.107), who ascribes its foundation to Tyrtaios. The texts in question are Plutarch *Lyc.* 21.3, *Inst. Lac.* 15 (=*Mor.* 238a–b), *Mor.* 544e, and the scholion on Plato *Laws* 1.633a, s.v. συσσίτια. Three choruses were present simultaneously. All the texts represent one of them as always made up of *paides*, and another as made up of old men (*gerontes*; *presbyteroi* in the scholion). As for the third, the names vary: Pollux and the scholion have ἄνδρες; Plutarch has ἀκμάζοντες in the *Lycurgus*; in the *Inst. Lac.* is ἀκμάζοντες ἄνδρες; in *Mor.* 544e we have – slightly surprisingly – νεανίσκοι; in the scholion the latter word is combined with ἄνδρες. We are left with the impression that our authors thought that these were young men (of around 30?). The first to sing was the old men's chorus: 'Once we were tough young men.' Then the ἄνδρες sing, 'But we still are – and we'll prove it, if you want to try.' Then finally come the *paides*, who thus have the 'last word': 'And we shall be much better still.'[36] In these passages there is no explicit connection between the *trichoria* and the Gymnopaidiai. Plutarch says only (though in two places, the *Lycurgus* and the *Inst. Lac.*) that this triple chorus took part 'in the festivals'; so if it did form part of the Gymnopaidiai, that was not the only festival concerned. What makes the *trichoria* a necessary feature of any treatment of the Gymnopaidiai is another passage: a fragment of Sosibios (595 F 5 [second century BC] = Athenaeus 15.678b–c) which is apparently a note on the Spartan crowns which were called θυρεατικοί.

Sosibios, Thyrea and the Gymnopaidiai

Here the text is far from clear. Authoritative warnings notwithstanding,[37] we venture a translation:

> *Thyreatikoi*: the name which the Lacedaemonians give to certain crowns, as Sosibios says in his *On Sacrifices*. He states that they are now called crowns of feathers, although in fact they are made of palm-leaves. They are worn, according to him, in commemoration of the victory at Thyrea, by the leaders of the choruses which are staged during the festival which also involves the Gymnopaidiai. The choruses are as follows: in front, the chorus of *paides*, and on the left the chorus of *andres*. They dance naked and sing songs of Thaletas and Alcman, as well as paians of the Lakonian Dionysodotos.

There is, first, a problem about the number of choruses. The text as we have it mentions only two, of *paides* and *andres*. Some historians believe that this is what Sosibios actually wrote.[38] Most commentators, however, take it that there is a lacuna after the mention of *paides*. The main reason why this has usually been assumed is not – *pace* Kennell – a desire to make Sosibios' evidence accord with that of Plutarch on the *trichoria*; that clearly would be bad method, since there is no reason to be sure that the *trichoria* were the same thing as the one described by Sosibios. The real reason for positing a lacuna is the run of the passage itself which, as we have it, reads oddly. It seems difficult indeed to describe the position of two choruses as being 'in front' and 'on the left'. If there are only two, and one of them is 'in front', the other is surely 'behind'. And if one of them is 'on the left', the other is necessarily 'on the right'.

There must, then, have been three choruses. But even so, it does not necessarily follow that the third chorus (the one 'on the right', as we argue) was made up of old men as in the *trichoria* discussed above. Indeed, the idea of a chorus of the elderly in any festival is problematic, since it was not normal in the Greek world for old men to compete in *agōnes*. It was for this reason that Bölte[39] made the putative third chorus consist of *eirenes*.

However, the currently-prevailing view seems best: that in Sosibios' text we should supply the idea of a chorus of old men after the chorus of *paides*.[40] The reason is not the *trichoria* of Plutarch, but is to do rather with another passage of Sosibios: Fragment 8.[41]

> We were too, once upon a time: a Laconian war cry. Mentioned by Sosibios in his *On Customs*. He records that this is what the old men used to say while dancing: *We* were too, once upon a time, ἀμές ποκ' ἦμες.

That the form of words is exactly identical shows that in context Sosibios was not only describing the *trichoria* but also was the source of what Plutarch and others say on this subject, especially as regards the words of the song. Very likely it was also this *trichoria* which was described in his *On sacrifices*; it is hardly likely that he described two separate *trichoriai* in two separate works.

In Fragment 5 of Sosibios, what is the relation between the Gymnopaidiai and the dance celebrating the victory of Thyrea?[42] The relevant sentence – on the subject of the crowns known as *thyreatikoi* – is as follows:

> φέρειν δ' αὐτοὺς ὑπόμνημα τῆς ἐν Θυρέᾳ γενομένης νίκης τοὺς προστάτας τῶν ἀγομένων χορῶν ἐν τῇ ἑορτῇ ταύτῃ, ὅτε καὶ τὰς Γυμνοπαιδίας ἐπιτελοῦσιν.

What is problematic is the phrase ἐν τῇ ἑορτῇ ταύτῃ. One possibility is that it refers to what has just gone before, the festival celebrating Thyrea, assuming either that such a festival was mentioned in the text immediately preceding the section quoted or paraphrased by Athenaeus or that the idea of a festival is implicit in the section that we do have, particularly in the words ὑπόμνημα τῆς ἐν Θυρέᾳ γενομένης νίκης. The other possibility, which I take as preferable, is that this expression, rather than referring to what precedes, introduces something which follows, something which becomes explicit in ὅτε...ἐπιτελοῦσιν. In effect the meaning thus would be: 'in the festival where the Gymnopaidiai also are celebrated'. In either case (though more clearly in the latter), it would seem that the festival in honour of Thyrea had been combined with the Gymnopaidiai, whether immediately after the victory or after a period in which it existed separately.[43]

Thus, thanks to Fragment 5 of Sosibios, we have textual support for the idea of a link between the *trichoria* (itself unique to Sparta, so far as we know) and the Gymnopaidiai. But what exactly was this link? At the start of the fragment Sosibios' subject matter is the festival in honour of Thyrea and the crowns which the chorus-leaders wore at that festival. The natural assumption, then, seems to be that the *trichoria* described immediately afterwards formed that part of the Gymnopaidiai which consisted of dancing and which originally celebrated the victory of Thyrea. And that would fit very well with the warlike nature of the words sung, which Fragment 8 describes as 'warcry', ἀϋτή. But this idea is refuted by Sosibios' description of the event. In the first place, we are told that the chorus-members are 'naked', and this naturally calls to mind the Gymnopaidiai 'proper'; had the nudity of the latter perhaps been extended to the part of the festival which celebrated the victory of Thyrea? But, even more seriously, the songs mentioned by Sosibios are works of Thaletas and Alkman and so antedate by far the victory of Thyrea.[44] We should then have to assume that, immediately after mentioning the Gymnopaidiai, Sosibios changed the subject and moved from the Thyrea festival to the Gymnopaidiai, and that when he describes the *trichoria* he is indeed talking of the Gymnopaidiai 'proper'. There is nothing in the text itself to indicate any such dichotomy. The problem arises not so much from Sosibios but from the way in which Athenaeus has represented his words. The *trichoria*, then, was apparently a triple chorus, sung and danced by a group of children, a group of men and a group of the elderly, and involving the singing of responses. This chorus happened at festivals, of which the Gymnopaidiai was the most famous. The evidence given so far might suggest that the *trichoria* constituted the totality of the dance-competition at the Gymnopaidiai. Another text, however, imposes a different conclusion.

Xenophon's evidence

This takes us back to the classical period. It shows that the Gymnopaidiai involved also a competition based on age-groups, in the normal way. On the day after the defeat at Leuktra, Xenophon writes,

> the messenger given the job of reporting the disaster arrived during the last day of the Gymnopaidiai, while the men's chorus was inside (Γυμνοπαιδιῶν τε οὔσης τῆς τελευταίας καὶ τοῦ ἀνδρικοῦ χοροῦ ἔνδον ὄντος). On learning the news the ephors were alarmed, quite naturally in my opinion, but allowed the chorus to continue with the competition. (*Hell.* 6.4.16)

Here there is no question of a triple chorus. The competition clearly lasts for several days, and there are several age-categories, including that of the *andres*. It seems that the messenger arrived just as the day and the competition were ending; the ephors' action was probably dictated by the desire to have the competition reach its conclusion. The men's chorus was, therefore, the last to perform. Questions raised but not answered by this passage are: How many days did the festival last? How many age-categories were involved, and what were they? Was there one day for each age-category? If not, how was the time divided?

Choruses of *paides* were almost certainly part of the competition. It is clear from Xenophon that, in addition to the *andres*, there was at least one other age-category; and the *paides*, who appear regularly in the sources for the Gymnopaidiai (sometimes, even, on their own) are the obvious candidates. For Athenaeus (14.631b) the Gymnopaidic dancing as a whole is dancing by *paides*. It is possible that these were the only two categories; the old are apparently excluded by the fact that they normally do not take part in competition (the *trichoria* may be a special case, since there the old men only make up a third of the chorus). However, if we reckon that the three choruses prescribed by Plato's *Laws* were modelled on Sparta, we may be justified in positing a third category, corresponding to Xenophon's *hēbōntes*. Plato's choruses consist respectively of children, young men and men between 30 and 60 years old (2.664c) and resemble the choruses of the Gymnopaidiai (apart from the *trichoriai*) in that they appear in succession.

The Gymnopaidiai were also no doubt structured according to one of the various ways of dividing the citizen body, whether by tribes, *ōbai*, 'phratries' or in some other way. (Tribes and 'phratries' occur as categories in the Karneia, as we shall see.) It is my belief that each social group put out four choruses: a *trichoria*, a chorus of *paides*, one of *hēbōntes* and one of *andres*. One sees how important a role was played at this festival by young people still in the education system.

Nakedness

It is tempting to see the 'nakedness', which is mentioned in various sources and is part of the very name of the Gymnopaidiai, not as literal nudity but as meaning only that the dancers did not bear arms. This is certainly suggested by the passage in which Athenaeus (14.630d–631b) defines the genre of the 'gymnopaidic dance'. He distinguishes between gymnopaidic and pyrrhic dancing, first with respect to rhythm (the pyrrhic has rapid and agitated movements, the gymnopaidic 'dignified and majestic') then by the fact that the pyrrhic is danced under arms, whereas in the gymnopaidic 'all the children dance "naked"' (γυμνοὶ γὰρ ὀρχοῦνται οἱ παῖδες πάντες). However, important though this passage is (albeit not *entirely* without ambiguity), the nakedness involved in the Gymnopaidiai was probably literal nudity. The lexicographers, who knew of many more ancient texts than we do, meant 'naked children' when they wrote of παῖδες γυμνοί without qualification, as in the two glosses in Bekker's collection. Even more clearly with Hesychius: he defines the Gymnopaidiai as 'when choruses stripped naked make their appearance' (πρόσοδοι χορῶν γεγυμνωμένων). Sosibios, a source to be taken very seriously, also writes of literal nudity (γυμνῶν ὀρχουμένων). It might be argued that originally the gymnopaidic dance was simply a dance without arms, and that only when there was a wish to give it an athletic quality (assuming that there was such a desire) was the event turned into a naked dance. But that would perhaps be to place too much faith in Athenaeus; there is no reason to think that he had particular information about possible 'primitive' Gymnopaidiai.

Athenaeus and the glosses in Bekker connect this nakedness only with *paides*. This connection probably arose from the name of the Gymnopaidiai. In any case, Sosibios in his description of the *trichoria* says that the choruses are made up of naked dancers (χοροὶ…γυμνῶν ὀρχουμένων). Nudity, then, was compulsory for all, including the group of old men who formed part of every triple chorus; the same probably applied to all the competitions of this festival. This is what gave its peculiarity to the festival of the Gymnopaidiai, and assimilated it to an athletic contest. And since the nakedness was not confined to the children, it is difficult to see it as an initiatory rite, as does Pettersson (1992, 47).

The Gymnopaidiai as an endurance test

Modern views of the festival see it as above all a test of endurance in the face of fatigue and heat, imposed upon children as part of their education. Even Pettersson, in his detailed study, conceives of it in this way (1992, 45–7). But this idea is seldom found in the ancient sources. Indeed, it occurs only once. Admittedly this is in Plato, but the idea is significantly not taken up by any subsequent ancient writer (with the possible exception of scholiasts on this passage). In Book 1 of the *Laws* (633c), in his list of forms of endurance tests (καρτερήσεις), Megillos refers to the Gymnopaidiai thus:

> And in addition the Gymnopaidiai too are a fearful act of endurance practised in our own community, where people have to hold out against fierce and stifling heat.
>
> ἔτι δὲ κἀν ταῖς Γυμνοπαιδίαις δειναὶ καρτερήσεις παρ' ἡμῖν γίγνονται τῇ τοῦ πνίγους ῥώμῃ διαμαχομένων.

As an *interpretation* of the Gymnopaidia this is indeed interesting, and suggests a link with endurance tests found in various archaic societies: tests imposed on boys during their initiation and involving exposure to intense cold or heat (see above, pp. 190–1). But it is questionable whether the Gymnopaidiai really amounted to a test of this kind. In one sense Megillos' view fits the facts; it is undeniable that this contest, which apparently took place during August, would in some years at least be a fearsome ordeal, though whether nudity made it harder or easier to bear the present writer can hardly say. But the aim of the competition was not to subject the performers to an endurance test of any kind. That it could be interpreted as such was not an aim of the event, but resulted from the time of year at which it was held. And the winners were not those who held out the longest but those who danced the best. Plato's character Megillos seems to suggest that this 'endurance test' was part of the 'breaking in' of young Spartans (of the other three examples in his list, two – the group fights and the theft of cheeses – involve the *paides*, while the third, the Crypteia, involves the *neoi*); but he is wrong: the dances at the Gymnopaidiai were performed equally by other age-categories.

With one significant difference, that all the performers are male, the Gymnopaidiai present the same overall character for our purposes as the Hyakinthia. The young did indeed play a notable role, but they did so alongside the adults. Thus even though initiatory themes can indeed be identified (such as the role of dancing, of nakedness, and the endurance-test aspect) the Gymnopaidiai should not be seen as part of an initiation rite for the young. The reverse is the case: this festival (and note especially the song in the *trichoria*) emphasized the future role of the young as full members of the citizen body.

The Karneia

On this we know even less than we do about the other festivals just mentioned. Our sources give us no more than snapshots, albeit fairly precise, of certain moments in the ritual. We can do no more than assemble and compare these sources. For the Karneia we cannot try to construct an overall schema as we attempted in the case of the Gymnopaidiai. It is certain that the Karneia were one of the most important festivals of Sparta; Brelich has even referred to them as 'the great festival par excellence' (1969, 148). They lasted for nine days, according to Demetrios of Skepsis, and several texts from the classical period make clear that the Spartans, like the other Dorians, made efforts to observe a truce during the occasion. The god in whose honour they were celebrated is always referred to at Sparta as simply 'Karneios', but Pausanias regards this as an epiklesis of Apollo (3.14.16). Here the only aspect of the festival which will concern us is, the role of young people in it.

The Karneatai

Here our only source is Hesychius (s.v.):

> Καρνεᾶται· οἱ ἄγαμοι· κεκληρωμένοι δὲ ἐπὶ τὴν τοῦ Καρνείου λειτουργίαν, πέντε δὲ ἀφ' ἑκάστης...ἐπὶ τετραετίαν ἐλειτούργουν

> *Karneatai*: the unmarried; chosen by lot for the service of Karneios, five from each..., they performed this service for four years.

The *Karneatai*, then, were *agamoi*. Clearly these people are not the same as the *agamoi* whose despised status is described by Plutarch (*Lyc.* 15.1–3). Hesychius' *agamoi* are being honoured: these are 'legal' bachelors. They were young men, not yet married but still within the age limit (probably between 30 and 35) after which it was a serious offence against Spartan custom to remain unmarried. To use Xenophon's terminology, they were *hēbōntes*, and perhaps among the oldest of that group.

What did the *Karneatai* do? Hesychius' term λειτουργία (*leitourgia*) certainly does not have the same meaning as in Athens, since liturgies in the Athenian sense seem not to have existed at Sparta.[45] Parker rightly interprets the term here as meaning the service of the god.[46] The service in question would be that of Karneios in general and not only with regard to the festival, though the latter most probably was the main area of responsibility. The *Karneatai*, then, were the organizers of the festival and the *agōnothetai* of the contests involved in it.

Hesychius writes of these men as chosen by lot from among the *agamoi* 'five from each...' The missing word here is usually supplied as φυλῆς, 'tribe', though other restorations are quite possible.[47] The idea of lottery is slightly surprising for Sparta; if Hesychius here is right, we could deduce that the Spartans regarded all *agamoi* as equally qualified for this responsibility, which in turn would mean that the financial liability was not great. The wording at the start of Hesychius' note, which seems to make *Karneatai* equivalent to οἱ ἄγαμοι, (note the definite article), was interpreted by Brelich as showing that, while the term *Karneatai* may strictly have meant 'organizers of the cult of Karneios' (1969, 149–50), it had come to be applied more widely, to all in the age-group of *agamoi*. But if the latter point were true, it would be hard to explain why the word in fact occurs only here.

The military rally

The most spectacular moment of the Karneia was a military-style rally which is described as follows by Demetrios of Skepsis (quoted by Athenaeus, 4.141f):

> Demetrios of Skepsis...states that the Karneia festival imitates military discipline. Nine positions are occupied, known as 'parasols' because they resemble tents. Under each of them dinner is served to nine men (*andres*); everything is done in accordance with the commands of the herald; each parasol includes three phratries, and the festival of the Karneia lasts for nine days.

Organizing this rally was certainly one of the main responsibilities of the

Karneatai. Our sole point of interest now is, Who were the *andres*? An obvious response is to distinguish them from the *agamoi*: that is, to see them as men over 30, of full citizen status and married (so Brelich 1969, 162). However, it is just possible that both categories applied to the same age-group, since Xenophon's *hēbōntes* are warriors and can themselves be called *andres*.

The staphylodromoi

For this episode in the Karneia our main source is a gloss in the *Lexeis Rhetorikai*, edited by Bekker (1, p. 305):

> σταφυλοδρόμοι ('the grape-runners'): during the festival of the Karneia, a man wearing sacrificial ribbons runs while uttering good wishes for the community; young men, called *staphylodromoi*, chase after him. If they catch him, this is a good omen for the crops in the community's territory; if not, it is a bad omen.

The agricultural meaning of this strange custom is clear enough, even though we are not informed as to why the name *staphylodromoi* was used. In an inverted form, it is a ritual of the scapegoat type: here the central figure is not chased away but is pursued in order to be caught; he is wearing ribbons like a consecrated victim for sacrifice, and he promises to bring good upon the community. For our present study, what matters is that the *staphylodromoi* are not only *neoi*, as the above text states, but they are also, according to Hesychius (s.v.), 'some of the *Karneatai*'. Here, then, is a ritual of obvious importance for the community, since it foretold abundance or shortage of food in the coming year; and young people are its organizers and (in some cases) participants.[48]

We can see, therefore, that the role of young people in the Karneia had certain striking differences from the two other festivals discussed above. For one thing, only young men over 20 are involved, a somewhat marginal group as regards formal education at Sparta. Also, and clearly related, there is the fact that these young people not only take part in the festival but actually organize it. This is all the more noteworthy when one recalls how in other respects this age group was excluded from certain things and treated as inferiors. The Karneia show that these young people indeed represent the future of the community.

We thus differ from Pettersson on the role of the young in the three great festivals of Apollo: the Hyakinthia, the Gymnopaidiai and the Karneia. For Pettersson, these festivals form three stages in a cycle of initiation. Now, the festivals do indeed have elements interpretable as connected with initiation:

in addition to those mentioned above, we may note the warrior aspect of the Karneia. These elements, however, are isolated; they have no connection either with each other or with any one particular function. Like Brelich, who also rejects the initiatory explanation, I note rather that here are three festivals of the whole community; young people play their part, but alongside other age-groups.

Where the young do have a special function, as in the Karneia, it is as *leitourgoi*, as representatives appointed by the community. It is characteristic of initiation rites to marginalize the initiands for a time, to set them at the periphery of society. Religion, on the other hand, integrates; it brings people into the heart of society – as here.

'Education and religion': does our chapter-heading mean that we think that the young Spartans were taught religion in a formal way? Certainly not – not, at least, in the modern sense of a subject labelled 'religion' with its own teachers. That would be alien to the whole nature of Greek religion. Religion was, of course, involved in the teaching which formed part of Spartan education, indeed of all education in antiquity. It was through Homer that Spartan children learned their *grammata*, and through Homer that they learned what they needed to know about the main divinities, their moral character and their history. *Mousikē* in its various forms – singing, dancing and poetry – was shot through with a form of religion which was more specifically Spartan. And it was their training in *mousikē* which equipped the young to play their part in the community's festivals. But, on the whole, religion was not taught formally. Young people learned it through osmosis, in every social context – starting with the family. It was the community as a whole which gave them their religious upbringing. Their practical training consisted of taking part in festivals. At Sparta the process of joining the community of citizens by means of religious activity started very early, probably at the age of *paidiskoi*. Taking part in religious life was just one aspect of training the young to live as citizens: and that training was the purpose of education.

Notes

[1] See above, p. 196. The name is found in various forms on inscriptions. For linguistic aspects of the names of Orthia, Sansalvador 1996.

[2] On the ephebic contests in the Roman Imperial period, Kennell 1995, 51–5.

[3] One ephebic contest of the Imperial period was known as Eubalkes (= Εὐϝάλκης, 'the strong one'). Eualkes is found as a male personal name in Lakonia during the classical period (*IG* 5.1.1124: Geronthrai, end of 5th century; 649: Sparta, very late 4th or early 3rd century), and this might seem to suggest that the contest existed at the period.

However, the name is also found in other cities (see, most recently, Bresson 2002, 30–1). Only if it could be proved that the contest existed at the time could one firmly suggest a link between its name and the personal name.

[4] What follows is an updated version of material first published in Ducat 1995.

[5] On such censorship at Sparta, Thuc. 2.39.1; 5.68.2.

[6] There exist several modern studies: Ducat 1995, 347–53 (reconstruction, with list of the main sources); Kennell 1995, 70–83 (reconstruction) and 149–61 (sources in text and translation).

[7] Bonnechère 1993, 16, and (with fuller argumentation) Ducat 1995, 356–7.

[8] The sequence of logic is: Lydians (procession) > Persian Wars > Plataia > Pausanias.

[9] Chrimes 1949, 262 argues similarly.

[10] Cf. Losfeld 1977.

[11] Den Boer 1954, 266–8.

[12] Kennell 1995, 77.

[13] Above, p. 185.

[14] Accordingly Xenophon observes that theft is carefully prepared.

[15] Diels 1896, 361.

[16] Graf 1985, 88–9.

[17] Namely: a Greek text, from the *Prolegomena* to Theocritus which go back to Theon of Alexandria, and two Latin texts, one by Probus the other by Diomedes. The texts are collected by Wendel 1914, 2–3, 14–17. See the study of these texts by Frontisi-Ducroux 1981.

[18] In Euripides' *Bacchae* Dionysos, who is portrayed as effeminate (ll. 253, 453–9), is said to come from Lydia (ll. 233–6, 464).

[19] Von Leutsch-Schneidewin 1839, 333.

[20] Others had previously observed the connection: Rose 1941, Vernant 1989, 197 n.58.

[21] Bonnechère 1998.

[22] To repeat, in summary: the verb occurs in connection with the Spartan ritual in Xenophon and Plato; and also in Plutarch concerning the aition of the ritual. It is found also in the context of the Kotyttia, in the proverb and in the explanation thereof. And there is more, as we shall shortly see, in the *bōmolochia* (scholia on Aristophanes).

[23] Frontisi-Ducroux 1984: on the Spartan ritual as a version of *bōmolochia*, see p. 32.

[24] *IG* 5.1.213. The most recent translation and commentary are in Hodkinson 2000, 303–7, whose concern is chiefly with equestrian victories as a sign of wealth. For the aspect of the inscription of relevance now, cf. Christien 1997, 64–5.

[25] See above, pp. 126–7 and 170.

[26] The fundamental study of these three festivals is Pettersson 1992; q.v. for the sources, bibliography and a brief summary of earlier scholarship. Cf. Richer 2004 and 2005.

[27] On the *neaniskoi* at Sparta in the Roman Imperial period, see Kennell 1995, 47. Note, however, that at p. 66 he expresses doubt as to whether this word had a precise meaning.

[28] Plutarch (*Ages.* 19.7–10) mentions deer and griffons.

[29] So Pettersson 1992, 42–56. In this respect Sergent 1993 is more helpful.

[30] A point taken up by Plutarch, *Cimon* 10.5. Cf. Hodkinson 2000, 78, 211, 342.

[31] The mention of Apollo Karneios, in a gloss from the *Lexeis Rhetorikai* (ed. Bekker, 1.234), is probably due to a misunderstanding.

[32] *RE* VII, col. 2087–9 (of 1910).

[33] This is probably the origin of the location by Aristoxenos of Tarentum concerning the Gymnopaidiai (fr. 108 Wehrli): εἰς τὸ θέατρον.

[34] 595 F 5, in Athenaeus 15.678b–c: see below, p. 269.

[35] In the sanctuary of Orthia a theatre was built in the 3rd century AD to accommodate spectators of the whipping. On the theatre of Sparta, see Waywell 1999.

[36] Here, for example, is the version found in the *Lycurgus*: ‘ἄμμες ποκ’ ἦμες ἄλκιμοι νεανίαι – ἄμμες δέ γ’ εἰμες· αἰ δὲ λῇς, πεῖραν λαβέ – ἄμμες δέ γ’ ἐσσόμεθα πολλῷ κάρρονες’. Only the scholion has the responses in normal Greek. The other versions are in good Laconian dialect. In the versions given by Plutarch there are slight dialectal variations but only one significant difference: at the end of the response of the ἄνδρες he gives αὐγάσδεο instead of πεῖραν λαβέ.

[37] Kennell 1995, 194 n. 127.

[38] Den Boer 1954, 282–3, Kennell 1995, 68.

[39] Bölte 1929, 125.

[40] As proposed by Wyttenbach and Kaibel.

[41] The text is preserved by Zenobios the paroemiographer (1.82), which explains the way it is presented; it had become a proverb.

[42] This is the Battle of the Champions, dated traditionally to 546.

[43] Most of the lexica (the *Souda*, *Etym. Magn.* and the glosses in Bekker I, pp. 32, 234) state simply that the Gymnopaidiai celebrated the victory of Thyrea.

[44] The paians of Dionysodotos, on the other hand, might belong to the part of the festival which commemorated Thyrea, if the latter remained distinct from the festival as a whole.

[45] Hodkinson 2000, 212.

[46] Parker 1989, 164 n. 7.

[47] For instance, ὠβῆς would have dropped more easily than φυλῆς which was understandable by every copyist.

[48] Nothing is known as to the age of the person pursued.

9

THE CRYPTEIA

Of all the institutions and social practices of classical Sparta, the Crypteia is one of the most talked about, doubtless because of its spectacular, even slightly theatrical, character, and also because our understanding of it is readily cited as one of the success stories of the anthropological approach. At the same time it should be borne in mind that, in the social organization and the initiatory-educational system of the Spartans, it was really only of secondary importance. It is even tempting to ask whether it may legitimately be included as one of the stages of education, so marginal do the age and small numbers of those subjected to it make it appear, relative to the object of that education – the forming of the citizen. But since, to view it from another angle, it could equally be regarded as the crowning moment, if not of education itself, at least of certain aspects of it, it seemed to me impossible to exclude it from this discussion.

The sources

What has, in recent years, struck some of the acknowledged experts on Spartan matters most forcibly is the disproportion that, in their view, exists between what modern scholars say about the Crypteia and what an objective analysis of the sources actually allows them to say. Thus, Whitby[1] emphasizes the uncertain nature of our understanding of this custom and, not without reason, tries to place its importance in perspective. The study which has offered the most shrewd statement of this problem is that of Lévy.[2] A critical scrutiny of the texts leads him to conclude that the images of the Crypteia conveyed by them are not only different but even contradictory. He puts forward the notion that the word Crypteia was used by ancient authors to denote several different things: a preliminary selection test, commandos deployed against certain helots, a patrol force on the ephebic model, and a specialized unit of the army.

All of this suggests that, although the Crypteia has been studied for over 150 years,[3] too little attention, perhaps, has been devoted to establishing precisely how it operated. Following Lévy, I shall re-examine the texts but in chronological order this time (one notable effect of which will be to detach the scholion to Plato from the text of which it is a commentary), to see whether the tradition on this subject does have a history. Each text will be considered in itself, and this with the aim not so much of exposing, at the outset, its documentary worth, as of analysing its construction and functioning. Only after that will a synthesis of the information be attempted. While taking care not to minimize the contradictions that emerge between the sources, rather than deducing from them that they reflect a plurality of things named 'Crypteia' I shall try to explain them, in the usual way, as testifying to the existence of several traditions.[4]

Plato's allusion

Here we find again the 'catalogue of *karterēseis*' drawn up by Megillos in Book 1 of the *Laws* (633b–c). He has already touched on the collective fights and the stealing of cheeses from the altar of Orthia:

> ἔτι δὲ καὶ κρυπτεία τις ὀνομάζεται, θαυμαστῶς πολύπονος πρὸς τὰς καρτερήσεις, χειμώνων τε ἀνυποδησίαι καὶ ἀστρωσίαι καὶ ἄνευ θεραπόντων αὐτοῖς ἑαυτῶν διακονήσεις νύκτωρ τε πλανομένων διὰ πάσης τῆς χώρας καὶ μεθ' ἡμέραν,

> There is also something called the Crypteia, which is an extraordinarily harsh form of training: in winter, neither footgear nor bedding; no slaves, so that each one looks after himself; and wandering all over the territory, night and day.
>
> (b9–c4)

The aim of the text is to illustrate, by means of some chosen features, which do not by themselves constitute a proper description, the arduousness of this 'hardening to suffering'. Hence, nothing is said about how long the test lasted nor about the age of the participants and the method of recruiting them. From this, the reader might gather that, as far as Plato was concerned, all young Spartans were subjected to it; this at least is what the logic of a military training would require, and it is thus that Girard understood it in his article *Krypteia* in the *Dictionnaire des Antiquités*. To illustrate the expression 'an extraordinarily harsh…training', which qualifies what is being presented in terms of a simple preparation for the supreme test, namely war, Plato resorts to four characteristics. (a) The flimsy nature of their equipment (lack of footgear and bedding, rendered the more cruel by the fact that the exercise could be taking place in winter – in fact, Megillos puts it as though it *always* took place in winter). (b) The absence of slaves: as we have seen, this refers not to pedagogues but, perhaps, to young slaves who served the boys and adolescents during the period of their education. (c) The abolishing of the diurnal/nocturnal rhythm; of course the participants must have slept, but this may have been at any hour, depending on the circumstances. (d) 'Wandering all over the territory' of the city.

By that, Megillos is not intending to describe the working of the Crypteia as an actual 'institution', but simply to conjure, in an allusive and almost poetic fashion, an image of the kind of life these youths led. It is characterized almost exclusively by negative features: in essence, the Crypteia constitutes asceticism, privation. The examples he uses of this privation are significant: not only do the young men have to endure extremely harsh living conditions, but to do so they are deprived of everything characteristic of the Greek citizen's existence – in other words, civilized living: footgear, slaves, bedding, an ordered life. The real test, in Plato's view, is the 'wandering' way of life, that is, being isolated from the life of the city.

The allusive presentation, the tone of which is set by the introductory phrase 'There is something...', does not mean that it was little known; it may even be to the contrary. Throughout the passage relating to the lawgiver's 'fourth device' Megillos' tone is mysterious, his terms veiled. This vagueness was entirely appropriate for institutions that appeared as very old and, at the same time, as of quasi-divine origin. But advocates of the anthropological approach could also point out that, throughout this passage of the *Laws*, the focus is on what we call initiation rites, and that what initiation requires of initiates is secrecy.

Two of the features to which Plato resorts are also attested in the field of education: the lack of footgear, and matters to do with bedding. On this last point there may appear to be a difference, since, according to Plutarch, boys slept not on the ground but on *stibades*, which they made themselves. But the *stibas*, an improvised bed, a simple heap of twigs or herbiage, is not inconsistent with the Crypteians' alleged lack of bedding. Plato's statement does not preclude the possibility of their having made *stibades*, and this is surely what used to happen; the *stibas*, a rough, almost animal, form of bedding-down, is as appropriate to the kind of life led by the Crypteian as it is to that of the soldier on campaign.[5] The recurrence of these two features should not lead us to suspect that confusion has crept in here. There is nothing to set against the notion that they really were common to both education and the Crypteia; the Crypteian thereby relived the tests he already knew, and, by his regressing to the savage state, he regressed to that of childhood.

On the question of what the Crypteian actually *did*, the verb πλανᾶσθαι is the sole indication supplied by the text, and it can only be translated as 'to wander'. In itself, wandering does not conflict with the idea of 'patrols', espoused by Lévy. There are in fact two kinds of patrol: those that aim to reconnoitre a particular objective, and those whose only object is to 'sweep' a certain tract of land, so as to observe what is going on there; this aim may perfectly well be achieved by 'sweeping' at random, that is, in a direction arbitrarily determined (sometimes as he went along) by the patrol leader.

The effectiveness of this type of patrol hinges precisely on the fact that its direction is arbitrary, thus unforeseeable. The verb 'to wander' does not on its own justify discarding Lévy's interpretation, but we should acknowledge that there is nothing in the text to support it, and that the idea central to this text, that of an endurance test pure and simple, does not draw the reader in that direction. Why should a patrol have been deprived of footgear, bedding, and slaves?

What is perhaps the most striking thing, ultimately, about Plato's allusion to the Crypteia is what he *does not say about it*: two features of it, which to us, given the sources at our disposal, appear fundamental, and which the philosopher does not mention. Firstly, there is nothing about the rule against being seen, which, by contrast, the scholion to this passage was to emphasize. This rule, nevertheless, forms part of the essence of the Crypteia, to the point where it has given it its name; Plato could not have been ignorant of it. It is, therefore, because he did not judge it useful to mention it. He is not compiling a notice, but he gives someone this speech, in the course of a certain argument which, here, concerns the tests. So, one might well say, Megillos should have mentioned it, because the rule against being seen *is part* of the test, and even constitutes the essence of it. All well and good; but Megillos' theme is more specific than that: preparation for war requires exercises to inure men to hardship (καρτερήσεις τῶν ἀλγηδόνων), and this rule is not one of them.

Plato says nothing, either, about the hunting of helots, which occupies so important a place in Aristotle's account, cited by Plutarch. The explanation put forward above does not appear to hold good in this case, since the test this hunting represents, although not, strictly speaking, an exercise to inure men to hardship, is still difficult and dangerous, and could perfectly well qualify as a preparation for war. So we should consider, provisionally at least, until we come to examine the scholion, the possibility that Plato might simply have had no knowledge of this aspect of the Crypteia. It only comes to light with Aristotle: perhaps it is he who found out about it and made it known.

Aristotle's description

Herakleides, fr. 10 Dilts = Aristotle, fr. 611, 10 Rose = 143, 1, 2, 10 Gigon.

> λέγεται δὲ καὶ τὴν κρυπτὴν εἰσηγήσασθαι, καθ' ἣν ἔτι καὶ νῦν ἐξίοντες ἡμέρας κρύπτονται, τὰς δὲ νύκτας μεθ' ὅπλων…καὶ ἀναιροῦσι τῶν Εἱλώτων ὅσους ἂν ἐπιτήδειον ᾖ.
>
> It is said that he [Lycurgus] also set up the Crypteia, whereby, even to this day, men go out of the city to hide by day, and by night in arms…and slaughter helots as they think necessary.[6]

Plutarch, *Lyc.* 28.1–7 = Aristotle, fr. 538 Rose = 543 Gigon.

1. In none of this is there any trace of the inequitable spirit and desire to dominate, for which some people censure Lycurgus' laws, saying that while they may be admirably suited to whipping up courage, they lack anything that might foster the practising of justice. 2. It is the so-called Crypteia (if, indeed, that really is one of Lycurgus' institutions, as Aristotle states) that may have inspired Plato in his opinion of the Spartan constitution and its author. 3. ἦν δὲ τοίαδε· τῶν νέων οἱ ἄρχοντες διὰ χρόνου τοὺς μάλιστα νοῦν ἔχειν δοκοῦντας εἰς τὴν χώραν ἄλλως ἐξέπεμπον, ἔχοντας ἐγχειρίδια καὶ τροφὴν ἀναγκαίαν, ἄλλο δ' οὐδέν· 4. οἱ δὲ μεθ' ἡμέραν μὲν εἰς ἀσυνδήλους διασπειρόμενοι τόπους ἀπέκρυπτον ἑαυτοὺς καὶ ἀνεπαύοντο, νύκτωρ δὲ κατίοντες εἰς τὰς ὁδοὺς τῶν Εἱλώτων τὸν ἁλισκόμενον ἀπέσφαττον. 5. πολλάκις δὲ καὶ τοὺς ἀγροὺς ἐπιπορευόμενοι τοὺς ῥωμαλεωτάτους καὶ κρατίστους αὐτῶν ἀνῄρουν.

This is how it worked: from time to time the authorities would send out into the countryside, though with no specific objective, those of the *neoi* whom they judged most intelligent, supplied only with daggers and essential rations, nothing else. 4. By day, dispersed in concealed positions, they stayed hidden, and rested; at night they came down onto the roads and cut the throat of any helot they could lay their hands on. 5. Often, too, they would range through the fields, killing the strongest and most influential of them.

6. Likewise, Thucydides records in his *History*... (there follows a summarized account of the massacre of the Two Thousand, 4.80.3–4). 7. Aristotle also states specifically that the ephors themselves, as soon as they enter office, declare war on the helots, so that anyone can kill them without incurring pollution.

Although on the surface it is simple, the sentence that constitutes §3 raises a problem of meaning. The most commonly accepted interpretation[7] renders τῶν νέων the complement of οἱ ἄρχοντες, which obviously then poses the problem of working out who these 'leaders of the *neoi*' could have been. On reflection, I have chosen the other possibility: it seems to me that by starting off the sentence thus, the genitive τῶν νέων must have a partitive sense ('among the *neoi*'), governed by the superlative τοὺς μάλιστα νοῦν ἔχειν δοκοῦντας...ἐξέπεμπον ('they sent out those who seemed to them the most intelligent'). *Exeunt*, therefore, the 'leaders of the *neoi*'; as for οἱ ἄρχοντες, this term presents no difficulty: Plutarch often uses it, in Spartan contexts, to designate a vague reality which might be expressed 'the authorities', but behind which we could also, in certain cases at least, set a specific institution – the ephors: thus, for instance, *Agesilaos* 17.2, and *Lyc.* 18.6 and 8.

A fair proportion of the indications given by this major text will not come in for comment here, since they will be brought to bear on the discussion about the operating of the Crypteia. For now, let us confine our attention to questions concerning the relationship between the text and its source.

Aristotle is only cited expressly on two details: the opinion (on which Plutarch casts doubt) that the Crypteia is a Lycurgan institution (§2), and the declaration of war (§7). These are somewhat marginal points, but, on the one hand, these two references 'frame' the text, which thereby seems to be placed fairly and squarely at Aristotle's door, and, principally, they confirm that he had devoted some discussion to the Crypteia in his *Lakedaimonion Politeia*. On the other hand, the limited nature of Aristotle's references shows that Plutarch is not citing him literally, but is probably summarizing a markedly longer text, which means that he could have altered it, either on certain details or even in its actual meaning: that is where the problem lies.

What is chiefly interesting about Herakleides' statement is that it confirms the Aristotelian origin of the main tenet of this discussion. It is, in fact, acknowledged that his 'extracts from the *Politeiai*' are made up of passages or *résumés* of passages from the *Politeiai* of Aristotle.[8] Now, this statement could pass for a *résumé*, a very brief but acceptable one, of what is contained in Plutarch's version. It leaves out some important details: the fact that the members of the Crypteia are chosen, the duration of the test (but then, Plutarch scarcely says anything about this!), the notions of 'highland' and 'lowland' which, in Plutarch's account, are linked to day and night. He alters one of the details, to do with weapons. This alteration seems to be a substantial one, since, in the classical era, ἐγχειρίδια are not classed as ὅπλα; but this probably amounts to no more than a slip. He even adds a detail, ἔτι καὶ νῦν, ('even to this day'); but it is easy to understand why this piece of information, if it does go back to Aristotle,[9] might not have survived in Plutarch's text. On the whole, however, the *résumé* preserves the essential point; but it does somewhat neglect the institutional aspect, in favour of concentrating on the Crypteians' activities, which are structured, as in Plutarch's account, by the opposition between diurnal and nocturnal occupation.

We can discern quite clearly what, in Plutarch's text, might correspond to his own interests and opinions. (a) The defence of Lycurgus (towards whom Aristotle should have been as critical as he is in the *Politics*), and hence the doubt cast (and made explicit at §13) on the Lycurgan origin of the Crypteia. (b) The idea that Plato's criticism of Spartan education rests essentially on the existence of the Crypteia; the idea is very largely erroneous, but it is true that Plato groups the Crypteia with the forms of training for war, and that it is because Spartan education is only a preparation for war that it comes in for his criticism. (c) The interpretation of the massacre of the Two Thousand as being connected in some way (which remains, moreover, completely obscure) with the Crypteia. It is evident that these points are marginal to the subject itself.

Concerning other points which, by contrast, are central to the subject, it is more difficult to determine which of them should be attributed to each of the two authors. They are, in order of increasing importance:

1. The connection between the declaration of war and the Crypteia. For Plutarch, legitimating the killing of helots by Crypteians was the sole purpose of this annual proclamation. One might be tempted to attribute to him the genesis of this interpretation, because it fits into the overall design of chapter 28, which is both to level criticism at the Spartans' treatment of the helots, and to acquit Lycurgus of responsibility for it. But it seems almost certain that the proposition 'so that anyone can kill them without incurring pollution', at §7, forms part of the quotation from Aristotle, which, here, is very short. Now, these words are, without possible doubt, an allusion to the Crypteia. So it really is to Aristotle that this explanation for the declaration of war is traceable; it is presented as a kind of wile, which emphasizes Spartan hypocrisy. Besides, it is not actually inaccurate, since the Crypteia was indeed one of the circumstances in which the declaration of war, which, according to Libanius' powerful statement (*Or.* 25.63), was the equivalent of a 'licence to kill', was implemented; but it was not the only one, and it served periodically to reaffirm one of the fundamental norms of the condition of helotage in general.[10]

2. The two versions of the killing of helots. I still[11] regard these as contradictory: either a helot was indeed taken at random (anyone the Crypteians came upon), or the victims were those already designated by the authorities (on the grounds that they were the most dangerous). The conjunctive phrase 'Often, too', as the means by which Plutarch tries to accommodate both of these methods, is purely a rhetorical device. Should this contradiction be attributed to Aristotle? Herakleides' *résumé* mentions only one version, but his mode of expression is vague enough to fit both cases. Nonetheless, it should be noted that he only indicates the number of victims, and not their circumstances. In any case, Rose ended his Aristotelian fragment 538 at ἀπέσφαττον, and in my opinion he was right. I view the ἄλλως of §3 as a confirmation of this: if the Crypteians had been sent on a mission with specific targets, lists, addresses, descriptions, how could Aristotle have said that they were sent out 'with no specific objective'?

Furthermore, Plutarch's twofold presentation rests on a contrast between κατίοντες εἰς τὰς ὁδούς/τοὺς ἀγροὺς ἐπιπορευόμενοι, which leaves us with a puzzle. These 'roads' and 'tilled fields' are both part of the same kind of space, 'the lowlands', where the Crypteians move about by night. Why, when helots were caught 'on the roads' was this done at random, yet when they were caught 'in the fields' it was by design? Lévy proposes an ingenious solution to this difficulty. Pointing out that at night the helots were probably in their homes, (in fact, without going so far as to talk, as Wallon does, in terms of 'a curfew', one must admit that 'home' would have been the best place for them), he translates τοὺς ἀγροὺς as 'the farms'. That has the merit of making sense, but is it not by forcing the Greek? If that was what Plutarch meant, he could have used Strabo's term κατοικίαι.[12] It would also raise the question of when and why the Crypteians switched from the first method to the second. Here, I shall confine myself to demonstrating the importance of this discussion. To state that helots were killed at random is to emphasize the senseless, wanton, savage character of these murders. The complexion of this custom alters completely if the Crypteians were doing no more than carrying out decisions instigated by the authorities. It is the very nature of the Crypteia, therefore, that is at issue here. This was already the subject of debate in antiquity, and the two scenarios combined by Plutarch correspond, in reality, to two opposing conceptions of the Crypteia.

3. Plutarch's text is constructed and written in such a way as to demonstrate that the killing of helots was the Crypteia's sole purpose. The notion of training and being tested, which is central to Plato's account, is almost wholly absent from Plutarch's. The Crypteians had provisions at their disposal, there is no mention of their going barefoot or sleeping on the ground. They are equipped with daggers, and even the rule against being seen (the etymology of ἀπέκρυπτον is self-explanatory) seems, logically, dictated by these killings: Crypteians have to rest, necessarily by day, without being seen by their future victims. This really is helot-hunting. Was this how Aristotle put it? Despite its brevity, Herakleides' *résumé* gives grounds for thinking that it was. Aristotle attributed the institution of the Crypteia to Lycurgus; to present it as a supremely cruel custom provided him with yet another occasion for criticizing the Spartan lawgiver; it is against this that Plutarch is rebelling.

Even so, the information supplied by Aristotle himself does not agree on every count with the interpretation of it (largely polemical, no doubt) which he then gives. If its chief purpose was to maintain the obedience of the helots through terror, why go about it in so bizarre a fashion? Why were the agents of this repression only active 'from time to time'? Why was their weaponry strictly limited? Why was their assignment complicated by the strange rule against being observed by, and hence communicating with, the rest of the citizen body? It seems to me that the adverb ἄλλως, which places all the action of the Crypteia under the heading of the random and irrational, testifies to the underlying presence, in this text, of that impression of wantonness which Aristotle would have received when faced with certain aspects of the Crypteia. Thus his description moves further, and in another direction, from the interpretation he espouses, precisely because his text is not a rational reconstruction, pure and simple (in those cases coherence is always admirable), but, unlike Plato's, is a true description of a complex reality.

The scholion to Plato (*Laws* 1.633b9)

ἠφίετό τις ἀπὸ τῆς πόλεως νέος ἐφ' ᾧτε μὴ ὀφθῆναι ἐπὶ τοσόνδε χρόνον. ἠναγκάζετο οὖν τὰ ὄρη περιερχόμενος καὶ μήτε καθεύδων ἀδεῶς, ἵνα μὴ ληφθῇ, μήτε ὑπηρέταις χρώμενος μήτε σιτία ἐπιφερόμενος διαζῆν. ἄλλο δὲ καὶ τοῦτο γυμνασίας εἶδος πρὸς πόλεμον· ἀπολύοντες γὰρ ἕκαστον γυμνὸν προσέταττον ἐνιαυτὸν ὅλον ἔξω ἐν τοῖς ὄρεσι πλανᾶσθαι, καὶ τρέφειν ἑαυτὸν διὰ κλοπῆς καὶ τῶν τοιούτων, οὕτω ὥστε μηδενὶ κατάδηλον γένεσθαι. διὸ καὶ κρύπτεια ὠνόμασθαι· ἐκολάζοντο γὰρ οἱ ὁπουδήποτε ὀφθέντες.

A young man would be sent out of the city, with orders to avoid detection for a certain length of time. He was therefore forced to live wandering the mountains, sleeping with one eye open so as not to be caught, and without being able to use slaves or carry provisions. This was also a form of training for war, since each young man was sent out naked, having been ordered to spend an entire year wandering outside the city, up in the mountains, and to keep himself alive by stealing and other shifts of that kind, and to do it in such a way as to avoid being seen by anybody. This is why it was called the Crypteia: because those who had been seen, wherever that might occur, would be punished.

On the whole there are no problems with the sense, except on two points, of differing degrees of importance. Lévy has translated ἐπὶ τοσόνδε χρόνον 'over so long a period'. Since the scholiast has said nothing as yet about the duration of the exercise, the supposition is that he is anticipating, as he thinks of what he is going to say. It is simpler to read, as Piérart does (1974, 279–80), 'over a designated period', that is to say, one fixed by the authorities: what follows shows this to be one year. On the other hand, Lévy, who regards the expression τις ἀπὸ τῆς πόλεως νέος as a single unit, translates it 'a young man of the city', and comments (1988, 249): 'the expression could indicate that the writer was hesitant about describing them yet as citizens'. In itself, this commentary is entirely unexceptionable, since, as we saw in chapter 3, the *hēbōntes* are not full citizens; but the translation is difficult to accept, and in any case Lévy, 2003, has abandoned it. That of Piérart, which I have adopted in this instance, is to be preferred for two reasons: first, and chiefly, because the Greek should be construed such that ἀπὸ relates to ἠφίετο and not to νέος; furthermore, if more is needed, because in the second sentence (which is really a second version of the text), ἀπὸ τῆς πόλεως is replaced by ἔξω and thus clearly means 'outside the city'.

Here we are tackling quite another kind of text, and one that is difficult to place in a temporal context. There is a strong chance that this scholion, probably composed, like its fellows, in the ninth century, reflects detail lifted from a commentary on the *Laws* by Proklos (fifth century). That said, it is among the better examples of what this very uneven genre has to offer. It is a genuine commentary on Plato's text. Firstly, it brings out its general idea and (apparently, at least) follows it accurately, as it attempts to show in what respects the Crypteia is actually a test and a form of military training, and it does that without becoming bogged down in a plodding repetition or paraphrase of the philosopher's statement. The details which appear in Plato are repeated, but in a manner both succinct and allusive; thus, everything he says about the 'negative' equipment of the Crypteia is summarized simply by γυμνός; the reference to winter is ostensibly omitted, but is actually insinuated in the stated duration of the Crypteia exercise, this being a full year. The absence of slaves, and the wandering life are also reiterated, and in clear terms. The scholiast does not mention the lack of mattresses, but, curiously enough, the result of that lack reappears here as the result of something else: for here, too, the Crypteian does not get much sleep, but this time the reason is psychological (the fear of being caught) rather than practical.

The scholiast is not content, however, just to follow Plato more or less; he furnishes explanations and supplementary information, as any good annotator should. He is able to deal with details such as the duration (very important), the mountainous location (Plato speaks merely of 'territory'), and the obligation to steal. He also deals with an absolutely essential point, the rule against being seen. This is a remarkable scholion, therefore, which deserves to be studied as a text in its own right.

Its structure is curious. It juxtaposes two descriptive discourses, separated by an explanatory sentence that takes up afresh Plato's general idea, that of training for war. Ostensibly, then, the first discourse is intended as a simple statement of what the Crypteia consisted of (from a standpoint which is also Plato's, namely the sort of life led by Crypteians), while the second, introduced by γὰρ, would have the function of justifying the interpretation which the scholiast, taking his cue from Plato, places on this custom. This is certainly what the author meant to do; but if we place the two discourses side by side, we discover that the content of both is practically the same: the first is every bit as explanatory as the second and, except where the duration of the test is concerned, it contains slightly more, even, in the way of detail. There is no real difference, then, between the 'description' and the 'explanation'; this arrangement is pure artifice.

The text presents another peculiarity, a more important one in that it concerns the content. The scholiast is following not just one lead, as he would like to make us believe, but two; one idea is displayed very clearly, since it is Plato's: that of the Crypteia as a military training exercise. So, the scholiast does his job, putting himself at the service of the author upon whom he is commenting, justifying his point of view, and also adding new material in support of it. Such, apparently at least, is the function of the second sentence. This intention accounts for the use of words from a military vocabulary, ἀφιέναι and ἀπολύειν, which are not present in Plato's text;[13] but, oddly, when he comes to describe the despatching of the Crypteian on an assignment, the scholiast uses verbs appropriate to a demobilization register, as though this were a case of granting leave of absence.

It certainly seems as though he really did think something of this kind. In fact, the second major idea, which is not displayed as the first had been, although neither is it introduced surreptitiously, is that the fundamental nature of the Crypteia hinges on the order given to the young man, that he spend a period of time without letting anyone see him: this is something of which there is not the slightest hint in Plato's text. It is articulated in the opening and closing sentences; hence this idea frames the text, just as the other constitutes the core of it. If the scholiast articulates it in the first place, it is because, in this too, he is doing his job. The rules of the scholiast's profession actually require him to begin by explaining Plato's *word*, Crypteia, and for that to supply its etymology. In his eyes, this task is his first duty to his readers; that is why he returns to it at the end, and this time in an absolutely explicit manner (διὸ καὶ… 'this is why it is called the Crypteia').

All the behaviour described in the first part of the text is presented as the logical consequence of the order given to the Crypteian ('he was therefore forced…'): to live in the mountains, to move endlessly from place to place, not to be attended by slaves but to remain on his own, and perhaps not even to carry supplies (because they would hamper his movements?). Now, this obligation to hide, an obligation so important that it has given birth to the name, proceeds neither from the character that is attributed to the Crypteia of a military training exercise (a hoplite has not the slightest need to hide), nor even from whatever might be useful or logical about it: the order is given, and that is that. Someone who presents the matter in this way can only have viewed the Crypteia as an absolutely gratuitous activity.[14] That the scholiast saw it very much in that light is confirmed, in my opinion, by one of the details he supplies about the Crypteian: he did not sleep deeply, he says, so as not to be taken by surprise. According to this conception of the Crypteia, it would be natural for the young man to sleep at night: there is no question here of the inverted bio-rhythm. Who on earth, then, would be in a position to surprise a young man, isolated in the heart of the wilderness, in the middle of the night? It is not the normal hour to be travelling in the mountains; this could not occur by accident. So the scholiast would appear to be suggesting that, after having sent the young men off to hide, the authorities would send others in pursuit of them (which is logical, after all);

the night was the favourable time to surprise the young men in their sleep. Lévy is quite right, then, to talk (1988, 250) of 'a sort of immense game of hide-and-seek'.

There is a discrepancy between the two main ideas, the two sides of the text: for, either the Crypteia was indeed a type of military training, hence something logical and functional, or it really was a kind of game (but a *serious* game). We have gained the impression that there is already a whisper of this incoherence in Aristotle's account, but it is much more perceptible here. It is all the more surprising to find the same information being used successively, to show first that the Crypteia was a sort of hiding-game, and then that it was a crisply organized course of military training. Between these two views, somehow, there hovers the word γυμνός. One might be tempted to interpret it in the technical, military sense, which, in the archaic and classical eras, it can have: without heavy armour. That is what Lévy (1988, 250) has suggested, and this interpretation could be relying on the fact that this notion of 'bareness' only occurs in that part of the text that seeks to justify the military explanation; but, as the content of the two parts is more or less the same, this argument does not carry much weight. I am more inclined, as I have already indicated, to think that this word is intended to encapsulate everything Plato says about the Crypteian's total lack of personal kit. The term is certainly extreme, and the scholiast uses it rather as a kind of metaphor. There is, however, in Plato's description, one part of the young man's body that is effectively 'bare': the feet. This detail could have struck the scholiast or his source, because it is charged with a meaning to which we shall return later on.

This is a remarkable text, then, and in many respects. One of the most striking of these is its originality relative to that of Aristotle, whose discourse on the Crypteia one might think had rapidly become the *locus classicus* on the subject. This text differs from it, firstly, on certain points regarding organization: the Crypteia lasts for a year, whereas in Aristotle's account it appears brief; rather than being a hunter, the Crypteian becomes, as Lévy so admirably expresses it (1988, 250), the quarry hunted by other men; instead of carrying provisions (this point is, here, categorically denied), to obtain food he must look to his own devices. These include stealing, to which the scholiast draws attention by presenting it both, implicitly, as a necessity consequent upon the duration of the exercise and the lack of provisions, and, explicitly, as the result of an *order* given by the authorities (προσέταττον). This last detail accentuates its resemblance to the stealing, likewise obligatory, that was practised as part of the course of education. Rather than regarding this as a confusion perpetrated by the scholiast or his source, it would be better to treat it, as in the case of Plato's text, as a revival (whether real or supposed is a separate issue), in the

Crypteia, of rules of conduct laid down during that education, and hence as a kind of regression to childhood.

There is one final, and absolutely crucial, difference from Aristotle: there is no question here of helot-hunting, nor, therefore, of weapons, nor of the inverted diurnal/nocturnal rhythm. This absence poses a very serious problem, since, if it can be assumed that the scholiast is restricted to repeating what is stated by his source, which could in this instance be the commentary of Proklos, it is difficult to believe that the latter would not have known what Aristotle had said about the Crypteia. Up until now, the only explanation that has been put forward is that the scholiast's silence, or that of his source, would have been the result of his faithful adherence to the text on which he is commenting. On reflection, this explanation seems to me scarcely credible. To suppose that, in adhering to his text, a commentator, whoever he might be – even a Platonist like Proklos – could have refrained from displaying his erudition by adding to his explanations details drawn from other sources, is to invest him with a rigour and an intellectual austerity that did not, in general, typify scholars of this kind. Our own scholar, moreover, makes no exception: the fact that Plato might not have mentioned the rule against being seen does not prevent the scholiast from not only speaking of it but even making it one of the principal elements in his notice. So we must infer that he *chose* to follow a source other than Aristotle, probably another *Lakedaimonion Politeia*, which, being more favourably disposed than he was towards Sparta and, especially, towards Lycurgus, gave a more anodyne image of the Crypteia by dint of remaining silent on the murder of helots. This in turn suggests that after the end of the fourth century, alongside the tradition stemming from Aristotle, and followed (with some adjustments on the subject of Lycurgus' culpability) by Plutarch, there also existed, in Greek historiography, a view of the Crypteia, perhaps an earlier one since we encounter it in Plato, in which there was no helot-hunting. Apparently, then, it was possible to conceive of the Crypteia without it. Why? It is one of the questions to which we will have to return.

Texts to be discarded

1. Phylarchos: the Crypteia as a military unit

Plutarch, *Cleomenes* 28 (in his account of the Battle of Sellasia).

> 2. Phylarchos, on the other hand, claims that treason was the chief cause of Cleomenes' defeat (...) 4. καλέσας δὲ Δαμοτέλη τὸν ἐπὶ τῆς κρυπτείας τεταγμένον, ὁρᾶν ἐκέλευσε καὶ ζητεῖν ὅπως ἔχει τὰ κατὰ νώτου καὶ κύκλῳ τῆς παρατάξεως, 'he summoned Damoteles, the commander of the Crypteia, and despatched him with orders to observe and investigate what was going on at the rear of, and around, the lines'.

§2 shows that, in this part of his account, Plutarch is citing or summarizing Phylarchos, so this is an excellent source.

Here, the Crypteia is manifestly something altogether different from what we encounter through Plato and Aristotle. This is a *corps* of troops, organized and certainly permanent, and doubtless made up of *neoi*. It specializes in a particular kind of mission, to observe without being observed, whereas the 'classical' Crypteian had only to avoid being seen and did nothing in the way of observation. This *corps*, as is usual in a military unit, had one commander and one only, whereas the Crypteians in the preceding texts had none, in the strict sense: all the authorities do is to choose them, and thereafter they appear to be equals, except where, for a specific operation, they might choose a commander between themselves. The Spartan army is thus endowed (at what period? Is this only after the reforms of Cleomenes, or before? We do not know) with a *corps* of observer-scouts. Phylarchos' account shows clearly that these are not sentries or look-outs, but *active* observers who go out into the field to gather intelligence.

This type of activity in the Greek armies is a subject that has only recently begun to attract interest. In the relevant chapter of his great work on warfare, Pritchett[15] demonstrates the near-absence of intelligence-gathering in the wars of the fifth century (notably the Peloponnesian), and again in the first half of the fourth century. Then, armies only had sentries; the first text to hint at active intelligence-gathering is a passage of the *Anabasis*, where what is being described is not a straightforward Greek war. As long as the Greek cities are relying on hoplite battle, active intelligence-gathering appears negligible. Thereafter, it begins to evolve.

Among the names used to designate members of these intelligence units, there has recently been occasion to claim a place for *kryptoi*, which is absent from Pritchett's list.[16] Thanks to the discovery of a new fragment, this is how Knoepfler,[17] taking up a suggestion which was made by Garlan but which no one had echoed since, interprets the word *kryptoi*, present in a decree of the *dēmotai* of Rhamnous honouring the general Epichares (268/7), to mean look-outs. These look-outs formed a permanent and specialized *corps* of troops, as is demonstrated by another decree in which the wording of the decision formula runs ἔδοξε τοῖς κρυπτοῖς. Knoepfler concludes, quite justifiably: 'To move from that to thinking of the *kryptoi* as having existed in most of the hellenistic armies (...) takes just a step, and an easy one at that'. In any event, it is clear that the Spartan *kryptoi* were not an isolated case in the second half of the third century.

In the circumstances, we can take it as read that this form of the Crypteia is something of a different order altogether from what Plato and Aristotle describe. I am not saying that the two were completely unrelated; that would be remarkable indeed, given that they have the same name. There are two possibilities to choose from. Either these two types of the Crypteia existed successively, the second having appeared coincidentally with the disappearance of the first, or even being formed after a 'hiatus'. Or, the two types actually co-existed, at least for a time, in which case, the 'old-style' Crypteia could have constituted a recruitment test or period of training that was aiming towards the other type.[18] The answer we choose may depend on the date at which we think the 'classical' Crypteia ceased to exist: this is yet another problem to which we shall have to return.

Be that as it may, it is now clear that this passage of Phylarchos can no longer be regarded as a source on the Crypteia as it is usually understood.

2. Justin on Spartan education

This text was cited above (p. 184). I agree entirely with Lévy's assessment that, here, Justin is speaking not of the Crypteia, but of Spartan education in general. What confirms this is his description, in another passage (13.1), of the Lucanians' education system, where he begins by saying that it 'conforms to the laws of the Lacedaemonians'. It seems, nevertheless, that the picture painted in these two texts may be powerfully influenced by the image of the Crypteia held by the author (Pompeius Trogus).[19] Education was conducted 'in the country' (Sparta), 'in the woods' (Lucania); the young men had to do without slaves (Lucania), clothing (Lucania), bedding (both texts); they did not eat coarse gruel (Sparta), they lived on what they had hunted, and drank only milk or water (Lucania). All of this bears a close resemblance to Plato's passage on the Crypteia, with elaborations which show that these descriptions are being used to draw attention to a *cliché*, that of 'life in the wild'. This is why Justin cannot in any way be considered a usable source on the Crypteia.

THE FUNCTIONING OF THE CRYPTEIA

Only three texts are of any use, therefore, when attempting a description of the Crypteia – Plato, Aristotle, and the scholion to Plato; but, on the one hand, anyone who takes an interest in Sparta will be no stranger to such a state of affairs (three texts could even be regarded as a lot); and, on the other, the texts are good ones. The scholion could, to a large extent, be regarded as forming a whole with Plato's text, even though it says more than the original; in which case, the number of versions would be reduced to two. Between these two, the contradictions are so numerous and so important (for example, with the helots, or without the helots) that to claim to be presenting a unique and coherent portrait of the Crypteia 'as it really was' seems dangerous; nevertheless, I shall try. What seems certain to me is that both are aiming to describe the same institution. My first conclusion, and this is important because the matter has been seriously called in question, will be that, in Sparta, there really did exist a custom known as the Crypteia, a custom which consisted of sending out of the city, at certain times, a certain number of young men to live for a certain length of time under difficult conditions, without letting themselves be seen by anyone. But, as soon as we attempt to go into detail, difficulties begin to arise.

The age of Crypteians

Only Aristotle gives any indication of this: these are *neoi*, that is, in Xenophon's terminology, *hēbōntes*. It would be nice to know whether their membership of the Crypteia took effect at the beginning or the end of this stage of their lives, but there is nothing for us to go on, and we do not even know whether there was a rule on the subject.

Recruitment

On this point, too, Aristotle (although the phrase is more probably Plutarch's) is very vague: there are 'the authorities' (οἱ ἄρχοντες) who 'send' the young men 'into the countryside', after having, undoubtedly, also chosen them. I think this is one of those cases where we might risk identifying these 'authorities' as the ephors: as we have seen, it is not the *paidonomos* who wields supreme authority over the *hēbōntes*, but the ephors. It is possible that, when making their choice, they may have consulted with the *hippagretai*; these must actually have known all the young men very well, since they had selected the *hippeis* from among them, with the obligation to justify their choice. On the criterion governing the recruitment of Crypteians, Aristotle supplies an interesting detail: it was not (or not only) physical strength, courage, or discipline, as was usually the case, but intelligence. This criterion reflects the way in which the authorities regarded the Crypteia and the qualities that it required: intelligence, in this instance, should be understood to mean cunning and even trickery. All the activity of the Crypteian thus comes under the heading of a cunning intelligence.

The Crypteians appear, then, as an elite who are being put to the test: they had first to be chosen, and then to show themselves worthy of that choice. The mechanism whereby this elite was chosen is somewhat reminiscent of that used for the *hippeis*, and we may assume that, in practice, the Crypteians must almost all have been drawn from among those who had already been recruited as *hippeis*, this *corps* being, obviously, much larger. The Crypteia thereby takes on a specific and almost institutional meaning, as a stage in the selection process that was permanently in operation among the *hēbōntes*. It is possible, moreover, that the business did not end there. Herodotos (1.67) says that from among the *hippeis* who were leaving their *corps* having reached the upper age limit (30 years), five *agathoergoi* were chosen annually, who remained in the service of the city for another year. Now from what we know of them, the missions of these *agathoergoi* are not unlike those of the Crypteia: they are often solitary, often carried on outside, and sometimes far away from, Laconia, they are secret in character and more akin to intelligence gathering or 'special operations' than they are to diplomacy. It seems logical, then, to suppose that the former Crypteians, already having been recruited for activities which called more for guile than for strength, constituted a kind of 'pool' from which the *agathoergoi* were later selected. The stages of a 'career' in the service of the city thus take shape.

Number

The number of those who were chosen each time is an important point, on which we have not a single piece of real evidence. In Plato's text, the argument of Megillos, who presents the Crypteia as a form of training for war, would logically suppose that all young men were subject to it, but that is certainly not what Plato believed. Conversely, the scholiast talks as if there was only one member of the Crypteia, but that is because, when he writes 'they sent a young man ...' he is anticipating what kind of life, according to *his* version, this young man will be leading. As for Aristotle, he is the only one to use the plural. So we can only construct hypotheses, based on the nature of the Crypteia itself. The implication seems to be that Crypteians were not very numerous, perhaps a dozen or so being selected at a time.

Frequency

The only author to touch upon this aspect is Aristotle, but the expression he uses, διὰ χρόνου, 'from time to time', tells us next to nothing. It might seem indicative of an irregular frequency, but we cannot be certain. The scholiast, who thought the test lasted for a year and thereby assimilated it to a sort of state 'duty', is perhaps also envisaging the frequency as annual; thus, in his view, there would always be members of the Crypteia in action. An annual frequency, comparable to that of a religious rite, seems to me the most plausible.

Duration

For the scholiast, then, this is one year. Aristotle says nothing on the subject, but the fact that, in his version, the Crypteians carried 'essential rations' seems to me to imply a relatively short duration. It appears, therefore, that, on this point, there is a distinct divergence between the two texts. The only way to choose is to assess their plausibility. It would be manifestly difficult for the Crypteian to survive for a whole year under the conditions described in the scholion, living on what he could provide for himself, particularly when he must do it without encountering a single human being. This, then, is a point in Aristotle's favour. The duration indicated by the scholiast may stem from his view of the Crypteia as a sort of *ephēbeia*. Plato raises the subject of winter, in terms, even, to suggest that the whole test took place at this time of year; should we infer from this that the choice of season was designed to make the Crypteia even more rigorous?

Place

Aristotle's indications are not detailed, but they are all logically connected: the Crypteians are despatched 'into the countryside', they are dispersed 'in concealed positions', and, finally, at night 'they come down' to search for helots. The picture that emerges is one of a wooded mountain. The scholiast twice specifies 'the mountains', a point on which he is in complete agreement with Aristotle. It is just the sort of place logic would suggest. The Crypteian is able not only to hide there, but also to find water and trap game. By virtue of his wandering the mountains, he is, to a certain extent, like the *orophylakes*, the 'mountain guards', who will be discussed further on; but, as the texts make plain, he guards nothing and he patrols nowhere.

It would be nice to be able to identify these mountains precisely. Cartledge[20] has posed the inevitable question: Laconia or Messenia? He opts for Messenia because, in his view, the Crypteia is a genuine agent of repression against the helots, and the most dangerous of the helots were probably those of Messenian origin. If the Crypteia was not like that, Laconia would be the better option: its mountains (Taygetos, Parnon) offered many a lonely spot favourable to Crypteian activity, and one might reasonably judge that to send young men, so few in number and ill-armed, far away from Sparta, would have been to take a serious risk.

Weapons

This subject is only broached explicitly by Aristotle, which is logical since, obviously, it bears on the killing of helots. The text transmitted by Plutarch is precise: the Crypteian cannot arm himself just as he pleases; he only has the right to carry 'hand weapons', ἐγχειρίδια. In one sense, these are well adapted to the Crypteian way of life, since they are not at all cumbersome and may serve as tools. Vernant has suggested[21] that these hand weapons may have been the sickles discussed above (pp. 212–14). At first glance, that scarcely seems probable, because, although capable of inflicting mortal injuries, they were not actual weapons which would enable the Crypteian, without fail, to get the better of helots equipped with farm implements, and also because they were the characteristic tools of the *paides*. But these arguments may be countered by another, namely that it was for these very reasons that the Crypteians were required to be equipped like this, so as to increase the severity of the test, and to make them regress, in a way, to their childhood. There would remain to establish, though, whether sickles could have been called ἐγχειρίδια.

Apparently, there is no question of weapons in the scholion, which is also logical because, in this case, the Crypteian has no one to kill. Nevertheless, it would be possible to maintain, as Lévy does (1988, 250), that γυμνός, the adjective which the scholiast applies to the Crypteian, has the technical usage 'unarmed' (more precisely, 'without heavy arms', which can agree perfectly well with what Aristotle says); I am more of the opinion, as I have already said, that what the scholiast intends by this word is to epitomize Plato's whole explanation concerning the Crypteian's 'destitution'. Be that as it may, this 'destitution' includes the lack of weapons, and that constitutes yet another difference between Plato and Aristotle.

Equipment

Aristotle makes a very succinct statement about the more-than-summary nature of the Crypteian's equipment: apart from his hand weapon he had nothing (ἄλλο δ' οὐδέν). Plato is much more detailed. There are two things the lack of which seems to him significant of this desire for destitution; he is discerning in his choice since they are two things of which the absence has an obvious symbolic value. The first is the mattress; that the Crypteian should not have merited one (and in any case, how would he have transported it?) does not mean that he had to sleep on the ground. There is nothing to stop him making himself a bed out of fallen branches, a *stibas*, to insulate himself from the bare earth. Now, the *stibas* has a twofold significance: it symbolizes the rugged nature of the soldier's life, and it has a part to play in certain rites of passage; all of this makes it eminently appropriate for the Crypteian. Moreover, as we have seen (above, pp. 26, 185), Plutarch recounts how, at a given moment in their education, the boys would make *stibades* for themselves out of reeds picked from the banks of the Eurotas: thus we meet again the theme of regression towards childhood.

The other missing item is footgear. This detail of *anypodēsia* also takes us back into childhood (above, pp. 7, 189). Likewise, on this subject, we may recall even odder equipment, which consisted in having one foot shod and the other bare; in such a case, the bareness, far from being played down, is, on the contrary, emphasized. This 'mono-sandalism', which often makes its appearance in initiatory contexts, has already been the subject of thorough study, and I shall only hark back to one episode, which is, itself, certainly 'historical': the breakout by the besieged Plataeans, reported by Thucydides.[22]

To embark on this, the Plataeans each wore only one sandal, allegedly to avoid slipping in the mud.[23] Certain details of this narrative are evocative of the Crypteia: the affair takes place at night, as do the Crypteians' activities according to Aristotle; the soldiers are armed only with daggers; the breakout is undertaken by volunteers, hence, men who are self-selected; it is winter; the standing order is 'never be seen'. To be sure, each one of these details may have a logical explanation; but we might also say, along with Vidal-Naquet, that 'they recall, quite naturally, the equipment that figures in rites of adolescence' – in other words, they are disguising themselves as Crypteians.

The absence of slaves

all agree

This is one of the features mentioned by both Plato (with particular insistence) and the scholion. Aristotle does not mention it, but it is hard to see how slaves could play a part in the Crypteians' life as he describes it. How might we interpret the presence to which this absence is opposed? It could mean the young slaves (*mothōnes*) who attended Spartan boys during their education (above, pp. 128–9), but Crypteians are no longer boys, and Lévy[24] is perhaps right to think of military life, where the citizen is normally attended by one or more slaves.

Food

On this subject, the sources are at odds in a quite categorical way, and one which, on the part of the scholion, seems intentional. Plato makes no reference to it; it is only the scholiast who affirms that the young man could not take provisions with him. This is a logical consequence of the duration he allots to the Crypteia: when faced with a whole year, what would be the use of the little he could carry? On the other hand Aristotle, for whom, apparently, the Crypteia was of short duration, says that the Crypteian took with him 'essential rations'. Thus the choice to be made between these two statements will merely follow upon the choice made about the duration, the likelihood being, as we have seen, on Aristotle's side.

Stealing

It is normal for this to be mentioned in the scholion, since it results alike from the duration of the exercise and the ban on carrying provisions. It is only the more remarkable that the scholiast feels the need to state, at the same time, that recourse to stealing was *ordered* by the authorities. Thus he seems to combine two explanations of stealing, the one as a practical necessity, the other as a quite arbitrary 'rule of the game'.

What was really going on? We may be content with Aristotle's silence, and regard stealing (of which Plato makes no mention) as having been inferred by the scholiast, or rather his source, from the rules applying to education, in order to explain how the Crypteian was able to subsist for a whole year on what he could find for himself. This is, surely, what would be most reasonable. All the same, to adopt Aristotle's view on the duration of the Crypteia does not necessarily mean that we must abandon the notion of stealing, which, here, would be a much-needed means of supplementing basic food, just as it was in childhood. I see two reasons to trust the scholiast on this point. Firstly, because, in our study of the Crypteia, we have already encountered, on several occasions, the theme of regression toward childhood. Secondly, because there seems to me to be a resonance between stealing and the untamed life of the Crypteians, to the extent that, when Xenophon describes the preparation for, and execution of, theft in boyhood,[25] we may come away with the impression that what he is describing is the life of the Crypteian.

Hunting

None of the texts we have used mentions this: it only appears in the passage of Justin on the subject of Lucanian education. If I allude to this, it is less on Justin's account than because, as I see it – and especially in the light of Schnapp's book[26] – in a way of life like that of the Crypteian, the pursuit of hunting is essential. Not the aristocratic kind, to be sure, but hunting by night, and with cunning, using nets and snares.

A solitary life?

At first glance, Aristotle and the scholion seem to be completely opposed on this point. The very language used symbolizes this: when they refer to the Crypteians' way of life, one uses the plural, the other the singular.[27] The Crypteians are despatched from the city in a body according to Aristotle, but individually (ἠφίετό τις…νέος) in the scholion. Nevertheless, this opposition is not as radical as it appears here. In Aristotle's version, the Crypteians number several at the time of their being selected, but there is nothing to stop us thinking that the same situation held good for the scholiast, who chose to omit this stage of the proceedings, and that, in his version, it was only when the Crypteian actually set out on his mission that he found himself on his own. In Aristotle's version, the Crypteians probably set off in a body, but, immediately afterwards, they adopt a form of behaviour regulated by the alternation of night and day. By day, each member lives isolated, which is logical since that enables him the better to find cover; this reasoning can be discerned from the text: 'dispersed in concealed positions'. What happens at night? It is far from obvious, and it could be maintained that, in Aristotle's account, when the Crypteians 'come down' to hunt helots, they do so one by one; in which case, there would be no contradiction between the two texts. But I do not believe that that is how Aristotle saw it. The fact that they should be described as 'dispersed' during the day, combined with the contrast, apparently systematic, between diurnal and nocturnal activity, seems to me to imply that after sunset they re-grouped to go hunting helots (which is also logical, as we shall see), although we cannot discover how they set about that re-grouping, nor whether they then formed a single band or split into small detachments. If that is what they did, then the two texts do conflict, and this, too, is logical: given that the scholiast has remained silent on the subject of the Crypteians' nocturnal activities and the murdering of helots, there is no reason why he should then have them re-grouping at night.

'*Never be seen*', μὴ ὀφθῆναι: it is the scholiast who has supplied the most accurate transcription of the standing order, which, undoubtedly, constituted the essence of the Crypteia (at least, during the first period of its existence), given that the name is derived from it. Certainly, from the linguistic point of view, Aristotle's wording, 'to hide (oneself)' (κρύπτονται, Herakleides; ἀπέκρυπτον, Plutarch) comes closer to the name itself, but the interpretation he then places on this obligation means that, in reality, it is not at all the same thing as in the scholion. In fact, Aristotle's Crypteia seems to be organized with one sole aim, to hunt helots, and if its members are required to 'hide', it is so that they may more effectively take them by surprise, just as hunters stay in cover so as not to be seen by their quarry, and as warriors mounting a raid camouflage themselves to gain the advantage of surprise. In the scholion, on the other hand, just as – so I am persuaded – in real life, the standing order is 'never be seen', and to hide is merely the *means* of accomplishing this. Put like this, the orders are not amenable to any rational explanation, and take on the aspect of some kind of ritual *taboo*: the Crypteian must, literally, make himself invisible. By comparison with usual taboos it displays this peculiarity, that, when there has been a transgression, it is not those who have seen that are punished, but those who have *been* seen ('wherever that should occur', adds the scholiast); it is as though the rule of the taboo is reversed. So, it is not to be seen in order not to be seen; this is reminiscent of the rules of a game, or of a ritual regulation. The scholiast's way of explaining this basic rule of the Crypteia is unquestionably much more true to life than the rationalized interpretation given by Aristotle.

Pursuers?

The scholion seems to imply that the Crypteians were sought and pursued day and night, if not by all the other Spartans, at least by some of them. It is obvious that Aristotle, who is silent on the rule 'never be seen', and for whom the Crypteia had one mission, to kill helots, could not have said anything of the kind; on this point again there is a contradiction. I do not know what it consisted of in reality, and the existence of appointed pursuers seems to me, at the least, doubtful. What is certain, however, is that, to have any meaning, the obligation to remain invisible and the sanctions that go with it assume a certain level of co-operation on the part of the people, such that we might expect that, if they could identify such and such a Crypteian, they would inform the authorities. This means that, here, the difference between the two sources is, all things considered, rather slender.

Wandering and exclusion

Wandering is one of the major themes of the Crypteia, and, in my opinion, one of the keys to understanding it, although only as it is described in Plato's version. In fact, 'wandering' does not really appear in Aristotle's account, where the adverb ἄλλως simply indicates that the Crypteians were despatched with no specific objective, without necessarily implying that thereafter they would have 'wandered'. By contrast, Plato and his scholiast use the verb πλανᾶσθαι, and it is significant that it should be Plato's text which, despite its brevity and its deliberately allusive character, devotes the most space and time to stressing this wandering nature (νύκτωρ τε πλανωμένων διὰ πάσης τῆς χώρας καὶ μεθ' ἡμέραν); to the extent that, in his allusion, it is this notion to which the philosopher accords pride of place. In practical terms, viewed from the perspective of having to remain invisible, this wandering habit is odd, since it would be better for the Crypteians, having once found a really lonely spot, to hide themselves away there and move about as little as possible. And yet, the scholion represents wandering as among the consequences that follow from this fundamental watchword, 'never be seen'.

It is thus quite clear that wandering, like the watchword itself, is purely a rule of the game, devoid of any rational purpose; it is suggestive of ritual behaviour. It takes place not only outside the city but outside the areas developed and travelled by people, at the outermost confines of the city's territory. In this wild region, the Crypteians wander, just as do, almost by definition in Greek eyes, exiles, beggars, stateless individuals. Wandering goes with their status; it is the necessary complement of their exclusion and of all the deprivations that set them apart from civic life and civilization: lack of bedding, lack of footwear, lack of slaves. It is a normal element in the picture of that life in the wild which young men, excluded for the time being from their city, are required to lead. Wandering thus resembles a metaphor of the exclusion that gives rise to the Crypteia and resembles ritual practices like those of the *pharmakoi* and the *ver sacrum*.

The diurnal/nocturnal rhythm

This is also a major topic, but, in contrast to the preceding one, it is in

Aristotle's text that it is most clearly implemented. The scholion certainly touches on the Crypteians' nights, but this is only in order to state that the fear of being taken unawares makes them rather unpleasant. In Plato's account, the normal rhythm of life seems to be suspended: the Crypteians 'wander by night as they do by day', and then sleep by day as they do by night, depending on the circumstances. It is with Aristotle that the rhythm is truly *inverted*: they sleep by day and hunt the helots by night. The author does not explain why, but it is easy to work it out: it is in order to have a better chance of surprising the helots that they mount their expeditions by night. Actually, it seems to me that this would almost be to complicate their assignment. The helots have no reason at all to be in the fields or on the roads at night, and, if they know that a Crypteia is operating in the region, they should be hurrying to go and lock themselves in their homes as soon as night falls; to winkle them out from there would certainly not be an easy job nor one free of danger. So the nocturnal character of the Crypteians' activity can scarcely be explained by practical considerations; it seems to be of the same order as wandering and remaining invisible (with which it also has, perhaps, a connection). The result of the suspension (in Plato's account) and, still more, the inversion (in Aristotle's) of the normal rhythm of human activity is to make the Crypteian withdraw, beyond the rough life discussed earlier, into the fierce animality of a nocturnal predator. That is why this subject, in its most complete form, is connected to the following one.

Helot-hunting

This is the last of the grand themes in the tradition concerning the Crypteia, and perhaps the most important, but it is also the most problematic. It is only featured in one of the texts, that of Aristotle. One solution, theoretically possible, and as simple as it is radical, would involve treating helot-hunting as a pure invention on the part of Aristotle or his source, devised, perhaps, on the basis of Thucydides' account (4.80.3) of the massacre of the Two Thousand, and designed to saddle Lycurgus with responsibility for an atrocity. No one, to my knowledge, has yet supported this hypothesis; everyone acknowledges that, at a certain time, this practice was actually in force.[28] But from when? The only reply that, at first glance, might appear at once simple and logical would be to say that it was between the time of Plato and that of Aristotle, let us say between 350 and 330. The problem with this is that between these two dates it is impossible to see either when or why such a change would have come about. Besides, on the one hand, it does not explain the scholiast's silence, and, on the other, if this measure had been so recent, Aristotle could not have claimed that the Crypteia as he saw it, that is, a Crypteia directed wholly towards the killing of helots, was an institution dating back to Lycurgus.

A date after the defeat at Leuctra has been proposed for this change;[29] it does provide the acceptable context of great peril threatening the state, but no longer allows us to explain Plato's silence, and, like the one discussed in the previous paragraph, is vulnerable to the argument attributing the change to Lycurgus. So we are driven further back in time. The most reasonable way to sustain the notion that helot-hunting was introduced into an already-existing Crypteia at a specific moment in history, is to set this moment after the Revolt of 464. It is possible, moreover, to claim that it is Plutarch himself who leads us in this direction when he asserts: 'For my part, I believe that the Spartans only gave themselves over to cruelties of this kind later on, and particularly after the Great Earthquake, when, say the historians, the helots revolted together with the Messenians, wreaking dreadful damage on the country and posing the worst of dangers to the city' (*Lyc.* 28.12). We do not, however, have to believe, as some have done,[30] that, in this passage, Plutarch is speaking of the introduction of helot-killing into an existing Crypteia: it is the Crypteia *in its entirety* that he considers to have been established at this time, as his next sentence indicates: 'For I cannot attribute to Lycurgus so abominable an act as the Crypteia (μιαρὸν οὕτω <τὸ> τῆς κρυπτείας ἔργον), since I judge his character according to the mild and just disposition of which he has otherwise given proof' (28.13). Why did he not hit on the idea of distancing the Crypteia from the murdering of helots? Because his knowledge was based on Aristotle, an author in whose view the murders were the Crypteia's *raison d'être*. So, to assign a date of about 464 for the introduction, into the Crypteia, of helot-hunting, is a modern hypothesis which has its merits but is not really supported by a single text.

Whether we choose the unitary view, which regards helot-hunting as having been part of the Crypteia since its inception,[31] or the dualist theory, according to which it was incorporated into it during the historical period, we have to answer the same question: why did the scholiast describe a Crypteia in which these killings do not feature? For Plato, who does likewise, it may be, as I have suggested, that he was unaware of them, the Crypteia being at that period still very little known. The scholiast, though, or, rather, his source, could not have been ignorant of what certain authors, beginning with Aristotle, had written on the subject. This shows that, from the end of the fourth century or later, there existed two traditions concerning the Crypteia.[32] One, which followed Aristotle, mentioned the murders perpetrated by Crypteians and presented them as the fundamental purpose of this institution. In this way the Crypteia became one further argument against Sparta, and more specifically against Lycurgus: Plutarch, by his very efforts to exculpate the lawgiver, creates an echo of these charges, which, we observe, were without appeal. The other tradition, which was favourable to

Sparta, had the choice of two possibilities: either to pass over the murders in complete silence, or, taking less of a risk, to claim that they had been added at a relatively recent date, and to present the description they give as being that of the 'true' Crypteia, that of Lycurgus.

Be that as it may, we can take it as read that the Crypteia of the classical era entailed the helot-hunting described by Aristotle. It remains for us to find out how it was conducted. As we have seen, Plutarch sets side by side two different scenarios for the choosing of the victim: he would be taken, he says first, at random; the fact that he describes this practice first ought to suggest that it was the most common. But 'often, also', the choice was dictated by the personal qualities of the helot, qualities that made him a threat to Sparta. The order in which Plutarch presents these scenarios seems to signify that the second was adopted when the first had failed to work, that is, when chance had failed to supply a victim. But that is absurd: if the Crypteians had with them hit-lists of helots, these would have to be given priority. If, then, we try to picture the procedure as Plutarch describes it, we end up with nothing of any coherence.

There is nothing surprising in this: the two practices that Plutarch combines are very different in character. The second is strictly rational: a preventative repressive measure methodically executed. In the case of the first, the objective is to kill a helot – any one will do. The second approach does not accord at all with the savage, primitive, regressive character of the Crypteian's way of life, as it is depicted by the text itself. Why, for so important and so dangerous a mission, take such pains, not in order to give those to whom it has been entrusted every possible means of carrying it out, but, by contrast, in order to *deprive* them of those means? This is why, wishing to spare Aristotle the charge of so contradictory a notion, I suggested above that only the first scenario, that of a random choice, featured in his text, and that the second is a rationalized version, perhaps created by making a rash connection with the massacre of the Two Thousand, which Plutarch or his source has paired with the other. I am convinced that, in reality, as in Aristotle's version, the victims were taken at random. In order to perpetrate these murders the Crypteians would re-assemble, which supposes a minimum of organization; this is also the point at which they 'come down again' into civilized space.

I have explained elsewhere[33] what place was occupied by this aspect of the Crypteia in the ritual demeaning of the helots; because it was gratuitous and perpetrated at random, the killing had a symbolic import. It is these characteristics, incontestable in my opinion, of the killing of helots, that lead me to prefer the unitary view of the Crypteia. Indeed it seems to me that if helot-hunting had been added to it at a relatively recent period, the motive for the modification could only have been the aim to intensify, for whatever reason, anti-helotic repression, and that in this situation, the executions would have been carried out in a rational and organized manner.

The end of the Crypteia

If, for us, the Crypteia has no beginning (in that we know nothing about it), it certainly had an end. The imperfect that Plutarch uses when discussing the subject shows that by the Imperial era the Crypteia had ceased to function; that seems to go without saying, but it is worth establishing more precisely that this was so, since other old Spartan institutions had survived into, or had been revived at, this period. The ἔτι καὶ νῦν of Herakleides is no proof that the Crypteia still existed in the second century BC, since he is only an epitomizer and adds nothing of his own; the information comes from Aristotle. Should we link the fate of the Crypteia with that of helotism, which seems to have disappeared at the beginning of the second century BC? Not necessarily. It may have ceased to exist before that (which I could readily believe); it may also have survived or have been re-established later, although, from then on, without the killing of helots.[34] We know that in 222 there existed, in the Spartan army, a scout *corps* known as the Crypteia, but that proves nothing one way or the other. All things considered, then, the end of the Crypteia is shrouded in almost as profound an obscurity as its beginning.

The Crypteia and its contradictions

If we recapitulate the points on which the two traditions concerning the Crypteia contradict each other, we come away with quite an impressive list; but it is possible to reduce it to two major points, of which the others are merely the logical consequences. The first bears on the duration, apparently brief according to Aristotle, and of one year in the scholion. This would be a secondary point if it did not, in reality, reflect a difference of interpretation, the Crypteia being, in the Aristotelian view, a test and a hunt, and something like a duty or *ephēbeia* in the scholion. But the remaining text of the scholion does not present it like that at all, and everything happens as if it was superimposing on the image of the Crypteia as a duty that of the Crypteia as an almost ritual test. What follows upon the view expressed about duration is that in Aristotle's version the Crypteian takes provisions with him whereas in the scholion he is strictly forbidden to do so. To subsist he must resort to shifts of his own, among which stealing is the most significant, though, of course, it is absent from Aristotle's account.

The other major contradiction is the one that concerns helot-hunting. It gives rise to three secondary contradictions. For Aristotle, the Crypteian carries a weapon (admittedly a strictly designated one), whereas in the scholion he is *gymnos*, a word that implies the absence of a weapon, in line with his general lack of equipment. The second contradiction is manifest in the way in which the name Crypteia is explained: if, with Aristotle, the Crypteian 'hides', it is so as to be better placed to surprise the helots, whereas in the scholion the standing order 'never be seen', which explains most of the young man's actions, exists for its own sake. As for the third contradiction, it, too, is a partial one: in Aristotle's account, the Crypteians each 'hide' alone but operate as a unit, whereas according to the scholion their life is wholly solitary.

This way of presenting the 'contradictions in the Crypteia' makes obvious, in my opinion, the fact that, according to a process familiar to every historian, they reflect only a duality of tradition, dictated, fundamentally, by the witnesses' attitude to Sparta in general and to the legislation of Lycurgus in particular. Viewed as a reality, on the other hand, the custom known as the Crypteia displays, despite its complexity (itself due essentially to the problem of the killing of helots), a robust unity.

The structure of a rite

The discourse of ancient authors on the Crypteia is structured according to a very rich set of themes. Let us recapitulate these subjects, beginning with those common (to varying degrees of intensity) to both versions.

– The Crypteian is *surrounded by prohibitions*. The most important is the visual one, but we have also encountered the ban on weapons (except, in Aristotle's version, daggers), as on almost all personal kit (and, in the scholiast's account, provisions).

– *Regression* is the trait whereby the Crypteian's way of life is best characterized. The prohibitions surrounding him have the effect of depriving him of what makes life civilized. Thus he re-experiences some of the conditions that characterized certain periods in his childhood. Finally, in Aristotle's version, the inversion of the diurnal/nocturnal rhythm, and the exclusively nocturnal nature of the Crypteian's activities, cause him to regress further still, into living like a beast of prey.

– *Expulsion and wandering*. Obliged to remain invisible and driven from the city, the Crypteian is excluded from all contact with other Spartans. He must go into exile far from the places frequented by citizens and seek refuge in the wilderness. In such a situation, as Plato emphasizes, all he can do is to wander indefinitely.

– *The murder of helots*. Certainly, we have been able to note, all the way through this analysis, that the Crypteia can quite well be conceived without this element of killing; on the other hand, this may equally appear as the crowning achievement of a custom in which it accentuates, in remarkable fashion, the character of a return to the savagery of primitive man, of an initiatory journey into the 'heart of darkness'.

These features, without any shadow of doubt, characterize the Crypteia as a ritual, as an ultimate test in a process of initiation. But Spartan society is so organized that, according to the process we have met time and again in the field of education, it has, at the same time, a function. This is actually a double function. On the one hand, in its proper place, which is a modest one, it fits into the process of the progressive and repeated selection of elites which begins during education, and only reaches its end with election to the Gerousia. On the other hand, as the executing by chosen 'representatives' of the superior community, of 'representatives' taken at random from the inferior community, it symbolizes and periodically renews the most fundamental structure of Spartan society.

The place of the Spartan Crypteia in the Greek world

Those who have treated the subject of the Crypteia seem tacitly to accept it as an entity peculiar to Sparta. This probably stems from the fact that that city is habitually regarded as essentially different from all others, except, possibly, those of Crete. But we cannot be content with this assumption merely on *a priori* grounds, and, before attempting to interpret this institution, we must see whether we cannot find parallels for it in a Greek world which, after all, has innumerable different facets.[35]

British Museum Papyrus no. 187

(2nd century AD; no. 114 in Milne, *Catalogue of the Literary Papyri in the British Museum*, 1927).

I offer the following translation from the best-preserved section:

> After having received a woollen coat (*chlanis*), a tunic of animal skin (*diphthera*), and a pair of coarse shoes (*kalbateinai*), they then spend two years during which they drink nothing but water, they endure the snow, they dig, they eat only the food issued to them, without following the instructions of doctors or of any regime (*diaita*), and without coming to expect any softness or luxury. Hegesilaos the Laconian was speechless with admiration...

That this might be a description of the Spartan Crypteia, as the original editors, Kenyon and Haussoulier, thought,[36] seems to be contra-indicated at the outset by the use of the ethnic 'Laconian' to refer to Agesilaos.[37] What is being described is an institution that displays some resemblances to the Crypteia but also some important differences from it. The main similarity is that the participants in both cases lead a rugged, almost savage, existence. The text does not specify the setting, but several details (the clothing, the snow, the earthworks) suggest that these are mountains generally situated at the territorial boundaries. The fact that the kit, which is uniform, should be 'received' by the participants, indicates that, like the Crypteia, this 'training period' was organized and supervised by the city.

Among the differences, the most obvious is that of *duration*. That of the Spartan Crypteia is not known to us, though we have seen that it was probably short. The two years mentioned in the papyrus show that this is quite another matter; it is not a temporary test, but a true ephebic or civic duty, like that carried out by Plato's *agronomoi*.[38] The quantitative difference here gives rise to a qualitative one.

The second difference – *equipment*. On the subject of the Spartan Crypteian, Plato is the author most insistent on this point, his aim being to emphasize the destitution which, for him, constitutes the whole rigour of the test. Certainly, our author's intention is akin to this: he means to demonstrate the extent to which the equipment of these 'trainees' is summary and coarse. But, actually, it is neither non-existent nor inappropriate – far from it. The clothing issued to them comprises both a cloth coat [39] and a kind of tunic, the *diphthera*, which is a rustic garment made from animal skin, both warm and waterproof; it is the typical dress of agricultural workers, both slave and free.[40] In contrast to the Spartan Crypteians, these 'trainees' do not go barefoot. They wear footgear called, in the papyrus, *kalbateinai*, the usual form of this noun being *karbatinai*. From several texts we are drawn to picture these as a form of rough protection, essentially consisting of a piece of animal skin, not stitched, but wrapped around the foot and lower leg and kept in place by straps. They were used by peasants, shepherds, and all who had to move about in mountainous terrain. It is clearly the author's intention, then, to underline the excessively rustic, even socially demeaning, character of this equipment, as a way of bringing out the physical and moral endurance of the participants. The anthropologist would most certainly bring in a major distinction between the woven coat, which belongs to the realm of culture, and the two items of equipment made from animal skin, which belong to nature; he would add, not without reason, that this ambiguity is symbolic of that which surrounds the status of these young men, who, presumably, are completing their journey towards being recognized in the rank of full citizens. The historian, for his part, would note that the rustic nature of this equipment does not make it any less complete and well-suited to the assignment laid on the young men, and he would emphasize that, in this respect, it stands in almost direct contrast to the Spartan Crypteian's destitution, which seems to have been devised in order to make his life as arduous as possible.

The third difference: *activities*. Apparently, the Crypteians had only one – the killing of helots, always assuming, however, that this is accepted as an integral part of the Crypteia. The Crypteians, say Plato and the scholion, 'wandered', and (in the scholion) the only order they are given is to avoid being seen. In the papyrus, there is no question of either wandering or hiding, and, moreover, nothing to suggest that the participants might have been known as Crypteians. Weapons and patrols make no appearance either, and the only activity that might be attributed to them is that of 'digging' (σκάπτοντες). On its own, this word would be incomprehensible were it not explained by the connection – made at the outset by Haussoulier – with the Platonic *agronomoi* who appear in the *Laws*. Unlike the Spartan Crypteians, the young men of the papyrus engage in work, probably carrying out tasks in the public service. To me it does not seem very probable, however, that these earthworks or highways, for which slave labour would have been quite adequate, would have constituted their only occupation; but the work that yielded this fragment doubtless omits to mention such things, given its strictly ethical and medical orientation. In the life of the 'trainees', the focus of interest was the *diaita*, thus the balance between diet and exercise, and, insofar as it was physical labour, 'digging' was, of all their activities, the one that came into the latter category.

It is thus not simply on account of the ethnic ὁ Λάκων applied to Agesilaos, but also for reasons pertaining to the description itself, that I am convinced that its subject was not the Spartan Crypteia. So, this text indicates that, somewhere other than in Sparta, there was an institution which both resembled and differed from it. In which city? This is not a simple question, since it involves others, concerning the nature of the work of which this fragment was an extract, its author, and its date. The attribution to Ephoros' *Cretan Constitution*,[41] put forward by Milne, should, in my view, be abandoned, and for three reasons. Firstly, a study of the vocabulary (notably the use of οὔτε alone, ἀνέθιστος employed in the sense of 'not used to', and the form *Hegesilaos* for Agesilaos) points to a date for the text in the late hellenistic era or later. Secondly, this work is definitely not of a historical nature. Girard had already (1898, 34) been struck by the tone, at once ethical and medical, of the text. Considerations of this kind take up almost half of this short description, since what is said about diet[42] already makes up part of it, even if the key word *diaita* only appears later, in the passage specifically devoted to 'medical' matters. In fact, rather than being a medical treatise, it seems to be a moral and philosophical work where medical considerations, which may be related to a particular doctrine, occupied an important place in the argument.

The third reason for abandoning the notion that this scene is set in Crete, is the sudden arrival of Agesilaos in the text. This sudden appearance is made intelligible through Milne's deciphering of the verbal form (κατεπλήττετο) that follows. Agesilaos, who himself was not only a Spartan, and one who had followed – king though he was – the public system of education, but who had, on top of that, attracted the admiration of one and all for the fortitude he had shown, despite his physical handicap, in this situation;[43] this same Agesilaos, then, who was the best judge imaginable on such matters, 'was speechless with admiration', undoubtedly for the rigours of this 'training period', for the way in which the participants endured it, and also, assuming we take account of the tenor of this text, by the physical and moral results it yielded. This suggests that Agesilaos may have spent enough time in the city in question to witness this test; now we have no knowledge of his ever having stayed in Crete.

It is difficult to go much further with the identification of this city. We might have considered a city in Asia Minor, since that is one of the sectors of the Greek world where there are the best attestations of institutions of the same type as the *peripoloi* and the *(h)orophylakes*, which are not dissimilar to what is described in the papyrus. But this is an extremely weak argument, and could just as easily apply to Acarnania, where Agesilaos conducted a campaign. Another proposition would be Thasos, where, as we shall see, there seems to have been an institution known as the Crypteia, but here, again, the obstacle is that, to our knowledge, Agesilaos never set foot on the island, but confined himself to crossing its *Peraia* on one occasion.[44] So it is better left like that; for the purpose of our enquiry the essential point is that there existed, in a place that was neither Sparta nor a Cretan city, something that, in certain respects, really did resemble the Crypteia in the form – and let us be quite clear about this, since it is important – in which Plato and, particularly, the scholion describe it, though not as it is depicted by Aristotle. To have verified this spurs us on to find out whether other evidence may not be tending in the same direction. And, in fact, there is an institution, frequently discussed, which the one described in the papyrus resembles far more closely than it does the Spartan Crypteia, but which is imaginary: the Platonic *agronomoi*.

The Platonic *agronomoi*

The place accorded these by Plato may cause some surprise; it is marked both by the length of the discussion he devotes to them [45] and by the role he assigns to them in his city.[46] Piérart explained the importance of this in the following way (1974, 283): Plato valued the *Agronomia* because it allowed him to reintroduce into the lives of his citizens, for a limited period and in a designated space, the community activities which, in all other respects, he had been obliged considerably to reduce since the *Republic*. No one would dream of claiming that this institution was purely imaginary; nor that it was based on only one model. The models for it probably included the Athenian *ephēbeia*, and particularly its *peripoloi* aspect; but even Piérart, who generally stresses the Athenian model in the *Laws*, emphasizes (1974, 273–5) that, here, it plays a more modest role. So, what other city (or cities) might have inspired Plato?

The usual response is: Sparta – the Spartan Crypteia. This answer seems inescapable, in view of the sentence with which Plato concludes his account: '...they, and their occupation, may be called Crypteians, *agronomoi*, or any other name one likes' (6.763b6–8). But, in order to make plain the connection between the *Agronomia* and Sparta, we must proceed from the assumption that by κρυπτοί Plato can only mean the Spartan Crypteians; otherwise, how could it be claimed that these κρυπτοί concern the κρυπτεία to which Megillos made no more than an enigmatic allusion way back in Book 1 (633b9–c4)? Certainly, there are some similarities, but the only one that might be both accurate and unquestionably intentional bears on a rather circumscribed topic, the absence of servants; since Plato insists on this detail both in Book 1 and in Book 6, and in practically identical terms,[47] this identity qualifies as a reference. On this point, Plato has indeed used what he knew of the Spartan Crypteia to make it a feature of the *agronomoi*' way of life, because he considered it a most valuable constituent of the 'test'. All the other possible similarities are subject either to limitation or to doubt. For instance, we might find one in the sphere of recruitment: the *agronomoi* and the Crypteians are chosen by officials (*archontes*); but where, in the case of the *agronomoi*, these officials are also those who direct the activities of the young, in the case of the Crypteia they certainly have nothing whatever to do with such things.[48] Let us take another point on which there may appear to be a resemblance. Crypteians and *agronomoi* are – and this is also emphasized by Plato in both cases – perpetually moving about the *chōra* of the city. But the nature of this mobility is not the same for both. The Spartan Crypteians are the only ones who truly 'wander', and, one might add, if they do this, it is because they are, for a time, excluded from the city and required to remain invisible. By contrast, the movements of the *agronomoi* do not take place at random; they are regulated in a way that really recalls astronomy, dictated as they are both by a strict calendar and by the way civic space is organized.

This example conveys very well the difference that sets the Crypteia and the *Agronomia* in diametrically opposed positions. The *Agronomia* is a true institution of the city; it fulfils specific functions in spheres as important as patrolling, developing, and defending the territory, maintaining the security of the rural population, dispensing justice. The Crypteia, however, serves no such useful purpose; it constitutes a dismissal to the margins of the city, its laws and its marked-out spaces, inflicted on some chosen individuals. Each

Crypteian is isolated, whereas there is nothing of the 'individual' about the *Agronomia*, and no equivalent, either, of the Crypteian's obligation to remain unseen. Where the *Agronomia* 'sends young men into the country' (6.778e1) so as to 'civilize' it, the Crypteia does it to make them savage. Both practices have an educational objective,[49] but the tendencies of each education run in opposite directions.

Taking cognizance of the fundamental difference between the Crypteia and the *Agronomia* leads us to treat as a *problem* the term *kryptoi* at 763b7: there being nothing of a secretive nature in the activity of the *agronomoi*, the term in itself cannot but provoke surprise. Was Plato really thinking only of the Spartan Crypteia? Were there not, in some other city, young men also known as Crypteians, whose activities were rather more like those of the *agronomoi*?

There is nothing to justify our thinking that the 'trainees' in the London papyrus might have been called Crypteians; having said that, for anyone seeking to identify the institution that inspired Plato's conception of the *agronomoi*, the 'trainees' are, in other respects, far stronger candidates than the Spartan Crypteians. There is, actually, one detail in the description of tasks assigned to the *agronomoi* that may give rise to some surprise, namely the importance of earthworks,[50] the characters and purposes of which are very varied. There is nothing along those lines in what we know of the Athenian *ephēbeia*. This unexpected and most unusual feature is what makes comparison with the London papyrus worthwhile: on the one hand, Plato alone enables us to understand what the papyrus refers to with a single word, 'they dig'; on the other, only the papyrus shows us that what Plato is dealing with is not purely the product of the philosopher's imagination, and that in this case, as in others, his model was real. Could this model have been the very city, for which, unfortunately, we have no name, to which the papyrus refers? It is true that they have other points in common: the duration is identical, and, therefore, the nature also (a genuine institution in the service of the city), and the communal way of life. But these resemblances do not go very far, which is not in the least surprising given the difference in point of view between Plato, who is describing his ideal city, and the anonymous author, for whom it is the regime (in the medical sense) that is under discussion. The responsibilities of the *agronomoi* appear infinitely more important and varied than those of the young men in the papyrus, who are more like forced labourers.

There is something else in the activity of the *agronomoi* that may strike us as surprising: that they should have, in matters of justice, powers which Plato explains in minute detail.[51] Certainly, *agronomoi* from the ranks only become involved in such matters in their capacity as assessors of the *archontes*, but that is precisely what leads to their knowing about the most important cases. As Pierart (1974, 288) has aptly observed, the idea of young men still under the age of thirty attaining office as judges is surprising by comparison both with the (usual) practice in Greek cities and with the very thinking of Plato himself. The only possible explanation for this singular notion is that, on this point also, the philosopher is consulting a real model. It may be that in the *neotas* of Gortyn we have, if not the model itself, at least something close to it.[52] I am well aware that the nature, the chronology, and the functions of this *neotas* may be, and have been, disputed, but it seems to me that, as often happens, its details and those of the Platonic *Agronomia* cast light on each other, even if the beam remains a flickering one. The *neotas* would be neither a Council rivalling the Gerousia and born of the civil strife current at the time of the war of Lyttos (or prior to, and having played a part in, it), nor a simple association, even a very formal one, functioning around a gymnasium, like those of *neoi* in general, but, rather, an authentic institution, maintained by 'the young', who were probably trained by grown men, as in Plato's scheme, and endowed with judicial powers, notably in the matter of markets.

Sparta, the city of the papyrus, Gortyn: have we, then, exhausted the possible models for the *Agronomia* of the *Laws*? That is not very likely, if only because we have still to explain the name *Agronomia* itself, which Plato seems to prefer to the others, and which does not appear in any of the three cases considered. In the *Politics*, Aristotle[53] mentions *agronomoi* on two occasions, and in almost identical terms: 'magistrates whom some call *agronomoi*, others *hyloroi*'. Since the *hyloroi* actually existed, I see no reason at all to suppose that, when speaking of *agronomoi*, Aristotle would have had in mind only those of Plato.[54] Besides, there is nothing surprising in the notion that they may have existed, nor that they may have had this name, if they were, as Aristotle says, the rural counterpart of the astynomes. We should acknowledge, then, that in certain cities there existed an *archē* of *agronomoi*; did there exist, in others, an *archē* of Crypteians?

The Thasian *archē*

This is only mentioned in one text, the scholion to l. 600 of Aristophanes' *Thesmophoriazousai*. In the Ravenna manuscript we read: ...καὶ ἐν Θάσῳ ἀρχή τις κρύπτεται. The last word, albeit barely intelligible, has been retained by some editors.[55] Others have preferred to correct it, whether to κρυπτεῖαι, as at the beginning of the scholion,[56] or κρύπται,[57] or κρυπτευταί.[58] Knoepfler[59] retains κρύπτεται, and offers this translation: 'On Thasos also there exists a magistracy which operates in secret'. One can see the extent to which he has to force the words, to make some sense of them. καί, here, does not mean 'also': there has been no prior discussion of magistracies operating in secret, and this καί simply follows two others that precede it where examples are given of uses for the word κρύπται. The words 'There exists' are added to the text. κρύπτεσθαι does not mean 'to operate in secret' but 'to conceal oneself' or 'to remain invisible'. It seems to me that the result of this attempt is that it demonstrates the need for correction. How, though? κρυπτευταί would be excellent, palaeographically, except that it does not exist. The phrase ἀρχή τις could be judged to be preceding an abstract noun, in which case, although Fritzsche's κρυπτεῖαι would be more satisfactory in palaeographic terms, the singular κρυπτεία, which, as far as I know, has never been proposed, would be the only one suitable. But the language of the scholia does not require this at all; in this kind of comment, the expression may well be followed by the plural noun for the 'magistrates'.[60] So, κρύπται, the most common reading, seems also to be the most reasonable; it would be an alternative form of κρυπτός.

What are we to make of this *archē* of *kryptai* on Thasos? Knoepfler has shown that any assimilation to the fifth-century Athenian *kryptoi*, who were 'sent on missions' charged with ensuring that foreign policy decided by Athens be implemented in the cities of the Empire, should be rejected.[61] What is meant by an *archē*? In its classical usage, the meaning of the word is – though far from vague – broad, and even more so where it has been used in commentaries and scholia: thus the comment cited above, n. 60, applies this term to the *agathoergoi* of Sparta, who are by no means what we would call 'magistrates'. Having said that, it seems to me that no ancient text, whatever its date, could use the term *archē* to designate an entity like the Spartan Crypteia. Yes, Crypteians share one characteristic with the holders of an *archē*, that of being chosen; but it is certainly the only one. They do not carry out a mission entrusted to them by the community as a whole, they do not have their own sphere of jurisdiction, in which they can wield 'authority' over the other citizens, they are not even of an age to be magistrates. That is indication enough that the Thasian Crypteia was something different from the Spartan. I would be tempted, on account of the word *archē*, to view them as some kind of *peripoloi* or *(h)orophylakes*, a rural patrol. But – you might say – on Thasos, an island constituting a single city-state, there are no frontiers to guard. True; but, on the one hand, danger may come from the sea, and there is a need in that quarter for look-outs and protection; on the other hand, and principally, there is what we might term 'the internal frontier', the mountainous interior, which forms an island within the island, where security must be preserved and respect for the laws of the city upheld. This is suggestive of watch-towers (a number of which are known), fortlets, patrols. Only, on Thasos, those who carry out this mission were called not *peripoloi*, not *agronomoi*, but *kryptai*, and there was certainly a reason for this, one that, in spite of everything, ought to have implied a certain resemblance to Spartan Crypteians. What was it? Did they, too, have to 'hide'? One cannot tell. One may wonder whether, on Thasos, the name 'Crypteians' might not have been a survivor from a past where this Crypteia resembled that of Sparta, before it evolved into something like an office that was entrusted, by the city, to certain young men.

From Crypteians to *peripoloi*

The preceding discussion invites us to draw up, on an experimental basis, a scheme that gathers together all the cases we have touched on: Sparta, the un-named city in the papyrus, the city or cities from which Plato drew the model for his *agronomoi*, and Thasos; to these there may be added some thirty cities where the existence of *peripoloi*, *(h)orophylakes*, or *phrourioi* is attested.[62] Their common underlying structure could briefly be described thus: young men, usually chosen – 'sent out of the city' (scholion) – for a designated period in order to 'wander about' or patrol in wild and uncertain regions. This scheme assumes the form of a fan or a rainbow in which each concrete instance occupies a particular place between the two extremes. The extremes are represented, at one end, by the Spartan Crypteia (the *structure* in the pure state), and, at the other, by the imaginary but plausible circumstance where the participants would be neither young men nor even citizens, but mercenaries (the *function* in the pure state: 'wandering about', now wholly functionalized, has become the itinerant guarding of civic territory).

It must be acknowledged that this attempt to construct a model runs into some serious difficulties. For a start, because this is an initiatory practice, the participants have to be young men; typically, ephebes. This is the case in Athens after the reforms of Lycurgus (and, perhaps, from about 370); the same goes for Apollonia by the Salbakē in the second–third century AD, where there are νεανίσκοι, controlled by a νεανισκάρχης (indicating that there, as at Gortyn, 'youth' is an institution), who are ὀροφυλακήσαντες (their function). But, in the majority of cases, it is impossible to be sure that the *peripoloi* or *(h)orophylakes* whom we see in action are ephebes. It might seem quite natural that they should be, but we should take careful note of the fact that in Athens, during the Peloponnesian War, the *peripoloi* were grown men, fighting as *psiloi* (Thucydides 4.67.2 and 5); they take part in the Sicilian Expedition (Cabanes 1991, 211 and n. 24); besides, mercenaries apparently could have been *peripoloi* (ibid., the case of Thrasyboulos of Calydon). One of the peripolarchs we know of in Epirus is a mercenary, as are the two secretaries of the 'college'. The Athenian examples, which show the *peripoloi* only as specialized troops, are the more worrying in that they are the earliest.

The second difficulty concerns function. It is a perfectly obvious one: it is not only natural, but imperative, for a Greek city to ensure that its entire territory be secure and under control. What first comes to mind is the foreigner, the neighbouring state, a possible, and often only too real, enemy; but we should consider also the 'internal enemies', above all the slaves, who, when they run away to escape their predicament, may reach the wild regions at the margins of the city's territory, either to find refuge there or to cross into the territory of the neighbouring city. It is when faced with that sort of danger that adjacent cities, when they are enjoying friendly relations, may arrange for their respective contingents of *(h)orophylakes* to collaborate: one may find an example of this in the agreement between Miletus and Heracleia.[63] It is obvious that, as they established, and reinforced, control over their territory (an effort that would endure for centuries), cities felt more and more acutely the necessity of organizing surveillance and regular 'sweeps' of their confines. So there seems to be no need at all to appeal to a common archetype, linked to initiation rites, to explain the fact that institutions like the *peripoloi* appear under inevitably similar guises in very different times and places throughout Greece. Similar necessity evokes similar response, and that response is an *institution*: a group of men carrying out a specific mission in the service of the city, taking orders from a leader, sometimes even having secretaries, and observing particular cults within the framework of their activities.

This explanation seems perfectly sound. And yet, the close resemblance between the theoretical model I proposed above, and the numerous cases, known the world over, of young men being sent, at some stage of their initiation, to spend a given period wandering 'in the bush', is incontrovertible and cannot be fortuitous. For the moment, then, it is appropriate not to espouse one of these ways of viewing it, but to keep both equally in mind. We may decline to choose between structure and function (that old debate!), by assuming that there may have existed (where? when?) an original model which the necessities that attend the development of the city caused to be reactivated in forms that were at once different *and* comparable.

Even within this global perspective, the place of the Spartan Crypteia remains a singular one. Perhaps there did exist, somewhere else in the Greek world, customs that really resembled it, but the present state of our knowledge does not allow us to make this assertion. As far as we know, it remains the only one that displays this character of a personal test, this absence of practical utility, this ritual aspect; what we encountered elsewhere are institutions, organized with a precise objective in view and provided with the means necessary to achieve it. Everything takes place as if (I put it like this to show that I am fully aware that what I am offering is a theoretical model, not a historical hypothesis) the Spartan Crypteia had preserved the original structure in its pure form, without its being mixed with the function of guarding the territory, this being accomplished by other means.

Exploring the Spartan Crypteia

Ancient interpretations

It would not be much to say that, of the ancient texts on the subject of the Crypteia, not one fails to put forward an interpretation of it: the principal object of the discussions offered in them is not, actually, to convey information on the subject, but to give an explanation of it, and the facts they present merely serve to justify this explanation. Two interpretations of the purpose of the Crypteia appear in the sources, and ancient opinion was probably divided between them.

The military interpretation

The first is the one that was, as we have seen, universally accepted in the fourth century concerning the system of education as a whole: the military interpretation. It is the one put forward by Plato and by the scholion; but between these two texts there are, from this viewpoint, some important differences. Plato does not believe that the Crypteia could really have qualified as a form of training for war, no doubt because of the place occupied in it by two entities which hardly lend themselves to this interpretation, namely the state of destitution and the wandering way of life. In his account, the military explanation is only in the background. In itself, he says, the Crypteia is a *karterēsis*, one of the four Spartan *karterēseis* for which Megillos makes the claim in his account; it trains them to endure rough living in the general sense. It is even the defining example of what a *karterēsis* actually is, θαυμαστῶς πολύπονος πρὸς τὰς καρτερήσεις; the whole passage is aimed at explaining in what respects it constitutes a test. What makes it military training is the fact that in Sparta, in accordance with the lawgiver's wishes, all tests of this kind were aimed at training warriors: it is their education as a whole that constitutes an education in the fourth kind of virtue, and in that kind only.

The scholion states it otherwise: it makes the assertion, directly and without subtlety, that the Crypteia is a training intended for war; the phrase ἄλλο δὲ καὶ τοῦτο γυμνασίας εἶδος πρὸς πόλεμον is the pivot around which the two components of the account are arranged. Nevertheless, its content, which describes the Crypteian's way of life (organized according to the topics we have analysed: invisibility, expulsion, wandering, destitution, stealing), can only with difficulty be considered a true justification of the military interpretation. The fundamental rule in this kind of game is 'never be seen'; now, every attempt to provide a military explanation for this standing order is, in my opinion, doomed to failure. In fact, while circumstances can arise where the mission assigned to a soldier or band of soldiers is, effectively, to observe something without being seen, the way things happen in the Crypteia is entirely different. There is nothing for them to observe, and even if, once in a while, there *was* something, while the Crypteian might perhaps see it without being seen, there is no way in which he could meet the third imperative of any intelligence-gathering, the one in which failure would mean that he might as well not have bothered: that is, to report it. It is not that he would be incapable of doing so, but, rather, that he is *forbidden* to, because he is forbidden to communicate with anyone. The standing order is 'never be seen', and *that is that*; it is rather like the rule of a game, or a ritual taboo, and it has nothing to do with a military exercise.

There are, moreover, other reasons for rejecting the military explanation. The most obvious is that, according to any sound logic, if the Crypteia had been a preparation for the rigours of life on campaign, it would have been imposed on all young Spartans. That it should be reserved only to some of them might prompt us to regard its objective as the selecting and training of an elite band, a specialized unit (we know, from Phylarchos, that one such existed in the third century, but this is manifestly not the case in the classical era, when the *hippeis* are able to fulfil this role). But in that case, this selection, too, must have operated among all young Spartans. The harshness of military life was real enough, but the Spartans, like other Greeks, did not consider that this required any special training; it was the pursuit of physical activities, marches, hunting, and, in the end, their whole system of education, that prepared them for this, and that was everybody's business. Lastly, one might say that the wandering way of life, on which Plato insists as much as does the scholion, makes the Crypteia something altogether different from a patrolling exercise.

The anti-helot aim

The other explanation that was in circulation in antiquity is the one we know of from Aristotle, via Plutarch: the 'anti-helotic' objective. Aristotle certainly accepted the Platonic view of the Crypteia as a form of military training, and, for him also, it constituted preparation for a rugged life which would be tackled virtually without means. But, to him, this test appeared principally as the framework for what he saw as the essential aim – helot-hunting. The other feature which he accepts – the obligation to hide – and which he cannot leave out because it is this that explains the name of the custom, was, according to him, subordinate to this purpose: the helots had to be taken by surprise. For Aristotle, too, the Crypteia is perfectly conceivable: it serves the purpose of killing helots, it is a staging of the slaughter. There remains one question, to which, at least in the state in which his text reaches us, Aristotle gives no answer, namely, why did the helots have to be killed, and why in this peculiar manner? As I have already explained, the very description he gives of the Crypteia seems to me to preclude the notion that the second version Plutarch supplies of these murders, the version whereby they represent the systematic execution of a plan to eliminate individuals considered to be a threat, goes back to Aristotle. In his view, the victims were taken at random; it is in this gratuitous element that the mystery of the Crypteia resides. As to what Aristotle thought of it, we can only construct hypotheses, of which the most plausible, when we take account of Plutarch's commentary, is that for him it was but one of numerous forms of 'ill treatment' the Spartans meted out to the helots, and that what they were aiming to do was to terrify them into being submissive. The Crypteia was, for the philosopher, yet another example of the 'savagery' of Spartan behaviour notably in the realm of education, the sense of the word 'savage' being at its most literal, since the Crypteian is compelled to act like a beast of prey who hunts by night. It is probably this idea, fundamental for him, of 'savagery', explicitly formulated in his account of Spartan education, that led him, when describing the Crypteia, to give pride of place to the murdering of helots, something of which Plato had been unaware or which he had left to one side.

Modern interpretations

The murder of helots

Almost all of them take, as their point of departure, the killing of helots. Numerous historians have been enticed by the apparent rationality of Plutarch's second version, and see in the Crypteia a kind of secret police whose function is to keep helots under surveillance and to eliminate those who had been marked out as likely troublemakers. As I have already remarked, this interpretation, besides appearing to me somewhat anachronistic, is contradicted by the very way in which Aristotle's text describes the working of the Crypteia. In order to make it possible to envisage, it would have substantially to be amended, for instance by perceiving in it an ancient rite, wandering or whatever you like, that has been *re-deployed* at a new target, that of anti-helotic repression; but this hypothesis also comes up against the fact that the killing of helots has a gratuitous and almost ritual character, making it the act of an assassin not an executioner. Two well-known cases of operations directed against helots, the massacre of the Two Thousand (Thucydides 4.80.3–4) and the pseudo-mission of Cinadon to Aulon (Xenophon, *Hell.* 3.3.8), demonstrate that when the Spartans had problems with some of them, the means they employed were varied, certainly, but well-tried, and far more efficient than isolated murders. Besides, if the executing of helots by members of the Crypteia had been justified for specific political reasons, Plutarch (following Aristotle) could not have condemned this practice as he does. I would be tempted to say that, of all the lines of thought one might propose to follow regarding the Crypteia – and we shall find that they are numerous – that of the 'anti-helotic secret police' is the only one devoid of utility. All the others are worth trying. Some of these lines of thought are merely 'Holzwege' and lead to nothing definite, but the route they take is, in itself, suggestive; others have a very limited explanatory force; but they are all of interest, if only because of their very multiplicity, which compels us to consider the Crypteia, a complex and perhaps composite reality, from a great many angles.

I shall begin with those where the main objective is the killing of helots. The first, one that is very familiar to me, is in a sense a variant of what we might suppose Aristotle's view to have been, but a variant that he himself would not be able to invent, because it calls upon sociological concepts. It is a fact that helot-hunting can, with validity, be regarded as an instance of repressive behaviour provided it is viewed as *preventive* repression, which not only accommodates the choosing of victims at random, but almost requires it. The reader will have recognized, in this, what I have called a conduct of contempt: the execution, apparently gratuitous in that there is not even an attempt to justify it by resorting to some allegation that the victim committed a reprehensible act, is the logical outcome of any conduct of contempt, because this conduct rests on denying the other his status as a human being. Aristotle was perhaps on the track of this concept. Plutarch has actually transmitted a highly significant feature of his way of viewing Spartan treatment of the helots: the annual declaration of war. For Aristotle, its essential aim was to render legitimate, particularly when it came to religious laws, the executing of helots by Crypteians: so it was only a means, and the execution itself was the end. Let us try inverting this reasoning, to dwell, rather, on the implications, for the society practising it, of the execution, 'gratuitous', legal and systematic all at once, of certain members of that society who were classed as inferiors. From this perspective, what is fundamental is the declaration of war, which amounts to a 'licence to kill', according to Libanius' expression, and hence a virtual death sentence for anyone it designated 'the enemy'. Thus it underlines one of the basic norms of the helot's condition, and it is the Crypteia that turns this virtuality into reality. It is on this practice of killing that the most fundamental ordering of Spartan society is established. For the helot, this is how his destiny is fulfilled; for the young Spartan who kills him, this is likewise his destiny, since the killing marks him definitively as a member of the superior community. 'To drench one's hands in helot blood', as Vernant has most aptly put it,[64] '...is, of course, to demonstrate the hard fact of the helots' inferiority...but it is also, and indeed principally, to draw between them and oneself a line which, from that moment on, may not be crossed'. One may try countering this interpretation, and many others as well, with the fact that only certain Spartans are members of the Crypteia; to this objection, which is ineluctable, the response, no less ineluctable, is that Crypteians do not kill on their own account but insofar as they are chosen 'representatives' of the group to which they belong, and which may be their age-class.

In order to interpret the Crypteia *qua* helot-hunters, use has also been made of ethnographic comparisons. The first to have adopted this approach is Jeanmaire, in his celebrated article of 1913. He compares this side of the Crypteia with the practice of probatory killing in certain societies in Africa (Gallas, Wanika) and, principally, the South Sea Islands (in Borneo and in New Guinea; 1913, 147–9), rightly insisting on the fact that, as in Sparta, this action is not an act of gallantry, but simply the execution of a human being. It might be said that the Crypteian is a helot-hunter, perhaps, but not a head-hunter,[65] and that he apparently loses interest in his victim's body. But in fact the expression 'head-hunting' only corresponds to one of the known forms of probatory killing, and, in the majority of cases, the young man does not have to bring back material proof of his deed. Other objections to Jeanmaire's interpretation are more serious. The first is the fact that it seems to bear only on one aspect of the Crypteia, an aspect, moreover, that we cannot be certain formed an integral, nor yet an original, part of it. In reality, if we read the whole article, we find that he has taken equal account of the other aspect, the wandering way of life, looking, first, for parallels with initiatory rituals, and then pointing out, with all due precision, that probatory killing generally takes place in the course of what is often, incorrectly, called an 'expedition' (this word is frequently prefixed with the phrase 'head-hunting', even though that is not always what it is). Thus, among the Wanika of East Africa, 'young men who have reached the age of manhood withdraw into the forest and remain there until they have had the opportunity to kill a man' (Schurtz, cited by Jeanmaire 1913, 147). As in Sparta, there seems to be a close connection between the practice of wandering outside the areas where people travel, and the killing of a man.

Another possible objection is one that is already familiar to us: this is the fact that not all young Spartans are Crypteians and thus cannot carry out this probatory deed. But we know from the record that, on this point, the situation in archaic societies varies considerably. There are those where probatory killing is a requirement for attaining full membership of the community. Jeanmaire cites several such cases; one (well-known) example from among the Dayak of Borneo, 1913, 148: 'In all the tribes, it is the rule that a young man cannot carry the *mandan* (the short sword of the Dayak), marry, or consort with women, if he has not taken part in several head-hunts' (Ratzel; we should, however, note the phrase 'take part'). But there are also many societies where, far from being prescribed for everyone, such killing is reserved for an elite. In a case cited by Brelich (1969, 157 n. 135), this hierarchy takes the institutionalized form of a ranked initiation. Among the Kwoma of New Guinea, all the young men undergo initiation with two degrees, which is centred on the cultivation of yams; a third degree, which is in fact a rank, is reserved for those who have killed a man in the course of 'head-hunting', and gives them the right *to plant* yams. The Spartan case appears to be different: the killing is carried out only by some of them, but these derive no special qualification or glory from it. Nevertheless, this assertion is open to criticism, and in two contrasting ways. First, if it is true that no text explicitly states that former Crypteians enjoyed particular prestige, the fact that to be chosen to undergo this test was already a great honour in itself cannot be contested, and one may judge, as I have done, that it was the point of departure towards a brilliant 'career' in the service of the city: which, in a political society, is the very adaptation we might expect of what, in an archaic society, is a higher rank of initiation. From another angle, it is also possible to maintain, again as I have done, that if, in Sparta, it was only certain young men who killed a helot during their time in the Crypteia, then they were not doing it on their own account, but only inasmuch as they were 'representing' their age-class, who, through their mediation, completely by-passed this stage, without its costing the community too dear. The real difference resides, rather, in the fact that, in Sparta, membership of an elite does not *result* from a killing, but, by contrast, is a *prerequisite* of it. Thus, the interpretation of helot murder as probatory killing proves, on examination, to be quite possible and attractive.

The comparativist method has the advantage of opening up new paths to understanding, but Greek data are more directly convincing, as the basis for an authentic interpretation, than those to be found in other civilizations. It is not in Greece proper, but in Macedonia,[66] that we find undeniable traces of probatory killing. According to Aristotle (*Pol.* 7.1324b15–17), 'There was also, once, a law in Macedonia, to the effect that anyone who had not killed an enemy should wear not a belt but a bridle', a visible sign of inferiority.[67] In a variant of this rule, a large game animal is substituted for the enemy. Hegesandros, cited by Athenaeus (1.18a), records that in Macedonia the only person who could recline at dinner was one who, out hunting, had killed a wild boar with a thrust of the hunting spear, without the aid of nets; those who had not done this had to dine sitting down, like children.[68] To kill an enemy, to kill a large animal, are two substitutes for probatory killing that are richly attested in archaic societies.[69] It cannot be said for certain, however, that the Macedonian data really confirm the interpretation of helot murder as probatory killing. Rather, they show that *normally*, in the Greek world, the murder is *replaced* by a substitute more acceptable to a society of this kind. So we would have to assume that, on this point, Spartan society behaved in a most unusual way in preserving, for this test, its original character, namely the executing of a human being. That is a possibility, but not an obvious one.

To stay in the Greek world a little longer: because of their wandering in the wilderness, I earlier likened the Crypteians to 'mountain warders' (*orophylakes*) or 'border guards' (*horophylakes*) whose existence is attested in numerous Greek cities. One of the principal functions of these guards was to recapture runaway slaves, particularly when they were trying to cross into the territory of a neighbouring city; this appears in a prominent position in the agreement, already cited, between Miletus and Heracleia, except for this slight difference that, there, the guards are not supposed to capture the slaves themselves, but only to take, and keep, custody of them. Who the 'hunters' are, we do not know. It was considered normal, then, for young citizens who were spending a period of 'wandering' at the frontiers of the city, whatever form that 'wandering' might have taken, to cope with the runaway slaves. Helot-hunting in the Crypteia could be regarded as a form, at once defunctionalized, ritualized and radicalized, of this perfectly rational and understandable activity. It would unquestionably be fanciful to claim this as an explanation of the Crypteia, given that the differences, which leap from the page, are so fundamental: the helots who occupy the Crypteians' attention are not runaways at all; the aim of the operation is not to return them to their masters, but to destroy them, which, from an economic point of view (a point of view to which the Milesian inscription accords considerable importance), is quite simply disastrous. It seems, nevertheless, that this comparison, which is in no way an attempt at an explanation, does have some meaning, that it may help to make the Crypteia conceivable, and that there is a connection, the exact nature of which escapes us, between these two modes of hunting slaves. It would be, perhaps, an indication in support of the notion that such hunting was originally part of the Crypteia.

Nevertheless, where its primitive character is concerned, it is – all things considered – more to the field of ethnology that helot-killing encourages us to turn; specifically, as Jeanmaire was already doing, to initiation rites (Jeanmaire 1913, 127). We noted, in a previous chapter (p. 217) that, for the initiands at certain times, the rules of society may be suspended or even inverted, and that they can (and therefore should) with impunity set upon property belonging to members of the community, to steal or destroy it. If we look at it from the point of view of law, helots are nothing more nor less than the Spartans' property. If truth be told, Crypteians are not initiands but *neoi* – to use a technical term, neo-initiates. Now, as we have also seen (p. 210), in certain societies such people are regarded as dangerous on account of the enormous amount of energy their initiation has discharged in them. To protect itself, society may make them lead, among themselves and for a certain period, a particular way of life, or may even exile them beyond the bounds of the city, to work off their aggressiveness there (Brelich 1969, 39 and n. 134). In the light of these comparisons, then, we might view the Crypteia as a kind of complement, in this objective of getting rid of aggressiveness, to the *hēbōntes*' individual bouts of combat that were examined earlier (pp. 102–3, 172–4). By temporarily expelling not the whole group but certain 'representatives' chosen from the neo-initiates, Spartan society would, according to this hypothesis, be protecting itself from their violence. Furthermore, ordaining that they should devote their energies to a manhunt (as H.G. Wells' *The Island of Dr Moreau* makes clear, for a hunter worthy of the name the only proper quarry is man) it provides them with the best possible way of discharging their aggressiveness, of shedding the savage element within them which their education – as Plato says – has failed to eliminate. In this way they enable their entire age-class to pass over a decisive step towards the status of full manhood and citizenship. Envisaging the Crypteia in this way has the advantage of considering the institution in its entirety, including the expulsion and wandering.

Wandering

It is plain, in fact, that this enquiry should not be confined to the murder of helots; every bit as important is the other aspect of the Crypteia, that of expulsion and wandering, to which Plato and the scholion give prominence. Here, also, certain initiation rites supply the material for significant comparisons: these are the ones that, together, come under the conventional heading of vagabondage. The best known form is the 'vision quest' which, among certain peoples, notably in North-West America, the initiands pursue, each in his own way. After a preparation which may have lasted several years, the young man leaves his tribe for a period of wandering that was liable to take him a long way from home. By giving himself over to this extremely harsh life, ridden with tests that may even have extended to auto-torture, he brought himself to a psychological state that enabled him to gain, at last, the vision that was the object of his quest, and in the course of which he entered into communion with his own tutelary spirit. This form of vagabondage is the most remarkable, because here the element of 'quest' (and even, in a sense, of a spiritual quest) is very pronounced and quite conscious; but it is a peculiar case in that it is linked to a complex of specific and highly elaborate religious beliefs.

In itself, the practice of initiatory vagabondage is quite widespread in human societies,[70] occurring also, as it does, in Africa, Australia, and the South Sea Islands. It can be collective, as in Australia, where it is a band of young men, sometimes accompanied by an adult, who wander 'in the bush'. In Africa, it is most frequently the individual on his own. The Spartan example seems to be a combination of the two, with the 'individual' aspect predominating. The length of time spent wandering and the distance covered are exceedingly variable. This is especially significant in Australia; in the case of the Wikmunkan, it lasted for two years, and the young men of the Karadjeri went more than a hundred miles away from their home ground; this feature is connected with the collective character of their vagabondage. Among the Warega of the Congo, where it was of the solitary type, it lasted for fifteen days, and for only five among the Babinga Pygmies of Gabon, who, like the American Indians, would set off in search of their spirits, attaining the requisite hallucinatory state by means of drugs. In general, vagabondage forms part of the initiation itself, but sometimes it takes place afterwards (after circumcision, for instance, among the Warega) or it opens the way to a higher rank (as in the case of the Wikmunkan of Australia). Where populations also practise probatory killing, this generally takes place during what is often called an 'expedition' but which actually bears all the hallmarks of vagabondage. So, sometimes this type of custom includes probatory killing, which now tends to be seen (though perhaps fallaciously) as the objective of 'wandering'. It is possibly with this model of initiatory vagabondage that we could link Greek practices to do with wandering by young men, practices that range from the Crypteia to the *(h)orophylakes* via the ephebic *peripoloi*.

Comparison with the world of initiation may allow us to make some sense of certain elements of Crypteian vagabondage that, otherwise, appear barely comprehensible. Perhaps the most characteristic example is 'trial by cold'. One cannot help feeling surprise at the way Plato insists on the fact that the Crypteians have to endure the cold, since, in itself, this detail seems to possess no particular importance. It does not appear in the scholion, and there is logic in that; since, as far as its author was concerned, the Crypteia lasted a full year, the Crypteians had to put up with all the seasons, and it goes without saying that this included the winter. This detail reappears, however, in the London papyrus, which leads to the conclusion that it played a structural role. Now, as we have seen (pp. 190–1), being tested by heat and cold constituted part of certain initiations; this detail had already been picked up by Jeanmaire (1913, 128), who cited, on the subject, an account relating to the Zulus.

The same applies to sleep. As we have found, all the texts about the Crypteia emphasize that there was something abnormal and disturbing about it: there are Plato's *astrōsiai* (the lack of bedding), Aristotle's daytime sleeping, and, more noticeably still, the scholiast's μῆτε καθεύδων ἀδεῶς. To sleep well or to sleep badly are very important matters indeed in real life, but this insistence on the part of the sources is surprising. Now, to be deprived of sleep, totally, over several days (six in the case of the Kru of Liberia), or partially, for a long period, is one of the most common initiatory tests; Brelich (1969, 73 n. 65, and 103 n. 144) cites examples borrowed from African, South Sea and South American societies. During periods of initiatory vagabondage, this is one of the ways of reaching the sought-after hallucinatory state.

It is likewise frequently the case that, during their period of segregation, young men are required to 'live off the land', as the scholiast says the Crypteians did. Jeanmaire gives several examples of this: Masai (1913, 126), Zulus (128), the 'labi' of several African societies (139); he concludes: 'Our young men lead the lives of young Robinsons, who are forced to get themselves out of their predicament by using, for food and clothing,[71] the resources of forest and moorland' (138).[72] Such a requirement is evidently the rule when the vagabondage is of long duration, as it is among the Wikmunkan and, even more so, in cases of a 'vision quest'. The means most frequently employed is hunting (on which cf. above, pp. 202–3), but there are also instances of stealing (above, pp. 201–7) and even of begging (Brelich 1969, 86 n. 104).

One of the most remarkable features of the Crypteians' vagabondage is that obligation to remain invisible which gave them their name. This feature is also found in some initiatory rites, but in a less radical form. Brelich (1969, 30) notes that, in general, it is only by certain categories of people that the initiands must not be seen; for example, by his parents, or women and children, or only certain categories of women (Brelich 1969, 68 n. 53). Jeanmaire, however, cites instances where the initiate must not be seen by anyone, as is the case among the inhabitants of the Admiralty Isles (138: 'If their father or the chief approaches, they hide in their cell and stay there until he moves off'), or in the case of the African 'labi' (139: 'Each ' labi ' must hide under a basket, a wicker watchman's-hut, a sort of large hamper which protects him from the gaze of the indiscreet'). These examples demonstrate that invisibility symbolizes and dramatizes the segregation that initiation calls for. The originality of the Spartan custom lies in the fact that here invisibility is implemented with extreme rigour, whereas in the initiations the youths who are segregated are generally surrounded by several adults or neo-initiates, which gives to their invisibility a character that is necessarily partial, and, by virtue of their resorting to contrivances like the basket that is supposed to render the 'labi' invisible, more symbolic than real. In Sparta, the Crypteian must literally and completely disappear.[73]

These peculiarities of the Crypteians' vagabondage, like the rest of the young Spartans' education/initiation, are arranged according to the two logics of inversion and testing (cf. above, p. 217). Everything, the exposure to cold, lack of sleep, lack of equipment, the obligation of invisibility, are considered as coming together to make the Crypteia the test *par excellence*. But what chiefly constitutes the test is the inversion itself, which entails being deprived of not only all the practical elements that go to make a civilized life, but even of all human contact, and which causes the Crypteian to regress into a state of animality and savagery. And that is how he becomes, once and for all, a man.

Notes

1 Whitby 1994, 105–6.

2 Lévy 1988.

3 See, for instance, Wallon 1850.

4 In this chapter I make use of certain elements from two articles, Ducat 1997a and 1997b, though with important modifications.

5 For an anthropology of the *stibas*, cf. Paradiso 1987, 261–4.

6 In Gigon's reading, there is no lacuna after μεθ' ὅπλων ; he simply omits καί.

7 Already that of Amyot, and now of Flacelière in the C.U.F. Likewise Brelich 1969, 156; Lévy 1988, 247; Nafissi 1991, 154; Birgalias 1999, 99.

8 See the introduction to Dilts 1971, 7.

9 Cf. below, p. 307.

10 Ducat 1990, 181–2.

11 Ducat 1990, 124.

12 Ducat 1990, 62–3.

13 Noted by Lévy 1988, 250 and n. 20.

14 A feature underlined by Lévy 1988, 249: 'The scholiast makes the Crypteia out to be a quasi-ritual test'.

15 Pritchett 1971, ch. 10, 'Scouts', 127–33.

16 Pritchett's list, *l.c.*

17 Knoepfler 1993.

18 This is rather what Lévy 1988, assumes. Cf., already, Jeanmaire 1913, 145: the Crypteians are 'ideally placed, for example in cases of a threat to the state, to supply a *corps* of auxiliaries and scouts. That this may have occurred appears from a passage of Plutarch...' We must, however, keep firmly in mind that this transition from a Crypteian in the literal sense towards a Crypteian in the military sense is pure hypothesis, and, if truth be told, not at all plausible in this form.

19 Cf. Birgalias 1999, 75.

20 Cartledge 2001, 88.

21 Vernant 1989, 194, n. 46.

22 3.22.2; cf. Edmunds 1984, with bibliography. In what follows, I combine comments made by Vidal-Naquet 1981, 116–17, and by Ellinger 1993, 55–8.

23 A comparable justification of anypodesy for boys is to be found in Xenophon, *LP* 2.3.

24 Lévy 1988, 249 n. 17.

25 *LP* 2.7; cf. above, p. 202.

[26] Schnapp 1997.

[27] It is Lévy who (1988, 249) has drawn attention to this opposition, and to the solitude of the Crypteian conveyed in the scholion.

[28] As for the idea that helot-hunting was dissociated from the Crypteia itself, it is neither recent nor uncommon: cf. Piérart 1974, 280–1, and Knoepfler 1993, 334.

[29] Christien 1997, 71.

[30] Birgalias 1999, 103 and 110.

[31] A variant of this would consist in assuming that the Crypteia did indeed exist from the outset without helot-hunting, but that this was incorporated in it at a very early date, for instance from the time when helotism first made its appearance, which is itself impossible to date.

[32] The scholion to Aristophanes *Thesmophoriazousai* l. 600 attests that several *Lakedaimonion Politeiai* dealt with the Crypteia. For a version favourable to Lycurgus, we might consider that of Dikaiarchos or Sphairos.

[33] Ducat 1990, 123–5.

[34] One hypothesis that would seem possible is that this Crypteia-without-helots was the inspiration behind the description given in the scholion; but the problem of Plato would still remain.

[35] In the following pages, I summarize part of an earlier article (Ducat 1997b, 20–38). This may be consulted, if necessary, for the detailed discussion and the documentation.

[36] In this they were followed by Girard 1890, who, moreover, decided to view it as a fragment from a *Lakedaimonion Politeia*.

[37] This was emphasized by Milne, endorsed by Piérart 1974, 283–5.

[38] The papyrus says nothing about the age of the participants; but it is only during their youth (whatever may be the actual reality defining that term) that we can envisage a two-year 'mobilization'.

[39] Although this would not be the most common usage, the word χλανίς can mean a thick, winter coat.

[40] Cf. Ducat 1990, 111.

[41] Ephoros did not actually write a work under this title; this refers to a lengthy discussion which occurs in Book 4 of the *Histories*.

[42] With the technical term ἀναγκοφαγεῖν, used by Philon of Alexandria, Arrian, and Philostratus to mean 'to eat according to a prescribed diet'.

[43] Cf. Plutarch, *Agesilaos* 1.2–2.2.

[44] In which case we would have to assume that the Thasian 'Crypteia' (if one existed) was conducted on the Peraia, which is highly improbable.

[45] *Laws* 6.760b3–763c2.

[46] In what follows, I make constant reference to the excellent account by Piérart, 1974, 259–91.

[47] *Laws* 1.633c1–2: αὐτοῖς ἑαυτῶν διακονήσεις ; 6.763a5–6: διακονοῦντές τε καὶ διακονούμενοι ἑαυτοῖς.

[48] To make, on this point, a minor correction to what Piérart says, p. 281.

[49] Especially for Plato, who saw in the Crypteia a process of toughening for war; which is also, to an extent, the case with his *Agronomia*: cf. Piérart, p. 281.

[50] 760e5–761c5 (earthworks for military purposes; highways; hydraulics). On the military earthworks, cf. the summary at 778e1–5.

[51] 761d6–762b6.

[52] For an account (simplified) of the data, see Piérart, pp. 288–91; he shows too much

caution, perhaps, in qualifying the comparison as 'risky'. The main texts: *IC* 4 (1950), nos. 162–4 (note, at 164, l. 3, νεοτατεύοντα, which shows that this is a true collegiate institution, an *archē*).

[53] Aristotle, *Pol.* 6.1321b27–30 and 7.1331b13–17.

[54] It is this to which Piérart seems to incline (1974, 273). I share the opinion of Knoepfler 1993, 334, 'that this title was in use in several cities at least, in the Greek world'. The hylores are only known in Thessaly (Thetonion, 5th century; Pherai, 3rd and 2nd centuries).

[55] Ed. Bekker, *Aristophanis Comoediae cum scholiis* 1 (1829) 275; Nauck, *TGF*, 2nd edn 1889, 712.

[56] Ed. Fritzsche (1838) 214.

[57] Ed. Dübner, *Scholia graeca in Aristophanem* (1842) 268; Blaydes, ed. of *Thesmophoriazousai* (1880) 195.

[58] Bernhardy, edn of Suidas (1853) 2, 1, 424; Rutherford, *Scholia aristophanica* 2 (1896) 476.

[59] Knoepfler 1993, 332; his aim is to show that there exists no attested instance of a form κρύπται.

[60] Cf. *Synagoge lexeon chresimon*, ed. Bekker, *Anecdota graeca* 1 (1814) 333, l. 30: ἔστι δὲ καὶ ἀρχή τις ἐν Λακεδαίμονι οἱ ἀγαθοεργοί.

[61] *Lexeis Rhetorikai*, s.v. κρυπτή; ed. Bekker, *Anecdota graeca* 1 (1814) 273–4.

[62] On the subject of these offices, some clarification and a guide to the bibliography may be found in Rousset 1994, 98–9. To my mind, the most useful studies are: on the *(h)orophylakes*, J. and L. Robert 1983, 101–9; on the *peripoloi*, Cabanes 1991; on the Thessalian *phrourioi*, Helly 1973, 140. *Orophylakes*: 'mountain guards'; *horophylakes*: 'frontier guards'.

[63] *Sylloge*[3] 633, ll. 87–99.

[64] Vernant 1989, 200–1.

[65] Vidal-Naquet once remarked to me that as a general rule the Greeks were not given to decapitation.

[66] This way of putting it does not suppose any particular stance on my part concerning the problem of 'the hellenism of the ancient Macedonians'.

[67] Hatzopoulos 1994, 58.

[68] Hatzopoulos 1994, 94.

[69] Killing an enemy: Jeanmaire 1913, 147. Killing a large animal: Brelich 1969, n. 68, p. 74.

[70] It could lie at the origins of a literary genre such as the novel.

[71] Cf. the *gymnos* of the scholion?

[72] In fact, the theme of a young man castaway on a desert island, as in *Robinson Crusoe*, or of a group of youths, as in *Lord of the Flies*, is typically that of an initiatory narrative. In my view, it would be possible to draw a comparison between Golding's novel and certain aspects of Spartan education – at least, as Aristotle saw it.

[73] Hatzopoulos (1994, 71–4) has collected certain Greek data which may be regarded as an adaptation of the obligation of invisibility imposed on the initiand. In certain manumissions from Beroia, Dionysos is called Epikryptos (and, in one instance, Kryptos); Hatzopoulos compares this epiclesis with the festival of Agrionia at Chaironeia, during which the women search for Dionysos who is hiding (κέκρυπται) in the *eschatia*, domain of the Nymphs and the Muses, as in Euripides' *Bacchae*. The god behaves like a young man undergoing initiation; he is carrying out his Crypteia.

10

CONCLUSION

A study such as this is bound to disappoint any reader who expects to find a complete reconstruction of the Spartan education system in the classical period. No such reconstruction will ever be possible. There were three elements in the making of a young Spartan. There was the process of initiation and education organized by the state. There were, as in other cities, the lessons provided by teachers. And there was the prolonged exposure to society: in the form of the family for the youngest children; then, increasingly, the young person came into contact with the *polis* in general. For a time the *polis* was represented, mediated, by the person of the *erastēs*, the lover. On the teachings given to children our sources are almost completely silent; not from a wish to hide anything, but because the interest of writers in the classical period lay in what distinguished Sparta from other cities – the education organized by the state. So with our main source, Xenophon: he gives little information on what we might consider the main point, how the system was organized.

To give one salient example: Xenophon does not help us to see how a child spent each day, or what activities made up the educational year. Nor can we see exactly where, or in what buildings, education took place. Numerous other examples could be given. Thus, we cannot tell whether in the classical period boys under 14 were grouped into age-classes of the same kind as those which, according to our (post-classical) sources, existed for young people between 14 and 19. Or whether, as in Crete, groups of boys took part in mock battles.

The near-complete silence of sources from the classical period on the instruction given by teachers makes it difficult to grasp the essence of Spartan education. This missing element – the 'hidden face' – amounts virtually to what at Athens was seen as the whole of education. Anyone who read only Xenophon would no doubt find Spartan education a very strange thing, dominated by the physical, steeped in brutality and setting the young to ferocious competition. One might question, with Plato and Aristotle, whether such a system even deserved the name of education. It must always therefore be remembered that all this was only a part of the reality: the most sensational part, certainly, and the most distinctively Spartan, but not necessarily the most important. It may have been above all that element of

Spartan education of which we hear nothing which most resembled what we understand by 'education'.

The hidden element of Spartan education was not so much the subject matter: that consisted, as elsewhere, of *grammata*, *mousikē*, and *gymnasia*. What is truly obscure is, how teaching was organized. Was it a public system, or did it depend on private initiative? With that question go others. Was the system compulsory or optional? Was it the same for all? It would have made sense for this aspect of education to have been public and the same for all, as some scholars indeed have thought that it was. *Gymnasia* prepare citizens for war. Song and dance make a contribution to physical and psychological training; they enable the young to play a proper part in the city's festivals and, as Greeks believed, they themselves are a preparation for war. Poetry, too, plays a part in forming the character of a citizen. It seems, then, that *gymnasia* and *mousikē*, if not *grammata*, ought logically to form part of state education. But did they? No text answers this question. In other cities such teaching was no less useful, and yet it there was left to private initiative. It was the father's job to make sure that his son one day would be fit to discharge his duties as a citizen. An effective test of whether an educational system is public or private is – who pays the teachers? If they are paid by families, the system can hardly be called public. Now, we know of no Greek city where teachers were paid by the state. And Diodorus (12.12.4) says that Charondas was the only lawgiver to propose this measure; Sparta is thus excluded. So in Spartan education the element which consisted of formal teaching was probably private. And that would have entailed a profound inequality: not every child had the means to attend a *gymnasion*, to take part in a chorus or even to learn *grammata*. Spartan education thus seems the opposite of what exists in modern states. In the latter, the element of formal schooling is compulsory and pretty well identical for all children. Allied activities, even when provided by the state, depend on parental decision. In Sparta the element which corresponded to our 'allied activities' (while having its own distinctive scale and application) was compulsory and was identical for all, whereas formal schooling depended on the family.

The distinctive element of Spartan education did not, then, consist in equality. Its strengths lay elsewhere. Chief among them, in my opinion, is what we might call 'participation'. This worked in two ways. On the one hand children, including girls, played a part in the life of the city – not only in its religious life (as happened in other cities, albeit in a less structured way), but also in social life, as for example when the *paidiskoi* were invited to certain common meals. On the other hand, and even more importantly, the education of the young took place where all could see; every citizen who wished could take part, every one felt involved. Thus it was not only during the *agōnes* of the young but at all times that the education of children by and for the community formed a spectacle for the community. This degree of participation and interest on the part of adults is found only in some archaic societies. Education is one of the spheres in which we can best see how Sparta contrived to be simultaneously a political society and a traditional society. In consequence the educational system was not a closed world but very largely opened itself to the life of the city.

Spartan education also had its negative aspects. One such, and perhaps the most alarming, was intelligently pinpointed by fourth-century philosophers: its exceedingly physical side, what Aristotle called *to thēriōdes* and what we have rendered as 'brutality'. This aspect was partly a result of another element of Spartan education, itself eminently questionable: the permanent competition which the system promoted among the young. The resulting tension was all the greater because the future of every young person was partly determined by his performance in this competition, and by the impression which he made upon adults. The rivalry between *hēbōntes* is the clearest sign of this combination of brutality and competition.

Our aim, however, has been not to pass judgement on Spartan education but to understand it; to this end of more value, perhaps, is a third kind of criticism directed at Sparta, namely that it moulded the young rather than educating them. This idea is more open to challenge than the previous two, because more subjective. The Spartan system has been variously compared with the traditional English boarding school, with the Hitler Youth and with the Soviet Pioneers. Such comparisons clearly reveal more about their authors, and about the intellectual climate in which they write, than about the reality of Sparta.[1] If Sparta is judged to be totalitarian, it can readily be asserted that Spartan education typifies what can be expected of such a state. If one deems Sparta to be the very model of a Greek state, one can similarly assert that its education system was perfectly adapted to produce citizens for such a state. But if one were to regard Spartan education as a process of moulding rather than of educating, one would be required to do the same with Athenian education. For Athens, if less obviously than Sparta, had a system which was widespread and effective in impregnating the young with the values of the city, in imparting the idea that the city was the supreme good, the place in which the happiest life could be led. In reality, every education is a process of moulding, of standardizing the young. The question, then, is not whether Spartan education moulded the young, but to what end it did so. What we have called the making of a citizen amounts in reality to planting in the minds of the young a model of behaviour, the same for everyone, which if closely followed will make the individual fit perfectly into the community of citizens, that is, of men educated in the same way and sharing the same values. So the ultimate aim of Spartan education is happiness, *eudaimonia*.

The happy city is, as Richer has shown,[2] a major theme of Greek political thought in the fourth century, one which reaches its fullest development with Aristotle. However, the term *eudaimonia* needs to be clarified. Does 'the happy city' mean one in which the citizens are individually happy, or is there such a thing as a collective happiness? Aristotle's reply is that the happiness of the city is completely identical with that of the citizens (*Pol.* 1324a5–13). But his case involves an ethical and philosophical idea of *eudaimonia* – for him, the thorough application of virtue (*Pol.*7.1328b38) – which is quite different from the normal meaning of the word.[3] The word is most commonly used to mean material prosperity, wealth combined with military and political power. This is the sense in which Xenophon uses the word twice in the Introduction to the *LP*, when he writes of the *eudaimonia* which has been produced at Sparta by the laws of Lycurgus (1.2). And the idea that the happiness, in this sense, of the city necessarily corresponds with that of the citizens is also present in the body of Xenophon's text. In Chapter 9 (§3), before describing the wretchedness of the Tremblers, he states that Lycurgus 'brought happiness (*eudaimonia*) to good men and unhappiness (*kakodaimonia*) to cowards' (§3: παρεσκεύασε τοῖς μὲν ἀγαθοῖς εὐδαιμονίαν, τοῖς δὲ κακοῖς κακοδαιμονίαν): he therefore means the happiness and unhappiness of individuals. This is not something that could be taken for granted; Perikles in the Funeral Speech on the contrary accuses Sparta of sacrificing the happiness of the citizens in favour of the power of the city.

Thus the Spartan citizen who followed meticulously the rules of his city was considered to have a happy life. There was more involved than merely an easy conscience or psychological contentment. Happiness here also had a physical aspect. In Xenophon and Plutarch there are several adjectives and participles referring to signs of this happiness. They tell of pride (γαῦρος, *Inst. Lac.* 40, *Mor.* 239d), gaiety (ἱλαρός, *ibid.*, Plut. *Mor.* 191f and 231b; ἀγαλλόμενος, Xen. *Hell.* 4.5.10), a radiant face (λαμπρός, Xen. *ibid.*; λιπαρός, Xen. *LP* 9.5; φαιδρός, Plut. *Lyc.* 25.6), a smile of contentment (μειδιῶν, Plut. *Mor.* 191f and 231b). These terms convey an image of a profound inner happiness, one so strong as to radiate externally.

In what circumstances did Spartan citizens show such happiness? Mostly when their happiness was contrary to what might have been expected; it is in circumstances where an ordinary man would have thought himself afflicted by the most dreadful ill-fortune that the Spartan showed his superiority by means of a radiant countenance. Thus young people (in the Roman period) under the lash at the altar of Orthia (*Inst. Lac.* 40); the *hēbōn* Pedaritos on learning that he has not been selected for the Three Hundred (Plut. *Lyc.* 25.6;

Mor. 191f and 231b);[4] relatives of soldiers killed at the battle of Lechaion (Xen. *Hell*. 4.5.10). Displays of happiness in such circumstances are recorded to make a moral point, but clearly happiness was regarded as the normal, permanent state of a Spartan citizen. Xenophon on the Tremblers confirms as much: the Trembler is unhappy and the good citizen happy (*LP* 9.3). The fact that Tremblers were forbidden to have a happy expression (*LP* 9.5, λιπαρὸν οὐ πλανητέον) implies that this was how good citizens normally looked.

This happiness involved more than a condition of mind and body. It derived from the possession or enjoyment of certain physical things endowed with symbolic value. These 'good things', taken together, are – in my opinion – what is meant by the phrase *ta kala* which occurs three times in Xenophon and was in all probability a local Spartan expression.[5] The expression is normally translated as 'the honours', but that begs the question of what honours could have been meant in the case of classical Sparta. Certainly not the crowns, *proedriai* and honorific decrees familiar from other cities. Magistracies, then? Using that term in a wide sense, to include military commands, election to the Gerousia and, for *hēbōntes*, selection for the *hippeis*, magistracies were undoubtedly part of what was meant by *ta kala*. But the meaning of the latter expression goes far wider. I believe that it means everything which contributed to making the life of a Spartan citizen 'beautiful', that is, noble and supremely free (μάλιστα ἐλεύθεροι, as Kritias said, D-K 37). Since the Trembler was by definition the opposite of the happy citizen, Xenophon's list (*LP* 9.4–5) of the things denied to the Trembler can be used to form an initial idea of what the 'good things' were: common meals, attendance at the gymnasium, street games, dancing, marks of respect from one's juniors. The fragment of Tyrtaios (12 W, ll. 35–44) which describes the intense happiness of the man who has fought heroically in the front line, mentions like Xenophon the display of respect which consists of the giving up of a seat to such a man. For Tyrtaios this is an example of something exceptionally precious: respect from the whole of society. There is no doubt that a good reputation, which in its highest degree might amount to glory, was a fundamental element in the happiness of the citizen. When Xenophon mentions the punishment which could be applied to a highly delinquent *paidiskos* (*LP* 3.3), he says simply that such a person would lose his reputation and would be 'completely *adokimos* in the community'. Sparta, then, was a society governed by honour and shame. To the list of 'good things' we should add conversation in the *leschē* and the *agora*. Sparta was a place where citizens were eminently provided with leisure to meet acquaintances and to discuss affairs of the day.

Finally, I believe that among the 'good things' of Sparta we should include the process of education itself. Two passages of Xenophon suggest as much.

At *Hellenica* 5.3.9 we read that the *trophimoi,* like the *nothoi,* 'had a share in the *kala* of the city'; the fact that they had taken part in the Spartan education, as we have seen, must be the main thing meant here. In *LP* (3.3) Xenophon states that the delinquent *paidiskos* 'will *no longer* participate in any of the good things' (μηδενὸς ἔτι τῶν καλῶν τυγχάνειν). Given the age of such a person, the *kala* in his case cannot mean anything other than education. It makes perfect sense that public education should have been seen as one of the good things that the city conferred on its (future) citizens. But this particular 'good thing' had an importance all of its own. For on it depended access to all the other good things to come, and thus to happiness.

The happiness of the citizen and the education the city had given him were thus intimately linked. Happiness flowed from the citizen's feeling that he belonged to, had almost melted into, a community of people like himself. This feeling would never leave him, but it was maintained and refreshed by certain activities within small groups which daily strengthened the social bond: the groups of those who ate together, of those who exercised together, of those who sang and danced together, who played together, who conversed together. For the citizen of Sparta the main thing seems not to have been, as it was for Aristotle's citizen, participation in politics; attendance at the assembly is notably absent from the list of good things which lead to happiness. Rather, the most important thing was to take part in the social activities which made citizenship a concrete reality. For this feeling of belonging to make a citizen happy, he needed to have internalized the rules of the city so thoroughly that they had become the dominant element of his character. And what brought about that internalizing of the rules was the process of education. One may indeed call this a form of moulding, but I in no way accept the widespread view that the Spartan citizen lived a grey, oppressive life.

Spartan education now appears as the product of two structures, which worked in parallel. One is almost entirely obscure to us with regard to how it operated, though its contents are clear. It consisted of teaching, probably mainly private, of the basic skills needed by every Greek citizen. It may not have been much different from that which existed at Athens, for instance. The other structure was what Xenophon represents as a public system of education (*paideia*). The fact that there existed on Crete a system which was – to some extent – parallel, means that the Spartan system was less unusual than it may appear. This public part of the Spartan education contained elements of preparation for life as a citizen, of training for war and of religious and cultural integration. It can therefore be more fully understood if we conceive of it as an unusually extended version of *ephēbeia*, which resulted from adapting, from 'translating', young people's initiation rituals (similar to those which operate in many archaic societies) to meet the needs of Sparta's political society. Each of the phases which Xenophon distinguishes can be seen to correspond with a distinct stage of this process of transformation. The two phases which mark the beginning and end of the process should be seen as periods of transition; the *paides* are still, in our terms, children, while the *hēbōntes* are junior citizens. It is the central phase, that of the *paidiskoi*, which, because of the age of the young people involved and also its strict organization into year-groups, most closely resembles the familiar model of *ephēbeia*. Its length, admittedly, makes it exceptional. But, interestingly, in the Roman period it did indeed become an *ephēbeia*. That this is how Greeks on occasion understood it can be seen from the glosses to Herodotos and Strabo when they say, 'from 14 to 20 years, the child is an ephebe.'

Notes

[1] A good example is Lazenby 1985, viii.

[2] Richer 2001b.

[3] On the distinction see (already) Xen. *Mem.* 4.2.34.

[4] On this episode see Ducat 2002, 14–19.

[5] *LP* 3.3, 4.4, *Hell.* 5.3.9. The latter passage has the phrase in a more elaborate form: 'the *kala* in the city', τὰ ἐν τῇ πόλει καλά. Plut. *Agis* 5.5 may contain an echo of it.

BIBLIOGRAPHY

Amigues, S.
1989 Théophraste, *Recherches sur les plantes* III–IV, Paris.
Angeli-Bernardini, P.
1988 'Le donne e la pratica della corsa nella Grecia antica', in P. Angeli–Bernardini (ed.) *Lo Sport in Grecia*, Bari, 153–84.
Arrigoni, G.
1985 'Donne e sport nel mondo Greco', in G. Arrigoni (ed.) *Le donne in Grecia*, Bari, 55–201; on Sparta, 65–95.
Baladié, R.
1978 Strabon VIII, Paris.
Bekker, I.
1814 *Anecdota Graeca* I, Berlin.
1829 *Aristophanis Comoediae cum Scholiis*.
Bethe, E.
1907 'Die dorische Knabenliebe', *RM* 62, 438–75.
Bianco, E.
1996 'Il capitolo 14 della *LP* attribuita a Senofonte', *MH* 53, 12–24.
Bingen, J.
1958 'Τριετίρης (*IG* V 1, 1120)', *AC* 27, 105–7.
Birgalias, N
1997 ' Ἔρις περὶ ἀρετῆς ', Ἑλληνικά 47, 35–52.
1999 *L'odyssée de l'éducation spartiate*, Athens.
Bölte, F.
1929 'Zu lakonische Festen', *RM* 78, 124–43.
Bommelaer, J.F.
1977 *Lysandre de Sparte*, Paris.
Bonnechère, P.
1993 'Orthia et la flagellation des éphèbes spartiates: un souvenir chimérique de sacrifice humain', *Kernos* 6, 11–22.
1998 'Le rituel samien décrit par Hérodote, III, 48, et la *bomolochia* spartiate', *EC* 66, 3–21.
Boring, T.A.
1979 *Literacy in ancient Sparta*, Mnemosyne Suppl. 54, Leiden.
Brelich, A.
1969 *Paides e Parthenoi*, Rome.
Bresson, A.
2002 'Un 'Athénien' à Sparte: Plutarque lecteur de Xénophon', *REG* 115, 22–57.
Bruni, G.B.
1979 'Mothakes, Neodamodeis, Brasideioi', in *Schiavitù, Manomissione e Classi*

dipendenti nel mondo antico, Pubbl. Istit. di Storia antica, Università di Padova, 13, 21–31.

Buffière, F.
1980 *Eros adolescent: la pédérastie dans la Grèce antique*, Paris.

Busolt, G. and Swoboda, H.
1920–6 *Griechische Staatskunde*, 3rd edn, Munich.

Cabanes, P.
1991 'Recherches épigraphiques en Albanie: péripolarques et péripoloi en Grèce du Nord et en Illyrie à la période hellénistique', *CRAI*, 197–221.

Cairns, D.L.
1993 *Aidos. The psychology and ethics of honour and shame in ancient Greek literature*, Oxford.

Calame, C.
1977 *Les choeurs de jeunes filles en Grèce archaïque*, 2 vols., Rome.

Cameron, A.
1981 'Notes on the erotic art of Rufinus', *GRBS* 22, 179–83.

Cantarelli, L.
1890 'I mothakes spartani', *RFIC* 18, 465–84.

Cartledge, P.
1978 'Literacy in the Spartan oligarchy', *JHS* 98, 25–37.
1987 *Agesilaos and the crisis of Sparta*, London and Baltimore.
1997 Review of Kennell, *The Gymnasium of Virtue* 1995, *CR* 48, 100.
2001 *Spartan Reflections*, London.

Cartledge, P. and Spawforth, A.J.S.
1989 *Hellenistic and Roman Sparta. A tale of two cities*, London and New York.

Chrimes, K.M.T.
1949 *Ancient Sparta. A re-examination of the evidence*, Manchester.

Christien, J.
1997 'Les temps d'une vie. Sparte, une société à classes d'âge?', *Métis* 12, 45–79.

Cobet, C.G.
1858 *Novae lectiones, quibus continentur observationes criticae in scriptores Graecos*, Leiden.

Curren, R.R.
2000 *Aristotle on the Necessity of Public Education*, Boulder, New York and Oxford.

David, E.
1979 'The pamphlet of Pausanias', *PP* 185, 94–116.
1992 'Sparta's social hair', *Eranos* 90, 11–21.
1999 'Sparta's kosmos of silence', in S. Hodkinson and A. Powell (eds.) *Sparta. New perspectives*, Swansea and London, 117–46.

Davidson, J.
2001 'Dover, Foucault and Greek homosexuality: penetration and the truth of sex', *Past and Present* 170, 1–51.

Dawkins, R.M.
1929 *The sanctuary of Artemis Orthia at Sparta*, London.

Delalande, J.
2002 *Cours de récréation: pour une anthropologie de l'enfance*, Rennes.

Den Boer, W.
1954 *Laconian Studies*, Amsterdam.
Diels, H.
1896 'Alkmans Partheneion', *Hermes* 31, 339–74.
Diels, H. and Kranz, W.
1960 *Die Fragmente der Vorsokratiker*, 10th edn, Berlin.
Diller, A.
1941 'A new source on the Spartan ephebia', *AJPhil.* 62, 499–501.
Dilts, M.R.
1971 *Heraclidis Lembi Excerpta Politiarum*, GRB Monographs 5, Durham.
Dover, K.J.
1978 *Greek Homosexuality*, London.
1988 'Greek homosexuality and initiation', in Dover, *The Greeks and their Legacy*, London, 115–30.
Ducat, J.
1990 *Les Hilotes*, BCH Suppl. 20, Paris.
1995 'Un rituel samien', *BCH* 119, 339–68.
1997a 'La cryptie en question', in P. Brulé and J. Oulhen (eds.) *Esclavage, guerre, économie, Hommages à Y. Garlan*, Rennes, 43–74.
1997b 'Crypties', *Cahiers du Centre Glotz* 8, 9–38.
1998 'La femme de Sparte et la cité', *Ktéma* 23, 385–406.
1999a 'La femme de Sparte et la guerre', *Pallas* 51, 159–71.
1999b 'Perspectives on Spartan education', in S. Hodkinson and A. Powell (eds.) *Sparta. New perspectives*, Swansea and London, 43–66.
2002 'Pédaritos ou le bon usage des apophtegmes', *Ktéma* 27, 13–34.
2003 'Du vol dans l'éducation spartiate', *Métis* n.s. 1, 95–110.
2004 'L'enfant spartiate et le renardeau', *REG* 117, 125–40.
Edmunds, L.
1984 'Thucydides on monosandalism', *Studies Presented to Sterling Dow*, Durham, 71–5.
Ellinger, P.
1993 *La légende nationale phocidienne*, BCH suppl. 27, Paris.
Finley, M.I.
1968 'Sparta', in J.P. Vernant (ed.) *Problèmes de la guerre en Grèce ancienne*, Paris and The Hague, 141–60.
1972 'Anthropology and the classics', lecture delivered in Cambridge, May 13, 1972, and first published in *The Use and Abuse of History*, 1st edn, London 1978; 2nd edn 1986, 102–19.
Flower, M.A.
1988 'Agesilaos of Sparta and the origins of the ruler cult', *CQ* 38, 123–34.
Fontenrose, J.
1978 *The Delphic Oracle*, Berkeley, Los Angeles and London.
Frontisi-Ducroux, F.
1981 'Artémis bucolique', *RHR* 198, 29–56.
1984 'La bomolochia: autour de l'embuscade à l'autel', *Recherches sur les cultes grecs et l'Occident* 2, *Cahiers du Centre Jean Bérard* 9, 29–50.

Fuhrmann, F.
1988 Plutarque, *Oeuvres Morales* III, Paris.

Furuyama, M.
1991 'Minor social groups in Sparta: mothakes, trophimoi and nothoi of the Spartiates', *Kodai* 2, 1–20.

Fustel de Coulanges, N.D.
1891 *Nouvelles recherches sur quelques points d'Histoire*, ed. C. Jullian, Paris.

Girard, P.
1898 'Un texte inédit sur la cryptie des Lacédémoniens', *REG* 11, 31–8.

Graf, F.
1985 *Nordionische Kulte*, Rome.

Hansen, P.
1989 *Carmina Epigraphica Graeca* II, Berlin.

Harvey, D.
1994 'Lacomica: Aristophanes and the Spartans', in A. Powell and S. Hodkinson (eds.) *The Shadow of Sparta*, London and Swansea, 35–58.

Hatzopoulos, M.B.
1994 *Cultes et rites de passage en Macédoine*, Athens.

Helly, B.
1973 *Gonnoi* I, Amsterdam.

Higgins, W.E.
1977 *Xenophon the Athenian*, Albany.

Hodkinson, S.
1983 'Social order and the conflict of values in classical Sparta', *Chiron* 13, 239–81.
1989 'Inheritance, marriage and demography: perspectives upon the success and decline of classical Sparta', in A. Powell (ed.) *Classical Sparta. Techniques behind her success*, 79–121.
1997 'Servile and free dependants of the classical Spartan *oikos*', in M. Moggi and G. Cordiano (eds.) *Schiavi e dipendenti nell' ambito dell'oikos e della famiglia*, Pisa, 45–71.
1999 'An agonistic culture?', in S. Hodkinson and A. Powell (eds.) *Sparta: New perspectives*, Swansea and London, 147–87.
2000 *Property and Wealth in Classical Sparta*, Swansea and London.

Hornblower, S.
1991 *A Commentary on Thucydides* I (books I–III), Oxford.

Humble, N.
2004 'Xenophon's sons in Sparta? Perspectives on *xenoi* in the Spartan upbringing', in T.J. Figueira (ed.) *Spartan Society*, Swansea, 231–50.

Huys, M.
1996 'The Spartan practice of selective infanticide and its parallels in ancient utopian tradition', *AS* 27, 47–74.

Ingalls, W.B.
2000 'Ritual performance as training for daughters in archaic Greece', *Phoenix* 54, 1–20.

Jeanmaire, H.
1913 'La cryptie lacédémonienne', *REG* 26, 121–50.

1939 *Couroi et Courètes. Essai sur l'éducation spartiate et sur les rites d'adolescence dans l'Antiquité hellénique*, Lille.

Jouanna, J.

1992 *Hippocrate*, Paris.

Kennell, N.

1995 *The Gymnasium of Virtue*, Chapel Hill and London.

Knoepfler, D.

1993 'Les *kryptoi* du stratège Epicharès à Rhamnonte et le début de la guerre de Chrémonidès', *BCH* 117, 327–41.

Kron, U.

1998 'Sickles in Greek sanctuaries: votives and cultic instruments', in R. Hägg (ed.) *Ancient Greek Cult Practice from the Archaeological Evidence*, Stockholm, 187–216.

Kukofka, D.A.

1993 'Die paidiskoi im System der spartanischen Alterklassen', *Philologus* 137, 197–205.

Lazenby, J.F.

1985 *The Spartan Army*, Warminster.

Le Roy, C.

1961 '*Lakonika*', *BCH* 85, 206–35.

Leutsch, E.L. von and Schneidewin, F.G.

1839 *Corpus Paroemiographorum Graecorum* I, Göttingen.

Lévy, E.

1988 'La kryptie et ses contradictions', *Ktéma* 13, 245–52.

1997 'Remarques préliminaires sur l'éducation spartiate', *Ktéma* 22, 151–60.

2003 *Sparta. Histoire politique et sociale jusqu'à la conquête romaine*, Paris.

Lipka, M.

2002 *Xenophon's Spartan Constitution. Introduction, text, commentary*, Berlin and New York.

Loraux, N.

1977 'La "belle mort" spartiate', *Ktéma* 2, 105–20.

1989 *Les expériences de Tirésias*, Paris.

Losfald, G.

1977 'Tyrophagie religieuse et mystique', *BAGB*, 257–77.

Lotze, D.

1962 'Mothakes', *Historia* 11, 427–35.

Lupi, M.

2000 *L'ordine delle generazioni. Classi di età e costumi matrimoniali nell'antica Sparta*, Bari.

2002 'Sparta compared: ethnographic perspectives in Spartan studies', in A. Powell and S. Hodkinson (eds.) *Sparta. Beyond the mirage*, Swansea and London, 305–22.

2003 'I presunti *eirenes* di Senofonte (*LP* II, 5 e 11)', *AION* 25, 157–68.

Luppino-Manes, E.

1968 *Un progetto di riforma per Sparta, la "Politeia" di Senofonte*, Milan.

MacDowell, D.M.

1986 *Spartan Law*, Edinburgh.

Marrou, H.I.
1948 *Histoire de l'éducation dans l'Antiquité*, 1st edn, Paris.
Michell, H.
1952 *Sparta*, Cambridge.
Millender, E.G.
2001 'Spartan literacy revisited', *Class. Ant.* 20, 121–64.
Murr, J.
1969 *Die Pflanzenwelt in der griechische Mythologie*, Groningen.
Nafissi, M.
1991 *La nascità del Kosmos. Studi sulla storia e la società di Sparta*, Perugia.
Napolitano, M.L.
1988 'Donne spartane e teknopoiia', *AION* 7, 19–50.
Nilsson, M.P.
1912 'Die Grundlagen des spartanischen Lebens', *Klio* 12, 308–40.
Ogden, D.
1996 'Homosexuality and warfare in Ancient Greece', in A.B. Lloyd (ed.) *Battle in Antiquity*, Swansea and London, 107–68.
Ollier, F.
1934 *Xénophon, la République des Lacédémoniens*, Lyon and Paris.
Paradiso, A.
1991 *Forme di dipendenza nel mondo Greco. Ricerche sul VI° libro di Ateneo*, Bari.
Parke, H.W. and Wormell, D.E.
1956 *The Delphic oracle*, 2 vols., Oxford.
Parker, R.
1989 'Spartan religion', in A. Powell (ed.) *Classical Sparta. Techniques behind her success*, London, 142–72.
Patzer, H.
1982 *Die griechische Knabenliebe*, Wiesbaden.
Pelling, C.
2002 *Plutarch and History*, Swansea and London.
Percy, W.A. III
1996 *Pederasty and Pedagogy in Archaic Greece*, Urbana and Chicago.
Pettersson, M.
1992 *Cults of Apollo at Sparta: The Hyakinthia, the Gymnopaidiai and the Karneia*, Stockholm.
Piérart, M.
1974 *Platon et la cité grecque*, Bruxelles.
Piper, L.J.
1986 *Spartan Twilight*, New Rochelle.
Pipili, M.
1985 *Laconian Iconography in the 6th Century*, Oxford.
Pomeroy, S.B.
2002 *Spartan Women*, New York.
Porter, W.H.
1935 'The antecedents of the Spartan revolution in 243', *Hermathena* 49, 1–15.
Pouilloux, J.
1954 *Recherches sur l'histoire et les cultes de Thasos*, Paris.

Powell, A.
1989 'Mendacity and Sparta's use of the visual', in id. (ed.) *Classical Sparta: Techniques behind her success*, London.
1994 'Plato and Sparta: modes of rule and of non-rational persuasion in the *Laws*', in A. Powell and S. Hodkinson (eds.) *The Shadow of Sparta*, London and Swansea, 273–321.
1998a 'Sixth-century Lakonian vase-painting: continuities and discontinuities with the "Lykourgan" ethos', in N. Fisher and H. van Wees (eds.) *Archaic Greece: New approaches and new evidence*, Swansea and London, 119–46.
1998b Review of Kennell, *The Gymnasium of Virtue* 1995, *Phoenix* 52, 173–4.
1999 'Spartan women assertive in politics? Plutarch's lives of Agis and Kleomenes', in S. Hodkinson and A. Powell (eds.) *Sparta. New perspectives*, Swansea and London, 393–419.
2001 *Athens and Sparta*, 2nd edn, London.
2004 'The women of Sparta – and of other Greek cities – at war', in T. Figueira (ed.) *Spartan Society*, Swansea, 137–50.

Preger, H.
1891 *Inscriptiones Graecae metricae*, Leipzig.

Pritchett, W.K.
1971 *The Greek State at War* I, Berkeley and Los Angeles.

Rebenich, S.
1998a *Xenophon, Die Verfassung der Spartaner*, Darmstadt.
1998b 'Fremdenfeindlichkeit in Sparta? Überlegungen zur Tradition des Spartanischen Xenelasie', *Klio* 80, 336–59.

Richer, N.
1998a *Les Ephores*, Paris.
1998b 'Des citoyens maîtres d'eux-mêmes: l'*eukosmos* de Sparta archaïque et classique', *Cahiers du Centre Glotz* 9, 7–36.
1999 'Aidos at Sparta', in S. Hodkinson and A. Powell (eds.) *Sparta: New Perspectives*, Swansea and London, 91–115.
2001a 'Un peuple de philosophes à Sparte?', *Quaderni del dipartimento di filologia... Augusto Rostagni*, Università di Bologna, 17, 29–55.
2001b 'Eunomia et eudaimonia à Sparte', *Dikè, Rivista di storia del diritto greco ed ellenistico*, Università di Milano, 4, 13–38.
2004 'Les Hyakinthies de Sparte', *REA* 106, 389–419.
2005 'Les Gymnopédies de Sparte', Ktéma 30, 237–62.

Robert, J. and L.
1983 *Fouilles d'Amyzon en Carie*, Paris.

Robert, L.
1962 'Bulletin épigraphique', *REG* 75.

Rose, H.J.
1941 'Greek rites of stealing', *Harvard Théological Review* 34, 1–5.

Roussel, P.
1939 *Sparte*, Paris.
1942 'Etude sur le principe de l'ancienneté dans le monde hellénique, du Vème s. av. J.C. à l'époque romaine', *Mémoires de l'Institut National de France, Académie des Inscriptions et Belles-Lettres* 43, 2, 123–227.

Rousset, D.
1994 'Les frontières des cités grecques', *Cahiers du Centre Glotz* 5, 97–126.
Ruzé, F.
2001 'La loi et le chant', in J.P. Brun and Ph. Jockey (eds.) *Technai: Techniques et sociétés en Méditerranée, Hommage à M.C. Amouretti*, Aix en Provence, 709–17.
Sansalvador, A.V.
1996 'Fορθασία, 'Oρθία y 'Άρτεμις 'Oρθία en Laconia', *Emerita* 64, 278–88.
Scanlon, T.F.
1988 'Virgineum gymnasium: Spartan females and early Greek athletics', in W.J. Raschke (ed.) *The Archaeology of the Olympics*, Madison, 185–216.
Schnapp, A.
1997 *La chasseur et la cité*, Paris.
Schwartz, G.S.
1976 '*IG* V 1, 213, the Damonon stele: a new restoration for line 39', *ZPE* 22, 177–8.
Sergent, B.
1986 *L'homosexualité initiatique dans l'Europe ancienne*, Paris.
1993 'Le sens d'une danse spartiate', *DHA* 19, 161–78.
Serwint, N.
1993 'The female athletic competition at the Heraia and prenuptial initiation rites', *AJA* 97, 403–22.
Shimron, B.
1972 *Late Sparta*, Arethusa Monographs 3.
Singor, H.W.
1999 'Admission to the syssitia in fifth-century Sparta', in S. Hodkinson and A. Powell (eds.) *Sparta, New perspectives*, Swansea and London, 67–89.
Spina, L.
1985 'L'incomparabile pudore dei giovani Spartani', *QUCC* 48, 167–81.
Stainhauer, G.
1998 'Unpublished lists of Gerontes and magistrates of Roman Sparta', *ABSA* 93, 427–47.
Stibbe, C.M.
1972 *Lakonische Vasenmaler des sechsten Jahrhunderts v.Chr.*, Amsterdam.
1976 'Neue Fragmente lakonischer Schalen aus Carveteri', *MNIR* 38, 7–16.
Tazelaar, C.M.
1967 '*Paides kai epheboi*: some notes on the Spartan stages of youth', *Mnemosyne* 20, 127–53.
Themelis, P.
1999 Ἀρχαία Μεσσήνη, Athens.
Tigerstedt, E.N.
1965–74 *The Legend of Sparta in Classical Antiquity*, 3 vols., Stockholm.
Toynbee, A.J.
1969 *Some Problems of Greek History*, Oxford.
Van Wees, H.
1999 'Tyrtaeus' *Eunomia*: nothing to do with the Great Rhetra', in S. Hodkinson and A. Powell (eds.) *Sparta. New perspectives*, Swansea and London, 1–41.

Vernant, J.P.
1989 'Entre la honte et la gloire: l'identité du jeune Spartiate', in *L'individu, la mort, l'amour*, Paris, 173–209 (= *Métis* 2, 1987, 269–300).
Videl-Naquet, P.
1981 *Le chasseur noir. Formes de pensée et formes de société dans le monde grec*, Paris.
Wallon, H.
1850 'Explication d'un passage de Plutarque sur la loi de Lycurgue nommée la cryptie', *Journal Général de l'Instruction Publique*, 470–3 et 487–90.
Waywell, G.
1999 'Sparta and its topography', *BICS* 43, 1–26.
Wendel, C.
1914 *Scholia in Theocritum vetera*, Leipzig.
Whitby, M.
1994 'Two shadows: images of Spartans and Helots', in A. Powell and S. Hodkinson (eds.) *The Shadow of Sparta*, London and New York, 87–126.
Whitley, J.
1997 'Cretan laws and Cretan literacy', *AJA* 101, 636–61.
Wide, S.
1893 *Lakonische Kulte*, Leipzig.
Willetts, R.F.
1955 *Aristocratic Society in Ancient Crete*, London.

INDEX LOCORUM

INDEX NOMINUM ET RERUM